Before Salem

# Before Salem

*Witch Hunting in the Connecticut River Valley, 1647–1663*

RICHARD S. ROSS III

McFarland & Company, Inc., Publishers

*Jefferson, North Carolina*

LIBRARY OF CONGRESS CATALOGUING-IN-PUBLICATION DATA

Names: Ross, Richard S., III, 1948– author.
Title: Before Salem : witch hunting in the Connecticut River Valley, 1647–1663 / Richard S. Ross III.
Description: Jefferson, North Carolina : McFarland & Company, Inc., Publishers, 2017. | Includes bibliographical references and index.
Identifiers: LCCN 2017011901 | ISBN 9781476666488 (softcover : acid free paper) ∞
Subjects: LCSH: Witchcraft—Connecticut River Valley—History—17th century. | Trials (Witchcraft)—Connecticut River Valley—History—17th century. | Witch hunting—Connecticut River Valley—History—17th century.
Classification: LCC BF1576 .R675 2017 | DDC 133.4/30974—dc23
LC record available at https://lccn.loc.gov/2017011901

BRITISH LIBRARY CATALOGUING DATA ARE AVAILABLE

ISBN (print) 978-1-4766-6648-8
ISBN (ebook) 978-1-4766-2779-3

Front cover image © 2017 iStock

Printed in the United States of America

*McFarland & Company, Inc., Publishers*
*Box 611, Jefferson, North Carolina 28640*
*www.mcfarlandpub.com*

# Acknowledgments

I would thank the following institutions for their contributions to this work.

Hay Library, Brown University, Providence, Rhode Island
Connecticut State Library, Hartford, Connecticut
Historic Winslow House Association, Marshfield, Massachusetts
Wellcome Library, London
The Library, Westminster Abbey, London
Trinity College Library, Hartford, Connecticut
Watkinson Library, Special Collections Division of the Trinity College Library

I want to also thank the librarians I have known over the years, especially the interlibrary loan librarians at the various academic institutions who assisted me in acquiring the numerous books and articles for my research. They are truly the unsung heroes of academia. For this book I am especially indebted to the interlibrary loan staff of the Trinity College Library and the staff in the Special Collections Division of the Watkinson Library.

I would like to acknowledge my parents Richard S. Ross, Jr., and Mary Plevell Ross, who without them this work would never have existed. I would also like to acknowledge my two children, Richard and Nicole, and my two grandchildren, Mitzie and Billy, who brought joy and laughter to the house in the midst of this serious subject. Finally, I want to thank my wife, Christine, whose editorial assistance, patience and advice allowed this book to finally come to completion.

# Table of Contents

# Preface

This book grew out of my long-time interest in witchcraft primarily in continental Europe and England. In 2005 I began to teach a class on witchcraft at Trinity College in Hartford, Connecticut. I decided to focus the course on the English origins of witchcraft in Colonial America with emphasis on the Salem trials to provide ready resources for my students. In teaching and researching for the course over a number of years the course evolved as I came to the realization Connecticut had its own significant share of witchcraft trials and executions prior to the Salem trials. Although not as resource rich as the Salem trials there was sufficient material for students to successfully investigate these earlier trials.

Salem has for a long time cast a shadow over the Connecticut witch trials. Its effect can be summed up in the words of the late nineteenth century author of *The Devil in Britain and America* (1896), who wrote: "The following are the known cases of witchcraft in Connecticut ... but as far as I can see, none present any particular feature of interest to the reader."[1]

Even today most people in Connecticut let alone New England are unfamiliar with the fact there were witch trials in the mid-seventeenth century Connecticut River Valley in which eleven individuals were executed, including the first witch hanged in New England in 1647 in Hartford, Connecticut.

As for my own research I began to see the unique situations in the Connecticut River Valley. There were obvious connections between the witch lore, the English demonologists, the legal system, and the trials in England and New England.

The book I have written takes a different perspective on witchcraft in early colonial New England. I place the origins of the witchcraft trials in what has also been called the New England wilderness from 1647 to 1662/63 not only in the unique conditions in the Connecticut River Valley but within the wider context of migrants who, while on the New England frontier, managed to maintain active communications with their homeland.

The connection to England was continuous during the period under this study. As the book shows the political, religious and social ferment in England during this period in conjunction with life on the New England frontier deeply affected the colonists, especially the ongoing and later outcome of the English Civil War.

The collapse of the central government, the ensuing power vacuum in England, and the witchcraft accusations between the Royalists and Roundheads led to a renewal of witchcraft accusations and trials in England, especially under the leadership of Matthew Hopkins in East Anglia. It was during this period when the New England colonies were left on their own that witchcraft statutes became part of the colonial legal systems. As the witchcraft accusations and executions in England increased the hysteria spread to New England. New tools and techniques for examining witches were quickly adopted by the authorities in New England.

Contributing to the general unease and suspicions in the New England wilderness were the Native Americans, who the colonists feared might attack them physically while clergy preached they were agents of the devil prepared to attack them spiritually with his aid. Additionally, they faced a harsh environment, famine, recurring epidemics, and an unforgiving religion which offered no relief from perceived *maleficia* by suspected witches, the devil and his demons. Later additional unease and fear was generated by rebellion, the continued threat of Indian attack, the legitimacy of land ownership without a Royal charter and for clergy the exclusiveness of congregationalism in New England and the governance of their churches as a result of the restoration of Charles II in England.

Unfortunately there are few records available for witch trials in the Connecticut River Valley. For later trials there are some depositions and other documents found in the *Samuel Wyllys papers* along with English legal manuals, printed reports from the colonies of Connecticut and New Haven, documents printed by the Massachusetts and Connecticut historical societies and other primary source publications available that allow us to piece together the history of witch hunting in the Connecticut River Valley.

The first witchcraft trials from 1647 to 1662/63 influenced both Increase Mather and Cotton Mather in their books on witchcraft in Colonial America and provide continuity and a connection to the later Salem witch trials. We find in these earlier reports demonic possession, bewitchment, countermagic, the type of accusations that rose to the level of witchcraft, legal issues confronting judges and juries, the clergy's role in suspected witch examinations, trials, and following conviction, the pact or covenant with the devil and the outcome and consequences of various trials. These reports undoubtedly provided some measure of guidance for good or for ill to the authorities and clergy in the years leading up to and including the Salem trials.

This book provides new material on witchcraft in the Connecticut River

Valley. I have been able to provide connections among individuals in Colonial America and England that show how and why individuals participated in specific events outlined in this book. A few other examples of new material I provide includes the origins and reasons for the execution of the first witch in New England; new information on the demonic possession of a young woman during the Hartford witch hunt, including her family's unique connection with the troubled Hartford Church; and a prior witchcraft trial in New Haven. Other material concerns background on the family of a young girl bewitched to death, initiating the Hartford witch hunt. Additionally, I explain the origin of the undated document *Grounds for Examination of a Witch* in the Connecticut State Library and thought to have been used as a legal document in a number of witch trials in the Connecticut River Valley. Most importantly the book sheds light on a dark aspect of colonial New England history that unfortunately took its cue from important events in England.

Over the years I have come to understand the quote "The past is a foreign country; they do things differently there."[2] These words could not be more accurate as we delve into and try to understand why witchcraft had such a hold on the people of England and Colonial America that allowed them to persecute individuals with such invective that their banishment or execution was the only relief for the community. The passions aroused and the self-righteousness of various groups in society who demand ideas and people be banished today because they do not conform to the "bee hive" mentality of those who believe they know the "truth" or what is best for all of us, this book is also a caution.

In keeping with the other theme, the past is a foreign country, you will find that most quotes are spelled as they were originally written. It was important to me that anyone reading these quotes understand it was an entirely different world than the one we inhabit today. However, in deference to the world we do inhabit I have made every effort to trace copyright holders.

# Introduction

The history of witchcraft and witchcraft trials in America has traditionally centered on the Salem Witch trials in 1692. Historians have focused
on a variety of causes for these trials. Their historical popularity remains
undiminished. However, what most people do not realize is prior to the
famous Salem Witch hunt in 1692, there was an earlier witch hunt primarily
focused in the Connecticut River Valley. This witch hunt resulted in at
least eleven persons tried, convicted and presumably executed or dying in
prison beginning in 1647 and ending in 1663. Historians have asked why
these witchcraft executions came to an end in 1663 but this study asks a
related question: Why did they begin in New England in the Connecticut
River Valley in the late 1640s? After all why during this outbreak did so many
accusations and trials end in the deaths of these victims? Meanwhile, the
eastern part of the Massachusetts Bay Colony had witchcraft trials during
this same time but not to the extent of the thinly populated Connecticut
River Valley.

One aspect of this first outbreak that is rarely considered is the unique
impact of conditions in the home country, England. Conditions there acted
as a catalyst for the outbreak for the first witch hunting mania in New
England. Culturally, it would seem obvious there was a direct link. New
England witchcraft trials were "produced by people whose culture belonged
to the Old World as much as the New—not the least their magical beliefs ...
[and] ... colonial authorities applied English accusatory justice, where the
onus for prosecution was on private complainants and suspects were examined without torture on the presumption of innocence."[1]

These first generation emigrants from England attempted to model their
agriculture, government and legal system on their home villages and towns
in England. They also brought their traditions and magical beliefs with them.
Ironically, in England following the stricter Witchcraft Act of 1604, witchcraft
prosecutions by 1640 had actually become "rare," not due to a decline in the
popular belief in witches and their ability to inflict harm, but to a growing

"cautiousness among the judges" and the successful stemming of the tide of witchcraft books and pamphlets under Charles I and his ministers. As Bishop John Hall wrote of the witch problem in England prior to the explosion of witchcraft accusations and executions in England in the 1640s, "Heretofore one of those clients of Hell in a whole Country was hooted at as a strange Monster ... [it was] some silly poore and ignorant old women [who] were thus deluded by that infernal imposter."[2]

From at least 1622 to 1642 the first generation emigrants to New England were not exposed to a new stream of witchcraft books, pamphlets and sensational trials in England which previously spread fear among the population. During the years 1618 to 1642 the English government had consciously inhibited the "persecution of witches" at least in comparison to the twenty years prior to 1618 and the five years after 1642.[3] The new emigrants did not carry the example of an activist "witch hunting mania" with them from England to New England.

A secondary topic of research in the causes of the Salem witchcraft trials is the series of conditions confronting Salem village in 1692. These included social, economic, political and religious dislocation and most importantly the Indian attacks in New England prior to the Salem outbreak. The Indian attacks sent psychologically unstable refugees (especially from Maine part of Massachusetts at the time) streaming into Boston and especially Salem.[4]

There is no doubt the direct cause of the witchcraft outbreak in the Connecticut River Valley was a result of specific actions taken by individuals that led to the accusations of witchcraft. However, like the recent research on the Salem witch hunt these early colonists existed in an even more hostile environment than the later inhabitants of Salem. The new environment was unsettling and unnatural compared to their original homes in England. They were under pressure to survive where food supplies were not stable, wild animals and hostile natives were a constant fear, weather conditions were unlike anything they had known in England and even land ownership was a constant challenge as a result of the various methods by which land was acquired in the New England colonies. This anxiety was especially acute in Connecticut as a result of the questionable methods in which Connecticut was settled and land acquired. This issue would not be settled for Connecticut residents until the early 1660s. In addition, their homeland, England, would soon face a civil war that would tear the mother country apart politically and importantly for most of these settlers religiously.

The rebellion in England gave rise to a variety of heresies and accusations in which each side vilified their enemies using invective like Satanists, papists, anti–Christ and witch. New England ministers and their congregations had a stake in the English Civil War and actively participated in the pamphlet war in England by siding with the anti-royalists against King

Charles. Once Charles I was beheaded in 1649, the Congregationalists on "both sides of the Atlantic had much to congratulate themselves on." The Anglican Church "had been dismantled root and branch" and the Scottish alliance with the king ended. This also meant "the threat of a Presbyterian establishment warded off."[5] For the chiliastic inspired congregational ministers in New England the overthrow of the king was expected to lead to a religiously reformed England (the end of the Church of England) and usher in the Second Coming.

When Charles I was executed, some of the colonists were disturbed by this act. Rather than being shocked like many in England, "New England leaders instructed the colonists in the necessity of the act." It was known that English Presbyterians (the enemy of the Congregationalists, especially those in New England) had wanted to gain power by making an "arrangement with the King." With the king's death there was no hope this would come to pass. After all, for years the king was portrayed as "the leader of anti–Christian armies that opposed the reform party in England." Loyalty to Christ as the one "true King of the English people transcended loyalty to the King." This provided the basis for justifying both the Puritan revolution and the regicide. These arguments were preached by two of the most important ministers in the Massachusetts Bay Colony, John Eliot and John Cotton. Although the ministers did not hold public office in New England they and the governing officials supported congregational religious principles and were anti-royalists.[6]

Because the civil war dissolved the national government in England local governments functioned without Parliamentary leadership. The weakened central government gave rise to local control and a consequent upsurge in witchcraft accusations, trials and executions primarily from 1645 to 1647.[7] This led most famously to the rise of the witch finders Matthew Hopkins and his associate Thomas Stearne.

The Witchcraft Act of 1604 was the legal statute for trying witches. In England, witchcraft was a felony, not heresy. A higher level of proof was needed for a conviction. Hanging was the method of punishment for a convicted witch. Under English law torture was not permitted. Matthew Hopkins introduced a variety of techniques to discover the proof the law required. He introduced sleep deprivation and watching. The witch hunt under Matthew Hopkins in East Anglia has been estimated at a low of 100 to a high of 200 executions for witchcraft. The new techniques quickly found their way to the Massachusetts Bay Colony as early as 1648 (their use described by Governor Winthrop) and undoubtedly were used in other cases where more traditional methods of determining witches had failed.[8]

Other issues faced by the colonists during the period under discussion included a demographic downturn because the rate of immigration to New

England declined during the English Civil War. Many settlers left New England and returned to England to participate in the action back home. Later, following the beheading of Charles I in 1649, New England colonists returned to serve in the new government. The war was also hard on the New England economy, resulting in a slump in trade during the 1640s.

In addition, there was the basic belief in witches as well as the religious and legal certainty of their existence endorsed by their betters.[9] There was also the chiliastic mentality of the ecclesiastical authorities who preached Satan and his minions would try to tempt and convert as many souls to the devil's cause before the Second Coming in the New England colonies. The clergy were certain Satan was incensed Christians had come to inhabit this land filled with his servants, the Indians. Ephraim Huit, minister in Windsor, Connecticut, on September 10, 1639, preached to his congregation that the Indians were in league with "the devil" and "an enemy to the holy colony."[10] For the clergy, Satan was working twice as hard to discredit and tempt these colonists who invaded his kingdom on earth. Clearly, the ministers and the people had to be on their guard. One alternative begun in the 1640s to frustrate Satan was to convert the Indians to Christianity. It was also believed that this would hurry the Second Coming.[11]

Finally there was the absolute certainty witches existed. This was based on biblical authority and written into the basic laws of the Massachusetts Bay, the Connecticut colonies and the laws and legal treatises of their home country. Even if the English government had recently restrained the persecution of witches, they still existed as a reality in the religious and legal worldview of the general population as well as among the elites. Even if the average person did not accept the religious understanding of the compact with the devil, witches had always existed in their magical folk beliefs.[12] It was at the level of common folk beliefs that witches continued to stimulate the imagination of the people in England, and this was especially true of the colonists from East Anglia (who primarily settled in the Massachusetts Bay area). The colonists from East Anglia have been seen as one of a number of factors that led to the Salem witch trials in Massachusetts. However, the first witchcraft accusations that led to trials and executions originated in Windsor, Connecticut, in the Connecticut River Valley. The majority of the Windsor settlers came from the West counties of Devon, Dorset and Somerset. This demonstrates that traditional folk beliefs were shared by all Englishmen and provided the necessary context to accuse individuals of the first stage of witchcraft, *maleficia*, or harming, and therefore cannot be limited to one region alone.[13]

To understand the influence of the English Civil War on New England and for our purposes the rise of the deadly witch hunts in the Connecticut River Valley during the end of the decade of the 1640s through 1662/63

requires background on the connections seldom noted but nevertheless documented between the New World colonists and their mother country. First
it is important not to see seventeenth century New England as the "seed bed
of a new nation" but more as an "outlier of the old country." Another historian
has noted the "transition from one continent to another was extremely conservative. Massachusetts was more a new 'England' than a 'new' England."[14]

New England (at least the first generation of settlers and even many in
the second generation) maintained social relations "that linked the colony
and the homeland. The early colonists were never as severely cut-off ... nor
did they fully turn their backs on old England. Migration, return migration,
trade, kinship, inheritance money and messages tied London to Boston ...
[as well as the other New England colonies like Connecticut] ... and sustained
a community of interest between provincial Massachusetts and provincial
England."[15]

In fact, the New England community of interest with England was an
understatement. During the 1640s and 1650s New England clergy and officials
wholeheartedly supported the Parliamentary forces. In May 1643 for example,
the magistrates of the General Court of Massachusetts removed the king's
name from the oath of allegiance.[16] During the period of the English Civil
War New Englanders forwarded a "steady stream of advice ... across the
Atlantic: sermons, treatises, private letters ... and numerous colonists
returned to England to personally lend their aid by serving in Parliament,
the Army and the ministry for the English Church." From England men like
John Winthrop and others even in the second generation "depended on the
flow of English books and correspondence, and sustained a ravenous appetite
for English news."[17]

With all these cultural, economic and political linkages as well as the
psychological investment on a successful puritan political and religious outcome of the civil war in England, one asks, what affect did these events have
on the political, psychological and religious stability of New England
colonists?

Certainly the resurgence of witchcraft books, lurid pamphlets, witchcraft
accusations, trials and executions after 1642 had to have had some impact in
stimulating witch fear in the colonies. We know that prior to "1640 witch-
trials had become a rarity and had it not been for the English Civil War they
might have faded from public life altogether."[18] By 1645, Royalist and Parliamentary publications focused on the "devil," 'witches," and "papists." Witches
were used by both sides "as a propaganda weapon" and several prominent
persons were associated with witchcraft, especially the Protestant leader
Oliver Cromwell and the leader of the Royalist forces, Prince Rupert. The
"imagery surrounding Prince Rupert was more lurid than that surrounding
Oliver Cromwell."[19]

Renewed interest in diabolical witchcraft generated hysteria, especially in East Anglia, and led to the deaths of between 100 and 200 people for the crime of witchcraft.[20] In a sermon preached in 1647 a minister in Suffolk, England, rejoiced that beginning in 1643 England saw the "extirpation of popery, prelacy, superstition, and heresy," and more specifically, "many witches have been discovered by their own confessions and executed."[21] The emphasis on witches and the invective language used in pamphlets, broadsides and sermons provided a highly charged atmosphere that inspired the witch hunts in England but also stimulated an atmosphere receptive to the witch hunts in New England in the period under discussion. For more on this we need to investigate the background to this new witch hysteria and determine how news of such events was communicated in England and to act as a catalyst spreading the witch hunt to colonial New England and especially to the Connecticut River Valley.

# 1

# The English Civil War and the Revival of Witch Hunting in England

By 1645 the terror surrounding the English Civil War created an untenable psychological situation for many individuals. As noted in the pamphlet *Signs and Wonders*, "Do we not see the bloody wars doth more and more increase in our three Kingdoms whereby every mans heart een trimbles to think what shall become of him." The uncertainty created by war and the language of the anti–Christ and the devil, the choosing of sides and the growth of heretical religious groups caused great anxiety. For many it seemed the "world was turned upside down." Surrounded by their enemies, people came to believe there were those who could "channel the powers of the Devil to affect and afflict people."[1]

For the Royalist forces the "witch" was if nothing else guilty of the "sin of rebellion." The Parliamentary forces were guilty of the same sin. In 1642 the Parliamentary forces accused the opposing Royalist leaders (including the king) of being in league with papists and the devil. They specifically attributed chief Royalist military commander Prince Rupert's successes in the English Civil War to the devil's influence. In one pamphlet his familiar was designated as a "white dogge" who was a "downright divil" that had once been a "Lapland lady" who "hath vowed to follow the Prince to preserve him from mischief."[2] Interestingly, in the same pamphlet the author concluded it is "impossible to destroy him, untill the Colonies of new England come in to helpe us: they know how to order these Dog-Witches better far than We." (This is probably a reference to the bounty for wolf pelts common in New England at this time.)[3] When Prince Rupert's "white dogge" or "familiar" was killed at Marston Moor in 1644, "a decisive battle for the Parliamentarians," a propaganda pamphlet was issued with an illustration showing the death of the "dog" with the words "Sad Cavaliers, Rupert doth invite you all that doe survive to his dog's funeral- Close mourners are the witch, the Pope and the devil."[4] Following the Battle of Newbury on September 20, 1643, that saw the defeat of Prince Rupert, the pamphlet's author described how a "witch chewed the bullets fired at her." As a counter-measure, Parliamentary troops cut "her face in the belief drawing blood would neutralize her power." The results of the artillery barrage because of this battle was said to have left "the troops in a brutalized state." Perhaps this imagery was used to help justify the massacre of women after the Battle of Naseby in June 1645. The troops slashed the faces of the women following the battle as if "to break the powers of the witches."[5] According to Davies, it was a common seventeenth century belief that bleeding the witch "deprived her of her magical powers." The Royalists, like Papists, were thought to practice the dark arts to defeat their enemies. The captured women in the Royalist forces would have been suspected as witches. The soldiers would have blooded the women to protect themselves, and killed those "most vehemently suspect and ... reserve the rest for a more leisurely investigation."[6]

Whatever the reasons for these brutal actions the pamphlets and popular ballads infused the language of deviltry and witchcraft not only among the illiterate but elites as well.[7] For the time being those arguing against the reality

A witch is pictured as one of the mourners of Rupert's dog, Boy, "killed by a Valiant souldier who had skill in necromancy" (from John Taylor, *A dog's elegy, or, Rupert's tears, for the late defeat given him at Marstonmoore, neer York, London, 1644,* frontispiece).

of witches and witchcraft were undoubtedly silenced or ignored because for the moment English society was in the throes of a "spiritual" as well as political crisis. One of the most formidable weapons was to accuse your enemy of being in league with the "forces of darkness." After all, the most important institutions were again confirming the existence of witches: the Church, the king and even the Parliamentary Army.

Fear of witches was not limited to a few backward counties nor was it limited to isolated cases. The conditions of the time gave birth to a full blown witch hunt that frightened those accused of witchcraft as well as those who stood to be accused. The high point of the witch hunting and trials occurred in 1645. In pamphlets one could read, or for the illiterate, hear, "have not a crew of wicked Witches, together with the Devil's assistance done many mischiefs in Norfolk, Suffolk, Essex and other parts of the Kingdom ... some were executed at Chelmsford in Essex." Meanwhile, the author of the same pamphlet noted other witches were being held for trial and some of them of the better classes.[8]

## Impact of Matthew Hopkins in the Colonial New England Witch Hunts

The inspiration for witch hunting in Colonial New England during the first wave of witch trials were the Matthew Hopkins witch hunts in the East Anglian counties from 1645 to 1647. To understand this, first some information on his background and activities.[9]

Matthew Hopkins was probably responsible for the most "savage witch hunt in English history." By later 1647 he and his partner John Stearne were responsible for the deaths of approximately 100 to 200 East Anglian women and men (mostly women) although even today it is difficult to obtain an exact number.[10]

The hunt began in Manningtree, a small town on the river Stour in northeastern Essex County, England, and the home of Matthew Hopkins. During the winter of 1644 a tailor named John River had visited a "cunning woman" to determine what ailed his wife. Her ailment, he was told, was caused by witchcraft. Major suspicion fell on her elderly neighbor, Elizabeth Clark. When Hopkins heard this he went to the justices of the peace to complain. Elizabeth was arrested. Her body was searched for devil's marks and three were found on her person. Hopkins and his partner John Stearne decided to keep her "awake at night and to watch her closely."[11] This led to a new approach for obtaining confessions through sleep deprivation, at the time not seen as torture. Torture was used on the continent for witchcraft, a heresy there, but in England witchcraft was a felony, and torture was not allowed as part of the English legal system.[12]

By the fourth night of "watching" Elizabeth Clark, the two witch hunters claimed to have seen a "succession of diabolical familiars enter the room." Later Elizabeth Clark confessed she "copulated with the devil and these monsters were their offspring." After her confession and execution the two men had found their calling. Accompanied by "Mary Phillips a Manningtree midwife" who was experienced in finding devil's marks, the legal proof for the witch's covenant with the devil, they began their witch hunting careers.[13]

They took their investigations into the counties of East Anglia, specifically Norfolk, Suffolk, Essex, Isle of Ely, Huntingdonshire and Cambridgeshire. In late July 1645 thirty-two women were indicted for witchcraft at the Chelmsford Assizes in Essex County, England. Nineteen people were convicted of witchcraft and hanged, three were acquitted and the "rest either died in jail either before or after being brought to trial." It was the Earl of Warwick, one of the great Parliamentary leaders, who presided over these most notorious Chelmsford trials during the Civil War. He was a close personal friend of Oliver Cromwell and was admired by many New England elites for his parliamentary leadership.[14] As one historian noted, he would probably also have been admired by some New Englanders for his punishment of the witches at Chelmsford. This historian attributed much of the Puritan emigration to the new world "as a protest of the toleration of witchcraft" in England by the government from 1618 to 1642.[15] It was generally known the Earl of Warwick's family was steeped in a variety of anti-witch connections to witches and witchcraft. For example, he had been at Cambridge in 1603 "at the time that the *Witchmania* at that University was approaching its climax." From 1610 to 1614 he sat in the "House of Commons for Maldon in witch fearing Essex," and his step-mother had supported Richard Bernard by partially subsidizing his education. Bernard was a "Puritan of the most nonconformist type," the author of the influential *Guide to the Grand Jury-Men* states. He had in fact taken part in the famous witch trial held at the Taunton Assizes in the west county of Somerset a year prior to the publication of his book in 1627.[16]

The trials at Chelmsford had created such a sensation a forty-four page pamphlet was published on August 19, 1645, describing the trials.[17] The pamphlet undoubtedly sold well not because of any "legal or theological implications" but more because of its "sensational content that included: curses, deaths, infestations and satanic pacts." In addition, since the collapse of censorship in England in 1641, the previous attempt by the government to prevent publications involving witchcraft and such had been unloosened and now during the Civil War there was an "obsession with cheap print" and "all the News in England, of Murders, Flouds, Witches, Fires, Tempests and what not."[18]

Before the printing of the *Chelmsford Trials* pamphlet the Earl of Warwick returned to the House of Lords and began to hear misgivings from other members of Parliament. Soon afterward the pamphlet was published. Joseph Hall wrote, there was a "marvelous multitude of Witches abounding in all parts ... now, hundreds are discovered in one shire; ... in a village of fourteen houses in the North parts are found so many of this damned breed ... now we have known those of both sexes ... drawne into this damnable practice."[19]

The weekly pro–Parliament *Mercurius Britannicus* in late August 1645 contained Royalist complaints about the excessive number of witches in the Parliamentary counties of Suffolk and Essex and of fourteen witches executed at Chelmsford. "Sorcery and dealing with the Devil is in Suffolk and Essex; which counties from the beginning were under Parliamentary control." The editor of the paper admitted there were problems in the two counties, "Yes, we grant there are too many mischievous persons ... [like Hopkins and Stearne] ... permitted in our Quarters."[20]

Parliament was aware of the criticism and following the Earl of Warwick's return was already willing to hear a petition from the women in Chelmsford who had been reprieved. It appointed a committee to look into the accusations before Parliament learned of a "witch craze" that broke out in Suffolk where a number of witches had been arrested and were to be tried. Meanwhile, on the religious front, the "Westminster Assembly of Divines" had been meeting and agreed witches deserved death and their "real crime was compacting with the devil."[21]

Both the Westminster Assembly and Parliament on the surface seemed to refuse to allow extra-legal measures to try witches. Initially a routine court commission for Suffolk was appointed to deal with the witches in the county of Suffolk. However, shortly after a "report was carried to the Parliament then sitting, as if some busie men had made use of some ill Arts to extort such confessions from them."[22] Parliament decided to grant a special court of *Oyer* and *Terminer* (to see and to hear), issued under the emergency powers of the Lord Chancellor and normally used to deal with "riots and seditious plots."[23]

The Court was led by Serjeant John Goldbot of Suffolk, a respected jurist, a number of county magistrates and the appointment of two clergymen instead of lawyers, Edmund Calamy and Samuel Fairclough. The latter appointments were done to ensure the "most special care taken ... wherein the Lives and immortal Souls of the many were concerned." It had to be legally proven the guilty had made an "express compact with the Devil, or an implicit one, by employing imps ... to the hurt of their Neighbors, in Life or Estate." Because the courts realized it was "very difficult to convict any person upon ... [the Witchcraft Statute] ... but such as shall confes themselves guilty; and now great care was taken, such confessions should be purely voluntary and unconstrained; and the truth thereof might also be evidenced by many collateral circumstances, and other concurring and convincing evidence."[24]

The trials after a number of delays began on August 26, 1645. The 150 prisoners held in Ipswich were delivered to Bury St. Edmunds, in Suffolk County, for trial. On their arrival there was much activity related to the trials, with carpenters preparing a gallows in the market square and the assize court clerk prepared a "gaol calendar and indictment file."[25]

The irony of this commission was it was established to ensure a fair trial but at the same time to follow the Witchcraft Statute and the prescribed manner of detecting witches. The reality for these officials was even though some of these individuals were probably innocent others were witches. This was demonstrated in the two sermons Fairclough gave the morning before the trials began in St. Mary's church before Serjeant Goldbold, Edmund Calamy, the justices named on the Commission and the other county magistrates. In the first sermon Fairclough preached there was "such a sin as Witchcraft, that is of men; dealing and contracting with familiar Spirits; and did then confute all those arguments, which either former or later Sadduces and Atheists have produced to the contrary." In the second sermon he spoke not on the reality of witchcraft because that was an accepted fact, but on the "heinousness of the sin of those who would violently prosecute or unduly endeavor to convict any person, except plain convincing evidence could be brought."[26] Perhaps some of the guilty would go free but at least those who were not witches would not be found guilty if the letter of the law was followed.

Fairclough's sermons had probably worked to make both Stearne and Hopkins, who were the chief accusers, uncomfortable in the courtroom.[27] Nevertheless the jurors considered the cases individually and by the end of the day of the accused that appeared on August 26 sixteen women and two men were sentenced to death. Samuel Fairclough was convinced at "least none had been condemned unjustly." The jurors at Bury St. Edmunds had been more cautious than those at Chelmsford, willing to convict "with strong evidence" and just as willing to "acquit when they smelt a rat."[28]

The Court was scheduled to reconvene the next day. However, "by reason of the neere approaching of the Cavaliers" the court was "compelled to adjourn." Those tried and convicted were to be executed the next day. Still there were "120 more suspected Witches in prison." There is no record of what became of them, and although some were undoubtedly released, others were tried and executed. Others probably died in jail, likely from the ravages of jail fever (typhus).[29]

The general level of skepticism from 1618 to 1642 in England had been overcome and the reality of witchcraft was supported by Parliamentary commissions, legal and religious authorities. Much of this can be attributed to the unloosening of censorship after 1642 and the rise of extreme religious views like the Puritans and others including the influence of the Scots entering the fray in England's civil war. What is of interest for this study is during the civil war the counties of East Anglia gave rise to the most severe witch hunts but more important was the witchcraft propaganda during the civil war, and the witch trials became familiar to the New England settlements. The evidence shows these colonists had for the most part kept up correspondence and communication with their family, friends and business associates back in these counties. The news of the outbreak of witchcraft undoubtedly frightened and pained those in New England and to the more religiously inclined these were further signs of the "end times."

Before we turn to the influence of the events in England on New England I would like to briefly discuss two books that not only had an influence on witch hunting in England but would also come to play an important role in the discovery and prosecution of witches in New England and especially the first wave of witch hunting from 1647 to 1663.[30]

## Legal Manuals "Refuting the Skeptics"

With regard to continental witch hunting one of the most notorious books responsible for inspiring the intense witch hunts and trials in Europe was the *Malleus Maleficarum* or *Witches Hammer,* first published in Germany in 1487. Although the book did not play a significant role in the witchcraft trials in England, for our purposes the value of this book was not so much its description of witches and why they exist but in the legal part of the *Malleus* that acted as a how-to manual for prosecuting witches. Much like the value of the *Malleus* we find developed in this period lacking witchcraft trials and new witchcraft publications in England the publication of two handbooks or manuals that purported to provide the legal proof witches existed and offered justices a method of obtaining real evidence for their conviction in the courtroom. These rules of evidence were quickly incorporated into English and American courts because they provided legal guidelines for discovery of the secret crimes of witches.

The strictly legal handbook that originally incorporated a small section on witchcraft was Michael Dalton's *Countrey Justice* (the first edition 1618). In the first three editions, Dalton limited himself to a "perfunctory statement of the provision of the Jacobean Statute of 1604" and placed witchcraft under "Felonies by Statute." However, Dalton recognized something more was needed for the magistrates: they "may not always expect direct evidence, seeing all their works ... [witches] ... are the works of darkness , and no witness present with them to accuse them." The solution was to provide better information for the justices to find the necessary evidence. Dalton incorporated material from the witches arraigned at Lancaster in 1612 "before Sir James

# MALLEVS
## MALEFICARVM,
### MALEFICAS ET EARVM
haeresim frameâ conterens,

EX VARIIS AVCTORIBVS COMPILATVS,
& in quatuor Tomos iustè distributus,

*QVORVM DVO PRIORES VANAS DÆMONVM versutias, præstigiosas eorum delusiones, superstitiosas Strigimagarum cæremonias, horrendos etiam cum illis congressus; exactam denique tam pestiferæ sectæ disquisitionem, & punitionem complectuntur. Tertius praxim Exorcistarum ad Dæmonum, & Strigimagarum maleficia de Christi fidelibus pellenda; Quartus verò Artem Doctrinalem, Benedictionalem, & Exorcismalem continent.*

### TOMVS PRIMVS.
*Indices Auctorum, capitum, rerúmque non desunt.*

Editio nouissima, infinitis penè mendis expurgata; cuique accessit Fuga Dæmonum & Complementum artis exorcisticæ.

*Vir siue mulier, in quibus Pythonicus, vel diuinationis fuerit spiritus, morte moriatur* Leuitici cap. 10.

### LVGDVNI,
Sumptibus CLAVDII BOVRGEAT, sub signo Mercurij Galli.

M. DC. LXIX.
CVM PRIVILEGIO REGIS.

The *Malleus Maleficarum* is usually translated into English as *The Witches Hammer*. It was first published in Speyer, Germany, in 1487. The authors were two Dominican monks, J. Sprenger and H. Institor. From the edition published by Claude Bourgent, Lyons, 1669 (courtesy Wellcome Library, London).

Altham, and Sir Edward Bromley Judges of the Assizes there." From this trial Dalton listed seven evidentiary examples of witchcraft: witches have familiars or a spirit that appears to them; the familiar has someplace on the body to suck; witches have pictures of clay or wax found in their homes; a dead body will bleed upon the witches touch; the testimony of a person upon his death; the examination and confessions of servants and children of the witch; and their own confession "which exceeds all other evidence."[31] Even with the legal evidence Dalton provided and the witchcraft laws on the books, by 1625 witch trials were likely "to fail for at least one or more of three reasons: the exposure of the accuser as a fraud; insufficient evidence; or a natural medical explanation."[32]

Nevertheless, even though the government suppressed witchcraft prosecutions the fear of witches remained alive among Puritans and the common people. Witchcraft accusations returned and were again taken seriously by the authorities during the Civil War in England.[33] Evidence for the continued and underlying fear of witches among the Puritans can be found for example in Puritan minister Richard Bernard's *Guide to the Grand Jury-Men* (1627) published in the middle of the government's suppression of witch trials and on the eve of the "Great Puritan Migration" to New England. Richard Bernard had been a protégé of Frances, Countess of Warwick, the stepmother of the Earl of Warwick, who presided over the Chelmsford trials in 1645 and condemned nineteen individuals to death as witches. Earlier as a vicar in Somerset, Bernard was a participant in a witch trial at the Taunton Assizes in the year prior to the publication of his book.[34]

In his book Bernard cleverly ceded some points to skeptics, including some diseases might be due to natural causes and there might be false possessions. But he was on firmer ground and refused to yield on the witches' mark. He wrote these witch marks were proof of a "league with the Devil." This was the evidence that a covenant with the devil had been made and this "compact between the witch and the Devil" was a certain truth. The witch mark was critical to his argument and here Bernard quoted from Revelations 13, "that the Beast will have his marke" (who is the Devil's lieutenant) and "Tertullian found this true, and saith, It is the Devils custom to mark his.... Ezek. 9, Rev. 7 and 14."[35]

The Puritan clergy's view of witches was not the same as that of the common person, the witch doing *maleficia*. Instead the witch committed a more heinous crime by sinning against God by making a compact with the Devil, as shown by the devil's or witches' mark. Bernard's book was the last complete attempt "to resist the Government's offensive against superstition." Shortly after the publication of Bernard's book, George Abbot, Archbishop of Canterbury (1611–1633), retired. He was replaced by William Laud, Archbishop of Canterbury, from 1633 to 1645. With Laud's ascension to the leadership

Richard Bernard, in his *Guide to the Grand Jury-Men*, wrote, "Satan marketh his." The upper panel shows the Beast, the Devil's lieutenant, marking the foreheads of his followers. From the manuscript *Book of Revelation*, ink and watercolor, 1420 (courtesy Wellcome Library, London).

post of the Church the government began to censor the press and prevented the publication of new books on witchcraft. However, government censors did not prevent "fresh editions of older books and in the passages newly inserted in them."[36]

Dalton's 1630 edition of *Countrey Justice* expanded the material on witchcraft from earlier editions. The book was about 10 percent longer than the 1619 edition; however, the space devoted to witchcraft was increased by 250 percent. Dalton added, "witches are the most cruel, revengeful, and bloudy of all the rest" and gives specifics on familiars that includes many common animals that can appear in their shape. Finally, he provided additional material by quoting wholly from Bernard and expanding greatly on the witchcraft material in previous editions of the book.[37]

Dalton provided more specific information on the nature of witches' marks, their location and a description of how they might appear. In the 1635 edition he wrote first of the witch's teat where the familiar suckled and then described the devil's mark:

> the Devil leaveth other marks upon their body; sometimes like a blew spot or red spot, like a Flea biting; sometimes the flesh suncke in & hollow (all which for a time may be covered, yea taken away but will come again to their old forme.) And these Devill marks be insensible & being pricked will not bleed & be often in their secretest parts, and therefore require careful and diligent search.

Dalton quoted Bernard that there are "two main points to discover and convict these witches ... [the witches' teat and devil's mark] ... prove fully that those witches have a familiar, and made a league with the Devil."[38] He also included for the first time in his legal manual the underlying Puritan belief that the greatest crime was not defined in the 1604 statutes but was the sin of making a compact with the Devil. This approach appealed to both the "saints" in England and those later Puritan emigrants to New England. It made it easier to prosecute witches because the marks identified the witch; proved the witch had made a covenant with the Devil a crime in itself; and avoided the more difficult need to prove *maleficia*.

The abridged Bernard in the *Countrey Justice* influenced the Hopkins trials and the early colonial New England witch trials from 1647 to 1662/63.[39] The evidence for Bernard's influence in the Hopkins-Stearne trials is provided by John Stearne's book, *A Confirmation and Discovery of Witchcraft* (1648). He copied "page after page from Bernard" without attribution. To be charitable, he also "enriches the discussion with a vast number of concrete details drawn from the great witch-hunt of his own period."[40] It was the later editions of the *Countrey Justice,* especially the 1630 edition, onwards with much expanded material on witchcraft that "was the law book most often imported into the first English North American Colonies."[41]

## Hopkins Defends His Methods

Where John Stearne's defense of his activities as a witch hunter consisted of a sixty-four page book, Matthew Hopkins published his defense in 1647 in a twelve page pamphlet titled *The Discovery of Witches: in Answer to Severall Queries, lately delivered to the judges of the assize for the county of Norfolk* (1647).

Hopkins defended himself against charges made in clergyman John Gaule's book, *Select Cases of Conscience Touching Witches and Witchcrafts* (1646). He criticized his witch hunting methods, especially watching, and described the procedure in his book,

> Having taken the suspected witch, shee is placed in the middle of a room upon a stool, or Table, cross legg'd, or in some other uneasie posture ... if she submits not, she is then bound with cords, there is she watcht & kept without meat or sleep for the space of 24 hours. For (they say) within that time they shall see her Impe come and suck; a little hole is likewise made in the door for the Impe to come in at and lest it come in some lesse discernible shape, they that watch are taught to be ever & anon sweeping the room, and if they see any spiders or flyes to kill them. And if they cannot kill them, then they may be sure they are her Impes.[42]

Mathew Hopkins defended this and other methods in his pamphlet written in the form of a dialogue. When asked how he obtained his skill and knowledge about witches, he wrote "from experience" and related his first encounter with witches in his home town of Manningtree.[43]

Regarding the variety of marks that could be found on the body, especially of the poor and elderly judged by "one man alone," he wrote this was not the case. Here he raised the idea of a twelve person jury for "never was any man tryed by search of his body, but commonly by a dozen of the ablest men in the parish ... and most commonly as many ancient skilful matrons and midwives present when the women are tryed."[44] Hopkins said he had been criticized for torturing the victims by sleep deprivation. He answered that in Essex and Suffolk the magistrates directed him to keep the witches awake because they would then be "more the active to cal their Impes in open view sooner." This was discontinued about a year and a half previously by the judges and magistrates but according to Hopkins "their own stubborne wills did not let them sleep."[45]

Other methods besides the "unreasonable watching" included thrusting a pin, needle or awl into the insensible witches' marks on the body of the suspected witch; walking the suspected witches until their "feet were blistered," of which he blamed others but not himself; and "swimming" suspected witches, but as he noted, this evidence was "never brought in against any of them at their trials."

Hopkins defended himself against the charge of obtaining a confession by torture, by cajolery and trickery, by using leading questions or if the person confessed to doing impossible things like flying through the air. Hopkins

Matthew Hopkins, Witch-Finder General, with two suspected witches calling out the names of their familiars. From a later etching in 1792, after an earlier woodcut from the frontispiece of his book *The Discovery of Witches* (1647), J. Caulfield, London (courtesy Wellcome Library, London).

explained he wanted a good complete confession but only after making the suspected witch understand what she had done and the "horribleness of her sin." Obtaining the confession should be done without any "hard usages or questions" and she does of her "own accorde" confess to when the Devil appeared to her, what transpired, what her "familiars and spirits" were, and their names. Further, where she sent her familiars and what "mischiefs" they had done. At the same time, she confessed "to the same parties for the same cause, and all affected, is testimony enough against her for all her denyall."[46]

The final complaint was Hopkins "doth fleece the country of their money." He answered he never went anywhere he was not asked to go, that he declared someone a witch after "her tryal by search and their owne confession," and he only took enough to cover his own travel expenses for him and the companions who accompanied him.[47]

Hopkins' pamphlet has been criticized as an "evasive, arrogant and superficial work and unlikely to have satisfied skeptics like Gaule."[48] However, this was not an age of skepticism and Hopkins pioneered a number of new methods that made it much easier to prove someone a witch.

## Hopkins' Methods Introduced into New England

Some of Hopkins' methods, although questionable in England, found their way to Colonial Massachusetts. For example, watching and sleep deprivation were introduced into Colonial Laws of Massachusetts in 1648. In that same year in the witchcraft trial in Boston of Margaret Jones of Charlestown, the General Court of Massachusetts added the following to its records: "The Court desires that the same course which hath been taken in England for the discovery of witches, by watching, may also be taken here with the witch now in question."[49]

Governor Winthrop later reported that "in the prison in the clear daylight there was seen in her arms ... a little child ... [her familiar]."[50] Along with other evidence described by Winthrop the most damning was the fact that she had "an apparent teat in her secret parts as fresh as if it had been newly sucked" found after a "forced search" and the evidence obtained from watching her. Margaret Jones was the first witch convicted of witchcraft in Boston (but not New England) and executed by hanging.[51]

## Witchcraft Beliefs in England and New England

Witchcraft traditional beliefs from England were imported into New England. The commitment of the early Puritan settlers to magical beliefs versus those who found an accommodation between the strictures of their ministers and the traditional beliefs they brought with them from England continues to be debated.[52] But that the emigrants brought popular beliefs concerning magic and witches is not debated. "At the end of the sixteenth century, the average Englishman believed implicitly in magic and witchcraft. There was no doubt in his mind spirits and demons existed. His neighbors believed, as did his masters. And the law of the land confirmed his belief-the practices of magic and sorcery were amongst the most serious of offences."[53]

Just as in England, the law of the land in the newly established colonies (plantations) in New England quickly incorporated witchcraft into their early laws. The rush to include witchcraft laws in the New England colonies led one historian to write, "The discontent ... [of the tolerance of witchcraft by the English authorities] ... of the out- and out Puritan is recognizable rather in the emigration to the New England States during the period before the Great Rebellion.... That this great emigration was in part a protest against the toleration of witchcraft is suggested by the conduct of the emigrants after they had crossed the Atlantic. Their long repressed fury against witches found immediate expression."[54]

While it is true in 1636 Plymouth included the punishment of death for compacting, or conversing "by Way of Witchcraft, conjuration or the like" with the Devil, and in 1641 the *Massachusetts Body of Liberties,* as well as the *Capital Laws of Connecticut* in 1642 stated witches should be put to death, there is no evidence of witchcraft trials prior to the English civil war. It was not until the pressure produced by the "outbreak of witchcraft activity" that came from England "between King and Parliament ... when hundreds of witchcraft accusations were made and at a minimum, one hundred witches were executed that the three New England colonies (the New Haven Colony had a law similar to the Connecticut law) re-enacted their witchcraft laws in 1646 and even Rhode Island enacted a witchcraft law in 1647."[55]

To equate the first witchcraft laws based on Mosaic law as a reaction to a more tolerant witchcraft policy in the home country is undoubtedly over-reaching in order to blame Puritans for the witchcraft actions in the new world. Witchcraft laws were on the books in England because for most people in England witchcraft was a reality. For the "elect" in New England it was an especial duty to seek out witches. After all, the Bible was proof of the existence of witches. The Bible served as the ultimate source of authority for the early settlers in New England, especially for witches, with the injunction "Thou shalt not suffer a witch to live."[56]

Finally "troubles with the powers of darkness were expected in New England." The colonists had embarked on a mission to emigrate to a land where the devil's minions lived and the "existence of all these devil-worshiping neighbors was a constant reminder of the possibility of the danger from witchcraft." However, during the period before the English civil war there is no evidence among the colonists in general of seeking out and trying witches. On the other hand, there is every reason to believe there was no lack of concern over the potential for the devil to have the Indians do his bidding or corrupt one of their own and therefore they included witchcraft as one of the more important crimes in their criminal code.[57]

The application of the laws of England in the colonies varied according to jurisdictions. There was no agreement on how the law should be applied. Some believed English laws should override colonial laws at all times, others "in the absence of a colonial law governing a specific crime in the colonies that British regulations of a general nature should be applied in every case," and finally provincial bodies should be allowed to make their own laws and that opinions by judges should "be accepted as legally binding." The need for colonial law arose from the unique environment in the colonies as well as the needs of the colonial administrators who found themselves in a land without a king or Parliament and without a centralized justice system. Instead they found themselves in "provinces organized under a maze of different charters, proprietorships and crown authorizations." As a result came the early attempts to "include witchcraft as a prohibited act." The wording of the laws was not as elegant as the English laws but by necessity they were "brief and harsh." For example in John Cotton's 1641 book, *An Abstract of the Lawes of New England as They Are Now Established*, "Witchcraft which is fellowship by covenant with a familiar Spirit to be punished by death."[58]

Although there were early laws passed in New England regarding the punishment for the crime of witchcraft there is little evidence that before the mid-1640s there were any trials in New England for witchcraft. The reason for this is threefold: the elites governing in the colonies needed to keep colonization an attractive option to continue to bring needed emigrants to settle in New England because emigrants from England had other more attractive places to settle in the English Atlantic World; at this time the elites up until the English Civil War needed to maintain good relations with the Crown in England because legally the colonies were expected to receive their charters from the Crown; and during the period of the 1620s and 1630s there was a conscious effort on the part of the English government to suppress witchcraft trials in England.

That is not to say witches and the devil's wiles were not outside the immediate experience during this quiescent period of witch trials of both the New England elites that included clergy, civic officials and the general population.[59] For example, Thomas Hooker, minister in Hartford prior to his arrival in New England had successfully performed a Protestant exorcism of "fasting and prayer" on a Mrs. Joan Drake of Surrey County, England. Thomas Shepard (son-in-law of Thomas Hooker), who left England in 1635 and became minister of one of the leading churches in the colonies, the First Church in Cambridge, wrote in 1633, while in England, he had stayed "in a house which we found haunted with the Devil…. For when we came into it, a known witch went out of it."[60]

Governor John Winthrop of the Massachusetts Bay wrote in his diary that when Mrs. Hutchinson dwelt in Boston, Mrs. Hawkins, a mid-wife and healer, "gave cause for suspicion of witchcraft, for it was certainly known, that Hawkins' wife … had much familiarity with the devil in England."[61]

While in England Mrs. Hawkins was probably viewed as a "cunning woman," the term "cunning" derived from the Anglo-Saxon *cunnan* (to know). Cunning men and women were an integral part of the social fabric in seventeenth century England. However, to Puritans they were "white witches," worse than "black witches" because cunning folk "enticed people into an implicit bargain with the devil by encouraging them to seek magical aid instead of putting their faith in God's will," thus corrupting their souls.[62]

However, it seems Winthrop during this earlier time could also take a more light-hearted approach concerning the supernatural. The Hartford clergyman Thomas Hooker wrote to him in December 1638 to complain about Connecticut's poor reputation among potential settlers. In the first part of the letter Winthrop seemed to find Hooker's complaints amusing. He wrote it "makes me a little merrye." Hooker concluded when colonists newly arrive to the shore they are told "choose any place … goe not to Conitticut." Winthrop replied in jest the complaints the "Cattle doe not thrive, that your ground is barrin etc," sound like the "speech of a prophet" and added it could have been worse had you "kept poluted night assemblys, and worshipped the head of an asse." Clearly, Winthrop is describing an imaginary witch's Sabbat and poking fun at Hooker's overwrought concerns. One can only imagine how this letter was received by Hooker.[63] Nevertheless, it would have been ill advised to use this imagery in a humorous vein after the outbreak of the English Civil War and the vitriolic language that emerged on both sides accusing each other of employing witchcraft for nefarious ends. Clearly by the 1640s one could not write of these things even in jest.

The witch trials in the 1620s and 1630s would not have been welcome prior to the outbreak of the English Civil War. They would become more acceptable with the dissolution of the authority of the central government in England, the rise of heretical Protestant sects and witch hunting in England justified by a strain of millenialism that not only infected Protestant groups in England but was especially rabid in the radical Protestant ministers who had migrated to Colonial New England. These clergymen came with the expectation New England would "mark the spot of the New Jerusalem."[64]

With the outbreak of the war, New England ministers preached and looked to the English Civil War as the beginning of the "end times" that would usher in the Second Coming "and Sion be restored (especially in England) to her former beauty, and a new Jerusalem come down from heaven."[65]

As a result of this millenialism they expected to see what was foretold in the book of Revelation "Satan would be set loose." This would explain the "multitude of witches abounding in all parts" in England that seemed puzzling to many but was easily explained: Satan's "time is short he rageth thus extremely," and this required a heightened "piety, vigilancy and zeale of the faithful ones." This theme would be picked up by the New England clergy as they began to witness increasing religious conflict and backsliding over the succeeding years of seventeenth-century New England.[66]

## Transatlantic Flow of Information— Witchcraft Trials and Accusations

The opportunity for news concerning witchcraft trials and accusations at both the elite level and the popular level from England to New England was delayed but not diminished by distance based on the circulation of letters, books, papers, newsletters and the arriving passengers from England with news. News was more regular and plentiful in the 1630s and primarily concerned family and business affairs. By the early 1640s political and religious events began to take a more ominous turn. As conditions deteriorated in England, news continued to flow to New England but was now more delayed and irregular.

Reports concerning witchcraft accusations and trials do not seem to have been reported in personal correspondence that has survived coming to or going from New England. There are possibly a number of reasons which I will note later. However we do know there was an active trade in newsletters, books and almanacs as well as information relayed from passengers and relatives coming to or returning to England during the 1640s. We have evidence some of this communication concerned the witch hunts occurring in England, especially in the newspapers. The most reliable evidence for this communication, as noted previously, was that in 1648 the Massachusetts General Court incorporated into the law "the same course which hath been taken in England for the discovery of witches."[67]

Correspondence although slow, helped emigrants from England maintain contact with family and retain their "common national identity." Both elites and even the non-literate maintained connections through this long distance communication. "The leading families of New England engaged in prolific transatlantic correspondence" while the common people wrote when "necessity" required it and often sent "news of their neighbors" or other acquaintances.[68]

The mail that traveled on ships between England and the colonies brought "news and correspondence." However, shipping was dangerous and slow and if a ship was lost, delayed or captured by pirates the mail would be delayed or completely lost. Many times the sender did not know if the mail had made it to its intended destination.[69] Because correspondence took weeks or even months to reach its destination any news would probably be old news by the time it arrived and explains why in much of the personal correspondence the writer would advise a better account of the news "could be obtained" by word of mouth from arriving passengers.[70] Another concern was the "danger of interference, censorship and confiscation at any stage" during passage. Sensitive papers were susceptible to interception by the colonial leaders or their enemies in England.[71]

Families like the Winthrops of Massachusetts and Wyllyses of Connecticut maintained an extensive correspondence and could be afforded some measure of privacy in their correspondence. Those who could not read or write depended on a minister, physician, merchant, neighbor or "employ [ed] a scribe to set their words to paper" but had little privacy.[72] It has been estimated in the colonies at this time less than 60 percent of the male colonists could sign their names and less than 50 percent of the women. For our purposes besides this lack of privacy these New Englanders also "lived closer than we have imagined to the credulousness word-of-mouth world of the peasant, closer to its absorbing localism, closer to its dependency on tradition and on the informed few." In other words, it was not a literate culture but an oral culture. News and information were spread directly by word of mouth or newsletters, pamphlets and other public communications and were read aloud in a communal setting.[73]

Besides letters relating family news and local events the elites also received printed books and newsletters. Book lovers who moved to New England were not "cut off from the literary culture of England and the printed polemics of seventeenth century England" than those with family and business dealings. Books reached the seventeenth-century New England colonies within a few months following their publication in England. The "colonists were disadvantaged" no more than those in some of the remote counties in England where "news" reached them slowly as well.[74]

Books traveled among the migrants personal possessions.[75] Consignments of books were shipped from England to New England. Throughout the colonial period "New Englanders could turn to imported books." They were loaned and circulated and kept for private enjoyment. Their circulation was especially "brisk among the community of divines."[76] Some books were most unwelcome, especially those "critical of government and religion." For the everyday person, besides gossip, other news from England was either sent or carried by emigrants or those who had traveled from England to New

England and brought or returned with "almanacs and diurnals [daily newspapers], gazettes and other prints."[77] Included among the gossip, correspondence, newsletters, pamphlets and chapbooks one can be sure the subject of witches, trials and executions were included because as we have seen sensational witchcraft trials had become so prevalent back home in England.[78] Like the war in England there is little doubt the outbreak of witchcraft would have caused great concern and raised questions whether there were witches in New England like the witches in England found especially in the communities of the most "godly."

By the middle of the 1640s "hundreds of New Englanders were in England ... some of them took pains to send printed newsbooks and manuscript newsletters, which helped satisfy the news-hunger of friends and kinsmen" in the New England colonies. In addition "printed gazettes and mercuries circulated in New England."[79] The English Civil War newspapers were particularly prized "especially among the governing elite." In May 1647, for example, Herbert Pelham wrote to John Winthrop, "I have sent the printed News to your Brother Dudley."[80] The governing elites, the Winthrops, Pynchons, Winslows, Dudleys and Haynes, "shared in a network of information" that covered Massachusetts to its western frontier and from Plymouth Colony to southern Connecticut and beyond.[81]

The discussion of witch trials and the outbreak of witchcraft trials in England do not appear in the private correspondence among these elites; however, they would have been exposed to some of this orally, directly from passengers arriving from England. There was a general caution in writing down controversial matters even in private correspondence (as earlier noted, there really was no private correspondence). For example, Stephen Winthrop wrote to his brother John Winthrop, Jr., "I canot inlarge to particular, passingers and Bookes will inform best."[82] As for writing about witchcraft it seems doing this might also cast suspicion on those lacking religious or scholarly credentials. For example, even in the *Parliaments Post* in the summer of 1645, a writer who reported on witchcraft wrote, "I am pursuing this discourse which did arise from the consideration of the witches, I am afraid the people suspect that I begin to conjure myselfe." At the time it was the common belief it was bad luck to discuss the "Devil's business" either publically or privately never mind writing it down.[83]

During the summer of 1645 official news reports from both those sympathetic to the Parliament and to the king reported on the outbreak of witchcraft in England. Primarily written as propaganda for each side it is still important to remember witchcraft was a serious charge. The news would have taken weeks to reach the New England shores but the elites in New England would have read in the *Diary or an Exact Journal of the Houses of Parliament,* "that the Devil is a busie & spiteful in the end of Times, as at the beginning of it, and surely this is bad news to all the World." Or in *The Parliaments Post*, "Here is an infection in wickedness; And the spirit of the Cavaliers because it could not prevaile with our men, hath met with some of our women; and hath turned them into Witches." The parliamentary paper, *A Perfect Diurnal*, reported on the trial of the "'Norfolke Witches about 40 of them, and 20 of them already executed and what strange prophecies some of them had before their deaths." The Royalists considered rebellion as a form of witchcraft and announced in the opening sentence in the August 10–17 edition of the *Mercurius Aulicus*, "The Rebels had almost forgotten their owne business, for till this last moneth they had omitted Witchcraft (an usual Attendant of former Rebellions)...." The article stated there had been no previously declared witches then reported "now the Rebels are so plentifully furnished, that they confesse 200 in Suffolke and Essex who were freely permitted as long ... as they bewitched Cavaliers ... so at last they began to practice upon friends, whereupon 14 of them were executed at Chelmsford and divers others at Ipswich, who (as tis printed in London) had their meeting with the Devill, whereof there are above 200 discovered of which 22 undertook to bewitch Prince Rupert [the military leader of the Royalists]."[84]

However, by September 1645 the parliamentary *Moderate Intelligencer* openly questioned Matthew Hopkins' activities in East Anglia:

> Whence it is the Devils should choose to be conversant with silly Women.... And sure there are those that are inquisitive enough and have wickednes enough to deal with him for these ends.... They will meddle with none but poor old Women: as appears by what we received from this day from Bury, 200 Indictments against such.... Life is precious, and there's need of a great inquisition before it be taken away.[85]

This criticism by the *Moderate Intelligencer* followed after the special Parliamentary Commission had been sent to Bury St. Edmunds to try the prisoners on August 26, 1645. Even with the special Parliamentary commission sixteen women and two men were condemned to death and executed the following morning. The trials of the others indicted were suspended due to the proximity of the Royalist forces and moved where they could be arraigned and tried later. The reality of witches was such even when one newspaper questioned what purpose the devil would have in corrupting old powerless women when it made more sense to "Assist a Prince or a General in a Cause against the True Religion." Nevertheless, this criticism could not sway people from their beliefs.[86]

The reference in the *Mercurius Aulicus* was to the pamphlet *A True and Exact Relation of the Several Informations, Examinations and Confessions of the late Witches arraigned and executed in the County of Essex* (1645). It appeared shortly after the executions in Chelmsford, on August 19,

1645. Whether this pamphlet was available in New England following its publication there is no evidence. However, as previously stated, it was extremely popular in England because of its "sensational content: curses, deaths, infestations, satanic pacts-all further proofs the times were out of joint."[87] This pamphlet would have had an appeal if for no other reason as curiosity to the elites in New England who had connections with friends and relatives in the counties involved in these witch trials. For example, the Reverend James Hopkins, the father of Matthew Hopkins, had written a letter to John Winthrop in 1632 that showed a close connection with John Winthrop as well as an intimate knowledge of his family and friends. Ironically, writing,

> Sir, I am so well affected by your plantation, that if I can not enioyce my libertie upon gods terms as I haue done, I haue a purpose to make my selfe a member of your plantation, and when I come I hope I shall not come alone; ... we hold our selues tied here, and dare not break loose till god sett vs loose.[88]

Unfortunately, for the victims of the witchcraft trials in East Anglia, James never moved his family to New England. Perhaps if he had done so bringing Matthew Hopkins to New England at the age of twelve, the history of the witchcraft trials would probably have been much more limited in scope and magnitude.

In addition, New England elites had connections with important figures like the Earl of Warwick who presided over the trials in Chelmsford.[89] They would have been curious about what had transpired at the trials and their involvement. As noted previously, there were opportunities to acquire these materials because there were correspondents in England like Pelham ready to supply them with any materials they wanted. For example, Pelham wrote to John Winthrop "if there be any thing yow have not scene yow may command them."[90]

Sensationalist pamphlets were popular among the lower classes in England and those emigrating to New England (at least those who were not Puritans) describing murders, monsters, evil portents, witches and conspiracies as well as the multitude of religious pamphlets that had arisen as a result of the war.[91] Some of these pamphlets likely made their way to New England to either be sold or carried by passengers and circulated among friends and family.[92] Charles Chauncey, president of Harvard, in a sermon given in 1651, wrote of the effect of these writings on the people "there is to be found in [New] N-England the contempt of the word of God and his ordinances, and listening to lying books and pamphlets, that are brought over into the country, whereby multitudes are poysoned amongst us."[93]

It had not taken long for the outburst of witchcraft to spread to New England in the troubling times of the late 1640s. The first recorded witchcraft accusations in New England began along the wilderness area in the Connecticut

River valley in the town of Springfield, Massachusetts, in 1645, however, subsequent criticism of this first recording suggests it may be "three or four years to early." Nevertheless, it is known on the eve of the war in England two ministers in Windsor, Connecticut, only a few miles from Springfield, Massachusetts, along the Connecticut River were giving sermons suggesting the devil was in Windsor. Not naming but suggestive of a witch among them.[94] The reverend John Eliot, in a letter dated July 4, 1651, from Natick, Massachusetts, that appeared in the London newspaper, *Mercurius Politicus*, wrote,

> The State of things here amongst us seems more troublesome; we have sad frowns of the Lord upon us, chiefly in regard of fascinations, and witchcraft…. Four in Spring-Field were detected, wherof one was executed for murder of her own childe, and was doubtless a witch; another is condemned, a third under trial, a fourth under suspition: One in Dorchester condemned, another under suspition, some say also that there are divers under suspition at Ipswich.[95]

Eliot also wrote that besides witchcraft there were other "Fascinations by strange errors, not a few; and there are also … [some Church members] … whom they call Shakers…. The Church has given them some admonition." Eliot offered his rationale that the fundamental cause of the discord was millennial enthusiasm in New England and in England,

> We are in expectation of the Reign of Christ … when Governors not only in Church but in the Commonwealth, shall deduce all their Acts and Orders from Scripture … whence come doubts, shakings, unsettlement but for want of this, and nothing will quiet England but this way, to reduce all unto Scriptures … and bring all to unity in Christ Jesus.[96]

Eliot wrote to remind Oliver Cromwell he had an opportunity to put the English "government in the hands of the Saints."[97] Eliot was not alone, as the New England minister John Cotton, in his first public sermon in support of Cromwell on January 10, 1651, defended "the act of regicide" and introduced "Oliver Cromwell as the agent of God purifying Old England." Other letters from New England clergy followed singing his praises.[98]

There were many reasons for New England's support of Oliver Cromwell, especially his congregational sympathies and the fact that he looked on the colonies as "models of the godly state." He had seriously considered immigrating to New England in 1631, and he had friends and relatives in the New England colonies. However, the most critical activity Cromwell undertook was to garner the initial support of the New England colonies in 1652 when the "Congregational ascendency" through Cromwell's support seemed assured in England" and other writings that demonstrated to the colonists in New England, "Cromwell was the champion of their churches as well as their congregational allies" in old England.[99]

Millennial enthusiasm for the new order under Cromwell ran high on

both sides of the Atlantic in the 1650s. Besides strengthening congregationalism and controlling various "sects" he was "making progress drawing
together Protestant powers on the continent" and "striking out against
Catholic Spain."[100]

All this progress was due to the efforts of Oliver Cromwell. His death
in 1658 endangered all that had been accomplished. New Englanders were
shocked by his death. Confidence in the future and seeds of doubt were
expressed. Had they "misinterpreted events" were the events they expected
"not to be fulfilled"? The imminent arrival of the millennium and the "end
times" that seemed to be assured in the early 1650s was cast in doubt. "The
decade of the 1650's, the decade of so many hopes, was coming to an end on
a note of doubt, perhaps even fear."[101]

The ascendency of Cromwell in England did not dampen the colonists'
enthusiasm for witch hunting and his death may have helped to indirectly
contribute to an increase in witch hunting activity not just in the New England
colonies but elsewhere as well.[102] However, in New England the trials and
executions of witches during this first period would later culminate in the
Hartford witch hunt of 1662/63.

# 2

## The "old serpent" Disturbs the Peace of the New England Churches

The religious tensions in New England were not only within the structure of the churches but in the DNA of the very founding of New England. This was combined with the unleashing of "heretical" beliefs during the English Civil War and the witch hunting "free for all" in the East Anglian counties in England. It occurred especially under the witch finder Matthew Hopkins, who introduced the new techniques and ideas of "searching and "watching" into England that were almost immediately adopted in the New England colonies. These exacerbated the already fragile community relations regarding religious heresy and the suspicion of witchcraft in the Massachusetts and Connecticut colonies.[1]

In reviewing the religious controversies in New England at this time one is struck by the continual mention of witchcraft as a first reference point. The "belief in the literal second coming of Christ pervaded New England Puritan culture." Although the extreme "theological and political positions" of some of the settlers were not held by the "majority of the ministers and the populace" there had been "important attempts" over the years to push for a "more thorough and rapid reformation of society than most New Englanders were ready to accept."[2] Thomas Hooker wrote what for many was a reason to emigrate to New England before the English Civil War that "England hath seen her best days, and the reward of sin is coming apace."[3] For some believers "the glory foretold in the Book of Revelation would be known by the present generation." In addition, "the gathering of the churches in a congregational manner necessarily preceded it."[4] To immigrate to the new world portended among other things "one's willingness to do battle with the Antichrist."[5]

New England ministers were concerned the heightened excitement could lead to "violence against those unwilling to accept an immediate rule by saints." To counter this potential violence New England Congregationalists advocated continuing to covenant in their churches because the "act of covenanting ... marked a significant step to the final days."[6] The chiliastic atmosphere of the last days just as in England certainly contributed to a higher sensitivity toward witchcraft beliefs and the confounding of heresy with witchcraft in New England. Legally witchcraft was not considered a heresy in England but a felony as a result of the English Witchcraft Act of 1562 and the harsher Witchcraft Act of 1604. The basic system of law in England applied as well in New England. Specifically neither courts nor the clergy in England at this time questioned the reality of witchcraft. They saw it as the "duty of the courts to extirpate it." Therefore "English law books now gave the most minute directions as to the means of detecting and the form of trying witches."[7]

Although the separation of heresy from witchcraft as felony may have been "settled law" it did not stop clergy in New England from invoking "the devil" and reference to his agents when referring to "heretics and heresies in New England." Cotton Mather later wrote, "The Devil does extreamly [sic] dread the approach of that Illustrious time, *When The Kingdom of God shall come*" and as the visible saints in New England the devil was especially pleased to turn his attention to leading them astray.[8] In addition he added, "I believe, there never was a poor Plantation, more pursued by the *wrath* of the *Devil*, than our poor *New England....* It was a rousing *alarm* to the Devil, when a great Company of English *Protestants* and *Puritans*, came to erect Evangelical Churches, in a corner of the World, where he had reign'd without any control for Ages; and it is vexing *Eye-sore* to the Devil, that our Lord Christ should be known and own'd, and preached in this *howling Wilderness*." He has "left no *Stone unturned*, that so he might undermine his Plantation, and force us out of the Country."[9]

## *The Anne Hutchinson Effect*

With "millennial excitement running high" some of the early settlers tried to seize the moment and ensure the "prophecy" was coming to pass. One of the earliest signs of this early fulfillment was evident in the Antinomian controversy in Massachusetts in 1637. Ironically, during Anne Hutchinson's examination by the Massachusetts General Court for heresy, she referred to the Reverend of the First Congregational Church of Hartford, Thomas Hooker's, sermon *The Danger of Desertion* and his core message "of England's progressive apostasy." Subsequently the "Holy Spirit" revealed to her "England should be destroyed" leading to the "Antichrist's fall."[10]

Anne Hutchinson and her beliefs derived from the "spiritist" or immediate revelations from the Holy Ghost. Her beliefs were not without supporters and were seen as a threat to the established New England clergy. Anne was banished from the colony in 1637 and in the following year she was excommunicated. During her trial it was evident the clergy had to "discredit and humiliate her" and not surprisingly, there was an attempt to link her with the devil. At her trial in 1637, the ideas she espoused were described as "an old method of Satan an ancient enemy of free grace." The clergy asked, was not that "old serpent" working after "his old method even in our daies." They accused her of insinuating herself into the community, especially her knowledge of and helping in childbirth (see pointed accusation below regarding this). Clergy asked how she knew her revelation was true or false and of God or Satan. To the clergy, with Anne's help, Satan had a commission to do his greatest to "undermine the Kingdom of Christ here ... and finally, the faithful ministers of the Church assisted by the Civil Authority, to discover this "Master-piece of the old Serpent ... would soon have driven Christ and the Gospel out of *New England* ... and to the repossessing of Satan in his ancient Kingdom."[11] Later at her hearing at the Church in Boston "she thought it needlesse to conceale herselfe any longer, neither would Satan lose the opportunity of making choyce of so fit an instrument, so long as any hope remained to attain his mischievous end ... disturbing the peace of his Churches."[12] When Hutchinson was banished from the Church the preface to the justification read, the "Lord had allowed the Churches to discover this great imposter, an instrument of Satan so fitted and trained to his service for interrupting the passage, Kingdome in this part of the world, and poysoning the Churches here planted."[13] She was cast out from the Church in Boston as an "unworthy member" and "this subtlety of Satan was discovered to her utter shame and confusion."[14]

Peter Bulkeley, minister of the Concord Church who served as moderator at the 1637 synod, was called to examine the "errors" of Anne Hutchinson. In March 1638 he was also one of the ministers who sat during the church trial of Anne Hutchinson, which resulted in her excommunication from the Boston church. He wrote of Anne, "that wretched Jezebell *whom the Devill* sent over hither to poyson these *American Churches,* with her depths of Sathan which she has learned in the school of the Familists ... she knew not that her glorious revelations were Satanical Delusions."[15]

Not content to besmirch her reputation with these accusations alone Governor Winthrop indirectly tied Anne to witchcraft and the consequences of heresy. He wrote around the time of Anne's trial that Mary Dyer, her friend, was "notoriously infected with Mrs. Hutchinson's errors had been delivered of a child some months before ... and the child buried (being stillborn)." Mrs. Hutchinson, the midwife, Mrs. Hawkins, and another woman were the only ones to see the infant. Rumors began to spread "the child was a monster." The authorities interviewed Mrs. Hutchinson before she left the colony. She said she had meant to report the death of the infant. The midwife was questioned and told the authorities the infant's "head was defective and misplaced." The authorities informed her Mrs. Hutchinson had given them a complete description of the infant and they intended to exhume the body. Winthrop wrote, "it was a woman child … it had a face but no head and the ears stood upon its shoulders … it had no forehead but over the eyes four horns hard and sharp … two mouths … instead of toes it had three claws on each foot … sharp as talons." The infant was exhumed though "much corrupted, yet most of these things" could be seen. Clearly, anyone who read of the description of the child could imagine it was the spawn of the devil.[16]

Concerning the midwife Mrs. Hawkins, it was discovered she had left the jurisdiction. Winthrop wrote it was time for her to be gone because it was known she "used to give young women oil of mandrakes and other stuff to cause conception; and she grew into suspicion to be a witch…."[17]

Later Winthrop established a more specific link between Mrs. Hutchinson and Mrs. Hawkins. He wrote in his diary in 1640 "when Mrs. Hutchinson dwelt in Boston [she] gave cause for suspicion of witchcraft…. Hawkins' wife (who continued with her; and a bosom friend) had much familiarity with the devil in England, when she dwelt at St. Ives."[18] Mrs. Hawkins was not only a midwife but she was likely a "good witch" or "cunning woman" because when she was in England she was consulted by a diverse group of people including "divines." As previously noted, to Protestant ministers in England and New England the "good witch" was the "more monstrous" because to obtain satisfactory results the devil used trickery to capture the soul of the person who benefited from his deceit and in so doing "killed" it.[19]

As if to confirm beliefs that Antinomians were in league with the devil, four months later, Anne Hutchinson on the Isle of Aquiday (Acquidneck or Newport, Rhode Island) in the Narragansett Bay, "after her time was fulfilled … delivered of a monstrous birth." To ensure the proper lesson was drawn from this "monstrous birth" it was communicated throughout the country. In Boston, the Reverend Mr. Cotton in an the open assembly, "upon lecture day, declared … [there] … to be twenty-seven several lumps of a man's seed, without any alteration, or mixture of anything from a woman, and thereupon gathered, it might signify her error in denying inherent righteousness, but that all was Christ in us." Clearly Cotton attempted to connect the birth as a punishment for Anne's heresy and her friendship with the witch, Mrs. Hawkins. Additionally, he also wanted to ensure this knowledge was spread throughout the colonies and did so from his pulpit in Boston.[20] Winthrop wrote, "these things are so well known in New England, that they have been made use of in public by the reverend Teacher of Boston, and testified to so many Letters to Friends, that the things are past Question ... this is now come to be known and famous over all the Churches, and a great part of the world."[21] For how news of Mrs. Hutchinson's "monstrous birth" could have been communicated throughout New England we have the example of John Josselyn's description of Mary Dyer's earlier "monstrous birth." In his first voyage to the Massachusetts Bay from England in 1639 on the ship *Nicholas of London*, he wrote, when they passed a ship near Cape Ann they yelled out for news of New England and the sailors told them of a "general earthquake" and of the "Birth of a monster at Boston, in the Massachusetts Bay, a mortality."[22]

Governor Winthrop requested Mr. John Clarke, a physician and preacher of Rhode Island, report on the birth. Winthrop received a detailed letter analyzing the contents of the "monstrous birth." His findings indicated there were "twenty-six or twenty-seven distinct lumps" of different sizes. The lumps contained "small round globes" about the size of a "small Indian bean." Two unlike the rest contained "congealed blood." According to Winthrop, Mr. Cotton on the next lecture day did acknowledge "his error," indicating he had gotten his "information by a letter from her husband." Nevertheless, Winthrop later concluded "she had vented misshapen opinions, so she must bring forth deformed monsters."[23]

The assault on the clergy and the heretical beliefs put forward by Anne Hutchinson were not quelled with her banishment and continued to spread throughout New England, including Hartford. Governor Winthrop reported in 1640 a young man named Mr. Collins came to Hartford having been hired as a teacher. His friend, Mr. Hales, had traveled to Aquiday and came under the influence of Mrs. Hutchinson. Mr. Collins wrote to his friend, Mr. Hales, to beware of Mrs. Hutchinson. Mr. Hales corresponded with Mr. Collins concerning Hutchinson's ideas. As a result Mr. Collins left Hartford "without leave" and was "taken with her heresies." Winthrop attributed this conversion to her relationship with the witch Mrs. Hawkins because it seemed that just as in Boston, people were easily swayed by her views and he saw this as attributable to the influence of witchcraft.[24]

The Reverend Thomas Hooker in Hartford, Connecticut, was no stranger to this controversy and had been a moderator at the Synod in 1637. In 1640, in correspondence with his son-in-law Thomas Shepard in Cambridge, Massachusetts, he recounted the following story. After speaking of Hutchinson, he said there were "severall persons by the seaside with us that way, but wether it be knowne to the rulers of that place, I know not. My heart is marvelous apprehensive of the hazards." Further, not many "Sabbaths ago had disputed with a Mr. Aspeynall on the meaning of revelation." The man supped with the Governor and told him the "gospel is the rule of revelation" and was all that was necessary for revelation and the matter was settled. This raised grave concerns for Hooker: "Myself and my brother Stone are making out what forces we may against it, for we fear a suddayne alarum; and ergo we would have our people have their weapons in readinesse. The elders here in the river conceave yt the printing of the synod would be now seasonable and singular use, to outface these delusions."[25]

The fear and tension surrounding this heresy was real. The fact Hooker would write they needed to have their "weapons in readinesse" was not just metaphorical. It was not just verbal attacks alone and the calling out of clergy on their various points during sermons, but as Thomas Weld wrote, "after our Sermons were ended at our publike lectures, you might have seen a halfe a dozen Pistols discharged at the face of the Preacher, (I mean) so many objections made by the opinionists in the open Assembly against our doctrine delivered, if it suited not their fancies ... and this done not once and away, but day to day after our Sermons."[26]

## Religious Toleration Advocated in the Connecticut Valley

As we have seen by the example of antinomianism there were other "heretical" opinions found, especially in Rhode Island, that included radical "spiritists" and Baptists connected to the "English sectarian underground." The clergy in New England later found themselves coming under increasing criticism for their support of measures against dissenters.[27] New England Puritanism was beginning to experience "ideological fragmentation like that of its counterpart in England." This siege mentality helps to explain the visceral reaction to William Pynchon who served as a magistrate in Springfield, Massachusetts, from 1641 until he was called to court to answer charges for his book, *The Meritorious Price of our Redemption*, published in England in 1650. Oddly enough an incident connected to a witchcraft trial originated in Springfield. According to one historian, "To its credit, the court did not openly declare the witchcraft episode linked to Pynchon's doctrinal aberrations, but the speed and severity of its condemnation of the book suggests it may indeed have perceived such a connection."[28]

William Pynchon was an early emigrant to the Massachusetts Colony coming from Essex, England. He arrived with the Winthrop fleet. He quickly established himself as "flourishing merchant" in the Massachusetts Bay. By 1635 Pynchon moved to the Connecticut River Valley and helped to establish the town of Agawam, later named Springfield after his hometown in England. Pynchon expanded the fur trade with the Indians and established an important trading post in what is now Windsor Locks. When the river towns along the Connecticut River established independent governments they sent deputies to the Connecticut General Court. Pynchon served as chief magistrate for Agawam.[29]

The relationship between William Pynchon and the de facto government of Connecticut, the Connecticut General Court, was contentious. When the General Court declared war against the Pequot Indians "at a meeting at which he was not present" the government cautioned Pynchon not to "betray" the General Court because of his "friendship" with the Indians. Meanwhile, one of his boats was pressed into service in the cause and a tax levied on Pynchon to help defray the costs of the war. A second area of contention occurred when the General Court granted one or two persons in each frontier town exclusive rights to the beaver trade of one shilling per skin, a monopoly Pynchon already enjoyed. Finally, the most difficult and critical was the controversy over a shortage of corn. The shortage was caused by a poor harvest in 1637 subsequently threatening famine in the Connecticut River Valley. To mitigate the shortage, Pynchon was ordered to purchase corn from the Indians by the General Court at five shillings per bushel. Others were not permitted to trade for corn with the Indians unless it was out of dire necessity. Pynchon tried to trade with the Indians at the fixed price but the Indians refused to sell their corn. He informed the Hartford authorities. The General Court sent "Captain John Mason, the conqueror of the Pequot up the river to obtain the necessary supply." Mason fared no better and "returned to Hartford convinced Pynchon was attempting to profit from the shortage." Shortly following his return Pynchon was charged with "unfaithful dealing in the trade of corne." He replied even when his "own family and neighbors were in want" he refused to pay more for the corn than was mandated by the General Court.

The General Court asked the Reverend Hooker and Samuel Stone for an opinion on the questions that had been brought before the court. Hooker accused Pynchon of refusing to purchase the corn until he could obtain a monopoly on the price and had in fact "broken his oath." Pynchon was fined forty bushels of corn. In the end Pynchon was shown to not have broken his oath because a few months later Mason with the threat of force had to pay "twelve shillings a bushel in order to obtain any corn from the Indians."[30]

Nevertheless this overreach by the General Court was resented by Pynchon because he had been judged and fined by the Court on Hooker's word that "Pynchon's conduct was immoral" and the court "acted without investigating the case any further or citing a specific statute."[31]

Oddly enough, in the summer of 1640, the Windsor Church in Windsor, Connecticut, summoned Pynchon to be tried on the old charge of "speculation in trade to the detriment of the public." It was most likely done to "withdraw from him the right hand of Christian fellowship." During this time there was a close connection between Windsor and Agawam. There was a question as to whether the Windsor Church had the jurisdiction to even hold a trial but does suggest the power the churches had at this time because a trial was held. Pynchon was summoned to appear. The trial was undoubtedly motivated by members of the church who were friendly to Captain Mason, a member of the Windsor Church. It was most likely an attempt to "make a demonstration against Pynchon for the morale effect." Pynchon was condemned by the Windsor Church for his actions in the earlier trade with the Indians. In addition the Church was also offended because Pynchon gave the magistrates his advice on "what policy to pursue" on this matter. Pynchon later replied to the letter of censure sent to him by the Church signed by the Reverend John Warham, the Reverend Ephraim Huit and Elder John Witchfield, by defending himself and pointedly asking, "Can a church or any else ... deny me the liberty to expound my own thoughts by way of advice to magistrates?" Clearly, Pynchon must have thought the local clergy both in Hartford and Windsor had overstepped their authority. But at the same time, it seems clear these ministers in their churches held the moral high ground and could be a threat even to a powerful man like Pynchon. Pynchon turned to his former church in Roxbury, Massachusetts, and the Massachusetts General Court to exonerate himself from the charges.[32]

Earlier in June 1638, as a result of his prior treatment in Connecticut, Pynchon attempted to seize the opportunity to get himself out from under the Connecticut General Court. He expressed a concern Agawam (later Springfield) "remain under the Massachusetts Bay government" because of a "pange of discontent ... upon a sensure hee then lay under by the Government of Connecticut."[33] Springfield was integrated into the Massachusetts government on June 2, 1641. William Pynchon was granted the authority to govern the people of Springfield. Although not much is known about Springfield under his authority it is known in 1648 tensions between the settlers and the Indians in the river valley were running high and it is probably thanks to Pynchon's legalistic approach to apprehending some Indians who murdered other Indians in the colony a major Indian war was avoided.[34]

Strangely enough, Pynchon has been linked with early witchcraft proceeding in the Massachusetts Bay. This was the case of Mary (Lewis) Parsons and Hugh Parsons (discussed in Chapter 7). In New England the law distinguished between heresy and witchcraft.[35] Yet, as a result of the Civil War in England and the rise of dissident Protestant groups more pressure was put on the New England clergy and magistrates from England to reduce their oppression of Protestant heretics, later including Quakers, while the prosecution of witches was not contested but heartily advocated by the authority of the "Westminster Assembly at the end of the Civil War." In their "semi-official commentary on the Scriptures" they noted, "Some have thought witches should not die unless they had taken away the life of mankind, but they are mistaken."[36] The results can be demonstrated by the reaction of the English dissident clergy to the treatment of William Pynchon and what would be seen by the Massachusetts authorities in his heretical book.

Although one chronicler wrote witchcraft accusations were common in Springfield almost since the founding in 1645 "rather of late more than one or two who was greatly suspected of witchcraft." The town minister, the Reverend George Moxon, and his family were not immune to the gossip of witchcraft. Two of his children were suspected of being bewitched. However, William Frederick Poole, in the late 1880s came to question the date of the witchcraft outbreak in 1645. The date of the witchcraft outbreak in Springfield may have been premature, but there was talk of witches in nearby Windsor, Connecticut, throughout the 1640s. These rumors of "deviltry" likely spread throughout the valley and influenced gossip in Springfield. Windsor is down river about ten miles from Springfield. The two towns were in direct communication with each other with significant business and family relationships. In addition, clergy from surrounding towns including Hartford and Springfield traveled to Windsor to give sermons in the Windsor Church. There is no doubt the later execution of the first witch in New England in 1647 (a resident of Windsor) followed after years of suspicion and rumors before the deadly accusations led to a trial for witchcraft.[37]

The first witchcraft case before the Springfield court occurred in 1649. It was a slander case involving Hugh Parsons and Mary Parsons. The two were married in Springfield on October 27, 1645. The trouble occurred in 1649 when Mrs. Marshfield (formerly of Windsor) brought a suit against Hugh's wife, Mary, for having called Mrs. Marshfield a witch. William Pynchon, the chief magistrate, found Mary guilty. She was ordered to receive twenty lashes or pay three pounds in fines, a figure equivalent to twenty-four bushels of corn.[38] As a result of this sentence Mary Parson's health seemed to deteriorate while at the same time her husband fell under suspicion of witchcraft. In February 1651, Hugh and Mary were arraigned before William Pynchon upon formal charges of witchcraft. Mary was accused of bewitching the Reverend Moxon's children. Hugh was accused of "practicing devilish arts." Following Pynchon's report she and her husband were later tried in Boston.[39]

However, when William Pynchon was examining the Parsons he came to be viewed with suspicion by the authorities in Boston as a result of having published his book in England in 1650, *The Meritorious Price of Our Redemption*. The book was written to show Christ did not suffer for us the torments of hell in order to redeem men's souls and he did not "bear the curse of the law" for our sins.[40] Essentially, this was a "protest against the Calvinistic theology as preached by the clergy of that day." Jesus was killed not as a result of God's wrath, but it was instead "the work of the devil through his instruments, the Jews and the Roman soldiers." The theory the guilt of the world was laid upon or imputed to Christ was denounced unsparingly.[41]

The book appeared in Boston in the second week of October 1650. After examining the book the General Court met on October 15, 1650, and wrote that it "did utterly dislike it and detest it as erroneous and dangerous," that the book should be answered by one of the elders, that the author be required to appear "before the next General Court" and that the book was to be "burnt by the executioner, or such other person the magistrates should appoint, in the market in Boston the next lecture day." Six of the members in the House of Deputies voted against these measures, including Edward Holyoke, sitting for Springfield.[42]

Ironically, William Pynchon attended the May session of the General Court in 1651 to take part in the trial of the accused witch Mary Parsons and answer the complaint about his book. At the same time, Pynchon was probably devastated his book had been burned because he probably thought he was bringing a message of a "more wholesome religious spirit than of the old theology" and probably did not realize he was to be accused of attempting to "overturn Christianity" and be "summoned to court like a common criminal." He was detained for two weeks and at the order of the court "conferred with leading clergymen about his alleged heresies."[43]

On May 22, 1651, William Pynchon confessed to some error and as a result on June 9, 1651, the Court permitted him to return home. He was expected to reappear on October 14, 1651, for the next Court session to conclude the proceedings. Clearly, William Pynchon was not about to wait around for a verdict (as noted earlier he had seen what happened when clergymen took the moral high ground both in Hartford and Windsor). Indeed, there had been no investigation after Hooker's pronouncement of his guilt on something as easy to prove as to whether he was cheating the colony. How much more difficult to argue and win over these "eminent divines" on a matter of theology. He realized the "theologians were not satisfied" and if he remained the "outcome would be disgrace, confiscation of his property and his plans ... for the career of his son."[44] William Pynchon ceded his estate to his son. He, his wife and the Reverend Moxon and his family returned to England.[45] It is probably safe to assume William Pynchon left before May 1652 because the Court records for May 1652 do not mention him. According to one source the Reverend Moxon and William Pynchon traveled through Hartford (staying out of the hands of the Massachusetts Bay authorities) in July 1652 on their way to England.[46]

Pynchon's influence did not end on his return to England. His ideas had influenced Edward Holyoke, an original settler, neighbor and friend who wrote a book titled *The Doctrine of Life, or Mans Redemption* (1658) in which he advocated "the individual's right to inquire into the scriptural foundations of his or her faith" and who directly referenced Pynchon's earlier condemned book. The "remarkable similarity between Holyoke's position on toleration and Pynchon's leaves little doubt the Connecticut Valley harbored a small but active group of Puritan rationalists who by the 1650's were beginning to broadcast their opinions ... [and] ... suggests that historians have underestimated the great variety of puritan thought in New England." Meanwhile, the true believers and clergy saw these new ideas being promoted by these antinomians and latitudinarians infiltrating their congregations and questioning their authority and the foundation of their faith. They began to draw a hard line against toleration, fearful of being undermined by these ideas.[47] Unfortunately for the latter as a result of the English Civil War and the Commonwealth of England that gave rise to dissenting religious viewpoints, the world of "English Puritanism was turning, and turning decidedly, toward accommodation with sincere dissenters."[48]

Pynchon had turned to his supporters in England for help but they had little influence over the legal proceedings in Massachusetts.[49] However, the next decade would lead to even more religious destabilization in the colonies by Quakers. The authorities in all the colonies were so fearful of the disruptive influence of the Quakers they passed a series of harsh anti–Quaker measures. In Massachusetts these measures included the death penalty. The overreach by the Massachusetts authorities would finally lead to a Royal mandate of toleration in the Massachusetts Bay Colony a few years after the ascension of Charles II to the English throne in 1660.

# 3

## Settling Windsor
## in the New England
## Wilderness

The recently formed settlement of Windsor in Connecticut in 1635 was ground zero for the first execution of a witch not only in New England but in the English colonies of the new world. This chapter introduces the unique circumstances of the settlers and their leaders that contributed to why this first execution for witchcraft occurred in Windsor in the heart of the Connecticut River Valley.

### West Country Origins of the Windsor Settlers

The Windsor settlement in 1635 was distinctive for a number of reasons and is found in the origin of the core group of original settlers who came primarily from the South West counties of England: Dorset, Somerset and Devon. Five years previously, although part of the migration organized by the Massachusetts Bay Company, they sailed on the ship *Mary and John* out of Plymouth, England, rather than out of Southampton with the Winthrop fleet. Unlike most of their counterparts in the Winthrop fleet they were not of East Anglian origin. These emigrants were assembled by the Reverend John White in Plymouth, England. He did not accompany them to their intended destination in the Massachusetts Bay Colony. However, their respect for John White was such they named their first settlement in the Massachusetts Bay, Dorchester, because it was "not only the country town of most of them" but also the "home and headquarters of John White." Initially they called their second settlement in Connecticut, Dorchester, but later changed the name to Windsor.[1]

The majority of the immigrants who founded Windsor originated from a "well defined part of west Dorset and South Somerset." The towns were fairly close to each other and included "Lyme Regis, Bridport, and the Brit Valley in west Dorset, Crewkerne, Chard and a half dozen satellite villages in south Somerset." Dorchester, approximately eight miles to the east, supplied immigrants as well.[2]

These West Country immigrants sailed from Plymouth harbor in England in March 1630 with fifty heads of families on board. They were later followed by ships sailing out of Weymouth, England, to Dorchester on the Massachusetts Bay.[3] The *Mary and John* immigrants were led by the ministers John Warham, White's choice "as minister for the gathered church of the *Mary and John's* ship company," and John Maverick. Many of the families traveling on this ship would find their way to Windsor, Connecticut, led by their minister John Warham. One of the most prominent passenger was Henry Wolcott of Tolland, a small village only a few miles from the great cattle and cloth market town of Taunton.

The Wolcotts were clothiers and Henry, who had taken a voyage to New England in 1628, was determined to leave Somerset for the new world. Other important passengers sailing on the *Mary and John* included Roger Ludlow, the owner of the ship, Edward Rossiter and Israel Stoughton. These men led this undertaking and later Ludlow and Thomas Newberry invested a majority of the funds to "found Windsor in Connecticut."[4]

Many of these emigrants were likely linked though marriage, due to their proximity with each other in the West Country towns and village. These extended families met at markets and fairs and did business with each other. In general, none of the families on this ship "came from a social stratum lower than husbandman or artisan or higher than minor gentry." The largest group belonged to the class of yeoman.[5] The passengers on the *Mary and John* were basically a "community of families." Only twelve were single men, there were no single adult women, and of the remainder, twenty-seven were married couples, of which the majority were middle aged or over forty. There were seventy-two children. There were no servants. There may have been some who saw this transatlantic voyage as a means for economic enrichment but for many there was undoubtedly "a strong religious motive."[6]

Even if some of the emigrants on this ship started out as strangers the crossing acted as a crucible that established more permanent relationships among the passengers.[7] Those who originated in the West counties and sailed on the *Mary and John* naturally developed into a more close knit community because of a shared culture and beliefs. In addition they were members of the same church founded by John White in Plymouth. They practiced a form of puritanism less radical than the East Anglian puritanism found among the colonists in the Massachusetts Bay Colony.

The same circumstances could not be said for the other ships sailing in the Winthrop fleet for New England. Those "Emigrants congregated from various parts of England and rarely had a chance to take stock of their travelling companions before they assembled on board."[8] Although the Winthrop fleet was the best organized it contained many individuals who were strangers to each other. In the case of the *Mary and John,* even though John White wrote in *The Planters Plea* on this ship there were "not six known either by face or fame to any of the rest," this was unlikely and was probably written "to support his denial that his emigrants were an organized band of Separatists conspiring to subvert the Church of England." The entire enterprise suggested an organizing agent.[9]

While most emigrants to New England "approached their journey with apprehension and fear … Stories of storms and wrecks" inhibited many from even taking such a perilous voyage.[10] However, for those preparing to travel on the *Mary and John* the voyage was probably not as fear inducing. West Country seamen had been crossing the Atlantic to fish in the Newfoundland waters for at least one-hundred years. The captains and seaman were a professional lot "committed to North Atlantic sailing … there was a fair amount of traffic" especially the fishing boats.[11] The ship was relatively spacious at 400 hundred tons and carried only 140 passengers. Still there was "little sanitation, lack of air and confined space." The worthy passengers traveled in separate cabins.[12]

Nevertheless, emigrants who traveled to America in the seventeenth century "underwent a crucial seasoning process" and no matter where they came from, their time at sea represented a community building process creating "alliances that shaped subsequent behavior" in America sometimes owed their origin to the enforced close company of the Atlantic passage. Strangers became acquaintances, acquaintances became firm friends and (sometimes enemies)."[13] As for the passengers on the *Mary and John* these were more than acquaintances and friendships. Also, for the seventy-two children on board, the voyage was probably the "formative experience" of their lives. Many of these children would do their growing up in Dorchester and Windsor. Later many of the young bachelors married daughters of their fellow passengers.[14]

The *Mary and John* landed in Nantasket, near Hull, in 1630. Roger Clapp, a passenger on the ship, wrote he had come "through the Deep comfortably; having Preaching or Expounding of the Word of God every Day for Ten Weeks, by our Ministers." They were put ashore at Nantasket Point instead of on the Charles River, the original destination. They were forced to "shift for themselves." After some hardship, they settled in Mattapan, later called Dorchester. Having originated in the farming counties of Somerset, Dorset and Devon, these settlers brought their own cattle with them. Dorchester in the Massachusetts Bay was an area "fit" to keep cattle.[15]

During the next five years, about 20 ships per year on average arrived from England, many carrying up to 200 passengers. By 1635 the population of the Massachusetts Bay swelled to nearly 8,000. The number of heads of families and individuals granted land by the town of Dorchester was just over 130. Many of these later arrivals are thought to have come from the West Country. Five years after the first landing the population of Dorchester, despite the first season of hardship, had increased dramatically. In addition, there was an increase in livestock, especially cattle, now the economic foundation of many of the West Country families. Unfortunately, the amount of land necessary to keep cattle was considerably more than was needed for "primitive subsistence farming." By 1634, settlers in New Town (present-day Cambridge) and farmers in Dorchester had complained about the "want of accommodation for their cattle."[16]

Knowledge about land in the Connecticut River Valley had been making its way back to the Massachusetts Bay for a while. The idea of moving to Connecticut had been talked about in the Bay towns. There was talk of lush meadows stretching along the Connecticut River, of fur and beaver trade, even talk of "good quality hemp," something of great interest to the emigrants from Dorset. Permission to leave the Massachusetts Bay was not easily obtained. Finally in early 1635 permission was given for emigrant groups from New Town and finally Dorchester to leave.[17]

The effect on Dorchester was significant. Of approximately 170 male inhabitants in 1635 about 56 "sold-out to newcomers and joined the exodus to the Connecticut." Fortunately for those willing to make the trek to Connecticut they were able to sell their land because 1635 had been a good year for immigrants coming from England who not only bought the land of the Dorchester pioneers but also infused the Dorchester Church that had been "weakened by departure of its pastor and most of his flock."[18]

## Settlement at Windsor in 1635

In the fall of 1635 sixty men and women traveled overland from the Massachusetts Bay to settle along Connecticut River Valley. The journey was through heavily forested territory along Indian trails. They carried their provisions with them for the winter and drove their livestock before them. Unfortunately, they had begun the journey late in the year. They were not able to plant their crops until spring. The supplies were low, the winter was harsh, and shelter was not adequate. The end result was some died of illness and one colonist drowned. Eventually the settlers were able to make their way back to the Massachusetts Bay. The settlers returned in the spring to make a second attempt at colonizing this area. They built homes and planted crops.

However, they did not have sole access to the site. There was another claimant, Plymouth Colony, the "owners of a patent granted by the Plymouth Council." They had already settled on the site and built a trading post. The Plymouth colonists were more interested in the fur trade than farming.[19]

A second patentee, Sir Richard Saltonstall, sent his representative Francis Stiles to Windsor. The Francis Stiles party was assembled in London and was made up of twenty men and Stiles family members. The party was "sent out from England largely at the private expense of Sir Richard Saltonstall … to prepare grounds and erect houses for himself and other patentees." At least sixteen of the original party are known to have settled in Windsor. The two male Stiles, two Stiles women, a woman, Jane Worden and two Stiles children, an infant of 9 months and a child of 3. Nearly all the remaining males were apprenticed either before or after arriving in America. Their ages ranged from 13 to 35 and as part of the Stiles party had sworn conformity to the rules and discipline of the Church of England in St. Mildred's Church in London before departing. The three groups spread out and settled on different parts of the west bank of the Connecticut River. The Plymouth party claimed 100 acres south of the Farmington River, the Dorchester group "settled alongside the bottom of the 600 acre Great Meadow, north of the Farmington River" and the Stiles men settled "further north at the top of the Great Meadow."[20]

The three groups lived together until the Pequot War in 1637. When the war broke out the Plymouth party returned to defend the Plymouth Colony. The Dorchester party and the Stiles parties joined forces. The residents left their scattered homes and concentrated in the Palisado, an area in the town surrounded by a stockade of densely packed logs. Some of the residents built homes in the Palisado and others waited to build their homes at a more convenient time. After the war the Palisado was retained in the event of another Indian war and became the town center.[21]

Two years after the Pequot War spring floods destroyed homes and crops in one section of town. An early bridge across the Farmington River was destroyed as well. The town substituted a ferry in place of the bridge. Although there were occasional floods the residents learned to cope with these and built their homes on higher ground. The town of Windsor was successfully established. The rights of the Plymouth Company were purchased and the issue was settled with land going to the Dorchester settlers and to the Saltonstall group.[22]

The immigration from Dorchester had been primarily a West Country affair. Of the fifty-four families that migrated to Connecticut the heads of forty of these families were West Country folk.[23] Besides land for their cattle other motivating factors prompted them to move to Windsor and likely included the fact that West Country immigrants stood out from the majority of

Massachusetts Bay inhabitants who were primarily of East Anglian origin. They were "different," their speech was much softer, they were more slowly paced and maintained "distinct ... rural habits and allegiances." Additionally they shared West Country folklore, customs, and were less religiously radical and still committed to the Church of England.[24]

From the beginning there was tension between the Dorchester men and Lord Saltonstall's party represented by Thomas Stiles. Roger Ludlow, the leader of the Dorchester party, told Francis Stiles to stay off the property Sir Richard Saltonstall claimed as a patentee four years previously.[25] In a letter to Governor Winthrop, Saltonstall wrote he had been abused and injured by Mr. Ludlow and the others from Dorchester who would not allow Francis Stiles' men to settle on the land he previously claimed in Connecticut. The basic question was who should occupy the Great Meadow? In the end, Stiles and his party were "crowded in and forced to settle to the extreme north end of the meadow." There was probably some doubt as to the exact location of the original land claim by Saltonstall.[26]

Nevertheless, there was continued resentment not only among the Dorchester settlers and the Saltonstall party, but as we saw previously, between the original Plymouth claimants to land in Windsor and the Dorchester settlers. This tension, although it appeared to be resolved through negotiation, was undoubtedly carried over into the early arrangements of the land distribution and ongoing settlements into the 1640s. This is evident in the fact that Windsor was not an integrated community. Wealth and prestige determined acreage and location but this was not unusual. What was unusual about Windsor was a third factor: families from the West counties in England tended to live next to each other and intermarry among themselves to the exclusion of those like the Stiles family and other settlers. The majority of the West Country settlers occupied the southern part of the town and most of Main Street. The section known as the Little Meadow and the Island contained "all of the gentry, most of the notables and the principle officers of the town, all West Countrymen: two magistrates and assistants of the colony court, the minister, the town clerk, the schoolmaster who was also a ruling elder, the deacon, and the constable." Of those who settled along the Sandy Bank along Main Street the "first thirty or so families with homes on Main street were old Dorchester people" and primarily from Dorset and Somerset. Those on Main Street included three members of the general court, a deacon and an elder. Finally the Stiles family and settlers with them, known as the "Lords and Gentlemen," settled together to the very North on Main Street. These two neighborhoods were in stark contrast to the neighborhoods of Backer Row and Mill Road where more modest families lived with the poorest on Mill Road.[27] Besides dominating the political offices, the West Country people also dominated the Church offices, although in 1638 with the arrival of the

Reverend Ephraim Huit, the successor to John Maverick, the church welcomed him and a number of mid-landers. However, Dorset and Somerset folks continued their preeminence in town politics and church membership.[28]

This control of the political and church authority by the original Dorchester Congregation established in Plymouth, England, in 1630 led to a psychological predominance of the community forged in a crucible of life and death experiences, bolstered by their faith. Specifically these included the Atlantic voyage, the Dorchester settlement, and the "wilderness trek and the grim winters" on the Connecticut River. Even with their settlement in Windsor these colonists would continue to experience events that would try their faith. The community would turn inwardly to look for the cause of their misfortune. They would try and execute one of their own townsmen as a witch and throw suspicion on three other women in their community. Windsor became the catalyst for the witch hunting mania along the Connecticut River Valley. Four women from Windsor were at one time or another suspected of witchcraft, and of the four women, three were eventually executed as witches. In addition, women with links to the suspected Windsor witches came under suspicion in the other towns in the Connecticut colonies.

Ironically, it was not from the radical "Separatist" and "Independent" puritan sects the witchcraft trials and executions were first initiated but, from this more moderate religious hamlet in Windsor, Connecticut, and from here it spread along Connecticut River valley and two other areas in the Connecticut colonies.

## Windsor: The Early Community

By the end of 1641 land distribution in Windsor was complete. The land grants went to the heads of ninety-four families and a few single individuals. Of these, sixty-three families came to Windsor from Dorchester, most in the great migration of 1635 and 1636. Of the remaining, five families came from other parts of the Massachusetts Bay and eleven others directly from England with the balance unknown. Dorchester people dominated the population of Windsor, comprising 70 percent of the population.[29] Others arriving later probably found Windsor settled in a most unusual way. The West Country colonists settled next to each other just as they had in Dorchester. The gentry and clerisy lived together in the "Little and Plymouth Meadows and the Island." This group would have included John Warham, the minister from Somerset, Roger Ludlow, the magistrate from Maiden Bradley, Wiltshire, and Bray Rossiter, the town clerk from Somerset. On the Island were individuals like Henry Wolcott (a magistrate and first constable) and his sons, William Phelps, a magistrate, all from Somerset. In addition, in this neighborhood was the whole Newberry family. The father, Thomas Newberry from Dorset and one of the principal investors in Dorchester, had unfortunately died before moving from Dorchester to Windsor. He left a widow with seven children and an estate of 1500 pounds. Newberry's widow, Jane, married John Warham, whose wife had recently died. There were seven lots side by side for the seven Newberry children adjacent to the Warham lot. Finally, there was Mathew Allyn, "a man of means" who was not from Dorchester but Devon and "thus an acceptable neighbor."[30]

The Main Street community was composed of men of position. Not unlike the gentry families who began to intermarry almost immediately, the families on Main Street also intermarried. If one looks at the "first thirty or so families with homes on Main Street" they "were old Dorchester people." Of the "twenty-four home lots" near the town center, ten were from Dorset, and six from Somerset. Of the Dorset families only two did not come from the "small Dorset neighborhood ... of the River Brit." The proximity to their neighbors was deliberate. For example, "William Hosford and Nicholas Denslow, both from the Brit Valley, had owned contiguous meadows in Dorchester and were again next door neighbors both in home and meadow lots in Windsor." The same desire for proximity to known neighbors can be found further up Main Street among the Somerset families who also hailed from towns and villages in Somerset close to each other.[31]

Main Street and the Plymouth Meadow families were in "marked contrast" to the neighborhoods of Backers Row and Mill Road. Those who lived in these neighborhoods were more modest people. The poorest section of town, Mill Road, came to be called "Silver Street" because people passing along that street in the early morning stopped to pick up silver sixpences and found they were only shad scales dropped by the poorer neighbors while carrying home shad in the night to avoid being seen by friends who fared more sumptuously."[32] Thomas Bascombe, brick maker and mason of Bridport, Dorset, was the only inhabitant on Mill Road from the West Country.[33]

## The Ministers in Windsor and Antecedents of Witchcraft Beliefs

Originally when John White recruited his colonists to New England he appointed two ministers to lead the party, the Reverends John Maverick and John Warham. After settling and establishing a church in Dorchester, John Maverick died in March 1635. Maverick had been against leaving Dorchester. Warham and many of his parishioners were eager to migrate to the more open pasture lands and what would be the less restrictive religious environment of Connecticut. With Maverick's death, Warham was free to move his flock to Windsor. He became the spiritual leader of the Windsor community in 1635 and remained so until his death in 1670.

John Warham was born in 1592 and was from Dorset. He went to Oxford and received his bachelor's degree from St. Mary's Hall (Oxford) in 1614. It is likely while at Oxford he was exposed to experiences and literature having to do with occult and witchcraft. For example, Thomas Cooper, the author of the *Mystery of Witchcraft Discovered* (1617), was a student at Oxford from 1586 until taking his bachelor in divinity degree in 1600. He wrote there were those interested in the occult at Oxford. While a student at Oxford his "Chamber-fellow was exceedingly bewitched with these faire views, and having gotten divers books to that end was earnest in the pursuit of that glorie which might redound thereby?" Cooper concluded the Lord used him "as a means to divert my Chamber-fellow from these dangerous studies?"[34] While at Oxford, Warham would have studied the writings of the puritan theologian William Perkins, one of the most eminent theologians of his time and the author of *A Discourse of the Damned Art of Witchcraft* (1608): "this treatise is good evidence as to what the views of a learned Englishmen were at the turn of the century." Perkins argued there are two kinds of witchcraft: "divining and working," and the "raising of storms, the poisoning of the air (which brings pestilence), blasting of corn."[35] Perkins was not only a firm believer in witches, but unlike many common people who consulted "cunning men and women" (or white witches who they believed were helpful), he held a special scorn for them. He wrote "it were a thousand times better for the land, if all Witches, but especially the blessing witch might suffer death."[36]

In 1639, the Reverend Ephraim Huit and his flock moved to Windsor where he was to become the teacher in the Windsor Church. Huit, like Warham, was an ordained minister and received his education at St. John's College (Cambridge University). Huit would have taken an orthodox puritan view of witchcraft. With the death of Huit in 1644, Warham was now sole minister and was assisted by the ruling elders in Church government who watched over church members and were responsible for disciplinary measures. The elders also visited and prayed with the sick and when the minister was absent expounded the Scriptures.[37]

In the fall of 1640 Warham and Huit began to give a series of sermons that suggested Satan was among and within the inhabitants of Windsor (see Chapter 6). Warham, especially with his sermons about Satan and the devil, began sowing doubt in his flock about who might be tempted to follow the devil. He helped create a climate of fear in the "wilderness community" of Windsor. The ministers by raising the specter of Satan and his demons could only have aroused suspicions and reawakened memories from Old England of the reality of the devil and witchcraft.[38]

To understand why the talk of the devil in sermons would have especially affected the Windsor colonists some background is necessary. The Lancashire witch trials of 1612 in England were the most famous witch trials throughout the country prior to the outbreak of the English Civil War.[39] As noted previously under Laud's regime the government actively discouraged witchcraft trials and the publication of new books on witchcraft.[40]

However, there was one trial held at the Taunton Assizes in Somerset in 1626 for the bewitching of Edward Dinham by Edward Bull and Joan Greedie that proved to be one of the most sensational witchcraft trials of this period.[41] It would have been recent memory of the reality and horror of the devil and witchcraft to the inhabitants of Dorset and Somerset. The location in Somerset would have allowed many of the 1630 immigrants or their family members to have attended the trial and participated in the local gossip concerning the extraordinary events related at the trial. The witchcraft acts described in the trial occurred in close proximity to the market towns in the old communities of the new Windsor residents. The evidence given in the courtroom "aroused widespread alarm." So great was the concern, especially by what appeared to be two spirits, one good and the other evil, "disputing over the ownership" of a bewitched man's soul that it seemed to confirm the reality of the devil.[42]

The depth of belief in witchcraft in the West Country that would have been carried by the settlers to Windsor is attested to by one writer on folklore in Somerset who wrote "the belief in witchcraft and the fear of it is widespread in Somerset, and I have, even in the last few years come across many counter-charms against witchcraft and traces of most of those beliefs which we find explicitly mentioned in seventeenth century witch trials."[43] That there are long held beliefs in witches in the West Counties is demonstrated in the number of witchcraft trials held in the West Country counties from 1559 to 1709.[44]

The events of this trial even persuaded the Reverend Richard Bernard of Batcombe, Somerset, to write his influential book on witchcraft in 1627. The title is usually shortened to a *Guide to the Grand Jury-Men*. However, the book is divided into two parts. The entire title illustrates the full content of the book: *A guide to grand-jury men divided into two bookes: in the first, is the authors best advice to them what to doe, before they bring in a billa vera ... [true and sufficient evidence] ... in cases of witchcraft, with a Christian direction to such as are too much given upon every crosse to thinke themselves bewitched. In the second, is a treatise touching witches good and bad, how they may be knowne, evicted, condemned, with many particulars tending thereunto.*[45]

For lawyers and other civil officials this book was highly influential. I believe it influenced Roger Ludlow one of the original Windsor settlers who trained as a lawyer in England just as it influenced another West Country

Witchcraft: a white-faced witch meeting a black-faced witch with a great beast. To Protestant clergy the "white witch" was more dangerous than the "black witch"; the white witches deserved death because in their practice "they deny God and are confederates with Satan." The image suggests there is no difference between the two in the devil's eyes as they meet on equal footing. The image is from *The History of Witches and Wizards: Giving a True Account of All Their Tryals in England, Scotland, Swedeland, France, and New England*, T. Norris, London 1720, p. 1 (courtesy Wellcome Library, London).

lawyer, Robert Hunt, who prosecuted witchcraft cases in Somerset, Wiltshire and Dorset in the 1650s and 1660s.[46]

The Taunton witchcraft case involved Edward Bull and Joan Greedie. Both were accused of bewitching Edward Dinham, possibly descended from an old noble Somerset family. The name would have been well known by Somerset inhabitants.[47] The circumstances were unusual and involved ventriloquism, possession and accusations of death by witchcraft. Edward Dinham would appear to lie dead for several hours. Up to six men could not move his head and they would "beat" his stomach and "thrust pins and needles into his hands and nostrils" yet he was insensible to the pain and no blood appeared. He would go into a trance and "two voices besides his own were to be heard carrying on a conversation."[48] In the trance he claimed Edward Bull and Joan Greedie were witches. They were both witches by descent (a belief that was also held true in a number of witchcraft accusations in New England). While in a trance Dinham claimed the two had perpetrated "much mischief," attacked Dinham and bewitched a person to death. For the first arrest, Dinham while in a trance described how Joan Greedie was dressed and when the authorities arrived at her home the "suspect was dressed as described." Later after further interrogation Edward Bull was arrested and Dinham was "delivered from his persecution." The two witches were indicted but there is no further information on the resolution of their trial.[49]

For the settlers from Dorset and Somerset their first-hand experience with a recent and sensational witchcraft trial and their neighboring minister, Richard Bernard—one of the most significant demonologists in England known to many of the more educated colonists and who had probably preached before them earlier and confirmed the reality of the devil and witches in their consciousness—these beliefs were easily re-awakened in the sermons of John Warham and Ephraim Huit.

## Two Worthies: Henry Wolcott and Roger Ludlow, Original Windsor Settlers

### Henry Wolcott

Henry Wolcott senior was one of the more prominent members of the colonists from Somerset who had traveled on the *Mary and John* to eventually settle in Windsor. Henry senior was born in 1578 in Wellington, Somerset, the second of three sons. Growing up, Henry led a comfortable life. He later acquired property in Tolland, Somerset. He married Elizabeth Saunders in 1607 from the nearby town of Lydiard St. Lawrence.[50] Wolcott was said to have spent his youth in "country past times" but later he turned to "religion and piety, under the instructions and 'labours'" of the Puritan minister, Edward Elton. This was said to have been a radical conversion.[51] At the age of fifty he became determined to leave his home in Somerset for the New World. In 1628 he made a voyage to New England, returned, sold his property and left with his family on the *Mary and John* in 1630. His abrupt departure has been generally linked to the "severe treatment of the puritans." Perhaps it was also the treatment of the books of his religious teacher and instrument of his conversion that foreshadowed hard times ahead for Elton's followers like Henry Wolcott and prompted his abrupt departure.

Two books by Edward Elton, who died in 1624, were burned at an open air pulpit (St. Paul's Cross) on the grounds of Old St. Paul's Cathedral, in the

City of London on February 25, 1625. The two books in question were *God's Holy Mind* (London, 1624) and *A plaine and easie exposition upon the Lords prayer in questions and answers by that faithfull servant of God,* (London, 1624).[52] As one court observer reported, "Last Lord's–day, after the Sermon at the Cross was Mr. Elton's book on the Commandments … burnt for containing schismatical doctrine of the Lord's-day and administration of the sacrament."[53] His books were considered "scandalous and seditious, teaching to innovation and to the subversion of religion and piety." They criticized the celebration of the Lord's Day, and the administration of the sacrament. The "errors attributed to Elton included a denial of the lawfulness of private communion, a number of extreme Sabbatarian opinions, a ban on marriage with papists, suspect notions about the validity of infant baptism and a denunciation of the use of the Lord's prayer and music in the worship of God."[54] Richard Montague, an enemy of the Puritans and fierce supporter of the Church of England, wrote to John Cosin, a confederate of Bishop Laud: "The next returne I shall heare by you what a goodly fire our Sabbatarian hereticks made at the Crosse" and in a second letter "Me thinke Elton should not father nor foster such prodigies…. It is well the books made a fire, though not all I doubt. But they are not burned that made the books."[55]

Additionally, Thomas Gataker, a Puritan minister of some note who had innocently written a two page preface, "To the Christian Reader" in Elton's book *Gods Holy Mind,* was "imprisoned in Fleet street." He was released through the intervention of the Earl of Manchester but he was later placed under "house arrest and suspended from his ministry by his majesty's special command."[56] What was occurring was an "ecclesiastical power struggle in the highest circles" and the high churchmen were attempting to associate their Calvinist opponents like the deceased Elton "in the King's mind" with the enemies of orthodoxy. The results had probably been more than they hoped for "Gataker was imprisoned … and Elton's posthumous reputation wrecked in a spectacular ritual display of anti-puritanism."[57] What ministers and their Puritan supporters perceived was the "godly" were increasingly at risk and undoubtedly Henry Wolcott as a follower of Elton saw himself as one of those at risk too.

Finally, one aspect of Elton's book on the Commandments was not raised but would have helped to inform Wolcott's views on witches: Elton's writing on their role in relation to the Ten Commandments. This would certainly have provided a religious context in line with his legal understanding concerning the reality of witches, the devil and witchcraft in his later capacity as a magistrate on the courts in Connecticut.

Wolcott's commitment and spiritual faith was strong enough to motivate him to leave England at the age of fifty and transport himself and his family to New England. A "godly man" and follower of Edward Elton's spiritual instruction, Wolcott would have undoubtedly had a familiarity with his *Exposition of the Ten Commandments of God* (London, 1624). In this book Elton expounds on the Ten Commandments. He includes witchcraft, magic and sorcery as activities that break a number of God's commandments. For example, in the first commandment one should not commit "Atheisme or the denial of God." Here he condemns "magicians or witches themselves … or by seeking to Magicians or witches, and using their help."[58]

Although there were a few ministers in the late and early seventeenth century that included sorcery and witchcraft in their discussions of the *Decalogue*, Elton not only included practitioners of witchcraft and magic but those who sought their help as persons who broke the Commandments.[59] The latter were probably seen by some as extreme because at this time it was common practice for individuals to seek out cunning men and women (also known as white, grey or "blessed" witches) for help for innumerable problems ranging from something as serious as lifting another witch's curse to merely finding lost articles.

Elton also makes reference to the sin of witchcraft in the third commandment, that they break the latter "when men use prayer to unlawful ends, as sorcery, enchantment" and so forth.[60] In the fourth commandment, keeping the Sabbath, he condemns activities like gluttony "drunkenness and whoredom" because by engaging in these types of activities the individual is not dedicating the day to God but keeping a "holy day to the devill."[61] For the sixth commandment he included "witch-craft, and by enchantments and sorcery, as when men either use the helpe of witches, sorcerers and enchanters, and by their helpe do kill another or others. Or when witches, enchanters and sorcerers, do of their owne accord by the help of the devill, kill another or others."[62] Finally, for the seventh commandment in the section on uncleanness and bodily defilement, he included unnatural acts between unmarried persons and against nature that include sodomy, bestiality and importantly, "By uncleannesse and defilement of the bodie, committed by a man or woman with the Devill, as Witches doe by their own confession."[63]

In summary we know the reality of witches and witchcraft was commonly understood based in the English legal system and for men like Wolcott the religious teachings reinforced by ministers like Edward Elton (and even in Windsor by Warham) in their writings and sermons. If there were any doubts as to what should be done about a suspected witch or those who frequented them a "godly man" like Wolcott could be sure in his own conviction that it was his duty "to punish the disobedient and to maintaine and defend all such as truly worship him against all that oppose him." This conviction would serve men like Wolcott well when faced with the reality of witchcraft in their colony.[64]

Although there is no direct information on Henry Wolcott's attitude toward witchcraft, based on the writings of Edward Elton it seems Wolcott as a recent convert and follower would believe in the reality of witches and their justifiable punishment. When this belief is coupled with the fact that in 1626, during the Taunton Assizes in England, Henry Wolcott was forty-eight years old and Taunton was a mere ten miles from Tolland. It is likely both he and his son, Henry Junior, would have been affected by the witchcraft trial that occurred there. The trial aroused widespread alarm through the West Country communities. If not directly affected at the time the long term effects of what had happened in Taunton would no doubt come back to him as he gained experience as an officer of the court in Connecticut. He was appointed constable in Windsor in April 1636 and served for three years. The constable was an important position at the time and was "entrusted with all the executive processes of the law and the power to apprehend suspicious persons without precept."[65] Later he was one of twelve Deputies sent to the first General Court of Connecticut that met in Hartford in 1637. The General Court had judicial functions and acted as an appeals court until the Particular Court "emerged from the shadows of the General Court in 1643." He was chosen for the magistracy and served from 1643 until his death in 1655.[66] In his capacity as a constable and service as a magistrate, Wolcott would have been familiar with Michael Dalton's *The Countrey Justice,* especially when trying Connecticut witch trials. Dalton's book was used as a guide for gathering evidence for proving witchcraft and used material on witchcraft taken directly from Bernard's book, inspired by his experience at the Taunton Assizes in England in 1626.[67]

As one of the leading members of the community in Windsor and later the Connecticut colony he would have had a variety of influences on his thinking concerning the reality of witchcraft and been in a position to elicit legal proof for trying witches. There is little doubt Henry Wolcott would not have been the least skeptical of the possibility a defendant in a witchcraft trial could actually be a witch and deserved death if convicted.

A man like Henry Wolcott, who was not only one of the chief planters of the towns of Windsor, Hartford and Wethersfield but a dignitary of the General Court, would have been influential in developing the first laws of Connecticut. After all it was the "ministers and captains, the magistrates and men of affairs, forceful in the new settlements from the beginning ... who took the lead in guided discussion" that led to the "Fundamental Orders" adopted in Connecticut in 1639. These same men also guided the adoption of the capital laws that originated from the General Court of Connecticut in 1642 and included the statute "If any man or woman be a witch (that is hath consulteth with a familiar spirit) they shall be put to death."[68]

## Roger Ludlow

Roger Ludlow was the second son of Thomas Ludlow of Maiden Bradley, Wiltshire, on the Somerset border. The Ludlow family was one of considerable rank and had as its pedigree a long line of lawyers in the family. Roger attended Baillol College, Oxford, for two years beginning in 1610 and was admitted as a student to the Inner Temple in 1612, where he trained to become a barrister, a rank he achieved in 1620.[69] He practiced law in London and until his emigration to New England devoted himself to "academic and legal training" that would serve him well first in the Massachusetts Bay and later Connecticut.[70]

Ludlow's family had a Puritan cast of mind. He and other family members found themselves in positions of responsibility on the "puritan side." For example, his father was uncle to Sir Henry Ludlow who later sat in the Long Parliament and another cousin, Edmund, was a judge at the trial of King Charles I. Roger also had two cousins who fought for the Puritans. Cousin Gabriel fell at the second battle of Newbury in 1644 (although as noted earlier one of the first instances of a pamphlet concerning the witches during the English Civil War was in reference to the first Battle of Newbury in 1643 in which the parliamentary forces overcame a "Royalist" witch and defeated the King's forces).[71] Another cousin, Robert, died after the Battle of York in 1646 as a result of "cruel treatment" by the Royalists. The fact that Gabriel's death was linked to such a notorious name, even if it was a later battle, would have re-awakened memories and perhaps earlier experiences he had in England regarding witches.[72]

In fact, Ludlow's home in Maiden Bradley was only ten miles from Batcombe, the village closest to the Wiltshire border in Somerset. It was here he likely came into contact with Richard Bernard, the parson in Batcombe and the author of the *Guide to the Grand Jury-Men*. Bernard was well known for his preaching and catechizing both in Batcombe and throughout the "adjacent market towns of Batcombe." He had been responsible for the "conversion of many souls" and was known for the "public exercise of his ministry" and gave public lectures along with other preachers until they were suppressed by the Bishop. There is little doubt Ludlow (and others) would have been quite familiar with Bernard's views.[73] In addition, because of his interest in the law, and the novelty of a witch trial adjoining his home county he would likely have attended or closely followed the Taunton Assizes witchcraft trial in England in the summer of 1626.[74] Bernard wrote he had written his book on witchcraft to disabuse other clergy and the judges from the idea he doubted the guilt of Edward Bull because a dangerous "rumor had spread, as if I favoured witches, or were of Master Scots erroneous opinion, that Witches were silly deceived Melancholics."[75] The "rumors" indicate his opinions actively spread throughout the West Counties and undoubtedly to London too. In order to dispel people of these rumors he wrote the *Guide to the Grand Jury-Men* and somewhat contritely dedicated the first part to the two judges, Sir John Walter and Sir John Denham, who sat at the summer Assizes at Taunton for the witch trial. The second book, or part II, was dedicated to Gerard Wood, Archdeacon of Wells, and Arthur Duck, Bishop of Bath and Wells, in which he wrote in the dedication, "the sin of witchcraft and the diabolical practice thereof is *omnium scelerum atrocissum.*" Ludlow could not have ignored the witchcraft rumors concerning such a highly regarded Puritan pastor like Bernard.[76]

An additional connection from Bernard to Ludlow was likely made through John White who had actively recruited for his Dorchester Company (the enterprise that Ludlow joined in 1629). White was a contemporary and friend of Richard Bernard.[77] It is likely Bernard was also "one of White's talent spotters and identified" Roger as right for his purpose.[78] Bernard had direct family connections with the Puritan community and the migration to New England. His "fourth son Masakiell, a clothier, went to New England with the Puritan minister Joseph Hull in 1636" and his "daughter Mary married the separatist Roger Williams" and together they emigrated to New England in 1631.[79]

Bernard was an active correspondent with the New England clergy and other officials. He corresponded with the Puritan minister John Cotton in Boston and was critical of the New England Congregationalists and what he considered to be their separatist ways. Ironically, Cotton also had to contend with Bernard's son-in-law, Roger Williams, who later founded the Colony of Rhode Island. Bernard corresponded with New England clergymen. John Winthrop wrote "about two years since, one Mr. Bernard , a minister at Batcombe, Somersetshire, England sent over two books in writing, ... wherein he laid down arguments against the manner of our gathering our churches etc., which the elders could not answer till this time, by reason of the many troubles about Mrs. Hutchinson's opinions."[80]

Unfortunately, Ludlow left little correspondence or any other records to determine if he corresponded with Bernard. He was undoubtedly familiar with Bernard's writings on witchcraft for two reasons: he probably knew him personally and may have discussed the Taunton trial directly with him. Also, Bernard was a respected Puritan divine. The latter gave him credibility with the Puritans in England like Ludlow, although as we have seen Bernard later came to disagree with Massachusetts Bay clergy over church matters. As noted earlier, Ludlow probably did not have radical Puritan views and this was an additional factor motivating him and the other Dorchester West County settlers to move from the Massachusetts Bay to Windsor, Connecticut. Bernard was not a minor clergyman only noted for his views on witchcraft; he was known among the clergy and other elites in New England for his religious writings as well.

Roger Ludlow left for New England at the age of forty as head of the Dorchester party on the *Mary and John*, the ship he had purchased. He settled with the other West Country emigrants in Dorchester and became a fixture in the Massachusetts Bay Plantation, rising to Deputy Governor. His residence in the Massachusetts Bay lasted five years. In 1635 after his failure to be elected governor of the Massachusetts Bay Colony he joined other Dorchester residents and emigrated to what would become the town of Windsor in Connecticut.[81]

Roger Ludlow was a trained lawyer and served in Connecticut, as he had in Massachusetts to help draft, originate, and frame the fundamental colonial laws. He served as a "magistrate, commissioner, legislator and jurist." As a member of the General Court, he was involved in drafting the *Capital Laws of Connecticut* in December 1642. The witchcraft statute was identical to the same statute in the *Massachusetts Body of Liberties*, adopted by the Massachusetts General Court in December 1641.

As a result, witchcraft became a capital crime in Connecticut with three Scripture quotations appended to the law. They are all excerpts from the Mosaic code. The law itself is a paraphrase of the first text from Exodus 22:18, "Thou shall not suffer a witch to live." The next quotation is from Leviticus 20:27 and orders that a witch shall be stoned to death. Lastly the verses of Deuteronomy 18:10–11 "forbid the children of Israel to entertain any that useth, divination, or an observer of time, or an enchanter, or a witch or necromancer."[82] The criminal code was based on Scripture. This made sense to Puritans like Ludlow, especially on the matter of witchcraft since "Not to have made God's law part of law of the colony would have defeated the purpose that brought Puritans to New England." However, the laws were not just a "restatement of Scripture" and care was taken to maintain rights "guaranteed under English law."[83]

As for witchcraft it was a secret crime and therefore the full measure of rights under English law could not always be maintained. Witchcraft differed from other crimes because to the colonists it was not the "harm allegedly done by the witch but the means employed to affect it."[84] To be a capital crime it required proof "that the accused was in league with Satan." The most important "proofs of witchcraft" throughout most of the seventeenth century in Connecticut were "witch marks, association with other suspected witches, self-confession and, sometimes the controversial "water test."[85] However, as a corollary, a trained lawyer like Ludlow would have been familiar with Michael Dalton's legal handbook *The Countrey Justice* and recognized Bernard's ideas on witchcraft that "had been incorporated wholesale" into it by Michael Dalton, first in the 1630 edition and then in subsequent editions.[86]

Use of this handbook would have been credible for two purposes: it gave the Connecticut court a way of proving that a witch was in league with the devil, and the author of the original recommendations in Dalton was a godly Puritan clergyman known by Ludlow and many others in New England.

In April 1646 at a session of the General Court, Mr. Ludlow was ordered "to take some paynes in drawing forth a body of Laws for the government of this commonwealth." The identical wording appears in Ludlow's *Connecticut Code of 1650*: "If any man or woman bee a Witch, that is hath consulteth with a familiar Spiritt, they shall be put to death." This statute continued to find its origin in the Mosaic code and scripture with the caveat that witchcraft was prosecuted under more expansive rules of evidence.[87] Suspicion alone could generate legal proceedings: absence from the scene of the crime was no defense because witches had the power to project their spectral presence and the "suspects character and even events that occurred many years in the past and not relating to the alleged offense counted as evidence." On the other hand, witches could only be prosecuted for "specific misdeeds against particular people."[88]

For our purposes two things seem clear: first, the Connecticut magistrates, including Ludlow, based the witchcraft statutes of Connecticut on the earlier witchcraft statute in Massachusetts in 1641, and Ludlow employed the identical statute in *The Connecticut Code of 1650*. Although the statute was on the books and was based on biblical passages, proving the act of witchcraft and finding evidence the accused was a witch was found in the passages from Bernard, incorporated by Dalton. One of the important questions facing those trying witches that Bernard had tried to resolve was to have the authorities not go forward with "unjustified accusations." It was possible harm by witches did not involve the witches at all. Harm could be attributed to the natural inclination of God or by the direct devices of the devil without the involvement of a witch. One way around this dilemma provided by Bernard can be summed up in these words: "Satan marketh his." As we will see in a number of these cases the courts will search for "witches' teats" that represent a suckling point for familiars. If the witch had these then it followed the witch also had devil or witch marks, insensitive marks on the witch's body where the devil had marked his own.[89]

Ludlow was an important personage in the early settlement and governance of Connecticut. He served in the Particular Court and was actively involved in a number of court cases as both a magistrate and litigant. He is most known to historians of witchcraft for his active involvement in at least two prominent witchcraft episodes, Goodwife Knapp in Fairfield in 1653 and his accusation that Mary Staples of Fairfield was a witch in the same year. For our purposes in this chapter and for all of Roger Ludlow's positive work in the colony, we can see he was not opposed to invoking witchcraft accusations he probably believed were true, and as we will see, as a magistrate and lawyer undoubtedly served or advised on a number of witchcraft cases during his career in Connecticut.

Like the town ministers in Windsor, Henry Wolcott, Roger Ludlow and other community leaders and churchmen throughout the Connecticut River Valley were steeped in their belief in witches and witchcraft they brought with them to New England. From the seventeenth century Puritan viewpoint the belief was based on a firm religious and legal foundation. It permeated the thinking of not only the clergy but the elites and common settlers. These beliefs were incorporated into the New England colonial laws. Most notably, thanks to Richard Bernard's work being added to Dalton's legal manual the courts in New England were armed with a method of discovering the crime of witchcraft, a crime formerly hidden and difficult to prove without self-confession. With this crime on the books it was only a matter of time as the colonies in New England were confronted with both external stresses and internal strains they would turn inward to find a cause for their turmoil. This would lead to the first trial and execution for witchcraft in New England of a Windsor, Connecticut, resident.

# 4

## Conditions in Windsor
## Increase the Fear of Satan

Besides the communal experiences of the first settlers of Windsor that affected the psychological attitude of these colonists, they also settled on the wilderness border and were surrounded by hostile Indians with no one to protect them but themselves. This fear of the native peoples, the Indians, is reflected in the initial laws that were passed regarding the colonists relationships with them. The colonists lived in fear of the Indians on two planes: the physical as they could be a deadly threat and the spiritual because they were believed to be the children of Satan. On the latter it can be linked with their fear of witches. After all, on the eve of the Pequot War, Roger Williams wrote to John Winthrop on the Pequot's boast they "heare of your preparations etc. and comfort themselves in this that a witch amongs them will sinck the pinnaces [a small boat]" and concluded that he hoped their dreams "shall vanish, and the Devill and his lying Sorcerers shall be confounded."[1]

The cause of the Pequot War was an Indian raid in Wethersfield on April 23, 1637. The Indians killed six men and three women, a number of cattle and horses, and took two young girls captive. This attack in Wethersfield followed a cruel incident in October 1636 concerning John Tilley of Windsor. He had been sailing in his canoe on the Connecticut River with a companion. They stopped to hunt for fowl about three miles above Fort Saybrook. When Tilley put himself ashore and fired his rifle he was immediately taken captive by Indians. His companion was killed. Winthrop wrote the Indians "cut off his hands, and sent them before, and after cut off his feet. He lived three days after his hands were cut off."[2]

These accounts show the reality of life on the frontier regarding the Indians for the colonists in the 1630s. Even after the colonists successfully concluded the Pequot War (a war that men like the commander John Mason from Windsor had taken a leading part in), it did not mean relations with the Indians and the colonists were settled. In Windsor, the fort at the center of town, the Palisado, was maintained for many years afterward.

During the 1640s the conversion of the Indians to Christianity was begun by ministers like John Eliot. This conversion activity served the purpose of leaving fewer followers for Satan's nefarious purposes. In the eyes of the colonists the Indians represented Satan and his minions. The fear was real and palpable. Testimony from the witchcraft trial of Goodwife Knapp in May 1653 shows the taint of Indian magic as an indication of witchcraft: "Goodwife Baldwin ... said that goodwife Knapp told her that a woman in ye towne was a witch ... she knew she was a witch, and she told her she had received Indian gods of an Indian."[3]

Cotton Mather showed evidence of the continuity of this Indian paranoia during the Salem witchcraft trials. He related accounts he received of the French and Indians in Gloucester, Massachusetts, in 1692. He wrote "the devil and his agents were the cause of this molestation which at this time befel the town ... [and] ... that those apparitions may not prove the sad *omens* of some future and more horrible molestation to them."[4]

The colonists' relationship with the Indians and consequent fear of Indians has recently become an important topic in the Salem witch trials in 1692.[5] The evidence indicates fear of Indians and their relationship with the devil may have been just as frightening if not more so in this earlier period of witchcraft accusations.

There was the constant fear of Indian attack, blood curdling rumors and the feeling among many of the colonists that they had been deserted and were isolated as a result of domestic priorities in England due to the civil war, especially during the 1640s. The latter could only have added additional stress to those settlers existing on the wilderness border and in particular the original Windsor settlers who had borne the brunt of a failed settlement in 1635 in Matianuck (Windsor) and a harrowing return to Dorchester, the second settlement attempt and the subsequent Pequot War in 1637. If nothing else, it left some of these colonists in Windsor with what would be diagnosed today as a form of post-traumatic stress disorder. Their unique shared experiences may also help explain why Windsor became the nexus for the witch hunting outbreak in the Connecticut River Valley.

As much as colonial officials tried to control their fellow colonists' relationships with the Indians, it was understood the Indians represented Satan and they were his followers. This is evident in the laws passed immediately in Connecticut and punishments meted out to both colonists and Indians who broke these laws. Even though Indians were considered "Devil worshipers" Indians were brought to court for various crimes but not for witchcraft. The distinction was clear in the minds of the English migrants. The "inward direction of witchcraft among New Englanders" was that the "worst work of the Devil" was "found-among their own kind."[6] Additionally, as the lawyer Thomas Lechford wrote, the "Powahe cannot work their witchcraft, if any English be by; neither can any of their incantations lay hold on, or doe any harme to the English, as I have been credibly informed."[7] However, the minister Roger Williams had a different opinion and thought it might be possible for Indian "witches" to negatively affect, for example, the war preparations of the colonists during the Pequot War, but held out the hope "the Devill and his lying Sorcerers" would be "confounded."[8]

There was an early attempt by the Indian Sachem Uncas in 1649–50 to involve the colonial government in judging Indian witchcraft. Uncas declared himself in danger from the bedevilments of hostile Indians and asked his English friends "that hee might be righted theirin." The "Commission of the United Colonies advised the authorities in Connecticut to appoint a commission to examine this charge. The results of the inquiry are unknown." But because the "Indians were generally supposed to be on familiar terms with the Devil, and the Puritans were probably loath to scrutinize closely the powowings" it was probably a judicious move on the part of the colonial rulers to "pay some attention ... to the wishes of their wily ally" but not extend it beyond an inquiry.[9] However, by 1675 the Connecticut Legislature reversed course and passed the following law in reference to the Pequot: "whosoever shall powau, or use witchcraft, or any worship to the divill, or any fals god, shall be convented and punished."[10]

Although Indians were not tried as "witches" during this period because of their relationship to Satan, they were a constant de-stabilizing force in the "puritan" community. (This no doubt explains why the ministers considered it a priority to convert the Indians to buttress their communities and to gain adherents in their constant battle with Satan). For some of the ministers their goal was to give "some light to those poor Indians who have ever sate in hellish darkness, adoring the Divell himselfe for their God."[11] But for others, the Indians were a constant reminder of the Devil and his works that operated as a continuing psychological weight on the settlers as they attempted to come to terms with a variety of other life and death issues affecting their communities.

## Economic Conditions in Windsor

The Hartford minister Thomas Hooker wrote to John Winthrop in December 1638 that Connecticut had acquired a poor reputation. People spoke of them as "rash creatures" who had rushed into a war with the "heathen" and people discouraged emigration to Connecticut with these sentiments: "Alas, do you think to goe to Conitticut, why do you long to be undone.

The early colonists feared the Native Americans as savages and servants of Satan. In this early image in the foreground we see a "powwow" performing a Devil Dance, while in the middle left two Native American prisoners are in the process of being beaten. The background appears to show a colonist being brought into the village as a bound prisoner. The image is from *Newe Welt und amerikanische Historien*, by J. Theodo de Bry, Frankfort, 1655, p. 598 (courtesy Wellcome Library, London).

If you do not, blesse yourself from thence; ther upland will bear no corne, ther meddows nothing but weeds, and the people are almost strarved."[12] Nevertheless, in the following year, 1639, Windsor experienced a "real estate" boom helped out by newly arrived settlers who came with the Minister Mr. Huit: "many passengers came over, severall of which settled at Windsor, and a general expectation there was at the time, as appeared by discourse [among themselves, on ship-board] of many more passengers to come, and some of note … by which means land at Windsor, nere the towne and redys for improvment, was at a high price." With the outbreak of the civil war in England the new settlers from England never materialized. Some colonists returned to England and others moved closer to the sea. Land in Windsor "fell very much in price."[13]

Henry Wolcott returned to England in 1639 following the death of his eldest brother, Christopher, to settle family matters. Christopher had died intestate and Henry inherited the family estate in Tolland, England.[14] In 1640 he partnered with Thomas Marshfield of Windsor and Samuel Wakeman of Hartford (the three were in England at the time). They bought interests in two ships, the *Charles* of Bristol and the *Hopewell* of London. It was a time of "slump in trade caused by the unsettled political conditions in England that would soon lead to the civil war."

These men realized there would be future difficulties for colonists to be able to depend on shipping their goods to England and obtaining needed supplies back in colonies. In order to prepare for the lack of these supplies from the mother country and perhaps make a handsome profit at the same time, Henry Wolcott and his partners made what they thought was a shrewd investment. In addition to goods, there was always a high demand for more colonists, especially in Connecticut, as noted by Thomas Hooker. It made sense from a businessman's viewpoint to have the ships carry as many passengers as possible and to delay sailing to maximize the passenger list. This investment did not materialize because of the bankruptcy and legal entanglements of Thomas Marshfield.[15]

The three partners chartered the *Charles* and *Hopewell* for sixteen weeks to carry 150 passengers to New England. Instead of 150 passengers there were 370 passengers as well as a cargo of wine, grain, meats, clothing, oil, muskets and gunpowder. The partners borrowed two hundred and thirty pounds from Nathaniel Patten who later sued them because "they carryed in sayd ship a great many more passingers to my remembrance and they the passingers were debarred of our beere and water before landing and if we had bin put to a long voyage we must needs have suffered much more than we did which I leave to the consideration of the Cort."[16] Patten later sued the three partners for living expenses, that he did not get his cabin as contracted, and for personal items never returned. The ship was scheduled to leave on May 24, 1640, but did not leave until June 18, 1640.[17] Marshfield had also borrowed additional funds from Patten: "For Mr. Patten, I conceive he hath received some wronge; I did receive one hundred and fiftye pounds allmost of him-not that that is all Due him."[18]

Marshfield got into more financial difficulties in Bristol, England, where he had "to sell his entire estate to pay his debts." In Windsor in October 1642 there were "many suts com into the Court agt Tho: Marshfield and he is wthdrawn and non soluit."[19] Henry Wolcott was appointed receiver and for the next ten years his time was taken up sorting out Marshfield's debt. Marshfield's bankruptcy on its own probably would not normally have been seen as anything unusual except for the extraordinary number of cases against him for debt that appeared in the Connecticut Particular Court from 1642 until May 1649. He had incurred debts from important men in Windsor like his former partner Henry Wolcott, and two church elders, John Witchfield and John Branker, his immediate neighbors.

Members of the community were constantly reminded of Marshfield's betrayal because his name was continually before the courts and consequently of the "fall" of one of their own, a man who had come over on the *Mary and John*, a member of the Dorchester Church in the Massachusetts Bay, a pillar of the Windsor Church and community. He had not only disappeared from his creditors but from his wife and children who were left to fend for themselves.[20]

Marshfield's betrayal and the decline in status of Mercy Marshfield, his wife, must have been devastating to her. It was unlikely that she would be accepted in polite society after this, especially the close-knit settlers that controlled the town from the West County. There is evidence that things had not gone well for her and that there was much rancor and resentment toward her because of her husband's "treachery." It is likely that she found herself befriended by other women (outsiders) who were not acceptable to the better members of the community. Evidence for this comes from the "Pynchon Court Record" for May 29 and 30, 1649, and shows hostile gossip had followed Mercy Marshfield to Springfield, Massachusetts, "it was reported to her by one in Towne that she was suspected to be a witch when she lived in Windsor and that it was publikely knowen that the divill followed her house in Windsor."[21]

## Epidemic Disease

Epidemic disease and its role in working out God's plan from the Puritan perspective cannot be underestimated. First, for the earliest settlers, epidemic disease among the Indians was seen as a positive sign indicating God's will favoring the settlement of New England by devastating the Indian population. Winthrop wrote in 1629 that "God hathe consumed the natives with a miraculous plague, wherby a great parte of the Country is left voyde of Inhabitantes."[22]

The minister John White of the Plymouth Church in England, the inspiration for the majority of the settlers in Windsor, wrote the plague visited on the natives in New England had "cleared ground for tillage, and large marshes for hay and feeding of cattle, which comes to passe by the desolatio hapning through a three yeeres Plague, about twelve or sixteene yeers past, which swept away most of the Inhabitants all along the Sea coast." To quiet potential recruits to New England, he concluded the plague had "not seized upon any others but the Natives, the English in the heate of the Sicknesse commencing with them without hurt of danger."[23]

Another writer was more direct and wrote because of plague there is "as yet a small number of Savages in New England to that, which hath beene in former time and the place is made so much more fitt, for the English Nation to inhabit in, and erect in it Temples to the glory of God."[24]

Nevertheless, the early years of the English settlements had not gone as predicted. Earlier colonies like Plymouth and Wessagusset were devastated by hunger and disease, "if the colonists really believed that God had blessed the English, then they had to admit that he moved in mysterious ways." Even though epidemics devastated the various Indian tribes in New England it seemed to the colonists that "enough of the Wampanoag and Narragansett survived to harass the Plymouth colonists for several years" as well as "disrupting plans for an English Plantation along the Connecticut River."[25]

Then in the summer of 1633 "pestilential fever, likely smallpox" struck in Plymouth. The impact was limited and only a few colonists died. However, the Indians were not so lucky and in its wake it "swept away many of the Indians" and spread throughout New England, New York and Quebec and was likely "the greatest epidemic ever to strike the New England Indians."[26] Plymouth traders in Windsor on the Connecticut River watched as the Indians that lived around the trading house "dyed most miserably."[27]

As the colonists had settled in prior to 1633 the Indians had continued to be a problem for them and it must have occurred to some that the earlier views of people like Winthrop, Bradford and White had been premature or wrong. However, following the smallpox epidemic in 1633 in which "God did shake his rod" over the Indians, the resulting demographic devastation revived the Puritan vision that the epidemics were the means "God hathe hereby cleered our title to this place." After all, "if God were not pleased with our inheriting these parts, why did he drive the natives out before us? and why dothe he still make roome for us, by diminishing them as we increase? And, "why hathe he planted his Churches here?"[28] In 1643, in a pamphlet published in England by friends of New England Men, we find the following thanks for "The sweeping away of great multitudes of the Natives by the small Pox, a little before we went thither, that he might make room for us there."[29]

Undoubtedly, this demographic disaster helped ease the settlement in Windsor, Hartford and Wethersfield in the middle 1630s. However, if as earlier historians noted of the Puritan writings that the epidemics were regarded "as the method by which Providence removed the savages to make room for Englishmen in general and for Puritans in particular," what about those on the wilderness border? They were in constant confrontation with the Indians and began to see the former plagues that had wiped out wholesale Indian communities as not as effective as they had been previously. They now observed the same diseases affecting both Indians and colonists.[30] On a general level one explanation for how the colonists came to terms with this paradox from a theological perspective is "Everyone—colonist and Indian— was flawed and thus vulnerable to divine judgment. Everyone had a mortal body, subject to hostile weather, inadequate food, and lurking disease. Colonists could rejoice when God favored them by removing American Indians, but they could also empathize with Indian suffering and regret their own responsibility for the calamity."[31]

However, on the local level the fear of Indians as "bond slaves to sin and Satan" and that the Puritans saw the slaughter of the Indians "as the destruction of devils" it is only fair to ask the question how might a local community respond to a devastating epidemic in their own midst.[32] Might they turn to supernatural causes and see their own sickness possibly caused by witches as Satan's revenge for what had been done to his Indian servants? We know the colonists in Windsor carried with them their belief in witches and probably become more sensitized to the supernatural and witches as a result of the "witch-hunting" that had broken out in England. If the Indians could be demonized and their religious beliefs condemned as "diabolical, and so uncouth, as if framed and devised by the devil himself," then witches in league with the devil capable of causing diseases and death were certainly not an unreasonable reach for the devil and his new followers in Windsor and the surrounding territory.

If we look at mortality in Windsor since the settlement in 1640, the number of deaths per year from 1640 to 1646 in Windsor were 1640: two; 1641: four; 1642: three; 1643: five; 1644: eight; 1645: four; 1646: six; and 1647: 27.

The number of deaths in Windsor in 1647 increased dramatically and was over six times the average number of deaths per year. The cause of the high mortality rate in Windsor as well as in other settlements was an epidemic sickness in 1647 that "passed through the whole country of New England, both among Indians, English, French and Dutch. It began with a cold, and in many was accompanied by a light fever."[33] The disease spread throughout New England, the English plantations and the West Indies. The mortality was not high as only a "few died not above forty or fifty in Massachusetts, and as near as many in Connecticut."[34] The disease may have been influenza.[35] Although the mortality rate was not high in New England according to Winthrop, a correspondent in Barbados, wrote in the following year, "The sickness was an absolute plague; very infectious and destroying, in so much that in our parish there were buried 20 in a weeke."[36]

We know disease was a common occurrence. Winter and spring colds were not unusual but generally not deadly either. We have an idea of how these seasonal colds were perceived through the verse of Samuel Danforth in his Almanac of 1647, printed prior to the outbreak of the "epidemical disease" of 1647. For March he wrote the following:

A Coal-white Bird appears this spring
That neither cares to sigh or sing.
This when the merry Birds espy,
They take her for some enemy.
Why so, when she humbly stands
Only to shake you by your hands?

The verse has been interpreted in a number of ways. One interpretation is that the "Coal white bird" simply "means white the fever common in the spring in colonial New England.... If by the bird Danforth means fever then ... his last line is a play on words, referring to the shaking caused by disease."[37]

Continuing with his somewhat light hearted approach to spring colds and coughs in New England with his allegorical verse Danforth wrote in April 1647:

That which hath neither tongue nor wings
This month how merrily it sings:
To see such, out for dead who lay
To cast their winding sheets away?
Friends! Would you live! Some pils then take
When head and stomack both doe ake.

Here he makes allusion to those who were sick during the winter and "grow better as spring comes."[38] However, treating typical winter and spring colds and coughs lightly in verse Danforth could not have foreseen the "epidemical disease of 1647" when composing his verses.

Interestingly, in Danforth's 1649 Almanac he composed a stanza about the 1647 epidemic;

An Arrow at noon day here once did fly,
Which wounded every man & family,
This poyson soon the body overspread,
And seiz'd upon the spirits, lungs & head.
'T is strange, such brittle vessels did not break,
When as the strongest scarce could help the weak.
How most were heal'd, some doe not understand,
'T was by a touch of one Physians hand.[39]

Two items of interest are, like Winthrop, Danforth reported that many of the sick recovered and not unusually it was thanks to Providence (the Physicians hand) this occurred.

Unfortunately, we do not know the exact dates of the deaths or the causes for those who died in Windsor. We know the epidemical sickness was reported to have begun in Massachusetts in June 1647. We also know that the first witch executed, Alice Youngs, was from Windsor and was hanged on May 26, 1647. It is likely that this "epidemical sickness" was influenza and it may have broken out earlier in Connecticut (late April or early May) than in

Massachusetts, and for some reason the death rate was significantly higher than that noticed in Massachusetts (after all it was significantly more deadly in Barbados too). Among the 27 in Windsor that died that year there were nine children, 10 women and eight men.[40]

## *"Magic Crosses the Atlantic"*

As we saw earlier, witchcraft beliefs were not new to the settlers from the West Country in Windsor. Their prior experience with witchcraft trials and knowledge of folk beliefs would have been carried with them from Old England, and the conditions in the wilderness of New England combined with their imagination and fears would have been stimulated in their hostile environment. The preaching of their ministers would have frightened them and their religious beliefs when dealing with their demonic adversaries left them both terrified and defenseless.

The majority of townspeople in Windsor were only a few years removed from their native West counties in England. They brought with them community norms. An example of this can be seen in a Somerset case in 1612 in which members of the community were at their wits end in what to do with a woman named Elizabeth Busher. According to the petition she led a lewd life, was the mother of "divers and base children" a disturber of the peace of her neighbors and "reputed and feared to be a dangerous witch," who was responsible for the "untimely death of men, women and children." Oddly enough, this was her second time before the courts. Her previous sentence had been to "humble herself" before William Bennett, a "man she had previously much abused" and to act in a "sober" and a "better governed" way. Now she was back in court again, accused of terrorizing her neighbors and of living in the woods and other "obscure places without obedience to the laws of God." The court issued a warrant for good behavior against her. What is interesting about this case is the tolerance that the courts had for her actions and the fact that even with these extreme accusations in the first case, the court expected her to rejoin the community with an "apology" and her own self-restraint. It appears that she was an extreme troublemaker and her excessive actions (at the end she seemed to be mentally ill) finally forced the community to take her to court for a second time.[41]

As Bissell noted in her study of Windsor it seemed that "deviance in one area" (here homosexuality) was tolerated in the community and "the town would try to use private means to control behavior" and as long as the individuals comported themselves with proper neighborly interaction they would probably not be taken to court.[42]

The community first tried to enforce good behavior on the part of someone who deviated from the norm and this might go on for a fairly long time. If they refused to participate in the community, the church, or be good neighbors, there was a solution and that was to take them to court. Although outright witchcraft would probably not be tolerated, accusations of witchcraft were probably built up over time for anyone who deviated from community norms probably through gossip and innuendo. If the accused refused to control his or her behavior or unexplainable events occurred then the next step was to accuse them of witchcraft and prosecute them in the courts. For the latter it "required a certain constancy of social relations" over time and a magistracy finally willing to prosecute the deviant or witch in the courts because the community was finally fed up with the unregenerate individual's actions or perceived *maleficia* in the case of a witch.[43] The New England courts were not apt to be as lenient as those in England for those suspected of witchcraft. The English courts required greater proof for a witchcraft conviction than the colonial courts in New England.

There does not seem to be any evidence of such unregenerate activities or black witches in the communities of New England. There were a number of reasons for this. However, the fact that the Windsor ministers began to preach about the devil as active in their community suggests the object of their preaching was likely Alice Youngs, who probably practiced healing using potions and charms which would have been anathema to the ministers grounded in Protestant theology. Her activities would have been less threatening (at least in the beginning) to some of the settlers who had likely consulted cunning men and women in their everyday life in England.

The position of cunning men and women was certainly different in England. They were tolerated by the authorities and worked within the norms of the community. These men and women also provided an important service to their communities by using counter-magic to neutralize the effects of the *maleficia* of "black witches" as well as providing a host of other services. Although counter-magic was frowned on by the clergy its use was common in England. Cunning men and women, "blessed witches" or "white and grey witches," were commonplace in England. There is not enough evidence to determine the extent of magical practice in early New England except to say that the nature of the migration and settlement of New England prior to the late 1640s "complicated magic's crossing" and anyone practicing magic outright in early New England communities settled by the Puritans, as in the Connecticut River Valley, would have immediately come under the watchful eyes of the local authorities, especially the clergy.[44]

In addition, the first settlers in New England had good contacts in England and anyone with an unsatisfactory reputation would have been discouraged from traveling and settling in the early New England towns, or if serious enough, would have been returned to England for trial. For example, in 1629 the Reverend Francis Higginson, who sailed on the ship *Talbot*, recorded in his journal, "for this day we examined ... five beastly Sodomitical boys ... we referred them to be punished by the Governor when we came to New-England, who afterwards sent them back to the Company, to be punished in Old England."[45] In another example, John Winthrop received a request from Newbury, Massachusetts, about the "scandalous reports" of a recent settler in the town from Bury St. Edmunds, England. The correspondent reminded Winthrop of a law passed in 1637 that because of the "godly intents" of the settlement in New England, those "whose lives were publickly profane and scandalous" should not be permitted to settle there and disturb "godes people."[46]

Secondly many of these first settlers were either family members or recruited and vouched for by friends, neighbors, and clergy. Even apprentices and servants were vetted.[47] As watchful as the settlers were, sometimes "disreputable" characters with less than noble motives did settle in New England.[48] As noted, John Winthrop had his suspicions concerning Mrs. Hawkins, the midwife and close friend of Anne Hutchinson, who practiced magic in England.[49] However, with the later broader settlement of New England, this situation changed, and New England began to see more "folk magic" with magical services in every kind of New England town, farming communities, seaports, and on the frontier."[50]

In Hartford, Katherine Harrison (who was later tried for witchcraft in 1669 while living in Wethersfield) arrived from England in 1651. She worked as a maidservant from 1651 to 1652 in the home of Captain John Cullick of Hartford. Neighbors and householders later testified in her trial about her unseemly lifestyle and supernatural abilities but what was of most concern was her "interest in telling fortunes." She admitted she was familiar with the astrologer Mr. William Lilly's famous "book in England" and it was suspected she had personal contact with him. Another example was found in Rowley, Massachusetts, where in 1652, John Bradstreet was fined for "telling dreams" and telling his customers that he "read in a Book of Magick."[51]

Those most suspected in early New England of being witches were generally not midwives because they were considered important members of the community and even called into court when the need arose.[52] However, those who only distributed potions, herbal remedies for sick individuals and animals or had knowledge of counter-charms, fortune telling or interpreting dreams would be suspected. Others suspected might include charmers who "rarely practiced" any other forms of magic (using only a healing touch, ownership of a healing object or the use of simple biblical verses). They rarely healed the bewitched or the possessed but were only concerned with "ailments, such as ague, bleeding burns bruising, snakebites, toothache, jaundice and scrofula."[53]

As we will see in the witchcraft cases in the following chapters many of those involved practiced some form of counter-magic. For example, one noted case involving accusations of bewitchment occurred in the New Haven Colony in 1657. A farmer used counter-magic to stop his pigs from dying. He was accused of cutting off a live pig's ears and tail and burning them, and later burned the pig alive. In court he said "it was a means used in England by some honest people to find out a witch."[54]

It is probably not surprising that remembered local customs and folk remedies were still invoked. Many of these people had only been in New England since 1630 and were still connected to their original communities in England.[55] It is unlikely that any of these cunning men or women were seen by the general public as "black witches." As we know the same could not be said for the clergy. No matter how helpful a cunning man and woman were they were considered more dangerous to the souls of their followers than black witches.

In order to bring a witchcraft case to court and obtain a successful conviction at least three things were needed: a community willing to admit that individuals had transgressed its norms; a body of evidence developed over time that *maleficia* had been committed against specific individuals, animals or property; and a magistracy willing to prosecute the crime. On the trial, suspicion by itself could trigger legal proceedings against an individual but much more was needed to gain a conviction. Evidence that would not have been possible to introduce in a regular crime was considered admissible in a witchcraft proceeding. The fact that the witch was not at the scene of the crime did not matter as witches had "the power to project a spectral presence across space while their physical body remained elsewhere." An individual's character and "events that occurred many years in the past and not related to the alleged offense counted as evidence." In fact, most of the actions attributed to witches if affected by means other than the witch having been "in league with the devil" the results would have been settled with "fines or civil damages." Because witchcraft was a secret crime proof had to be determined by a confession, witnesses to the witchcraft or marks on the witch herself.[56]

There is little doubt the settlers in New England and especially along the Connecticut River Valley wilderness in the 1640s lived in a chiliastic time expecting the "end times" in England ushering in a new godly era. Meanwhile, hordes of witches were being discovered, tried and executed in England. The Puritan settlement in New England was a sign that the end times were near, they lived in expectation that the devil and his servants, the Indians were conspiring against them and the devil would make his last stand in his kingdom to drive them out. In addition, they faced poor economic conditions, disease, and were being told that in the Valley the devil was recruiting servants from within the Windsor community. Furthermore, their lives were harsh and danger lurked everywhere from wild animals to the natives. Their religious leaders and strict church doctrine offered little worldly comfort. The settlers lived in constant fear of their lives in this world and for their souls in the next. There was little they could do about the external adversary beyond their control but if they could discover the enemy within, "the witch" was not beyond their control.

# 5

# Old England and
# the Origins of Witchcraft
# in New England

As one historian wrote, "In spite of local excitements, the minds of these remote pioneers continually turned to England and even in the wilderness" that at the time was the Connecticut River Valley.[1] Although written in reference to religious conflict in England during the 1640s it also applied to the social, economic, business, and political issues of the day. In point of fact, these settlers saw their New England as not located in a different country but more like a "detached English province."[2]

The mid–1640s in New England was ripe for witch trials and executions. Prior to the English Civil War begun in 1642, New England authorities had to remain in the good graces of the English regime in order to maintain the support of the authorities under Charles I. In addition, when the king named the autocratic William Laud as Arch-Bishop of Canterbury in 1633, Laud continued his active discouragement of books on witchcraft, witchcraft accusations and witch trials stemming from his earlier position as Bishop of London. Richard Bernard's *Guide to the Grand-Jury Men* (1627) was one of the last new witchcraft publications before Laud became Archbishop. The book gave recommendations on how to proceed against witches. His views were incorporated in Michael Dalton's legal manual *The Countrey Justice.* Under Laud, new books on witchcraft were forbidden but it was possible to publish new material on witchcraft in "fresh editions of older books and in the passages newly inserted in them."[3] Dalton's book was an example of an earlier edition freshly updated with long passages on witchcraft taken directly from Bernard. Dalton's book came to function much like the third part of the *Malleus Maleficarum* or *Witches Hammer* had earlier on the continent. *The Countrey Justice* provided guidance for conducting a trial and discovering the evidence needed to prosecute a witch for a secret crime in which evidence under English felony law was normally difficult to obtain in order to get a conviction.

With the outbreak of the English Civil War the English authorities, king and Parliament were in a weakened position and power devolved to local authorities. As the war progressed polemical pamphlets attributing satanic and witchcraft motivations to both sides in the civil war became common. The combination of a weak central government, local communities in religious conflict and a weakened justice system led to witchcraft accusations and local trials in England beginning in 1644. The trials developed under the leadership of Matthew Hopkins, a self-styled witch hunter in Essex County, England. His reign of terror lasted until the spring of 1647. The Civil War in England, the witchcraft propaganda resulting from the war and the outbreak of a significant witch hunt in England freed local authorities in New England to pursue their own witches. After all, witches were a reality based on biblical authority and English legal statute. Anti-witch statutes were incorporated into the earliest New England legal codes. Previous restrictions suppressing witchcraft accusations and trials under the English king had been removed. The settlers were no longer beholding to the authority of a king or an unfriendly Parliament in England. Finally, the belief in the reality of witches in England and in New England doing harm on a personal level was an idea that had never been eliminated. Given the general pressures and psychological instability, the everyday proximity to the devils agents, the Indians, previously described in the Connecticut River Valley, there is little doubt as to why the number of the first witchcraft executions in New England occurred in this "New England" wilderness along the Connecticut River.

Because of the limited information on Alice Youngs that led to her accusation as a witch it would be helpful to use the previous experience (with better documentation) of how certain types of women were treated in the New England and the West Country in old England to suggest why Alice Youngs came under suspicion of witchcraft in Windsor.

## Women Healers Under Suspicion in the New England Colonies

In New England we can find the attitude of elites to outspoken women and non-traditional healers like Anne Hutchinson and Jane Hawkins expressed in the writings of John Winthrop. Anne Hutchinson appears to have practiced "charitable medicine" while her friend Jane Hawkins engaged in dangerous "magical medicines" while living in Massachusetts. In addition, another healer, Margaret Jones, of Charlestown, Massachusetts, was hanged as a witch in 1648 in Boston. For Alice Youngs we have the unusual sermons of the Windsor ministers John Warham and the teacher Ephraim Huit during the period when she first moved to Windsor with her husband and daughter.[4]

The English writer James Howell wrote at the time of the English Civil War: "But since the beginning of these unnatural wars there may be a cloud of witnesses produced for the proof of this black tenet: for within the compass of two years near upon three hundred witches were arraigned, and the major part executed in Essex and Suffolk only."[5]

While the authorities supported accusations against witches who did harm to people or animals, at least this had to be proven in court. Protestant ministers were more concerned with the relationship the witch had with the devil and they were especially critical of wise men and women, or cunning folk, who they described as worse than "black witches." As Perkins wrote, "so the Ministers of Satan, under the name of Wise-men, and Wise-women are at hand by his appointment, to resolve, direct and helpe ignorant and unsetled persons, in cases of distraction, losse, or other outward calamities." Perkins condemned wise men and wise women as "horrible and detestable Monsters" because of the two types of witches, the bad witch only hurts the body, but the good, "though he have left the body in good plight, yet he hath laid fast hold on the soule and by curing the body, hath killed that. And the partie thus cured or helped cannot say the "...*Lord is my helper;* but the devill is my helper; for by him hee is cured. Of both kinds of these witches the present Law of Moses must be understood."[6]

According to Bernard, "Good witches (untruely so called) may be Sundry ways known":

1. By their unwillingness to confere with 'godly or learned divines of their Faith and good prayers, by which they profess to doe such cures, or with godly and learned Physicians about such medicines ... [but] their works of darkness should come to light and they be discovered as witches.
2. By professing to bee able to help such as be bewitched and forespoken for the supernatural work of the divil....
3. By saying certain prayers ... which be ... Popish prayers, many of them as so many Creeds, Ave-Marias and Pater-Nosters as a witch confessed to me.
4. By only touching the party....
5. By Charmes and Spels which ... have no power from natural working, nor from ordinances of God, and therefore must needs from the Divell.
6. By the remedies which these prescribe.... Charmes, popish prayers, popish superstitions and by Witcheries themselves.

7. By foreknowledge.
8. By showing the suspected in a Glasse....
9. Lastly by requesting Faith, ... they profess they cannot ... heale such as do not believe in them."[7]

Bernard concluded, "none ought to goe to these Wizards, Witches, blessers, healers, cunning men and women for helpe."[8] These cunning folk are in "league with the Divell, they are for all these pretexts to bee detested, and their villanies before God to be abhorred."[9]

However, for ordinary people cunning folk were indispensable and consulted on "health and lost property." Problems of a more personal nature were also considered. People were willing to travel great distances to consult with cunning folk.[10] Nevertheless, their primary importance was curing the bewitched. Cunning folk were common throughout England. As John Melton, the English writer and politician wrote in 1620, "you have not only scattered these in or about the Citie, but in the country: for many Towns have been pestered with these Wise-men."[11] Cunning folk were found primarily in the towns and in London the latter was especially rife with cunning folk. They provided a "concentrated customer base and greater anonymity from the authorities."[12] On London, Melton wrote, "the cunning man on Bank side, Mother Broughton in Chicke-Lane, young master Olive in Turnebole -street, the shag-hair'd wizard in Pepper-Alley ... and many such imposter, that like birds of Wonder flye the light of the citie."[13] "Conjurors" could even be found on London Bridge.[14]

For example, we have the case of a community divided over a cunning woman, Joan Guppy of Dorset, England. The question was whether or not she was a "black witch" because she refused to cooperate in "unbewitching" a neighbor. She found herself in court forced to defend her reputation. As a result of the examination of Joan Guppy, it was difficult to convince those that had been helped by her she was a true witch. Perkins wrote that ordinary people "hate and spit at the damnifying Sorcerer, as unworthy to live among them; whereas the other is so deare unto them, that they hold themselves and their country blessed that have him among them."[15]

The latter holds true for Joan Guppy, even while accused of witchcraft, her neighbors signed a document in her support. What is of interest to us is that it articulates the witchcraft powers and practices she was accused of in Dorset. The accusations were not supported by the people who knew her. A response acknowledging she was not a witch was made by four commissioners appointed by a court at Crewkerne in Somerset on April 9, 1605. A certificate confirming Joan Guppy was not a witch was subsequently signed in July 1606 by the parishioners and neighbors of the accused in the parishes of South Perrott, Stoke Abbott and Mosthorne.

The case was as follows: Margaret Abington was "suddenly taken and tormented with a strange swelling and hardnes within her body." She could obtain no relief from the doctors or medicines they prescribed for her. She believed she was bewitched and her "harme came by wytchcrafte." She turned to a local "wise woman" Joan Guppy because she was known for having cured bewitched people and animals. She would take the clothing or hair of the bewitched and remove to a secret room. She would return and answer her clients by indicating whether they were "bewitched, sometimes that they were overlooked ... or taken with Faireis." At the same time she would give them powders and tell their future as to whether a sick person would "lyve or dye." She was continually "haunted by the ignorant country people" as though she had a rare "Spiritt of Prohecy or Dyvynation." And she received "money and Rewards for these things she taketh in hand."

Margaret Abington was determined to consult with Joan Guppy but she refused to help her. Margaret was convinced Joan wanted nothing to do with her because she had bewitched her and "appeared to hate her." Neighbors who sided with Margaret accused Joan of seeming to know everything "done or said in many houses" and "possessed some Malignant Spiritt of sorcery." Besides that, she "seldom attended Church or received the sacrament, and when asked to recite the Lord's prayer, she was unable to say it."[16]

Margaret convinced her neighbors to prick Joan "to draw blood" because "to scratch and fetche blood ... is a means to cure them that be hurte." They attacked Joan and pricked her, but she was able to get away.[17] After Joan was pricked Margaret was "revvied eased and amended in the state of her body." Joan in turn became ill and "fell into lyke Torments and Stitches within her body..." and "lay two or three dais and nights ... as the passing Bell went for her."[18] Margaret's father scolded her for what she had done and she "grew sorry" for Joan. Joan began to recover and Margaret became "worse again."[19]

In order to defend herself, Joan Guppy sought the protection of the courts and accused Margaret and others of bringing an "imputation upon.... Johane Guppie that she should be a witch ... to bring your said subject Johane into contempt and disgrace amongst her honest neighbors, and ... notoriously to defame and abuse ... Johane."[20]

The end result was what was believed to be a unique document titled "Certificate That Joan Guppy, of South Perrott, in the County of Dorset, Was Not a Witch. 1606." As the following shows Joan Guppy was fortunate to have other neighbors who could vouch that she had lived a good life in her community, was well known for curing people and animals and had never hurt anyone, practiced sorcery or witchcraft or could use such things. Nor was she ever thought to be that type of a person. The certificate basically read:

To all Christian people to whome this presente certificate shall come wee the parishioners of South Perrot in the county of Dorset [where] Johane Gupie, the wiefe of Thomas Guppie, nowe dwelleth and of Stoke Abbot where the said Johane was borne [and of oth]er parishes neere theer aboutes ... signifie affirme and declare that the said Joane Guppie duringe all the tyme of her aboade and dwelling ... doth behave herself in all thinges well and honestlye and never did to our knowledge or as wee have heard eyther hurte or damage to anye person or persons whatsoever by waye of enchantment sorcerye or witchcrafte nor was ever accompted reckoned or knownen to be a woman that ever could use anye such thinge or to be a woman of that sorte condicon or quallitie, but contrariwise she hath donne good to manye people aswell in curinge of dyvers peoples woundes and such like thinges as in drenching of cattell and such like exercise and always hath lyved of good name and fame without anye spott or touch of enchantment sorcerye or witchcraft.

... And in wytnes wherof wee the said parishioners and inhabitants have herunto subscribed and our names and sette our signes markes and seales.[21]

Joan Guppy was fortunate to have her neighbors stand up for her. It seems evident she had lived her entire life in this area, had helped her neighbors and their animals (especially cattle) through a variety of illnesses and had an excellent reputation among certain neighbors. This was strong enough to dispel the witch accusations of others based on rumors and innuendo.

Cunning or wise women and men were, for Protestant ministers, an abomination. Earlier we saw evidence of the attitude of the governing elites in New England toward these "cunning" people even in a man like John Winthrop who referred to one woman who appeared to him as more than an ordinary midwife as a healer and a witch.[22]

It is probably not surprising the first witch executed in Massachusetts in 1648, Margaret Jones, could be described as a "cunning woman."[23] Conditions in England for cunning people were more propitious because of the variety of services they supplied to ordinary people. William Wycherley, a tailor and "conjuror," upon examination in court declared, "he cannot express how many the tymes; for people ar so importune upon hym dayly for this purpose, that he is not able to avoyde them."[24] Even in the ecclesiastical courts there are examples of individuals who sought out cunning men to help them with what they believed were bewitched animals. Thomas Ward sought the help of a sorcerer "having lost certain cattell and suspecting that they were bewitched, he went to one tailor in Thaxted, a wysard to know whether they were bewitched or not and to have his help." His punishment was fairly light and he was ordered to heartily acknowledge he was sorry to have done this.[25] Another author wrote, "they be innumerable which receive helpe by going to the cunning men."[26]

Respect for and attitudes toward "cunning folk" or "blessers" had undergone a change, especially following the writings of Puritan ministers like

Perkins and others.[27] The period from 1588 to 1618 was one of "terror of witches by the literate classes in England." The reaction to the terror increased the demand for books on witchcraft, books supplied by Protestant theologians, and these in turn "increased the terror" by undermining cunning folk who provided services ministers and physicians could not.[28] What was the cause of a person's loss or affliction? The latter had no answers while cunning folk offered an explanation that helped people make sense of their lives. What were acceptable magical practices to ordinary people, a Protestant theologian saw as an affront to God, "Let this instruct the godly magistrate to have an eie [eye], especially to the Blesser, that raigneth among us: And to draw the people to the true and harmful meanes of helping soule and body by rooting out the Good witches, which are rife almost in every parish."[29] It was of course during this period ministers like Warham and Huit in Windsor, Connecticut, as well as other ministers trained in England received their divinity degrees and later emigrated to New England as Puritan ministers.

We have an excellent example of this negative attitude toward a cunning woman, a healer or wise woman. Margaret Jones of Charlestown, Massachusetts, tried and hanged in Boston in 1648, was described as a "strong minded woman and practitioner of medicine" who used "simple remedies and small doses, yet produced extraordinary results." She was also accused of foretelling because she predicted the results of cases that proved to be true. There was no formal charge in court that she bewitched anyone, however, her neighbors were convinced she had used her skills to bewitch or sicken their animals. The minister John Hale, who was boy of twelve at the time, wrote, "She was suspected partly because that after some angry words passing her and her neighbors on their creatures, ... or the like and partly because some things supposed to be bewitched, or have a charm upon them, being burned she came to the fire and seemed concerned."[30]

The main evidence as reported by one of the judges, John Winthrop, was based on the new techniques introduced by Hopkins and Stearne in East Anglia, England, the regional home of many of the Massachusetts settlers. The main evidence consisted of the discovery of "imps" that served her and were detected by "watching her."[31]

English law books and demonological tracts stated, "every witch had familiars or imps, which were sent out by the witch to work deeds of darkness" and "they returned to the witch once a day, at least for sustenance, and usually at night." By watching the witch it was believed the imps could be seen on their return for feeding and this would show the proof needed to declare the accused witch guilty.[32]

The imp or familiar, according to Dalton's book the *Countrey Justice*, was as follows: "the witches have a familiar, or spirit ... the familiar hath some big or little teat upon their body, and in some secret place where he sucketh them." There is also a separate distinguishing spot called the devil's mark on the witch's body, "sometimes like a blue or red spot, like a flea biting." The devil's marks are "insensible, and being pricked will not bleed, and be often in the secret parts, and therefore require diligent and careful search."

Importantly, "these first two are main points to discover and convict those witches; for they fully prove that those witches have a familiar." Most importantly for the ministers and the elites, they "make a league with the Devil."[33]

Following the admonitions of Perkins, these wizards were the "most pernicious enemie of our salvation, the most effectual instrument of destroying our soules, and of building up the devills kingdome; yea as the greatest enemie of God's name, worship and glorie that is in the world, next to Satan himself."[34] It is no wonder given opportunity and proof, ministers and other elites believed they were doing God's work in ridding their land of not only "black witches" but "good witches." Perkins wrote, white witches deserved death because "they deny God, and are confederates with Satan."[35]

The Massachusetts court ordered for Margaret Jones "that the same course which hath been taken in England for the discovery of witches, by watching, may also be taken here with the witch now in question, and therefore do order that a strict watch be set about her every night, and that her husband be confined to a private room, and watched also."[36]

The ordeal Margaret and her husband (who was also accused) likely underwent is graphically described by the clergyman, John Gaul, who wrote about the practice in England: "Having taken the suspected witch, shee is placed in the middle of a room upon a stool or Table, crosse legg'd, or in some other uneasie posture to which if she submits not, she is then bound with cords, there is she watcht, and there she is kept without meat or sleep for the space of 24 hours. For (they say) within that time they shall see her Impe come and suck; a little hole is likewise made in the door for her Impe to come in it. And lest it might come in some less indiscernible shape they that watch are taught to be ever and anon sweeping the room."[37]

The main evidence against Margaret Jones, wrote John Winthrop, was she had "such a malignant touch, as many persons, (men, women, and children) whom she stroked or touched with any affection or displeasure ... were taken with deafness or vomiting, or other violent pains or sickness." Her practicing physic and her medicines (by her own confession) were harmless, being such things as aniseed, liquors etc. yet had extraordinary violent effects. She would tell those who did not make "use of her physic" that they would never be healed, and accordingly their diseases and hurts continued, with relapse beyond the ordinary course, and beyond the "apprehension of all physicians and surgeons." Also, she had the ability to foretell things she could not have known such as "secret speeches, etc. which she had no ordinary means to come to the knowledge of."[38]

These charges were probably exaggerated by witnesses and well within the skill set of an experienced "cunning person" in England. However, the proof required by the court that she was a witch without a self-confession came as a result of the examination of her body where was found "an apparent teat in her secret parts as fresh as if it had been newly sucked, and after it had been scanned, upon a forced search, that it was withered, and another began on the opposite side."

Finally, the observance of a familiar or imp "in the prison, in the clear day-light, there was seen in her arms, she sitting on the floor, her clothes up, etc., a little child, which ran from her into another room, and the officer following it, it was vanished. The like child was seen in two other places, to which she had relation; and one maid that saw it, fell sick upon it, and was cured by the said Margaret, who used means employed to that end."[39]

Margaret did not confess to being a witch. On the day of her execution Hale and some of her neighbors "took great pains to bring her to confession and repentance." She would not confess and said she was innocent of the crime. Her neighbors "prayed her to consider if God did not bring this punishment on her for some other crime," and asked whether she had "been guilty of stealing some years ago." She replied, "she had stolen something but it was since" and she had repented and there was "Grace enough in Christ to pardon that long agoe, but as for Witchcraft she was wholly free from it, and so she said unto her Death."[40]

As a final justification and a presumption of witchcraft Winthrop concluded Margaret was "very intemperate, lying notoriously and railing upon the jury and unto witnesses etc., and in the like distemper she died." According to Perkins this was a presumption of witchcraft. If there was any doubt of her guilt outside the courtroom, Winthrop wrote, "that same day and hour she was executed, there was a very great tempest at Connecticut, which blew down many trees, etc." further evidence Margaret was a witch because according to Perkins, a sure proof of a witch was to have raised tempests.[41]

Finally, the General Court that convicted Margaret Jones of witchcraft was made up of many of the original founders of the colony: John Winthrop, governor; Thomas Dudley, deputy governor; John Endecott, Richard Bellingham, Richard Saltonstall, Increase Nowell, William Hibbins (whose widow was executed for witchcraft in 1656), John Winthrop, Jr. (who would later play a prominent role in witchcraft trials in Connecticut), and William Pynchon (shortly afterward he conducted witch examinations in Springfield).[42]

There is little extant correspondence mentioning witches in surviving materials from this time. This should not be surprising for the early witch trials in Massachusetts and Connecticut Court records are full concerning crimes of less interest but give little detailed information on the early witch trials.[43] However, there is no doubt information about witch accusations and trials was passed among the elites in New England. For example, Emmanuel Downing wrote to his nephew John Winthrop, Jr., in Pequoyt (New London, Connecticut, since 1658) from Boston on June 13, 1648, in a reference to Margaret Jones, "The witche is condemned, and to be hanged to morrow being Lecture Day."[44]

As noted earlier, even discussing witchcraft was a dangerous endeavor, especially if one of the individuals showed doubt. For example, for accused witch Hugh Parsons of Springfield, Massachusetts, his attitude toward witches probably contributed to his being "suspicioned" of witchcraft. His wife testified during her examination the two had spoken about a Wethersfield, Connecticut, couple, "Carrington and his wife, that were now app'hended as Witches." She said she hoped God would "purge New England of all Witches." Later her husband took up a block to throw at her because of what she had said but instead threw it at the chimney hearth. She said this expression of his "Anger was because she wished the Ruine of all Witches."[45]

The early 1640s was a difficult time for the residents of Windsor. Expecting an influx of new immigrants to increase the price of land and add to the size and wealth of the community, as well as to help defend the town, the residents were disappointed when this did not happen.[46] The Civil War in England had caused the migration to New England to dry up and the reverse occurred as New Englanders began to return to England to support the Protestant cause and take up prominent positions in new model army.[47] The crisis in England also affected the Puritan clergy in New England who opposed the king and the Anglican Church. Besides a host of what they deemed heresies that were unleashed was their antipathy toward Presbyterianism. Included with this was the unleashing of witchcraft accusations and anti–Christ vituperative pamphlets and accusations.[48] After 1642, witchcraft trials and publications that had been suppressed by the government of King Charles I returned with a vengeance. By 1644, witchcraft cases were being tried back home in England and new methods to determine who was a witch and the ability to observe witches interacting with their unholy familiars had made its way to New England.[49] Undoubtedly, the most immediate and unsettling events in Windsor during the early 1640s that set witchcraft rumors swirling around already suspected witches were the epidemics and local Indian attacks that pushed the people in the Connecticut River Valley to look within to their own neighbors for the cause of their misfortune. The advantage to doing this was that the community could at the least act to rid itself of whoever was causing this discontent and disharmony bringing God's wrath down on their community.

## The Influence of the Clergy in the Connecticut River Valley

There is little doubt clergymen of the education and status of Warham, Huit, Hooker, Stone and Moxon, who all visited and preached in Windsor, would have been familiar with William Perkins' book, *A Discourse of the Damned Art of Witchcraft (1608)*, especially chapter seven, in which he advised on the examination of a witch by "the Magistrate, making special enquirie of the crime of Witchcraft." The State Library of Connecticut contains an undated document titled the *Grounds for Examination of a Witch* as part of the Wyllys Papers in the Connecticut State Archives. The heavily edited handwritten document is based on chapter seven in Perkins' book. (See the Appendix for more information). It is edited in a way that suggests more certainty of guilt where Perkins' original text is less certain. Perkins' book would have been readily available and known especially to local clergy and by the magistrates in Connecticut.[50]

The first transcription may have been originally written out and edited by Roger Ludlow, who famously worked on important Connecticut legal documents at the time and had an interest in witches. The original document provided ready guidance to examine witches throughout Connecticut from the earliest cases to come before the magistrates of the Hartford Particular Court.[51] In Connecticut guilt by association was one of the grounds for examination for witchcraft and is featured prominently in *Grounds for Examination of a Witch*. Guilt by association is a less prominent feature in Dalton's legal manual *The Countrey Justice*.[52]

Guilt by association is especially prominent in the Windsor witch trials and later trials following the execution of Alice [also Alse] Youngs. Alice Youngs' husband was a carpenter and was undoubtedly known to another suspected witch Goody Bassett, who also lived in Windsor before she moved to Stratford, Connecticut. Thomas Bassett (her husband) was also a carpenter. Lydia Gilbert (born Bliss), wife of Thomas Gilbert, partner of Henry Stiles (another carpenter), was also a suspected witch. These men and their wives had the opportunity to re-acquaint themselves with each other "in Hartford where the artisans from both towns gathered."[53]

Mercy Marshfield may have become friendly with these women as she lost status in Windsor with the clannish West Country settlers as a result of the consequences of her husband's misfortune and the desertion of his family. Two of these women left the Windsor community with the taint of witchcraft following them. Goody Basset was later hanged for witchcraft and Mercy Marshfield was accused of witchcraft but not convicted. Lydia Bliss (Gilbert) remained in Windsor and was later convicted of witchcraft and hanged.

The taint of witchcraft and fulminations from the pulpit concerning Satan's wiles and guilt by association was probably never more direct than in Warham's sermon delivered on September 13, 1640. In speaking of the temptation of Christ in the wilderness (apropos to their own situation) he addressed the Windsor congregation, "it is possible the prince of devils might here tempt you? ... there is one devil that is their captain. [The] reason he is called the tempter because of his dexterity ... what shall we think of those men who are not content to be wicked themselves alone but must draw others to be wicked ... they are the children of the devil ... then answer your temptations ... [with] ... hatred of devils."[54] Seven days later he told the congregation the devil was in Windsor.[55] The fulminations against these wicked persons from the pulpit raised suspicions about Alice Youngs and eventually others in the town that followed these women culminating later in at least three convictions and executions for witchcraft.

If Alice engaged in unusual practices considered to be harmless and or helpful by many people it would have been the clergy who objected to what they considered "diabolical practices." Secondly, not unlike Margaret Jones, she may have been forthright in her tone and speech. Over time this would also have been a contributory factor to a witchcraft accusation among the ministers, elites and even some of the ordinary town folk.

## Conditions from 1640 to 1647

The period from 1640 to 1647 was a time of high tension and insecurity in both New England and England. The New England clergy supported the anti-royalists and many saw the end result of a victory as ushering in the Second Coming. Ministers like Warham and Huit, especially in the early 1640s when communications with England were relatively open, preached sermons declaring days of humiliation in support of England. In July 1640, Warham showed how closely the fate of "Connecticut was tied to England" and said, "our welfare lies in England's welfare."[56] With the invasion of the Scots into England and with the calling of a new Parliament conditions changed rapidly. There was an expected thorough reformation and those migrants who might have left for New England stayed in England while others returned to join the revolt. However, by 1640/41 both ministers began to preach critically about England with Warham in February 1640/41 comparing England to Babylon.[57]

Clearly the thoughts and sympathies of the settlers were linked to their homeland and when news was available it was eagerly received. Although the economic conditions of Windsor were hard in the early 1640s as a result of a lack of colonists and the decline in trade, conditions began to improve once they began exporting their agricultural goods to the Caribbean. While the general economic conditions in Windsor improved some of the more important citizens of Windsor were affected by the major bankruptcy and scandal of Thomas Marshfield. His business failure was tied up in the courts in Hartford and England for most of the 1640s and led to the forfeiture of his land in Windsor and as noted previously a loss of status to his wife and family who he appeared to have deserted.

On May 6, 1641, George Wyllys, in Bristol, England, wrote to his father, Governor George Wyllys in Hartford,

> Mr. marshfeild of windsore hath beene in a great trouble here & was inforced to make over his wholl estate to one mr. Tarry for the payment of his debts here and old accounts for the ships yt he & Goodm wakema were undertakers in the last yeere so yt his coming is as yet somwt uncertaine and they wil not I suppose gayne so much as is supposed."[58]

As we saw in the previous chapter, Marshfield's troubles began in the spring of 1640. He went into the shipping business with Henry Wolcott of Windsor and Samuel Wakeman of Hartford. The partners were sued by Nathaniel Patten who alleged the ships he booked passage on did not leave port when they were scheduled, were overloaded with passengers and did not carry adequate food supplies. Mr. Patten complained he was not reimbursed for all his losses.[59]

On October 14, 1642, when charges were brought against Thomas Marshfield in the Court at Hartford the court noted he had "withdrawn and not returned." This first case was the beginning of a drawn-out bankruptcy that affected some of the leading men in Windsor and Hartford as well as others in England. The case extended throughout the 1640s and appears to have been especially disruptive of the Windsor community. The fate of Marshfield's lands and the changed attitude of the community toward his wife eventually forced her to leave Windsor for Springfield, Massachusetts, with the taint of witchcraft about her person.

On October 14, 1642, the court ordered Henry Wolcott and Thomas Ford to "Take into their chardge or Custody all the Estate gods & Chattells of the said Tho. Marshfield ... for the use of the creditors." On June 1, 1643, his creditors were listed as well as the amount owed. They included the captain, William Torrey in England, of the ship *Charles*; Mr. Patten, a recent arrival to New England; his partner Henry Wolcott; and reputable Hartford gentlemen like William Whiting and Thomas Allen; his neighbors, including John Brancker the schoolmaster, John Witchfield, a church elder, William Hubbard and Thomas Ford.

Other creditors were involved so much so that the court on June 16, 1643, ordered Mr. Marshfield's estate be priced and an equal distribution among his creditors be made with "a portion to be set aside to belong (to such creditors fro old England as may challing [challenge] ... provided they appeare within 14 months."[60]

Wolcott was back in court on June 6, 1644, asking for damages that amounted to 43 pounds. On December 6, 1644, Mr. Wolcott, Mr. Webster and Mr. Whiting asked for an "equal distribution of Marshfield's Estate to several creditors." On March 5, 1645, Wolcott was back in the courts again and asked to "gather up the debts" and "husband the Estate" of Mr. Marshfield's for the benefit of his creditors and "be alowed resonable satisfaction."

On December 2, 1647, the court required Wolcott "give notice to Thomas Marshfield's creditors that Thomas Marshfield's estate was to be divided among his creditors "by the 24th of June next." The estate of Thomas Marshfield was finally settled on December 5, 1650, following what had been nearly a decade-long series of court battles over his creditors. Henry Wolcott had been entrusted by the court "to take Care of the Estate of Tho: Marshfield and to pay over and distribute it to the severall Creditors of the said Marshfield according to the proportion of the debts." Wolcott settled the debts in accordance with the orders of the court; Marshfield land was sold and for his "paines and service in the business" he was allowed "seventeen Acres of upland, and six Acres of Swamp."[61]

The extent of this business failure and its effect on the citizens of Windsor and Hartford was dramatic and led to the forfeiture of all Marshfield's property in Windsor. The effect of this ongoing battle in the courts concerning this business failure was a constant reminder to the Windsor community that even "a gentleman of good standing" as John Winthrop wrote of Mansfield [Marshfield], could lose his "godliness and his wealth."[62]

For a small town like Windsor the ongoing court cases throughout the 1640s were constant reminders of its failings in having trusted a man like Marshfield, who it seems early on had "difficulty in the Church," had lost everything in a business venture, deserted his neighbors and creditors in Windsor, New England and England then deserted his wife and family, never to be heard from again.[63]

Following the business failure that appears to have affected many of the solid citizens in Windsor and Hartford the early to middle 1640s was one of increased fear of the Indians. There was also the chiliastic mentality of the ecclesiastical authorities who preached Satan and his Indian servants would try to tempt and convert as many souls to the devil's cause before the Second Coming in the New England colonies. As we saw earlier, Huit, on September 10, 1639, while preaching in Windsor, said the Indians were in league with "the devil" and were "an enemy to the holy colony."[64]

The power of suggestion by the clergy should not be underestimated. For example in a case brought to trial in New Haven in 1653 the accuser stated she thought one woman a witch "because [Reverend] Mr. Davenport about that time had occasion in his ministry to speake of witches."[65] For the ministers, the devil worked twice as hard to discredit and tempt their godly settlers who had invaded the devil's kingdom on earth. The ministers and their congregations had to be on their guard to frustrate the devil. Clergy were actively converting the Indians to Christianity to turn them away from the devil and thus hurry the Second Coming.[66]

The devil was also capable of corrupting one of their own who might act in league with the Indians. For example in the New Haven trial previously mentioned, a Mrs. Godman was not only accused of being a witch but her husband the Indian arch-fiend "Hobbamocke."[67] As we will see, there were a number of cases involving witchcraft accusations that stemmed from either real or speculated relations with the Indians.

The Indians were a constant reminder of the devil and his works. The fear of the Indians operated as a continuing psychological weight on the settlers as they attempted to come to terms with a variety of other life and death issues affecting their communities. The tensions concerning the Indians continued to plague the colonists of Connecticut during the 1640s.

In 1643 an Indian uprising had begun between the Dutch settlers in present day New York and the Indians. A Dutch settler was killed by an intoxicated Indian. In return a Dutch captain slaughtered between seventy and eighty Indian men, women and children. The Indians in return killed approximately thirty Dutch settlers. In the summer and fall of 1643 the Indians killed fifteen more Dutch and drove out all the inhabitants both English and Dutch west of Stamford. At the same time, the Indians sought out Mrs. Hutchinson, who had settled in New Netherlands with her family in 1641 in what is now the Bronx in New York. She and most of her family and neighbors, approximately eighteen persons, were slaughtered by the Indians. By 1644, Connecticut was on a war footing and every family in which there was a man capable of bearing arms was obligated to send one armed man on each "Lord's day, to defend the places of worship."[68]

The settlers of New England were faced with a two-front war, a "bloody and merciless Indian" war on one side while "civil discord" raged in England. The Indian war in the colonies and the civil discord in England were both physical and spiritual wars. The stakes were eternal. For the Puritan settlers they saw either the triumph of God or the devil and his followers in both venues. In regard to the conditions in England, the settlers turned to "fasting and prayer" and in January 1643/44 the Connecticut Colony ordered a monthly fast, an activity "practiced throughout the united colonies, during the civil wars in England."[69]

The Indians continued to rise up against the English settlers. In the spring a settler was murdered between Fairfield and Stamford. The Indians did not turn over the perpetrator and tensions continued to increase between the English and the Indians. Next followed a horrific crime in Stamford on June 3, 1644: "itt appeares, thatt a woma of thatt towne hath of late beene cruelly wounded if nott murdered by an Indian, so thatt itt is thought thatt the Indians being so bolde and insolent are miscieviously bent to begin a warr against the English...."[70] John Winthrop shed more light on crime: "At Stamford an Indian came into a poor man's house, none being at home but the wife and a child in the cradle, and taking up a lathing hammer, as if he would have bought it, the woman staying down to take her child up out of the cradle, he struck her with the sharp edge upon the side of the head where-with she fell down and then he gave two cuts more which pierced her brains, and so left her for dead, carrying away some clothes which lay at hand." The woman recovered and was able to identify the culprit but later "lost her senses." The accused was not immediately delivered up by the Indians for a trial. This increased tensions. He was finally turned over to the authorities for trial. He was condemned to death in New Haven. The executioner cut off his head. It took "eight blows at it before he could affect it, and stirred not all the time."[71]

The tensions between the colonists and the Indians continued to simmer. In 1646 an Indian plot was uncovered to kill Governor Hopkins, Governor Haynes and Mr. Whiting, a prominent magistrate in Hartford. The Indian hired to assassinate them was a Waranoke Indian, considered a friendly tribe. Thus the exposure of the plot was even more troubling. However, the Indian determined it was better to expose the plot rather than be hunted down and executed for carrying it out (in the same manner as other Indians who had killed settlers). However, that same year, Indians from the Waranoke tribe attacked Windsor and "burned up the tar and turpentine," destroying "tools and instruments, to the value of a hundred pounds or more." The Hartford magistrates "issued a warrant" and approached one of the Indians who they thought was guilty, but the Indians rose and made an assault upon the officers, and "rescued the criminal from justice."[72]

Messengers were sent to the Waranoke Indians to seize the delinquents "who had done the mischief at Windsor." The Waranoke insulted the messengers. They "boasted of their arms, primed and cocked their pieces in their presence ... and threatened to rise and fight." The officials at the time determined it was not "expedient" to fight the Indians because of the "state the Indians were in" and to "proceed any further than to issue a resolution that for any more transgressions they would demand satisfaction in a peaceable manner."

Relations with the Indians deeply affected the inhabitants of Windsor as well as the other surrounding communities. The atmosphere prior to the first serious witch accusations in Windsor and Hartford was charged and as one historian wrote, the "Indians at the time were mischievous and gave

much trouble to the plantations." The trouble continued and a little later
when the town of Milford, Connecticut, was first settled the Indians set
the adjacent country on fire wishing to "burn down the newly established
town."[73]

From the first settlements the Puritans were certain New England and
its native inhabitants belonged to the devil and this was a basic belief of the
Puritan clergy who arrived with the settlers. An anonymous author writing
in 1643 wrote these "Indians ... adoring the Devil himselfe for their God"
needed to be saved, "Yet (mistake us not) we are wont to keep them at such
a distance (knowing they serve the Devil and are led by him as not to
imbolden them to much or trust them to farr."[74] The relationship between
Indians, the devil, witches and the supernatural occurs in a number of the
witch trials in mid-seventeenth century Connecticut and is a theme echoed
in the later Salem witch trials.[75]

## Epidemic Disease During the 1640s in Windsor, Connecticut

The settlers in New England saw it as God's judgment that epidemic
disease had virtually wiped out the Indians allowing a somewhat peaceful
settlement of the New England Plantation.[76] Nevertheless, there seemed to
be plenty of Indians still around to confound the Connecticut settlers. They
observed the Indians were not dying with the same frequency and the settlers
were being afflicted as well.[77] This could be explained by the fact they too
were being punished for their own sins.[78]

Starting in 1642, the deaths in Windsor as reported by Matthew Grant,
although not exceptionally high, heavily affected the minister Mr. Huit's family. For example, in 1642 there were three deaths (including Huit children
Sara and Nathaniel); in 1643 there were five deaths; in 1644 there were eight
deaths (including the Reverend Huit); in 1645 there were four more deaths
(including Susanna, another daughter).

The Reverend Huit's family was witnessing an inordinate number of
deaths. We know he also had railed against the devil and Satan from the pulpit. In 1646 there were six more deaths but in 1647, 27 persons died and in
1648 another 25 persons died. By 1649 the number of deaths in Windsor
returned to pre-epidemic levels of between 4 or 5 people and peaked again
in 1655 to 17 that year.[79]

It is likely the death of the Reverend Huit and three of his children only
increased the suspicions of the townspeople about Alice Youngs and her
acquaintances. The death of their teacher minister, three of his children and
then the onset of an epidemic in 1646/47 must have been a final psychological

blow to the community. Alice Youngs was hanged in May 1647 at the beginning of the epidemic. It is not unlikely she was blamed for this calamity. For example in those areas of Africa today where belief in witchcraft and sorcery is especially strong, witchcraft is "used to explain rapid deaths in the early stages" of the outbreak of a disease.[80] If there were any doubts about whether anyone was a witch or if they were under assault by the devil this would have been the *pièce de résistance*. Any strange or peculiar incidents attributed to an individual in the community were likely gossiped about. Over a long time and if this person or persons worked as a healer or cunning woman in the community the aroused suspicion of practicing unorthodox methods that included potions and charms (not unlike Mrs. Hawkins or Margaret Jones) could suggest to people their healing woman could be practicing black magic just as their ministers had warned them.

## Witchcraft Abounds

Nevertheless, witchcraft was in the air in Windsor, in New England and England. In Windsor, Warham "lectured often on the subtlety of Satan's temptations."[81] One chronicler later oddly wrote of Warham, in poetical form, though without direct reference to the witches of Windsor about his broader battle against the "Antichrist" in the wilderness. This stanza does not reference the Indians (ministers and others were not shy about comparing them directly to the devil and calling their "Powwows" witches) but seems to be written about his battle against the devil and his parishioners.[82]

> With length of dayes Christ crowned hath thy head.
> In Wildernesse to mannage his great War,
> 'Gainst Antichrist by strength of him art lead;
> … This mighty Monster, that the Earth hath taken,
> With poysons sweet in cup of Gold drunke down;
> Dead drunke those lie whom Christ doth not awaken.
> But Wareham thou by him art sent to save,
> With words of truth Christ to their soules apply,
> That deadly sin hath laid in rotting Grave
> Dead, live in Christ here, and Eternally.[83]

In one of Huit's last sermons found in *Grant's Diary* based on 12 Hebrews [he added a reference to Belial] he preached they must not give their "heart … to the creatuer … beli" [probably Belial or the devil]. The sermon is about the spiritual health of his congregation and that they not become too encumbered with the pleasures of this life. Huit lists five reasons that "occasioneth … them … to become the instruments of evil in his hands, unthankfulness, unfruitfulness, hipocrasie, security, and pride."[84] Of the five "distempers" to the parishioners, "pride" would have suggested witchcraft because from the Puritan viewpoint "pride was Satan's most grievious sin." The congregation would have been familiar with 1 Samuel 15:23 where witchcraft is equated with rebelliousness and pride.[85] However, Huit also said no matter "how impregnable thy sowle is with out thy selfe, The Devill though a spirit, could never quonquer it."[86] Essentially, if you are not willing to let the devil take your soul he could not have it.

The mid–1640s continued to be years of troubles both in England and New England. The English Civil War continued to affect the settlers in New England politically, economically and religiously. Religiously, the congregational ministers in New England had been in a struggle with the ascendant Presbyterians in England but at home had to contend with a the heretical views of Samuel Gorton. Gorton was a danger because of his "spiritist ideas and his belief that God literally dwelled in the heart of a true Christian." John Winthrop received the following report from Salem, Massachusetts, in April 1644:

> We haue heere divers that are taken with Mr. Gorton's opinons....
> There is one of them hath reviled Mr. Norrice ... [the Minister] ... and spoken euill of the Church. I thought it good to aduize with you whither it were not best to bynde the partie ouer to Boston Court, to make such a one exemplarie, that others might feare,
> For assuredly both with you and with us and in other places, that heresie doeth spread which at length might proue dangerous.

In a subsequent letter a former parishioner of Mr. Norrice's, a Lady Moody who wished to return to his jurisdiction, was called a "dangerous woman" because "she questions her owne baptism and it is doubtful wither shee will be reclaimed, she is so farr ingaged. The lord rebuke Satan the aduersarie of our soules."[87]

The ecclesiastical portion of the 1650 law code of Connecticut was written by Roger Ludlow, who was influenced by the heresies and disharmony in the churches in the 1640s. Ludlow was involved in the religious dissension arising out of "Gortonism." Governor Endecott wrote, "My brother ... [brother-in-law] ... Ludlow writ to mee that by meanes of a booke shee sent to Mrs. Eaton, shee questions her own baptisme."[88]

To exacerbate the religious turmoil and the underlying threat to the clerics in New England in the middle 1640s, there was in 1646 a strange apparition in the sky, two images of the sun and a rainbow, that some saw as a sign to "overthrow all the ordinances of Christ, under the name of Newlight, and that there could be no restoration of Religion, till new Apostles come."[89]

In New England by the mid–1640s officials feared the effect the spread of these radical religious ideas would have on the churches and government of the New England plantations. In a series of sermons, Peter Bulkeley, minister in Concord, Massachusetts, forcefully criticized this movement away from the "old truths delivered to Abraham, Isaac and Jacob" and wrote, "there is a generation in the Land, that are altogether looking after new light, and new truths.... But let us take heed lest while we gape after new light, and new truths, we drinke not in old poysoned errors, and be fed with windy fancies in stead of bread."[90]

The result of this fear and the punishment for transgressing the duly ordained ordinances of the church for example, is articulated in the Connecticut Code of 1650. These ordinances would not have been incorporated in the Code unless these activities were a threat to the peace and harmony of the Connecticut churches. As we have seen repeatedly, for the Puritans any disharmony in the church was a result of Satan's influence. Satan's policy most recently was to "keepe men from that one way, by the which hee applies himself to the soule.... First in dividing betweene the word, under pretense of a legall Gospell, by persuading people their Ministers were legall preachers, teaching them little better than Popery, and unfit for Gospell Churches denying them to be any Minister of Christ."[91]

When Roger Ludlow wrote the Connecticut Code of 1650 he dutifully incorporated the following in the ecclesiastical section of the Code and began by writing that anyone who challenged the duly appointed ministers with open contempt is committing a sin against the state and the church: "Forasmuch, as the open contempt of Gods word and messengers thereof, is the desolating sinne of civill states and churches." He explained the role of ministers and their importance to both God's plan and the civil state. Because of this, he continued:

> It is therefore ordered and decreed, That if any Christian, so called, within the jurissdiction, shall contemptuously beare himself towards the word preached ... either by interrupting him in his preaching, or by charging him falsely with error, which he hath not taught in the open face of the church ... any reproach to the dishonor of the Lord Jesus, whoe has sent him, and to the disparagement of that his holy ordinance, and making Gods wayes contemptible and rediculous ... for the first scandall bee convented and reproved openly, by the magistrates.... If a second attempt ... they shall either pay five pounds to the publique treasury, or stand two houres openly, upon a block or stool ... with paper fixed on the breast written with capital letters, AN OPEN AND OBSTINATE CONTEMNER OF GODS HOLY ORDINANCES, that others may feare and bee ashamed of breaking out into the like wickedness.[92]

This unsettled atmosphere ranging from the economic, political, and religious tensions in New England, as well as fear of Indians and diseases, especially in the wilderness areas along the Connecticut River Valley during the 1640s, influenced settlers, clergy, and magistrates to take witchcraft accusations more seriously. Besides being assaulted on many sides now, the assaults could be blamed on the devil through his agents, witches. Witchcraft trials had become a sensation in England. New methods were now available to ferret out witches. The trials in Chelmsford (Essex) in July 1645 created such a sensation that a forty-four page pamphlet was published within a month of the trial to satisfy the insatiable curiosity of the public on the subject matter of witches.[93]

Notices and reports about witches were published in the newspapers. Settlers in New England, as they received the news in print or by word of mouth, would have learned there were an excessive number of witches in the Parliamentary counties of Suffolk and Essex and of the "Sorcery and dealing with the Devil" in the two counties.[94] They would also have learned of a "witch craze," as reported to Parliament, that broke out in Suffolk. Meanwhile, the Westminster Assembly of Divines, a committee composed of theologians and members of Parliament to restructure the Church of England following the news of the witches in Suffolk, agreed "the Witch deserves present and certain death," and "the real crime was not causing harm but compacting with the devil. This was high treason against God, the devil's chiefest enemy."[95] Due to the extraordinary number of accusations of witchcraft in Parliamentary held areas, Parliament ordered a special court held under the auspices of the Lord Chancellor, a court normally used to deal with "riots and seditious plots."[96]

Men like John Winthrop and the Minister John Davenport in New Haven, as well as other elites of the first generation of settlers, received a steady flow of books, newspapers and correspondence from England.[97] Concerning witchcraft safe discussion among the elites was probably limited to the experts, the ministers. However, from the legal perspective new methods were quickly adopted for detecting witches in New England and added to the Colonial Laws of Massachusetts in 1648.[98] There is little doubt "By the time the first witchcraft trials were held in New England the primary method of detecting a witch were 'searching' and 'watching.'"[99] These methods were likely used in the earlier Connecticut witch trial in 1647. As for the lower class settlers, witchcraft accusations and stories were left to gossip and whispered accusations. Even these discussions were considered harbingers of bad luck or could be used to accuse someone of guilt by association. For example, when Mary Parsons of Springfield, Massachusetts, accused her husband of sympathy for witches because he became angry when "she wished the Ruine of all Witches."[100]

In Windsor, Alice Youngs appeared as a threat to the ministers and later the people of Windsor. Ironically, the minister's complaints followed soon after the Anne Hutchinson trial. Her heretical views were seen as a direct threat to the clergy. Surely, Edward Johnson articulated in his book an extreme clerical view but not one unsympathetic to most clergy, especially concerning any threat to their authority. Due to Hutchinson's teachings "the weaker Sex prevailed so farre, they set up a Priest of their own Profession and Sex ... abominably wresting the Scripture to their own destruction ... being also backed with Sorcery of a second ... [Mrs. Hawkins called a midwife, healer and witch] ... who had much converse with the Devill by her own confession."[101]

On the latter the implication is that Mrs. Hawkins had worked with the devil to influence Mrs. Hutchinson to twist the meaning of scripture and sow confusion among the "godly." The ministers likely did not see Alice as a Mrs. Hutchinson but more a Mrs. Hawkins working in the background causing dissension with her practices in their "godly" community.

In summary, witchcraft was from the beginning a "continuous presence in the life of local communities" in New England and "widely dispersed among the general population." Actions were a different matter and varied markedly over time. The range of actions went from "personal comments" to formal trial proceedings." In Windsor, what probably began as local gossip concerning Alice Youngs and her acquaintances had found its way to the pulpit in the fall of 1640. However, the time was not propitious for bringing a witchcraft suit to court. But by having the ministers lecture on the subtlety of Satan's temptations local gossip was reinforced. Alice Youngs' trial was preceded by years of "preparation, during which suspicion intensified and spread, gossip flourished and relations between accused and accusers gradually deteriorated." In addition, by 1647 conditions had radically changed and fear of witches bordered on hysteria in England and New England. The courts and society were now more inclined to accept the reality of witchcraft based on new and improved legal techniques for discovering witches.[102]

The years leading up to the witchcraft trials were tumultuous ones for England, the colonies and especially the Connecticut River Valley communities. It is now time to turn to the specific witchcraft trials in the Connecticut River Valley.

# 6

# "The devil is amongst thee now"

The nineteenth century historian of Windsor, Henry R. Stiles, in his book *The History and Genealogies of Windsor, Connecticut, 1635–1891*, wrote about the ongoing controversy in Connecticut over the date and place where the first witch was hanged in New England. The issue had arisen as a result of two articles published in the *Connecticut Post* of Hartford on August 11 and 18, 1883, under the heading of "A Witch of Windsor" and "Our Witch History." The writer claimed a woman, Mary Johnson, was convicted of witchcraft and hanged in 1648 and was from Windsor.

Stiles answered this claim in an article in *The Hartford Evening Post* on July 29, 1885. He complained about the "frequent allusions in the *Connecticut Post* newspaper, of late to the 'Windsor Witches.'" He argued Mary Johnson was not from Windsor but from Wethersfield, Connecticut, as stated in the court record: "Mary Johnson for theuery is to be pr'sently whipped and to be brought forth a month hence at Wethersfield and there be whipped."[1] He raised the question as to whether "Mary Johnson was the first person hanged as a witch in New England?" He cited the entry in *Winthrop's History of New England*: "One [blank] of Windsor arraigned and executed at Hartford, for a witch."[2] He argued Winthrop offered no evidence and was "a writer in Boston, one hundred miles from Windsor, and wholly unsupported by contemporary records or statements, is all that has been brought against the good fame of Windsor in that respect." Stiles listed a number of other New England historians and discussed what they had written about the "first case." Most agreed Margaret Jones of Charlestown, Massachusetts, was the first person hanged in New England in June 1648.[3] Stiles continued with a litany of other witchcraft cases, errors and unknowns reported by other writers concerning witchcraft cases in Connecticut. He concluded, "When Hartford and Wethersfield shall have been fully worked, the experience there gained may help in the Windsor hunt." He prophetically wrote: "This not ought to be seriously difficult, for Matthew Grant the first [actually the second] town clerk of Windsor whose veracity has never been questioned, was in the habit of putting on record every occurrence which was of interest to Windsor people."[4] He finished the article by saying that if the records show the facts surrounding the first witchcraft case "then we must accept them as true, even if they involve the best families of the colony."[5]

Historians of Connecticut like James H. Trumbull in 1850 compared Connecticut's witchcraft history favorably to other states. In 1904, Sherman W. Adams and Henry R. Stiles argued only two people had been executed in Connecticut but "it is certain that the Connecticut Colony was not swept by the whirlwind of superstition that disturbed the Massachusetts Colony." Later, John M. Taylor (1908) wrote that in comparison to Massachusetts there were "more cautious and saner methods of procedure ... in the government of Connecticut." Charles H. Levermore refused to engage in Connecticut "boosterism" at the complete expense of Massachusetts. He wrote, "Democratic Connecticut for a good part of her history was more guilty than ... [Massachusetts] ...and was saved from further guilt not by 'popular enlightenment' ... but during the last thirty years of that century by the moderation and humanity of the magistrates."[6]

Stiles later wrote he had heard "that upon the inside of the cover of a diary kept by Matthew Grant in his own handwriting, is an entry to the effect that on a certain day in 1647, 'Achsah Youngs was hanged for being a witch'; and that the date corresponds with about what would be the date intimated in Winthrop's entry." Stiles had probably not seen the diary and questioned the accuracy of the information. He wrote, "Such a record, by Matthew Grant, giving the name of the person, executed, with a date fitting in with the imperfect record of Winthrop, would be quite conclusive; if our information, as to the Grant record was fully satisfactory." Stiles wrote he had written the article to obtain more information on what seems to have been a "witch case" that could be credited to Windsor. However, "In the lack of any further testimony, we proceed to tell what we know concerning the real Windsor witch case, which however, dates as late as 1653–4." Oddly, Stiles wrote, this "real original, Windsor witch case, the author is happy to say, is intimately connected with history of his own ancestry." The family "can at least claim the honor of an ancestor killed by a witch!" Here he referred to the trial of Lydia Gilbert of Windsor in which the court concluded who with the help of Satan "hast killed the Body of Henry Styles besides other witchcrafts ... thou deservest to die."[7]

## The Matthew Grant Diary Confirms the First Witch Executed in New England Was from Windsor

Matthew Grant of Windsor, Connecticut, was a resident of the town and lived there from 1635 until his death in 1681. He emigrated from England as a passenger on the *Mary and John* on the same voyage that brought other Windsor luminaries to the Massachusetts Bay Colony from Plymouth, England, in 1630. He and his first wife originated in the West Country. Matthew was by training a surveyor. He was appointed the second town clerk of Windsor in 1652, succeeding Dr. Bray Rossiter (who later figured prominently in the Hartford witch panic in 1662/63).[8]

Stiles had hinted about the contents in Matthew Grant's Diary in an earlier article and in his book. This information had probably been shared with Stiles as well as other historians and genealogists by Trumbull, the first Connecticut state librarian, who deciphered the *Grant Diary*. Trumbull "published an abridgement of Thomas Hooker's *Thanksgiving Sermon* on page one of the November 28, 1860 issue of *The Hartford Evening Press*. The accompanying article reports 'within the last week' a memorial of Hooker has come to light,—a Thanksgiving Sermon, preached at Hartford on Thursday, October 4th, 1638, carefully transcribed (from the author's own manuscript, probably) by Matthew Grant of Windsor."[9] The existence of the *Diary* and its contents establishing "the identity of the first individual executed as a witch in New England was not widely known until after Trumbull had deciphered Grant's diary. Following his death, Trumbull's daughter, Annie Eliot Trumbull published an article entitled *One Blank of Windsor*."[10] By publishing it in a major newspaper "she disseminated to a wide audience the connection between Grant's entry that "Alse Young was Hanged" on May 26, 1647 with the first execution of one accused of witchcraft in New England."[11]

The information is contained on the fly leaf of the *Matthew Grant Diary* where the following is written:

> may 26.47. alse younges was Hanged
> desim.. [December] ... 15.47. John newbery was Hange[d]
> mar. 19.50. carington and his wife war Hange[d][12]

Alice Youngs, Carrington and his wife were hanged for witchcraft while John Newberry admitted to bestiality and was hanged.[13] There is nothing in the record about why Alice Youngs was accused of witchcraft or her trial. However she was not the only resident of Windsor "suspicioned" of witchcraft and who paid the ultimate penalty. There were three other women in Windsor besides Alice Youngs suspected of witchcraft. They included Lydia Bliss, later Lydia Gilbert, [Mercy] Marshfield, wife of Thomas Marshfield, and Goody Bassett, who lived in Windsor "before removing with her husband" Thomas Bassett to Stratford, Connecticut. Goody Bassett and her husband seem to have left Windsor sometime in 1640–41 when Thomas Bassett sold his lot.[14]

Goody Bassett might have briefly known Alice Youngs in Windsor or later became acquainted with her through her husband. He was a carpenter like Alice's husband, John Youngs, as well as a number of others later accused of witchcraft including John Carrington of Wethersfield, Connecticut. As Mercy and Goody Bassett moved away from Windsor the suspicion of witchcraft followed them. In the case of Lydia Gilbert, who remained in Windsor, she could not escape the original suspicions and was hanged for witchcraft in 1654. That is not to say all the accused witches were related or directly connected in some way. However this group of witches seemed to be connected and had a commonplace origin in Windsor. Alice Youngs, Goody Bassett, Lydia [Bliss] Gilbert and Mercy Marshfield were all likely acquainted with each other in Windsor. Given the environment and background previously discussed it now becomes a little clearer as to what might have happened to cause Alice Youngs to be the first person convicted and executed for witchcraft. We only have limited circumstantial evidence as to what happened in Windsor to cause Alice and the others to be accused of witchcraft. Like a virus, the witchcraft accusations that began in Windsor reached beyond Windsor to the entire Connecticut River Valley and infected other communities causing panic and the execution of other suspected witches.

## The First Witch

Thomas and Alice Youngs moved to Windsor sometime around 1640/41. Thomas purchased the land formerly owned by William Hubbard on Backer Row. The Backer Row neighborhood held secondary status to the impoverished "Silver Lane." The Youngs migrated from London a few years after the arrival of the Stiles party and likely had a connection to the members of the Stiles party while they were in London.

The original Stiles party had taken the oath of "Allegeance and Supremacie" at the Church of St. Mildred, Bread Street before they were "transported to New England" on the ship *Christian de London*. The party was led by Mr. Francis Stiles. Nearly all the males on the ship were apprenticed "some before and some after coming to America."[15] Francis Stiles and his brother were both master carpenters.

John Youngs was also a carpenter and when he passed away in 1661 (having left Windsor in 1649 or about two years after the execution of his wife, Alice), he left a "modest estate" including "carpentry tools."[16] I believe I have found evidence his daughter Alice Youngs was christened on March 2, 1633/34, in St. Margaret's Church in Westminster, London, only seven miles from the church of St. Mildred on Bread St. This suggests John Youngs may have known Henry Stiles and his brother or other members of the carpenter's trade in London.[17]

As further evidence, an "Alis" Young (the s had been dropped later) married "Symon" Beamon on December 15, 1654, in Springfield, Massachusetts.[18] There were no other last names of Young or Youngs in Windsor

**Baptism Record of Alice Youngs, March 2, 1633/34. St. Margaret's Church, West-minster, London (Copyright: Dean and Chapter of Westminster, London).**

or Springfield (both names were rare at this time in colonial New England). When Alice married in 1654 she would have been about the age of 20, the average age of marriage at that time in colonial New England and approximately twenty years following her baptismal record.[19] John Demos located further evidence Alice was most likely the daughter of the woman hanged for a witch in 1647. He wrote in 1677, "Thomas Beamon, the son of Alice [Young] Beamon sued another man for slander—specifically for saying his mother was a witch, and he looked like one."[20] That "witchcraft was hereditary" was a common belief among the general population and reinforced by the most learned divines. According to Bernard, "The common report of neighbors of all sorts, is with all the suspected be of kin to a convicted Witch, as sonne, daughter, brother, sister, neece or nephew, or child ... or of familiar acquaintance with such a one. This is a cause of suspicion." Perkins had earlier concluded after listing kin and acquaintances "that a Witch dying leaveth some of the forenamed, heirs of her Witchcraft."[21]

Strangely, about the same time as the Youngs' arrival in Windsor in the fall of 1640, the two Windsor ministers Warham and Huit began preaching sermons that the devil was among the inhabitants of Windsor. Warham, especially with his sermons about Satan and the devil, began sowing doubt in his flock about who might be tempted to follow the devil. This would have been a strange thing to do on his part, to suddenly begin accusing members of his flock of being influenced by the devil because most of the inhabitants in Windsor had traveled from Plymouth, England, with him. The new immigrants that arrived in 1639 included a number of "excellent families from" the new minister Ephraim Huit's church. This group came from the midlands of England and the people were hardly candidates to be tempted by Satan's wiles. Even with these new arrivals, Windsor continued to be dominated by the original Dorchester settlers, who still made up approximately 70 percent of the population.[22]

However, there were a small number of immigrants who were not of West Country origin, including the Youngs. John and Alice were likely friendly with the Stiles settlers, fellow Londoners who lived in the north section of the town above the Great Meadow. In addition, there had been a continuing undercurrent of animosity toward the Stiles party since the latter's arrival. The Stiles party were referred to sarcastically by the West Country settlers as the "Lords and Gentlemen." Because of their ties to the Stiles party, the Youngs were probably not warmly welcomed into the West Country dominated church or community.[23]

At the time of Alice's arrival both ministers began preaching sermons concerning the devil and his temptations. Ephraim Huit was no stranger to discussing the evil of witchcraft and had previously written, "Evil stirring … the torments of hell … its impossible that the soule beholding God out of Christ, should ever swimme out of the griefe of despaire. Thus Saul runs to the Witch of Endor."[24]

We may never know exactly what activities Alice Youngs and others may have done to prompt these early sermons. Based on some clues provided and the concern expressed early on by the two ministers, as well as similar language expressed toward other woman in New England, we can speculate what Alice and the others had done to cause the ministers to speak out immediately on her arrival. Also, witchcraft accusations were usually spread out over many years without the accused being brought before the magistrates until some event finally prompted an examination and trial.

## Alice Youngs Suspicioned As a Witch

It does not seem inappropriate to conjecture that Alice was attacked from the pulpit by the two ministers in Windsor who probably saw her healing skills as a threat to their community. It is highly doubtful she would have practiced "black magic," but as a healer with some skills, she would have drawn the ire of the two ministers who considered a "white witch" more evil than a truly malevolent witch.

For both the ministers and other settlers their suspicions about Alice could have been brought about due to the unusual medical condition of her husband. John Winthrop, Jr., described the disease "of one John Yong [formerly of Windsor] of about Stratford his wife was hanged for a witch at Conecticut." Although, there is no additional information beyond our knowledge they were husband and wife, she was likely his caretaker and experienced in the use of herbs, potions and salves (likely acquired in London) gaining this experience over the years nursing her husband's unusual condition. The following is a description of "John Younges disses,":

> 20 yeares Ago being sike in A plurisi he wase exstroodanary swet so much that it ron throught his bead; yit being carlesly tended he wase taken out of that swet and presently put on his cloth being so sike he cold not set up. Thay put him into his wet bead without driing or warming: by which means he toke a gret sorfit [excess] in his blud: After a doctor gave him phisike which cost not: when the doctor saw it did not work he judged it would case sume il efect: and ten yeares After he was taken with this disease which now he lyeth under: and hath bin somewhat free only some reed spots now and then on his body and it is ten yeares sinc he lay by it last and now is as bad Agayn. His dissese is this. A hot berning all over his body and his skin stripeth all of from head to feet. When on skin is gon and An other com it goeth of Agayn and so he constantly kepeth striping. His nayles goeth of and his hear: yet not sike inwardly and A good stomick to his meat: all places of his body is Alike. His Age is 59 years.[25]

Youngs' illness could have been ascribed to pulmonary tuberculosis when he was 39 but the later episode of "exfoliative dermatitis, with loss of skin, hair, nails" according to one physician, was probably related to tuberculosis. But it can also be seen as an "allergic reaction to medications," and in the 17th century, "most people had access to various herbal potions."[26]

During the 1640s John Youngs had intermittent bouts of the disease. The criticism perhaps by a doctor that John had been carelessly tended and then later the doctor mentioning he could do nothing was probably not unusual. Doctors were skeptical of healers (as quacks) but many people trusted healers as more effective than doctors. Thomas Hobbes wrote he had little faith in doctors and said many times "he had rather have the advice, or take physique from an experienced old woman, that had been at many sick people's bed-sides, then from the learnedst but inexperienced physitian."[27] In fact, some folk cures would later be shown to have had a "basis of science behind them."[28]

It is possible that unknown to Winthrop, John Youngs had the same extreme symptoms on occasion and that he seemed inwardly normal with a healthy appetite but lost his skin, hair and nails again and again frightening the townspeople in Windsor (later Stratford). Initially, in Windsor this may have suggested witchcraft to the inhabitants, especially if his wife seemed to be able to cure him with salves and potions and used the same skills to help animals and others suffering in the community. In doing so she would have come under the suspicious eyes of the ministers not as a helpful "cunning woman" but as someone practicing witchcraft. There is also the suspicion she may have tried to help those who thought they were bewitched. For example, later in Springfield, Massachusetts, there was gossip about Mrs. Marshfield, who was likely an acquaintance of Alice Youngs. Because Mrs. Marshfield had come with her husband from the Dorchester church and was likely a member in good standing she initially had high status in the town. As she lost status in Windsor she likely turned to Alice and others who lacked status in Windsor for friendship. The gossip that followed Mercy to Springfield implied she also was a witch and was sought after to "try a witch" or to lift a curse, an action expected of a cunning person or "white witch." In addition, she appears later as a witness who was helping an accused witch's victim who complained of suspicious pains following childbirth.[29]

As we saw in the previous chapter there were a multitude of cunning folk in England and they were especially numerous in London. Alice emigrated from London and may have acquired healing skills while living there. Examples of other women who settled in Hartford with origins in London who may have innocently practiced some of these "helping" skills and later came under suspicion included Katherine Harrison and Judith Ayres. Both had lived in London. Katherine Harrison was first suspected of witchcraft in the 1650s. The charge that she was a "fortune-teller and healer" and had used her "cunning for malevolent and benevolent purposes" were accusations that continued to haunt her well into the next two decades.[30] Katherine claimed to have a knowledge of the famous English astrologer William Lilly and of "Mr. Lilly's book in England; others inferred a more personal tutelage."[31]

Judith Ayres was accused of witchcraft during the Hartford witch hunt in 1662. One witness testified "goody Ayres Sayd when she lived of London in England" told tales of meeting the devil there.[32]

In general, in England it was only when the "cunning folk clashed with the direct interests of other professional groups, particularly the clergy and doctors, that their activity has been recorded."[33] In Windsor the religious motivation may have taken precedence over more pecuniary interests. The ministers John Warham and Ephraim Huit may have determined Alice' skills as a cunning person were a threat to their congregation inviting devilish arts into their godly community and corrupting the souls of their congregation.

It is highly doubtful any of the original emigrants vetted by the Protestant ministers White, Warham and Maverick would have accepted a cunning person for passage. In fact we know Alice arrived later with her husband. She was not hand-picked by a minister. Her skills were unlikely to call much attention to her in London but would arouse the suspicion of the ministers in Windsor. Her skills would have been especially useful in Windsor and in demand. Cunning folk seemed to have been called upon to help cure sick or bewitched animals, especially cattle. The people of Windsor brought their cattle with them from England on the *Mary and John* and one of their reasons for moving to Windsor there was not enough land for cattle farming in Dorchester.

Consulting cunning folk in England was a common practice. Unlike the Protestant ministers who saw cunning folk in league with the devil, ordinary people were generally not convinced this was the case.[34] The latter seems

For Puritan ministers in England and New England they would have seen the origin of the "healer" or cunning person's knowledge coming from the devil. The image shows the devil bringing medicine to a sick man or woman. Woodcut, 1720 (courtesy Wellcome Library, London).

reasonable to assume because of the changing nature of their sermons, the focus on the devil, and the devil's presence in Windsor expressed in the minister's sermons shortly after Alice's arrival.

Other reasons the original Dorchester settlers moved to Windsor was because they did not get along with their more religiously strict East Anglian neighbors in the Massachusetts Bay. In addition, the West Country settlers spoke more slowly with a distinct dialect different from the East Anglian dialect.

Alice from London would have had a London dialect, like the Stiles immigrants, with speech foreign to her West Country neighbors. However, there was one significant difference: there were only two women in the original Stiles party—the rest were the Stiles men and a group of male apprentices. As one of the few females in Windsor originating in London, Alice would have stood out. They might have viewed her more rapid London speech pattern and dialect as sharp if not rude and overly opinionated (similar to Margaret Jones later). This would not have suggested witchcraft but it might have been a contributing factor combined with her London ways and "cunning skills" that prompted the two clergymen to speak out from the pulpit. What may have been perceived by some as useful or "benevolent" skills to the ordinary townspeople were seen from the pulpit as deviltry. In early New England the Church carried significant moral weight in the community with the authorities. This criticism over time may have begun to negatively influence the ordinary people's attitude toward Alice and her associates.

In addition, if this was interpreted by the ministers as unregulated female speech then her behavior may have been seen as a threat to the religious and civic authority in the town, a common concern in colonial New England. As George Webbe, an Anglican minister wrote in 1619 "The tongue is a Witch … it is full of evil poison."[35] In colonial Massachusetts, "the spoken word had a kind of power…. People measured their own worth by the way their neighbors, servants, trading partners, and families talked to and about them."[36]

Language was an important area to "suspicion" witchcraft, especially in women. Perkins listed seven categories where witches would arouse suspicion "five of these centered on the spoken word." They included: "Notorious defamation … if a fellow-witch or Magician give testimonie of any person to be a witch … if after cursing there followeth death, or at least some mischiefe, … if after enmitie, quarreling, or threatening, a present mischiefe doth follow … [and] … if the partie examined be unconstant … to himself in his deliberate answers, it argueth a guiltie minde and conscience which stoppeth the freedom of speech and utterance."[37]

New England clergy had recently become especially sensitive to women's "disorderly" speech. The recent experience with Anne Hutchinson in Boston as far as the clergy and civic leaders were concerned "could have been the undoing of New England's fragile social and religious order."[38] Clergy in Connecticut and Massachusetts would have been sensitized to the profound effect that slanderous and cursing speech could have on their communities. Huit, for example, in a sermon delivered on October 2, 1640, in Windsor, said "contentions that are amongst us are from a cursed spirit."[39] Locally, it was generally a "contentious verbal exchange" that tipped neighbors off a suspect might be a witch. Wishing that bad things would happen to a neighbor was "contentious speech" and when taken for diabolical intent led to witchcraft accusations. West Country settlers were familiar with individuals suspected of witchcraft who feared being "ill-treated by their neighbors" and may have been reduced to threatening their neighbors. If the threats led to "death, illness, or misfortune then observers could readily persuade themselves that witchcraft had been employed."[40]

The opposite was also true. "Pretended kindness" and then a sickness or death that followed was also suspicious.[41] Finally, the woman's neighbors saw the witch undermining everyday activities like butter churning or the health of farm animals and children. The clergy and educated elites heard words that threatened the "social hierarchy" and their authority while the neighbor heard words that threatened them with physical harm.[42] It was most likely the quick response of the ministers and even the deacons in Windsor in their preaching recognized some kind of verbal threat from Alice but were in no position initially to act immediately on her transgressions. It does appear the ministers felt someone was an immediate threat to their godly community and began to warn their parishioners around the time of the arrival of John and Alice Youngs. It is likely at first her neighbors perceived her activities as benevolent but later saw them as malevolent.

Nevertheless, at about the time of the arrival of the Youngs something was surely amiss. Unfortunately no one is named in these early sermons as the cause of the trouble in Windsor yet the sermons are clear there is a real evil presence in the town. That this concern would be articulated by the ministers was not unexpected. The Church was the "center of community life" in Windsor, and even more "the town was emphatically the church, and the church was the town." The "ecclesiastical history of Windsor" cannot be separated or understood as "distinct from its civil history."[43]

## *"For the devil is amongst thee now"*

The ministers and related religious leaders in Windsor were significant in their number and authority in town and in the Windsor Church. Besides the governance of the Church by its two ministers, the community had an inordinate share of ruling elders, deacons and the sons of or settlers related to clergy as a consequence of its early organization in England by the minister John White.[44]

The summer and fall of 1640 seemed to have been a pivotal time in Windsor for the introduction of ideas about Satan and the devil into the Windsor community barely removed from similar ideas in their previous homes. These ideas about evil and the devil were introduced in various sermons given by the ministers in Windsor during that time.[45]

When John White recruited his emigrants to New England he appointed two ministers, the Reverends John Maverick and John Warham, who led the party across the Atlantic on the ship the *Mary and John*. The two ministers settled and established the church in Dorchester; John Maverick had been against moving to Connecticut. When he died in March 1635, this gave John Warham free reign to lead the parishioners to settle in Windsor in that same year. He remained the spiritual leader of the Windsor community until his death in 1670.

In August 1639, the Reverend Ephraim Huit and his flock emigrated from England to Windsor. He became the teacher in the Windsor Church. Huit died in 1644 leaving Windsor with one minister to care for the church. This was in place of the traditional two ministers hired for a church, one responsible for spiritual care and the teacher responsible for explaining doctrine and scripture. Like Warham and while he lived in Windsor, Huit, would have taken an orthodox Puritan view of witchcraft. With the death of Huit in 1644, Warham was assisted by the ruling elders in the church, John Witchfield from Exeter, John Branker from Somerset, and William Hosford from Dorset. The elders assisted in church government, watched its members and were responsible for disciplinary measures. They also visited and prayed with the sick and, when the minister was absent, expounded on scripture.[46]

Of special interest to us were the sermons given primarily in the Windsor Church during Sunday services and on lecture day in the summer and fall of 1640 by the clergy of the Windsor Church. Strangely enough prior to the fall of 1640, Warham and Huit referred to the devil or Satan only on rare occasions. For example, in a sermon on September 10, 1639, preached as day of humiliation "for the soldiers gone forth against the Pequots" one of the justifications for their actions against the enemy was "the devil is the enemy to a holy colony." Again, on July 29, 1640, a day of humiliation for England, we find Huit proclaiming in Windsor the king's "reigning sins do let in raging plagues." He argued the king's commands are "contrary to God," they are in "conformity with the devil," and that "we should rise up in the face of evil times to suppress the reigning raging power thereof."[47]

However in a sermon given on June 28, 1640, Warham introduced the idea "we may not do evil to keep ourselves out of evil" (a reference to those who use charms and potions in keeping with the Puritan belief all magic was bad whether it was performed by a white or black witch) and "God hates evil works and workers."[48] Other than these instances we find few references to Satan or the devil in either the sermons of Warham or Huit given in Windsor until the fall of 1640 when they increase with greater frequency.

On September 13, 1640, Warham introduced the theme of Christ's temptation by the devil in the wilderness (the idea of their sojourn in the wilderness deep in enemy territory was surely not lost on his congregation). The same theme continued for over three months suggesting something was amiss in Windsor. Warham began, "it is possible the prince of devils might here tempt you? There is one devil that is their captain ... those men are not content to be wicked themselves alone but must draw others to be wicked ... they are of the devils calling ... the devil sets them to work as they are children of the devil so to the devil they shall go."[49]

One can imagine sitting in the congregation and hearing these words trying to understand after all your sacrifices to create a sound and godly community that your beloved minister is telling you there are those in your small community who could be tempted by Satan and perhaps are recruiting for him as well. On September 20, 1640, Warham said to his flock the "devil is the great tempter of the world ... unto the men of the earth for the devil is amongst thee now he doth as well tempt to sin as raise it."[50] Huit, on September 13 and again on September 20, 1640, attempted to be more positive about the power of the church and offered hope to the "community of saints" and preached the devil carries an "irrecoverable hatred against the body of Christ" and the church will not be "seduced."[51]

Clearly, the attempt by Huit seems not to have quieted paranoia and suspicion in Windsor. Suspicions were reinforced by folk beliefs and customs carried from England and found even today in the folk beliefs of the West Country people. It seems Warham attempted to quell some of this suspicion himself and on September 27, 1640, told his congregation "although the devil is the great tempter of the world ... though the devil be a spirit and a great adversary yet he is but a tempter therefore we should not go to far that way ... [and become frightened] ... we should not fear the devil too much."[52] On October 2, 1640, Warham told his flock "the temptations of Satan are many" but the "devil cannot force us to sin."[53] On October 18, 1640, he continued with the theme of Christ's temptation: "Satan hath the power and ability given unto him whereby he is able to make known his thoughts and desires to the sons of men ... to confute the apprehension of those Christians that question whether they are true or no because of the evil thoughts that are in them." The "many temptations of Satan are subtly contrived and have a depth of hellish policy."[54] Huit concluded this same theme on November 1, 1640, on an upbeat note preaching "God's own spiritual policy is the thing the devil mainly envies? And one of the critical attributes of the church is it "doth nourish spiritual courage and manliness to fight against Satans kingdom" as well as act as a "reproof of those that act the devils work helpers."[55]

The ministers by raising the specter of Satan and his devils could only have aroused suspicions and re-awakened memories from Old England of the reality of the devil and witchcraft. These suspicions fell on fertile ground. John Warham's early regular preaching on the "subtlety of Satan's temptations even to the best Christians" no doubt contributed to the later suspicions of witchcraft in Windsor. After all, it was "with a woman in his town that the witchcraft suspicions ... began and, of the following six trials [in Connecticut], at least two, perhaps three others accused lived in Windsor either before or at the time of the suspicioning."[56]

John Warham and Ephraim Huit's preaching would have reminded these emigrants from Dorset and Somerset of the recent sensational witchcraft case at the Taunton summer Assizes in Somerset, England, in 1626. The reality of witchcraft had been in their midst in their home country and the inhabitants of Dorset and Somerset were now thrown into a land inhabited by Satan's servants who they knew wanted to undo their colony. Urged on by the sermons of a minister who had been with them from the beginning of their sojourn it would not have taken much for them to begin to suspect some of their own neighbors (likely the strangers or outsiders in their town) had succumbed to the wiles of the devil and were witches.

John Warham preached regularly of Satan and warned his parishioners not to "deify the devil as ignorant papists who worship the devil because of miracles." He also warned them not to "judge to readily the meaning of Scripture since the many passages "are misapplied in England to maintain their superstitions." To the ministers, it was known cunning folk used Catholic prayers many times in garbled Latin in their charms.[57] Charms could also include Christian themes and remnants from the pagan past. For example here is a charm to cure argue from Lincolnshire, England:

> Father, Son and Holy Ghost,
> Nail the devil to the post,
> Thrice I strike with holy crook,
> One for God, and one for Wod and one Lok

In this charm "Woden and Loki are invoked as well as the Trinity, and the instrument used is the Hammer of Thor."[58]

For the people of Windsor the most damning and frightening words heard that fall and undoubtedly set Windsor on edge for many years were the fateful words from the pulpit in September 1640, "the devil is amongst thee now."[59] These words, direct and accusatory, told them it was not just the Indians in Satan's grasp but the devil had breached their "godly" community and recruited witches from among their neighbors.

On November 1, 1640, Warham preached, "Satan is marvelous subtle in his temptations … [in the] … use of direction in some of Satan's wiles and remedies to help us therein."[60] Can we suspect that here in his sermon there is an oblique reference to some magically based healing practiced in Windsor?

Further Warham lectured on the "subtlety of Satan's temptations even to the best Christians …" and moreover "the Holy Ghost never led men to suspect except where there was cause." The latter "must have proved a confusing philosophy when credulous members of his congregation later appeared as their neighbors' jurors."[61]

Huit also spoke of Satan's threats throughout October 1640 and concluded on November 1, 1640, "unsuffering spirits are unfit material for church communion … reproof … those that act the devils work helpers … cast forth the devils malices … [and] … take heed that we give the devil no advantage."[62]

With the clerisy responsible for discipline and expounding scripture this constant reminding of the devil's tempting members of the community to become witches and undermine the Windsor colony had to have had a

Witches (the original subjects of this illustration, Joan Flower and her daughters Margaret and Philipa) with their familiars: a cat, a dog and a bird, woodcut circa 1619. In the Connecticut document *Grounds for Examination of a Witch,* "If ye pty suspected be ye son or daughter … familiar friend, neer neighbor … of a knowne or convicted witch this alsoe is a prsumcon, for witchcraft." This image is from *The Devil in Britain and America,* John Ashton, London, 1896 (courtesy Wellcome Library, London).

profound effect on the daily life of the community. Who could they trust and who were the "unsuffering spirits" that should with the devil be given "no advantage"? Whatever activities initially caused the Windsor settlers to suspect Alice as a witch eventually led to the suspicion of three other Windsor women for the same crime. The ministers had a ready answer for their parishioners as to who they should "suspicion" of being a witch, "if the partie suspected ... the familiar friend, neere neighbor, or old copanion of a known and convicted Witch. This may be likewise a presumption." This held true especially after Alice's conviction and death.[63]

## The Alice Youngs' Trial in Hartford, Connecticut

There is no information or record of Alice Youngs' examination or trial in 1647. We only have the brief note by Winthrop, her mention in the *Mathew Grant Diary,* and interestingly, the notation in John Winthrop, Jr.'s letter written in 1652 confirming "one John Yong of about Stratford his wife was hanged for a witch at Conecticut."[64]

I believe Alice was brought to Hartford as a result of accusations by the West Country townspeople in Windsor influenced by Warham and the other clergy of the Windsor Church. There is some evidence of internal strife in the Windsor Church at this time too. For example, Thomas Stoughton later wrote to John Winthrop, Jr., "Soone after Mr. Huits death wee were said in preaching to be enemies of Gods trueth ... [there] ... was much disquiet."[65] To the Puritans, strife in the church was a result of the devil's influence and one example of its cause was undoubtedly the gossip and increasing invective surrounding the suspicion that Alice was a witch.

As stated previously, the first accusations from the pulpit were made concerning witchcraft when witchcraft accusations and trials were actively discouraged in England. In addition, the reputation of Connecticut at the time was poor. Thomas Hooker wrote to Governor John Winthrop that people said, "Alas, do you think to goe to Conitticut, why do you long to be undone ... their upland will bear no corne, ther meddows nothing but weeds, and the people are almost starved." In New England and in Old England, "ther is a toung battell fought upon the exchange ... [to] ... keepe passengers from coming, or to hynder any sending a vessel to Conitticut."[66]

Winthrop replied to Hooker somewhat tongue in cheek, in what can only be described as a reference to a witches' sabbat, "it is well they have no worse matter to laye to your Charge if they added that you kept poluted night assemblys, and worshipped the head of an asse etc."[67] Winthrop could not have known how prescient his "amusing" reply to Hooker for colonists not to come to Connecticut would be.

## The Alice Youngs Trial

Although there is no evidence about Alice Youngs' trial based on subsequent trials we can glean some information on what probably occurred.

In 1604 the penalty for witchcraft in England was made more stringent than it had been under the Elizabethan statute. In the past, for first time offenses, especially when no death resulted, the accused was not put to death. Since 1604 the new statute ordered the "mere intent to cast a spell or converse with a spirit was deemed so evil as to warrant execution." In the colonies the question of the exact degree as to how English law should be applied there was a subject of disagreement. For many, local or provincial laws in the colonies should be "agreeable" to English tradition. The reason, English law and the many court systems in England could not easily be applied to the provincial colonies is because unlike in England they were a hodgepodge of charters, proprietorships and crown colonies. The legal issues were different in the "pioneer environment and were unrelated to conditions in England."[68]

The solution was to base New England colonial justice on "courts of general jurisdiction." How the accused proceeded through the system was dependent on the sophistication of the local authorities. However, colonial justice was based on the ideal of the "basic concept of liberties granted to British citizens for centuries." They were the "direct confrontation of the accuser, examination of witnesses, fair and speedy trials, right of appeal, grand jury, oral testimony, writs, subpoenas, and trial by jury."[69]

In the case of witchcraft these rights were generally taken into account. However, the end result could be influenced by rules of evidence that probably would not have always stood up in an English court of law. These rules were acceptable in the more unsophisticated colonial courts that also carried a bias toward Mosaic Law or Church influence. This bias was most dangerous for one accused of witchcraft. There are a couple of reasons for this. Thomas Lechford observed in the legal system in Massachusetts in the late 1630s and the same would apply to cases in Connecticut, that the church had a peculiar influence on the trial system in New England. Magistrates and other officers had to be church members and freemen and "most of New England are not admitted of their Church ... when they come to be tryed there, be it life or limb ... they must be tryed and judged by those of the Church, who are in sort their adversaries."[70]

Churches did have a say in some issues that might not go before the legal system. For example, "for erroneous opinion" the teacher would denounce and recommend an "admonition or excommunication"[71] and for "ill manners the pastor denounceth." Ruling Elders rarely passed any sentences but Lechford wrote he had "heard, a Captaine ... [Israel Stoughton] ... delivered one to Satan, in the Church at Dorchester ... [the church originally formed by the Windsor Church in Dorchester, Massachusetts at their first settlement] ... in the absence of their Minister."[72]

Even in the legal system the influence of ministers and the church was paramount. The inherent bias can be demonstrated by John Winthrop's remark that the "church should take precedence over all criminal matters." He concluded "this does not really occur."[73] Lechford argued differently. To him it was obvious the ministry had influence because ministers in Massachusetts, for example, voted in all elections for magistrates. Ministers "advise in the making of Lawes, especially Ecclesiastical, and are present in the Courts, and advise in some special causes criminall, and in Framing Fundamental Laws.... Any Fundamental laws must be made according to the Lawes of England or not contrary thereunto." Nevertheless, in the early Massachusetts laws ministers played a prominent part. In 1641 the Boston minister John Cotton published *An Abstract or The Lawes of New England as They Are Now Established*. This included "Witchcraft which is fellowship by covenant with a familiar Spirit to be punished by death" and "Consulters with Witches not to be tollerated, but either to be cut off by death or banishment." He included the appropriate biblical verses (Deuteronomy, Exodus, and Leviticus) listed beside the crime."[74]

The General Court decided all cases civil, criminal and ecclesiastical. It could "put to death, banish, fine men ... and these for Ecclesiastical and civil offenses ... and without sufficient record." The latter was a particular criticism of Lechford's because "the proceedings were not entered at all and to the constitution of juries, such as it was, no practical check existed in form of facilities for challenging them."[75] This lack of documentation in the courts was especially true of the early witch trials in Connecticut too. In New England, the General Court in each plantation was the highest Court of Appeal.[76]

Before discussing the colonial court system in regard to handling witches, a word about the defense and lawyers in early New England is necessary. The accused had to defend themselves in the early New England courts. Even in England no defendant at this time was allowed to have counsel to plead for him. Counsel was not granted for felony cases until 1836 in English trials.[77]

Not only were lawyers not permitted to defend the accused in the New England courts but practicing lawyers were looked down on by the elites in New England. For example, the minister John Cotton in the midst of a sermon offered a reproof of lawyers, calling them "unconscionable Advocates" such as "bolster out a bad case by quirks of wit, and tricks and quillets of laws ... and for men that professe Religion (as many Lawyers do) to use their tongues as weapons of unrighteousness unto wickedness ... to plead in corrupt Causes, and to strain the Law to that purpose."[78] According to John Winthrop,

"Magistrates should not give private advice, and take knowledge of any man's cause before it came to a public hearing." This was, according to Winthrop, debated in the General Court and was opposed for a number of reasons, the first being if we allow this, "we must provide lawyers to direct men in their causes."[79]

Secondly, even though there was a structure for all trials including witch trials there were few trained lawyers in early New England (Lechford being one and he returned to England in 1641). One critic noted that there was no doubt that trials were conducted without reference to the "fundamental principles of the Common Law." For example in the trial of Anne Hutchinson in 1637 she was quoted as saying, "I have no things heard to my charge" and more directly in the later Quaker trials in Boston in 1661, the defendants appealed to the laws of England and the reply was, "You have broken our laws and we shall try you." It seemed that English common law was also binding only so far as it was expressive of the Law of God. All early cases frequently cited scriptural authority but on the subject of witchcraft this was most ominous for the outcome because these scriptural references would readily fall on the knowing ears of the godly church members who were magistrates and jurors.[80]

Nevertheless, there was a "similar pattern" concerning witchcraft trials "regardless of geographical location" in the New England colonies and this gives us a good idea as to what probably occurred in the trial of Alice Youngs.[81]

The first order of business was a formal complaint made against the accused. The accuser would state they were a victim of sorcery. The accusation would be made to a magistrate or some other officer in the town who could call a preliminary hearing "to investigate the alleged crime." The magistrate would decide after investigating the allegation whether to allow the suspect to "remain free in the community" or be detained by the sheriff prior to further examination. Although there were few jails in most settlements the Particular Court of Connecticut that met in Hartford did order a prison be built in 1640. It was completed in September 1641 and served as the jail for the towns of Hartford, Windsor, Wethersfield and Farmington.[82] Generally there were few jails in "seventeenth-century, settlements, prisoners were usually quartered in the sheriff's home and restrained from escaping by irons, ropes or other physical bonds." The confinement was short because the magistrate convened a hearing almost immediately following the decision to proceed with the case.[83]

Hearings were generally "informal and open to the public." The goal was not to judge the "guilt or innocence of the accused, but to determine if an incidence of witchcraft had taken place and if there was reasonable proof the crime had been committed by the detainee." In the case of witchcraft the magistrates "were vested with special powers."[84]

Citizens could be subpoenaed to give oral or written testimony. This could lead to grand-jury activity. The courts were careful with written testimony and the expectation was accusers and witnesses would give oral testimony before the court. Written testimony could only be used as evidence if a witness died or could not attend. The local magistrate could take sworn testimony and collect evidence that included ordering the home of the accused be searched for "puppets," charms and other supernatural objects. The magistrate could order the body of the accused be examined for incriminating marks on the body. This included a thorough examination of the body including the private parts of the accused for witches' marks or devil's marks. The magistrate's court was not the end of the case for those found guilty. The magistrate's opinion and evidence of guilt was sent on to a grand-jury for indictment. The grand jury was all male, composed of free men, church members and landowners.[85]

The grand-jury was empowered to call all witnesses for their testimony. The hearing was generally short and "rarely took longer than a day." If the evidence was "insufficient to sustain charges of witchcraft then the word *ignoramus* was written on the bill of indictment." If the evidence was sufficient for a guilty charge then *billa vera* or true bill was written on the indictment and the case would go to the highest court.[86]

Now armed with Dalton and Perkins the trial for witchcraft could get underway. The trial of Alice Youngs would have been held in Hartford at the Particular Court. Undoubtedly, the trials held in England and the new methods to determine guilt introduced by Hopkins and Stearne in England were used the following year in Massachusetts and would have been known in Hartford as well, especially among elites like Roger Ludlow, a trained lawyer, who would later become involved in a series of witchcraft trials in the 1650s.

> Immediately after the court convened the defendant was brought forward to face the bench. The indictment was read to the prisoner and sometimes a less formal summary of charges was given, … the judge called for the entering of a plea. If the prisoner called out guilty, sentence was pronounced without delay. If a claim of not guilty was made, a jury was impaneled and the trial began.[87]

Following the plea the judge might give his opinion as to "what constituted punishable witchcraft." The jurors were instructed on the level of importance. In general, procedures for whether the accused was to be brought before the bar for witchcraft followed the seventeen points articulated by Perkins.[88] Evidence showing the defendant had a previous history of dealing in the "black arts" was "damaging and carried significant weight." Witnesses were called to the stand to give oral evidence. The judge and jury could question the witnesses. The defendant had the ability to question the truthfulness of the witnesses and make "private inquiries as to possible errors of fact."

The defendant could ask the sheriff to bring in witnesses to the court by force if necessary witnesses who could possibly contradict "unfavorable testimony." No matter was too trivial and most "testimony took for granted that magic had been used."

As for physical evidence, this was generally seized during a search of the defendant's house and could consist of "poppets" books on witchcraft, or "containers of evil smelling potions or unknown substances." The court also received petitions on behalf of the defendant and most critically for witchcraft cases (because the clergy were seen as experts on witchcraft) in New England courts, the clergy served as *amicus curiae* and gave "expert advice on the ethical or moral aspects of criminal infractions," especially witchcraft. Although their opinions carried no legal weight they could and did "influence the thinking of both the judges and juries."[89]

After the evidence and opinions had been rendered the jury retired to

Witches meeting with the devil and giving him poppets. In New England the local magistrate could order the suspected witch's home be searched for poppets, charms and other supernatural objects. From *The History of Witches and Wizards: Giving a True Account of All Their Tryals in England, Scotland, Swedeland, France, and New England*, T. Norris, London 1720, p. 15 (courtesy Wellcome Library, London).

consider the verdict. The deliberations generally lasted only a few hours. The court accepted the findings of the jury, releasing the innocent and sentencing the guilty.

The case of Alice Youngs raises a number of interesting issues. As noted earlier, accusations of the devil being in Windsor were made by Windsor's clergymen at the time Alice and her husband arrived in Windsor. It is unlikely Alice was seen immediately as a witch by the community but more as a "cunning woman" or a "blessed witch" who, like Margaret Jones in Charlestown, may have practiced "healing" using herbs and charms and believed in the efficacy of her cures for humans and animal. Alice, like Margaret Jones and Jane Hawkins probably "aroused suspicion" because all three "required patients have faith in their cures."[90] She probably informed her patients in no uncertain terms an unsuccessful cure was their own fault because of a lack of faith and not following her directions. This would have been anathema to the ministers because of the suspicion she was using charms and magical potions in her healing. Warham noted in an early sermon in November 1640 that "Satan is marvelous subtle in his temptations ... [in the] ... use of direction in some of Satan's wiles and remedies to help us therein."[91] Could this be an oblique reference to some magically based healing being practiced in Windsor?

As Perkins wrote, and the clergy in Windsor would have agreed the "blessed witch" was more dangerous to the soul than the "black witch."[92] That there was a belief the two types of witches could exist in one person was demonstrated in the testimony of a Mrs. Jane Sewall in 1681, who said William Morse of Newbury, Massachusetts, whose wife had been accused of witchcraft, said "that his wife was accounted a Witch, but he did wonder that she should be both a healing and a destroying Witch."[93]

Unfortunately for Alice, she may have been initially acceptable to the Windsor non-clerical members of the community but over time and with events earlier noted occurring in Windsor, including the death of the Reverend Huit in 1644, who appeared to have a wasting away sickness, combined with tensions in the Windsor Church (attributed to the devil's influence), the community finally had it with Alice. We do not know what the tipping point was, but she was finally accused of witchcraft and brought to court in 1647.

It is important to note Alice's activities should not be confused with a midwife. Midwives were taken seriously on the continent, in England and in New England. For example on the continent there were few midwives accused of witchcraft "whereas there are plenty of cases where the accused was described as a *medica* or *Artzin* although this may mean little more than the English term cunning woman."[94] In England it was not midwives who were accused of witchcraft: "they were more likely to be involved in checking the alleged witch for signs of the Devil's mark."[95] In England, a licensed midwife "was firmly fixed in this position by her duty to investigate rape, bastardy, and infanticide."[96] In support of this position we have an example of a copy of a legal certificate "concerning a monster brought forth by Mrs. Haughtend, Papist living in that Parish." This was witnessed by Edward Fleetwood, pastor, and W. Gattaker, midwife.[97] In England, the midwife and matron traditionally appeared in court and to give expert testimony on all matters concerning the "examination of the belly."[98]

In England and New England it was unlikely for a midwife to fall under suspicion of witchcraft. The more common route was for a "healer" [not a midwife] who "rashly diagnosed a sick person as being either possessed or bewitched and, when he failed to improve after she administered magical remedies, worsening instead, she fell under suspicion of having caused his bewitchment. This was the usual course of events when a healer [blessed witch] was accused."[99]

Although cunning folk were rarely persecuted in England for witchcraft, in New England the suspicion of witchcraft was rife for what appears to have been marginal woman practicing healing. Accusations of witchcraft in New England followed a common pattern. For example, Anne Hutchinson, Mary Dyer, Jane Hawkins and Margaret Jones were all accused in some form or other of witchcraft and none of them except Jane Hawkins were midwives but she and Margaret Jones went further and practiced magical healing.[100]

This was not the case for midwives who were rarely suspected of witchcraft. There was an aura of respectability given to midwives in England, and even unlicensed midwives "required the confidence of patients and neighbors, they too had to give evidence in court cases."[101]

Alice did not function as a midwife in Windsor because Mrs. Fyler, the highly respectable wife of Walter Fyler, was the midwife. Both Walter and Jane Fyler had migrated from Dorchester to Windsor. They were church members and lived in the Palisado. Alice and her acquaintances were marginal women in Windsor and probably practiced some form of healing and thus were suitable targets for witchcraft accusations.[102]

It seems unlikely Mrs. Fyler would have seen Alice and her activities as a threat to her midwife duties but as a church member her suspicions would have been aroused by the early accusations of the Warham and Huit, the unrest in the church during this time and the deaths of four of her six children in the 1640s. It is most likely Jane Fyler, suspicious of Alice, would have been asked to lead the physical examination of Alice to look for a devil's mark and witches' teats. Unless she confessed during watching or familiars were discovered, witches' teats were probably discovered on her and Alice was remanded over for trial.[103]

In May of 1647 there were three courts held in Hartford on the 19, 21 and 24. We know trials lasted one or two days.[104] On May 19, Governor Hopkins presided over one trial. Henry Wolcott and Mr. Welles served as two of the four magistrates; on May 21, there was another trial that consisted of a series of minor cases. Walter Fyler sat on the jury. On May 24, Roger Ludlow served as moderator for yet a third trial that month. Henry Wolcott and Mr. Welles served as magistrates. The case involved Mrs. Willis, a plaintiff, against Francis Stiles, defendant. The jury consisted of twelve men that included Walter Fyler. Three of the jurors on this trial (this did not include Walter Fyler) also served on the witchcraft trial of John and Joanne Carrington on February 20, 1650, in Hartford. The latter two were also convicted and hanged for witchcraft.[105]

It appears those with the most experience and knowledge of witchcraft were in Hartford for these trials (Ludlow, Wolcott and undoubtedly as a friend to the court Warham and midwife Fyler to give evidence). Alice Youngs was tried and convicted at one of these trials. Most likely the trial held on May 24, 1647, with Ludlow as moderator because I believe this first witchcraft case was a delicate matter for Connecticut and had to be handled with care. Ludlow had the most experience and legal knowledge concerning witches and he was trained as a lawyer.[106]

The defendant Alice and those in the courtroom heard those fateful words comparable to what would be said in later witchcraft trials in Connecticut: Alice Youngs of Windsor

> thou art indited ... that not having the feare of God before thine eyes thou has Interteined ffamilliarity with Sathan the great Enemye of God and mankinde and by his helpe hast done works above the Course of Nature for which both according to the Lawes of God and the Established Lawe of this Common wea[lth] thou deservest to dye.[107]

Alice was taken to the Hartford jail, which was a wooden building about 24 feet long by 16 or 18 feet wide near the meeting house. She would have been attended by William Ruscoe, the jailer, and placed in iron "gyves and fettered with chains." Her stay would have been short, perhaps a day or two. Her family would have had to bring her any supplies she needed. Alice probably would have been visited by a minister and some of her accusers (perhaps some of the women that examined her for witch teats or devil's marks), especially if she did not confess to being a witch. They would have asked her to confess before she was executed and to name other witches either in Windsor or in the surrounding towns.

On May 26, 1647, she would have been taken outside of the Hartford "town-plot" along what is now Albany Avenue on the road toward Simsbury "where the witches were executed."[108] There a crowd would have assembled to watch the spectacle of the hanging of a witch. Hanging was "death by strangulation rather than the more humane broken neck of later executions." There was no benefit of clergy.[109] Her body was likely thrown into a waiting unmarked grave or given back to the family for a discreet burial.

The testimony at the earliest Connecticut witch trials was "either not taken down in writing or later destroyed."[110] Oddly enough there are references to the witchcraft trials in the Connecticut Court records beginning with Mary Johnson on December 7, 1648.[111] It was only the first trial of Alice Youngs that there is no mention in the court records even though there were three separate trials held in May 1647.

The trial of Alice Youngs as a witch led to the first execution for witchcraft in New England and for whatever reason, no written record was kept not even as an entry in the Connecticut court records. This may have been the result of the request of the minister of the Hartford Church, Thomas Hooker, who, noted earlier, had written to Winthrop in August 1638 about how Connecticut was being badly perceived in England and Winthrop had made his prophetic reply concerning "poluted night assemblys" and worshipping "the head of an asse."[112] The bad effect on migration to Connecticut that Hooker and his acquaintances had worried about was probably allayed by the later witchcraft trial in 1648 of Margaret Jones in Massachusetts (although Hooker did not live to hear of the trial in Boston as he died in July 1647). However, in 1648 the trial of the self-confessed witch Mary Johnson was entered into the Connecticut court record. As more witchcraft trials followed in Connecticut the verdicts were rendered in the Particular Court records. As one historian noted, not until seven executions had taken place did we finally find out what the witches were actually accused of.[113]

However, the trial had immediate ramifications for three women who were her acquaintances as well as her descendants. Although the trial was undocumented the results fueled gossip throughout the years. Shortly after Alice's execution, Thomas Hooker preached his last sermon in the Windsor Church in June 1647 and died in July 1647. His sermon was one of reconciliation. There was no reference to the hanging of Alice Youngs. Instead, Hooker developed the theme of an issue dividing churches at the time, the thorny problem of baptism of the children of church members who were qualified to take communion (visible saints) versus baptism of the children of those who attended church but had not become members and were not qualified to take communion.[114]

In August 1647 John Warham returned to Windsor. He preached a sermon and made references his congregation would have understood related to the witch, Alice Youngs. In the beginning of the sermon Warham preached a man may appear to be "visably good" and refers to two men, one of them being "simon magus," or Simon the magician. Warham's congregation would have understood the reference because they knew that Simon Magus fooled the people into thinking he had power from God "whereas he did all by the devil.... He being a good witch did more hurt by seducing the people of God."[115] It appears from the text that Alice Youngs served as an example to his congregation as to why she could not live in their community. He preached, "the church is a garden in closed, thay must not live in vissiable profainnes vissiable rebelles against Christ are satans subjects, and are not fit to be of the vissable kingdome of christ."[116]

Whatever had caused dissension in the Windsor Church and whether the dissent and tension in the Church had been finally put to rest with Alice's death is difficult to ascertain. Huit died in September 1644 and one phrase on his epitaph suggests he had been a stabilizing force in the Windsor Church: "Who was ye Stay of State, ye Churches Staff."[117] Meanwhile, concerning John Warham, Cotton Mather wrote that he was a pious man "yet Satan often threw him into those deadly pangs of melancholy, that made him despair" of salvation. For example, "when he administered the Lord's Supper to his flock ... yet he has forborn himself to partake of at the same time."[118] His example was hardly a sterling or inspiring example to his flock on a hostile frontier. However, as noted earlier, a contemporary of Warham's wrote of his heroic labors for Christ against the "Antichrist" in the Connecticut wilderness.[119]

On October 23, 1647, the Windsor Church established a new covenant. Warham, who earlier had warned his Church members not to "deify the devil as ignorant papists.... [Who] ... worship the devil because of miracles" or to try to determine the meaning of scripture because many passages "are misapplied in England to maintain their superstitions," was comparable to demonologists like Bernard, who gave examples of how to know a "good witch." His examples concerned popish prayers combined with charms, etc.[120] In the closing passages of the new covenant for the Windsor Church the issue of prayer is addressed and the first three examples given in the covenant notes that prayer will not be efficacious "if you pray not to god only ... if you conceive not of god aright ... [and] ... if you pray not in the name of Christ at least implied."[121]

The trial and hanging of Alice Youngs set off a series of related witchcraft accusations that continued to haunt Windsor and the Connecticut River Valley during the late 1640s and 1650s. During this period not all those tried for witchcraft were executed but a significant number of those with any relationship to Alice Youngs were accused, convicted and hanged.

# 7

# "Ah! Witch! Ah! Witch!"

William Pynchon, a charter member of the Massachusetts Bay Colony who helped "obtain a royal charter in 1629 for the undertaking" and assisted in the preparation and sailing of John Winthrop's fleet, had become an important and successful merchant in the Massachusetts Bay Colony. He obtained a fur trading monopoly and began to look west to the fertile Connecticut River Valley as a place to increase his fortune.[1]

In 1635 he moved west where he established a trading post on the Connecticut River twelve miles below Springfield just below the rapids. The area became known as Warehouse Point. Both Indian hunters and farmers brought goods to Warehouse Point and it became a commercial hub for the Valley. In 1636 the General Court of Massachusetts granted the right to make settlements in the Connecticut River Valley.

The founding of the town of Agawam soon followed. Agawam would later be named Springfield in 1640 after Pynchon's home town in England. Springfield was approximately seventeen miles upriver from Windsor.[2] In 1640 a road was built connecting Windsor with Springfield. This permitted active intercourse between the two towns for both personal and business reasons.[3]

While Pynchon was settling Agawam, Roger Ludlow and others settled the towns of Windsor, Wethersfield and Hartford. Pynchon's relations with the Connecticut towns quickly deteriorated due to the attitude of Thomas Hooker in Hartford and Pynchon's involvement with the "corn controversy" during the famine conditions of 1637/38 in the Connecticut River Valley. A later disagreement over the boundary between the Massachusetts and Connecticut colonies prompted Pynchon to ask that Agawam, under the jurisdiction of Connecticut, be brought under the "jurisdiction of the Bay." Connecticut had no choice and in "late winter 1638/39 Agawam inhabitants "formalized their separation" and elected Pynchon as "the magistrate of the plantation." Following the separation the name of the settlement was changed from Agawam to Springfield.[4]

Springfield was initially settled by young single men, some from Wales, but the majority of settlers were from England. The population did not begin to increase until after 1640. Families with children included William Pynchon, the minister George Moxon and other well-known founders. Unlike other early towns in the Connecticut River Valley settled for religious reasons, Springfield was settled as a business venture and the population of the town and its growth reflected an emphasis on trade. Pynchon imported artisans (many as indentured servants) to support the growing infrastructure needs of his business concerns.[5]

The inhabitants of Windsor and Springfield as well as other Connecticut towns conducted business, intermarried, migrated and appeared in each other's courts. Gossip and news traveled throughout New England and in the towns by Indian messenger, travelers and visitors.[6]

It was no wonder with the business failure of Thomas Marshfield and the likely gossip surrounding the innumerable bankruptcy appearances in both the Hartford and English courts that Marshfield's widow had been marginalized in Windsor and likely had befriended Alice Youngs and her acquaintances. After all, in the words of John Winthrop, if Thomas had "lost his godliness" so had his once respectable wife, Mercy Marshfield. Perhaps after Alice Youngs' conviction she sought refuge with her older children in Springfield. However, the gossip that Mercy was a witch followed her to Springfield.[7]

The first witchcraft accusations in New England that led to a trial, conviction and hanging began along the wilderness area in the Connecticut River Valley as early as 1640 in the town of Windsor. However, in a letter written by John Eliot and published in a London newspaper on July 4, 1651, Springfield rather than Windsor was prominently mentioned as rife with witchcraft. He wrote:

> The State of things here amongst us seems more troublesome; we have sad frowns of the Lord upon us, chiefly in regard of fascinations, and witchcraft…. Four in Springfield were detected, wherof one was executed for murder of her own childe, and was doubtless a witch … another is condemned, a third under trial, a fourth under suspition.[8]

There are documents and court records accusing Hugh Parsons and his wife, Mary Parsons, of witchcraft. John Hale, who wrote after the Salem witch trials, referred to "two or three of Springfield, one of which confessed … to familiarity with Satan." As for the other two unnamed witches Eliot mentioned in Springfield, we learn from the examination of Hugh Parsons the other two likely witches were named Bessie Sewall and Sarah Merrick.[9]

A few years later in 1654, Edward Johnson's, book, *Wonder-working providence of Sions Saviour in New England* appeared in London. He reported, "There hath of late been more than one or two in this Town [Springfield] greatly suspected of Witchcraft, yet have they used much diligence, both for the finding them out, and for the Lord's assisting them against their witchery, yet have they as is supposed, bewitched not a few persons, among whom two of the reverend Elders children."[10]

## Witchcraft in Springfield, Massachusetts

Springfield experienced the most extreme form of witchcraft accusations during the late 1640s and early 1650s. The storm was unleashed when Mary Parsons, wife of Hugh Parsons, accused the widow Marshfield (formerly of Windsor) of witchcraft. Initially, Mercy Marshfield and Mary Parsons were brought before William Pynchon, the magistrate, on May 29 and 30, 1649, on a complaint from the widow Marshfield that Mary had accused her of being a witch. The initial trial later escalated into a full examination of Hugh and Mary Parsons, who were both accused of witchcraft.[11]

The evidence of this examination is contained in a surviving manuscript referring to two examinations, one dated March 1, 1651, and one later, on March 18, 1651. The manuscript contains statements made before Pynchon under oath on "thirteen different days," starting as early as February 25, 1650/1 and extending to April 7, 1651. It indicated Mary Parsons was also examined by Pynchon on the same suspicion but no record of her examination appears to have survived. Whether the examination was initiated by Pynchon or from a complaint made by a neighbor is not clear. However, once the examination was begun thirty-five persons excluding Hugh Parsons "testified under oath or volunteered information." The case against Hugh Parsons rested primarily on his main accuser, his wife.[12]

The transcript of the examination of Hugh Parsons held in Springfield not only revealed an undercurrent of greed, vengeance and abnormal deviance but attempts at counter-magic and diabolism. There was a pattern of examination in the court that followed Perkins' recommendations, notorious defamation by the report of the people, testimony of another witch, death or mischief following cursing, mischief after quarreling or threatening, guilt by association and the search for devil's marks or witches' teats for suckling familiars.[13] The court itself used Dalton's *The Countrey Justice* as its legal manual, a text which Pynchon was familiar with.[14]

The witchcraft trial of Hugh Parsons was not the first witchcraft trial Pynchon had served on. He previously sat on the General Court in Massachusetts at the 1648 witchcraft trial of Margaret Jones of Charlestown. The latter was the first case resulting in capital punishment in the Massachusetts General Court for witchcraft.[15]

There is not much known about Hugh Parsons except he was a wood sawyer and brick maker. We have more information on Mary (Lewis) Parsons, who represents an interesting case. She was not English but Welsh and had been originally married to a Catholic. These two factors alone made her suspect to her English Protestant neighbors. Other significant factors that colored her reputation for the English settlers was the support in Wales for the Royalists in the Civil War and that they spoke a foreign language.

The suspicion of the English regarding foreigners and their languages is shown in a 1622 grammar book by John Brinsley, an English educator, who wrote in its introduction "for all those of the Inferior sort, and all ruder countries or places; namely for Ireland, Wales, Virginia … for their more speedie attaining of our English tongue." On the matter of Catholicism, an English Protestant minister wrote, "The whole world knoweth with what efficacie and powers of Satan it hath bin upheld: how busie Satan was, how oft he appeared in Goblins, Fayries, walking Spirts & for the strengthening and supporting of it." Closer to home, John Warham in Windsor regarding Catholicism, preached, "ignorant papists worship the devil because of miracles."[16]

Mary Lewis [Parsons] was originally a servant in the William Pynchon house when he lived in Dorchester, Massachusetts. On June 2, 1645, Pynchon affirmed she was currently a servant in his stepson Henry Smith's house. Mary wanted to re-marry and had made the case her first husband "a papist," had deserted her over seven years ago, and she wished to marry again.[17] Pynchon seems to have gone out of his way to support Mary Lewis in her endeavor to marry. He wrote Governor Winthrop while in Wales that Mary was married to a papist that "used her extremely badly: and at last her husband went from her & she hath not herd from him thes many yeres…." He asked her if she wished to marry again and if she was "free from all intanglemente she saith she is and that she will kepe her so."

Pynchon entreated Winthrop to "consult about her case." Given the attitude toward "papists" in New England, Pynchon probably expected nothing less of Mary's cruel "papist" husband and he was no doubt sympathetic to her plight; however, this did not mean her neighbors had complete trust in her or her new husband.

Pynchon wrote he had a witness who could vouch for Mary Lewis. The witness, a church member in Springfield, said he knew Mary Lewis in Wales five years ago when he lived there. He said she was a "herer" in Mr. Wroth's ministry. She often complained "her husband was away from her," and that "she could not tell where to find him." He also heard her say her "husband was a Ranke papist and his 2 sisters … that she lived in continuall danger of her life for he did often threat to do her mischeaf if she would not be a papist and do as he did, or else depart from him."

Mary Lewis said a letter had been written on her behalf "to ps her as a sister and see her placed in some godly family." If the letter could be found it would be proof she had attempted to find her husband and with the "counsel and advice of godly ministers." Advised to come to New England, she went to Bristol, England to depart for New England. She was advised to return to Wales to find her husband. She came over to New England six weeks later. It was now "near seven years since her husband left her."[18]

Mary continued to press Pynchon and on September 15, 1645, he wrote to Winthrop admitting Mary had "falen into a leauge of amity with a brickmaker of our Towne [Hugh Parsons]." She had been persuaded that according to the laws of England she could marry. Pynchon entreated Winthrop to "answer … my letter … most haste." Hugh Parsons and Mary Lewis were wed on October 27, 1645. On November 4, 1645, Pynchon wrote to Winthrop, "I received yours about Mary Lewes … [she] … is now newley maried to a brickmaker."[19]

Hugh and Mary Parsons produced three children: Hannah, born on August 7, 1646; Samuel, born on June 8, 1648 (who died in September 1649); and Joshua, born on October 26, 1650. Following the birth of Joshua, Mary became sick and her husband was "suspicioned" of witchcraft by his wife. The testimony of this "sick and insane" woman was taken as legal evidence against Hugh Parsons and later used against her. Because her sickness came on immediately following the birth of Joshua the child was "deprived of the Care it required" and he was "said to have been killed by his mother on March 1, 1651."[20]

Following the child's death accusations of witchcraft increased further against the father who already had a reputation as being "rough spoken," quarrelsome and quick to anger at any slight. According to the court transcript he constantly threatened his neighbors.[21]

As a servant in the Pynchon household Mary was closely acquainted with the family and seems to have been able to pressure Pynchon into obtaining a quick answer from Winthrop so she could marry. Ironically, after all Pynchon's help in getting her married to Hugh and his intimate knowledge of her past life, a few years later he found himself examining the two for witchcraft. Ironically, this exposed the town in the courts to their dysfunctional marriage that was on a downward spiral of continuous quarreling that finally ended in Mary accusing Hugh of being a witch.

## *Mary Parsons vs. Mercy Marshfield for Slander (Witchcraft)*

On May 29 and 30, 1649, the widow Marshfield made a complaint against Mary Parsons of Springfield for "reporting her to be suspected for a witch." Mercy produced two witnesses, John Mathews and his wife, who swore Mary Parsons told John Matthews "how she was taught to try a witch by a widdow woman that now lived in Springefeild [sic] and that she had lived in Windsor and that she had 3 children and that one of them was married and at last she said it was the widow Marshfeld."[22] This accusation raises a number of puzzling questions not addressed in the proceedings. Mary Parsons went to the widdow Marshfield not to bewitch someone but to "try a witch." This means that she wanted to find out how to "unwitch" someone or determine who had cursed someone "to try and know a witch." This was something expected of a cunning person or white witch.[23]

Undoubtedly the widow Marshfield was sensitive about being taken for a witch (even a white witch) as she was well aware what happened to her acquaintance Alice Youngs almost two years earlier to the day. Her friendship with Alice Youngs probably cast a shadow on her and was a case of guilt by association. She may have been seen as a white witch who "could both bless and curse." Mary seemed desperate and had turned to the widow Marshfield for help. When rebuffed she turned on Marshfield because she knew even a white witch was a "dangerous person to cross" and probably feared she would be cursed for seeking her out.[24] She told John Mathews Marshfield was a witch. Mathews did not believe this and said Mary Parsons answered him,

> you need not speak so much for Goody Marshfeild for I am sure ... she hath envied every womans child in the end till her owne daughter had a child and then ... their child died and their cow died: and I am persuaded ... they were bewitched: and ... moreover it was reported to her by one in the Towne that she was suspected to be a witch when she lived in Windsor and that it was publikely knowen that the divill followed her house in Windsor and for aught I know ... followes her here."[25]

Goodwife Mathews said Mary Parsons went to her house and she asked what had become of a ball of yarn. Mary said she could not tell but a "witch had witched it away." Goodwife Mathews said, "I wonder ... that you talke so much of a witch doe you think there is any witch in Towne." Mary said,

> An Stebbinge had tould her in Mr. Smiths Chamber that she [Mrs. Marshfield] was suspected to be a witch in Windsor and that there were divers stronge lights seene of late in the meddow that were never seene before the widow Marshfeild came to Towne and that she did grudge at other women that had Children because her daughter had none and about that tyme (namely of her grudging) the child died and the cow died."[26]

Mary Parsons denied the Mathewses were telling the truth. Pynchon believed the Mathewses because they had given their testimony under oath. He concluded Mary had "defamed the good name of widow Marshfeild" and sentenced Mary to be "well whipped on the morrow after lecture with 20 lashes by the Constable unless she could procure the payment of 3 [pounds] to the widow Marshfeild for and towards the reparation of her good name."[27]

Unfortunately for Hugh and Mary Parsons this was only the beginning of a long examination and trial that eventually led to Mary's death and Hugh's

later departure from Springfield. Hugh and Mary Parsons both had prob-
lematical backgrounds. They were not fully accepted by their neighbors. Their
neighbors became their most vehement accusers, they included Rice and
Blanche Bedorthe, Benjamin Cooley, Jonathan Burt, John Lombard, Griffen
Jones, John Mathews and George Lankton.[28]

## The Accusations Begin

Hugh Parsons did not think the court's punishment for his wife's accusations against the widow Marshfield was right and threatened Marshfield. Marshfield testified on March 22, 1651, when Hugh came "to tender the said Corne,
he said, I here that you will abate 20 s of the Money." She told him she "would
not abate any Thing" because she heard "his Wife had said the Witnesses had
taken a false Oath." He told her, "if you will not abate … it shall be but as Wildfier
in y [our] Howfe, and as a Moth in y [our] Clothes." He uttered these "threatning Speeches … with much Anger: and shortly after, in the Spring, about May."
Marshfield said her "Daughter began to be taken with her Fitts of Witchcraft."

Marshfield had accused Hugh Parsons of bewitching her daughter after
making threatening speech towards her. Her son, Samuel Marshfield, also
testified in support of his mother's accusations. He said after the corn was
paid his sister was taken with strange fits [bewitched] and added "but neuer
so bad as when Mr Moxon's Children were taken," clearly an attempt to implicate Hugh in the bewitching of Moxon's children too.[29]

A fellow townsman, John Lumbard, testified he had heard Hugh Parsons
and his wife say, "the Corne w ch they paid to ye Widdow Marshfeld for the
Slander, would do her no Good, and that it had bin better she had never
taken it." Further he heard this said "seuerall Tymes" and Hugh often stated,
"when he hath been displeafed w th any Body, that he would be euen with
them for it."[30]

Hugh Parsons attempted to defend himself, although not from the
charge of witchcraft but for his harsh speech. He was present at the hearing
and asked "when did I giue such threatening Wordes." He was told when he
paid his corn. He said he did not remember making these threats. That lawfully the corn was due Mrs. Marshfield but the reason for his "Speeches" was
because both believed his wife was falsely accused. Mary Parsons was also
present at the hearing and testified "when her Husband came Home, he tould
her what Speeches he had used to the Widdow Marshfeild, namely, according
to ye Testimonies she said it might well be so, for she was falsely accused."[31]

The historian Samuel Drake suggested a conspiracy against Hugh Parsons.
Undoubtedly this began with Mary Parsons' allegation when she told her
neighbor John Mathews in May 1649 just prior to her libel trial that her

husband was a witch. Since it came from the man's wife there is little doubt Mathews repeated it to his wife and the rumor spread throughout the town. Thus John Mathews stated before the court, on February 27, 1650/51,

> a little before the Tryall with ye Widdow Marshfeild, which was about May, 1649, being in Talk with Mary Parsons about Witches, she said to me that her Husband was a Witch: I asked her how she knew it, she said the Diuill came to him in ye Night, at the Bed, and suckt him one Night and made him cry out one Tyme, she could not tell what it should be else but the Diuill. She said also that her Husband was often tormented in his Bowells, and cryed out as though he were pricked with Pins and Daggers, and I know not what else it should be, unlesse it were the Diuill that should torment him so.[32]

Drake dismissed these and other accusations made in the Hugh Parsons' trial as "a Collection of childish Nonsense." However, as we will see, it was not so much his neighbors' accusations that helped build a case against Hugh Parsons but the perceived intent taken together that followed the advice in Perkins and Dalton for how to identify a witch.

Hugh Parsons had many enemies. He was "shrewd" in his business dealings. For example, he had difficulty with "Mr. Moxon, the Minister, respecting the Bricks for the Chimney of his House." Moxon became one of his accusers. Parsons had a habit on more than one occasion of making remarks (seen as threats) when he felt he had been disadvantaged. For example, "it would do him no good" or he "would be Even with him." Certainly with his veiled threats and the strange happenings reported in Springfield combined with rumors started by his wife, Mary, Hugh Parsons was a prime suspect for a witch.[33]

A second factor putting neighbors on edge in the Connecticut River Valley was the recent trial of John and Joanne Carrington of Wethersfield in February 1650/51. That witches were a general topic of discussion is demonstrated in the court transcript. During her husband's trial, Mary Parsons stated, "She saith that you tould her that you were at a Neighbors Howse a little before Lecture, when they were speaking of Carrington and his Wife, that were now app' hended for Witches." In addition, when he told her about the discussion she felt he did not speak strongly enough against witches and said to him, "I hope that God will find out all such wicked Psons and purge New England of all Witches." Later the argument reached the point where Hugh threatened to throw a "block" at her but instead threw it into the hearth. Mary testified he became angry "because she wished the Ruine of all Witches."[34]

John Carrington and his wife of Wethersfield, Connecticut, were tried and found guilty of witchcraft on March 6, 1651, in Hartford and hanged.[35] In addition, there was even more witchcraft afoot or, as Drake put it, "Commotion by Witchcraft" over the upcoming trial of a witch in Stratford, Connecticut, Goodwife Bassett, formerly of Windsor, who was also accused of witchcraft and whose trial was held in May 1651.[36]

## The Bewitched Pudding

On March 1, 1650, Hugh Parsons was brought into court on a suspicion of witchcraft. During his second examination his neighbor George Lancton and his wife, Hannah, testified on February 21, 1650, and again on February 23, that they brought home two puddings. Each one was cut "as smooth as any Knife could cut it, namely, one Slice al alonge, wantinge but very litle, from End to End." They were certain the pudding was bewitched. Hannah Lankton somewhat innocently stated a neighbor came into her house. She showed it to him, and the "Neighbor took a Peece of it and threw into the Fier: and she saith that about an Hower after, phapps a little more, she herd one mutter and mumble at the Dore."[37]

Burning a bewitched item was a well-known counter-magic technique and was used to determine who had bewitched the pudding and as a way to ferret out the witch.[38] This was the same technique described in the Margaret Jones witch accusation in Boston and used by her neighbors.[39]

One has to imagine this was a set-up. Goody Lankton had called on someone who probably knew something about counter-magic. Goody Sewall just happened to be in her house at the burning of the pudding. In later testimony Goody Sewall is named by Mary Parsons as one of three people who took the shape of a cat and was possessed by the devil.[40]

Goody Lankton "asked Goody Sewell who was then at her House (and neere her Dore) who it was" and she said Hugh Parsons. He asked her if Goodman Lankton was at home. Goody Lankton said he was not at home and he went away. However, he "left not his Arrand, neather did he euer ... signifie his Arrand."[41] Hugh Parsons had shown up at the burning of the bewitched pudding. This would have made sense to his neighbors who suspected him of being a witch. It was confirmed when he refused to explain his reason for coming to the Lankton's door.

During his trial Hugh Parsons was asked why he came to the Lanktons' door that day. After being asked three times he said he wanted to buy hay from George Lankton. Lankton said Parsons never asked him to buy hay. Parsons said he did not ask him because John Lumbard told him Lankton could spare no hay.

Lumbard contradicted Parsons and said in passing he had spoken to Parsons on the previous Wednesday and told him Goodman Lankton told him he could spare no hay because he had sold more to Goodman Herman than he could spare. He said "he should now want himself." Also, John Lumbard said the Friday after, when the said Pudding was so strangely cut, "he tould Hugh Parsons that Lankton had no Hay to sell."

Hugh Parsons did not reply any further. It was evident to his neighbors that his coming to the door of Goodman Lankton after the pudding was burned and after Lumbard told him that he had no hay to sell, that his "Arrand to gett Hay was no true Cause of his coming Thither but rather that [the] Spirit that bewitched the Pudding brought him thither."[42]

His neighbors believed the counter-magic had worked and the proof was not only that Hugh Parsons had shown up at the Lanktons' door for no reason but that he lied in court and it was found out. According to Perkins, "lying notoriously" was further proof of a witch. While lying and the successful working of counter-magic was evidence of his guilt to some of his neighbors it was not sufficient evidence for a conviction in a court of law.[43] However there was additional evidence of a more diabolical and serious nature that brought Hugh and his wife into court for witchcraft.

For William Pynchon as the court magistrate, Samuel Drake wrote that the testimony was "childish Nonsense ... and how a Man of Sense, as Mr. Pynchon is supposed to have been, could have sat, day after day and listened to it, is as astonishing as the Matter itself is puerile, absurd and ridiculous." Henry Burt wrote "the testimony heard by the magistrate was nonsensical in the extreme." However, much of the testimony must have been unnerving to the townspeople and the magistrate because it closely followed the observations for the "discoverie of the Witches" in Dalton's *The Countrey Justice*.[44]

Dalton warned the magistrates they may "never expect direct evidence, seeing that all works are the works of darknesse." There will be no witnesses to accuse the witches because they are the "most cruel, revengefull, and bloudie" of all magic practitioners.[45] Also, the "two maine points to discover and convict these Witches; for they prove fully that those Witches have a familiar, and made a league with the Devill" are that the witches have a "little teat on their body ... in some secret place" and a devil's mark. Another important factor was the testimony of other witches, "confessing their owne witchcraft and witnessing against the suspected that they have spirits or markes; that they have beene at their meetings; that they have told them what harme they have done."[46]

In the case of the Hugh Parsons' trial his main accuser was his wife. Within the transcript it becomes clear Mary Parsons gave information that led the authorities to suspect her of being a witch as well. On April 3, 1651, Thomas Cooper testified that when he was appointed to watch Mary Parsons she told him she suspected her husband of having a familiar or spirit. One of the witnesses, John Mathews, at the first hearing said that at the first trial with the widow Marshfield, Mary Parsons and he were talking about witches. He repeated what Mary had told him of the devil coming in the night to her husband's bed, sucking him and his crying out.[47]

Thomas Cooper testified after hearing Mary Parsons complain about her husband and calling him a dog that he said "why do you speak so of ye Husband." Thomas Cooper may have had some doubts as to whether Hugh Parsons was a witch because Hugh had been searched for witch marks. Cooper said, "if he were a Witch there would some apparant Signe or Mark of it appere vppon his Body, for they say Witches haue Teates vppon some pt or other of their Body, but as far as I heere there is not any such apparant Thinge vppon his Body."

Mary Parsons may not have been surprised there were no marks on Hugh's body because while offering an explanation for the lack of marks she incriminated herself, her husband and two other women as witches. She described their participation in a witch's meeting [Sabbat]. She said she was visited by the devil and she and the other witches were transformed into animal familiars. She claimed she had no witchcraft skills like her husband, but the "Night that I was at Goodman Ashlies: the Diuill may come into his Body only like a Wind, and so goe forth againe, for so the Diuill tould me that Night, (for I think I should haue bin a Witch afore now but that I was afraid to see the Diuill, lest he should fright me.) But the Diuill tould me that I should not Feare that, (I will not come in any Apparition, but only come into thy Body like a Wind, and trouble thee a litle While, and p' sntly go forth againe:) and so I consented."[48]

This was a voluntary self-confession of guilt which Dalton wrote "exceeds all other evidence."[49] According to Cooper, she continued, "and that Night I was with my Husband and Goodwife Mericke and Besse Sewell, in Goodman Stebinges his Lott: and we were sometymes like Catts and sometymes in our owne shape, and we were a plodding for some good Cheere; and they made me to go barefoote and mak the Fiers, because I had declared so much at Mr. Pynchons."[50]

Mary Parsons admitted the devil had entered into her and the other witches as a wind, they all had assumed animal or "familiar shapes," had participated in a "witches meeting" and she was punished by the other witches being made to go barefoot and forced to light the fires because she had admitted her husband was a witch at the examination.[51] She seems to have had the presence of mind not to have mentioned the widow Marshfield when she related this story to Thomas Cooper.[52]

## Hugh Parsons Learns His Wife Will Be His Chief Accuser

Initially Hugh Parsons did not realize his wife was going to be his chief accuser. Jonathan Taylor testified Hugh Parsons asked him outright if he knew who his accusers were? He said, "Was it euer known, said he, that a Man should be accused and not know his Accusers: Tell me who they are, for what euer you tell me shall be as in [your] owne Breft.... [Taylor] I will not tell you any Thinge; but, faid I, I beleeue [your] Wife will be [your] biggest

Accusar: at this Speech he saw his Wife goe by to be examined, then said he, it is like I shall be examined [for a witch now]."⁵³

The bitter animosity between the two was such that Hugh said of Mary these words, "considering the Relation that is betweene vs : and if any Body bespeake Euill of me she will speake as ill, and as much as any Body else ... [and] ... she would be the Meanes to hang ... [him]."⁵⁴

During the examination of Mary Parsons she was asked what reasons she had to suspect her husband for being a witch. The first reason was that he seemed to know things she had confided to her friends only; second, he would go out at night and she would hear noises about the house and the door; third, "he useth to come Home in a distempered Frame, so that I could not tell how to please him; sometymes he hath puld of the Bed Clothes and left me naked a Bed, and hath quenched the Fier [either in the hearth or had sexual intercourse?]; some-tymes he hath thrown Pease about ye Howse and made me pick them up."

Other signs of his witchery were that he made a garbling noise in his sleep and when she asked him what he was saying he said "he had strange Dreames; and one Tyme he faid that the Diuell and he were fighting, and that the Diuill had almost ouer-come him, but at last he got the Mastery of the Diuill." Finally, she was asked a critical question, did she see her husband "doe any Thing beyond the Power of Nature." She replied she saw his familiar. "I saw a Thing like a great nasty Dogg by the Path Side. I suspected it was donn by Witchcraft from my Husband."⁵⁵

Hugh's familiar was corroborated by his neighbor, Blanch Bedorthe, who swore her two-year-old child had seen a dog that scared him. When "his ffather asked him where the Dogg was, he said it was goun under the Bedd: his ffather asked him whose Dogg it was: he said it was Lumbardes Dogg: his ffather said that Lumbard had no Dogg." The child said it was Parsons' dog. Goody Bedortha said the child had originally meant it was Parsons' dog because when Parsons came to the house the child called him Lumbard. The child was frightened of this dog and talked about it all the time "and yet Parfons hath no Dogg, neather was there any Dogg in the Howse: but the Earnestnesse of ye Child, both then and since, doth make me conceive it might be some evill Thing from Hugh Parsons." (Hugh Parsons did not answer this charge). Rice Bedortha, the child's father, testified he was so "earnest" about the dog that he "often made me afraid."⁵⁶

## After Individuals Were Threatened, Evil Events Followed

Blanche Bedortha testified two years before Hugh Parsons' indictment that he had been at her house and he threatened her husband in an argument over some bricks. When she remarked about the bricks Hugh Parsons turned on her and said, "you neded not have said Anythinge, I spake not to you, but I shall remember you when you little think on it." Her husband told him "that it was no good Speech; but I have often herd him use such Threatninge, both against myself and others when he hath bin displeased." Samuel Marshfield testified he was there when the threats were made and evil events followed not long afterward.

Blanche Bedortha testified soon after the threats she saw a strange light behind her, "Wastcote made of red flag Cotton," as bright as a candle even though the fire was blocked by a "double Matt betwixt her and the Fier." She attempted to duplicate the effect several nights since and could not.

About a month later she said when "in Child Bed: and as well as most Women … about an Hower or more after, she awaked, and felt a Sorenesse about her Hart, and this Sorenesse increased more and more … the Paine was so tedious, that it was like the pricking of Knifes … and this Extremity continued from Friday in the Forenoone till Monday about Noone … the Paine began a little to abate, and by Tusday it was pritty well gon : and suddenly after, my Thoughtes were, that this Euill might come vppon me from the said threatning Speech of Hugh Parsons."

The widow Marshfield (helping out as a healer?) testified that when she attended to Blanche Bedortha, upon returning the next morning "she was in lamentable Torment; she grew worse and worse for two or three Dayes, and she cryed out as if she had bin pricked with Knifes in such a lamentable Manner that I did much feare her Life."[57]

Perhaps of all the threats made against anyone the one with the most serious repercussions for Hugh Parsons (aside from the charge of having bewitched one of his children to death) was that made against the minister, Mr. Moxon.

In court Hugh Parsons was informed his wife said she suspected him of causing the "evil [bewitchment] that is befallen to Mr. Moxons Childerne, your wife suspects you because when you spoke to her about the agreement concerning the bricks for Mr. Moxon's chimney you said I will be even with him, or he shal get Nothinge by it." John Mathews said under oath that Hugh Parsons commonly used words to that effect and Mr. Moxon, who was present at the hearing, testified the same week Hugh Parsons spoke to him about the bricks, "my Daughter Martha was taken ill wth her Fittes."[58]

On March 1, 1650/51, Hugh Parsons was asked "if there was not some Witchcraft in the Distemper of Mr. Moxons Children." He answered, "I question not that there be Witchcraft in it: but I wish the Sadle may be sett uppon the right Horse, being demanded who was the right Horse, and whether he knew of Anybody else, he said no, I am cleare for myself, neather do I suspect any other."

Parsons did not question witchcraft was involved but he was not responsible, he did not know who was responsible and he was suspicious of no one. Unfortunately, he lied because when he was asked if he suspected his wife he answered he did not and had never "such Thought of her." The court produced witnesses that testified he had suspected her of being a witch, leading to her being accused of witchcraft too.[59] Parsons was also accused of drying up a cow, spiriting away a cow tongue and bewitching a trowel and a beer barrel.[60]

But it was the bewitchment of Mr. Moxon's children that was doubly frightening because ministers represented a threat to the devil in this pagan land and if a minister's children could be bewitched by Satan's agents what about their own children or themselves? Secondly, what shield did they have against Satan and his evil followers if their minister was powerless? If the minister would not use white magic, the people of Springfield had no qualms about using counter-magic themselves. Mary Parsons had resorted to white magic to "try a witch" other neighbors used counter-magic to identify the witch.

## Other Unnatural Activities on the Part of Hugh Parsons

There were many other incidents reported of people bewitched by Hugh Parsons in Springfield. Samuel Marshfield testified his sister Sarah Miller was taken with strange fits, but at least he added they were "never so bad as when Mr Moxon's Children were taken."[61] Thomas Miller testified while his wife was in one of her fits she cried out, "get thee gon Hugh Parsons … if thow wilt not goe, I will goe to Mr. Pynchon, and he (shall have thee away)." Other neighbors confirmed his testimony.

Prudence Morgan said that when Sarah Miller was visiting her, between her fits she said, "look you, there is a Man, at Goodman Coopers Barne, I said no there is no Man there that I can see." She asked her, "who is it, she said it is one in a redd Wastcote and a lynd Capp. It is like Hugh Parsons; … he points his Finger at me; he would have me come to him." The testimony indicated Hugh Parsons was away at the time and the jury was to infer he had sent his apparition to tempt Sarah Miller, who she identified by his red waist coat and cap.[62]

Samuel Marshfield testified that when he came into Prudence Morgan's house Sarah Miller "said there he is I said to her there is no Body there that I can see; she said yes, there he is, two or three times over, but there was Nobody there that we could discover, though she did often affirme it."[63]

William Brooks testified on March 18, 1650/51, the day Hugh Parsons was arrested, that when the constable passed by her door with Hugh Parsons

"Goody Stebbing[s] ... was first taken w[i]th her Fitts, and cryed, Ah! Witch! Ah! Witch! just as he was passing by the Gate."[64]

John Stebbings testified on March 18, 1651, that his wife had fallen into one of her fits (it seems this was relatively common for his wife). "And with a Gesture of strange Wonderment, O deere! there hangs Hugh Parsons uppon yt Pole (for there stood a small Pole upright in ye Chimny Corner) and then she gave a start backward, and said, Oh! He will fall uppon me: and at that Instant she fell downe into her Fitt." (See the following chapter for the occult significance of the hearth and chimney in 17th century New England). His testimony was confirmed by Rowland Stebbing who was present on the same day.[65]

## Mary Parsons Accuses Hugh Parsons of Bewitching to Death Two of Their Children

Mary Parsons was at the second examination. She said she suspected her husband of being a witch because anything he sold did not "prosper." She felt sorry for Thomas Miller after Hugh sold him land and he cut his leg.[66] Also, she said Hugh could not "abide that any Thing should be spoken against Witches."[67]

Hugh was asked if his wife had ever asked him to confess to witchcraft. He replied not that he could remember. His wife said, "did not I speak of it to you uppon the death of my Child: did not I tell you then that I had [j]ealousies that you had bewitched y[our] owne Child to Death." Hugh did not answer.[68]

Hugh asked Anthony Dorchester, their lodger, if he remembered if Mary had ever charged him with bewitching his child. He said he could not remember if she spoke to him directly of this but she had "[j]ealoufies that he had bewitched his Child to Death." Mary accused Hugh of bewitching their latest child and the other child who had died earlier and she had spoken "of it to him, and to other Folkes, together above forty Tymes."[69]

The fact Hugh Parsons did not show the proper respect for his dead child led to the idea he bewitched his child to death. His wife and neighbors gave examples of his lack of sorrow. When his child was near death he lay in the long meadow and when he heard the next morning the child had died "he never shewed any Sorrow for it."[70]

Earlier, George Coulton testified he had gone to Hugh Parsons' house and seen his wife with the child. He was "amazed at it, for ye Childs Secretts [sexual organs] did rott, or were consuminge: and she said, though my Child be so ill, and I have much to do with it, yet my Hufband keepes ... at me to help him about his Corne." Coulton's evidence for witchcraft was that Mary berated her husband in front of Coulton and said "such Things against him as are not ordinary for Psons to speak one of another, and yet he beinge p'ent said Nothing." Hugh said he heard "such Speeches from her dayly, and therefore he made the best of it now…. I have often blamed her for doinge Worke, and bidd her do lesse."[71]

Anthony Dorchester testified the only time Hugh asked Mary to do less work was when she helped his wife. Parsons was never afraid to "greeve or displease his Wife any Tyme." When Parsons' was asked if he ever did anything to comfort his wife on her child's death "he answered not."[72]

George Coalton testified as to the strange actions of Hugh when he learned of the death of his child: "He was not affected with it but he came, after a light Manner, rushing to my Howse, and said, I here my Child is dead: but I will cutt a Pipe of Tobacco first before I goe Home." His callousness at the death of his child was so striking Coalton said "after he was goun my Wife and myself did mch wonder at yc lightnesse of his Carriage, because he shewed no Affection or Sorrow for ye Death of his Child."[73]

Although Hugh Parsons said privately he was sorrowful over the loss of his son, his neighbors testified that in no instance did he show any sorrow after his death. Hugh Parsons said when the child was first sick he ran "barefoote and barelegged, and with Teares to desyre Goody Cooly to come to his Wife, because his Child was so ill."[74]

Mary Parsons and her neighbors questioned the nature of the child's illness and blamed Hugh Parsons for bewitching the boy. Mary said her husband came for help because he was fearful his son was "suddenly and strangely taken with a Trembling, beginning at the Toes, and coming upwardes, and so it stopped the Childes Breath." Goody Cooly testified that when the child first became ill there was talk "that it might be bewitched, for these that are now bewitched have often Tymes Something rise up into their Throates that doth stopp their Breath." Two other neighbors, Mary Ashly and Sara Leonard, testified "they saw the Child in ye Tyme of its Sicknesse, and that they app' hended the Secrets of the Child to consume and wast away." Coalton testified that at the time he understood the child to be "strangely taken."

Following the testimony concerning Hugh Parsons' lack of grief on the death of his son and the possible bewitchment of the boy that caused his death the court inquired after Mary Parsons why she suspected her husband was a witch (see above).[75]

## Mary Parsons Also Suspected of Being a Witch

Mary was taken into custody during Hugh's examination. She would have been immediately suspected of being a witch once she named her husband as a witch. In addition, she previously admitted to consorting with the devil and participating in a witch's sabbat with her husband, goodwife Mericke and Besse Sewell.

In addition, she recently interpreted a dream for her guard, Jonathan Taylor, who believed he was bewitched. On April 7, 1651, Jonathan Taylor swore two nights before Mary Parsons was taken to the Bay [Boston] to be tried for witchcraft, she said two things to him while he was watching her. First, she forgave him for the "Wrong you have done me." The other was about a dream he had about three snakes. He had been ill ever since the dream. She told him the meaning of his dream: "the three Snakes ... they were three Witches." Taylor asked who were the three witches and "shee said one was my Husband. I asked her who were the others, she said I have pointed at them already: but you will not beleeve me; I am counted but as a Dreamer: but when this Dreamer is hanged, then remember what I said to you: ye Towne will not be cleere yet."[76]

Hugh was in "Chaines" in the custody of the constable on March 2, 1651, and transported to Boston for trial. Mary Parsons had been taken into custody in early April. She was transported to Boston shortly after but not before her threatening words that there were more witches in Springfield that needed to be identified.[77]

There is no record Mary was officially examined for witch marks although it is likely she was examined. That this was a common method of discovering a witch can be seen by the fact both husband and wife tried to examine each other for these marks. Hugh Parsons "suspected his Wife to be a Witch, that he would have serched her ... she resisted for she tould him it was an imodest Thinge."[78]

Mary Parsons being overly suspicious of her husband being a witch secretly looked for witch marks on his body. Benjamin Cooley testified Mary Parsons told him that she "feared her Husband was a Witch, and that she so far suspected him that she hath serched him when he hath bin asleepe in Bedd, and could not find Anything about him unlesse it be in his secret Ptes [parts]."[79]

As noted earlier, Thomas Cooper's testimony suggests the examination for witch marks was probably undertaken by court officials. He told Mary Parsons of her husband, "me thinkes, if he were a Witch there would some apparant Signe or Mark of it appere vppon his Body ... as far as I heere there is not any such apparant Thinge vppon his Body."[80]

## Trial by the Massachusetts General Court, May 8, 1651

Following Hugh Parson's examination in Springfield he was remanded over for trial in Boston. There is nothing in the *Pynchon Record* concerning an examination of Mary. However, it appears the "offences charged" for both "were beyond Pynchon's jurisdiction to hear and determine." Mary was sent for trial in Boston also.[81] She was tried on May 8, 1651. The indictment read, "Mary Parsons wife of Hugh Parsons of Springfield, being committed to prison for suspition of witchcraft, as also for murdering her oune child, was this day called forth and indited for witchcraft." Her examination went beyond witchcraft and included the murder of her own child. She was tried for both crimes in Boston.

The only specific accusation in the indictment was that Mary was accused of "consulting with a familljar spirrit … [and ] … making a covenant" with the devill, as well as other "devilish practices by witchcraft to hurt of the persons of Martha and Rebekah Moxon." Mary was not accused of this act by any of the witnesses in the Hugh Parsons transcript so in the missing transcript of the examination of Mary in Springfield she must have been accused of bewitching Moxon's daughters. Perhaps there was an earlier relationship between Martha and Rebecca Moxon during her service in William Pynchon's household and his stepson's household that caused suspicion to fall on Mary as the cause of their bewitchment. The Reverend Moxon was close to William Pynchon. He settled with him in Springfield and left with him when Pynchon returned to England.

Mary pleaded not guilty to being a witch. The court concluded "the evidence were not sufficient to prove her a witch; and therefore she is cleared in that respect."[82] But "the Court understanding, that Mary Parsons now in prison accused for a witch, is likely through weakness, to dye before trjall if it be deferred, doe order, that on the morrow, … she be brought before, and tried by the General Court, the rather that Mr. Pinchon may be present to give testimony.…"

On May 13, 1651, Mary was indicted for murdering her child. The Court, after finding her guilty by "hir oune confession … proceeded to judgment: You shall be carrjed … to the place of execution, and there hang till you be dead."

Although Mary was not guilty of witchcraft the Court had no qualms about invoking the devil in the indictment. "The Court record stated she "being seduced by the devil" did "about the beginning of March last, in Springfield … wilfully and most wickedly murder your oune child, against the word of God." Mary acknowledged she killed her child. Hale later expanded on this and wrote, concerning one of the witches in Springfield, "one of which confessed" said the occasion of her becoming familiar with Satan was due to the loss of her child. She was "discontented" and wanted to see her child again and "entered into covenant with Satan and became a Witch."[83]

The death of a child and the temptation to consort with the devil was not to an unusual response and was brought on by the "searing grief experienced by grieved mothers" leading to cases of "disturbing grief." For example, Increase Mather's brother Nathaniel wrote to his brother concerning Mrs. Lake of Dorchester, who he heard "the devill drew in by appearing to her in the likenes, & acting the part of a child of hers then lately dead on whom her heart was much set" or in England for example in the case of Margaret Moore accused by Matthew Hopkins of being a witch and who "surrendered her soul to the Devil" because "shee would save the life of on[e] of hir children ... upon Contract."[84] In addition, it was not uncommon at this time for "mothers who wanted to kill their children frequently found the thought so troubling they believed it had been implanted in them by the Devil or witchcraft." In the event an infant or child died the woman was undoubtedly racked with guilt. The seventeenth century physician Richard Napier recorded at least "25 consultations with patients who blamed witches or demons for infanticidal urges."[85]

Most commentators on this trial believe Mary was deathly ill and probably insane at the time of her trial. According to the record Mary Parsons was reprieved until May 29, 1651. It is believed by some she probably died in prison as there is no record that she was hanged.[86] However, Justin Winsor wrote that she was undoubtedly hanged and based his conclusion on Eliot's letter to the English newspaper, the *Mercurius Politicus* in which he wrote "fascinations and witchcraft.... Four in Springfield were detected ... one was executed for murder of her own child, and was doubtless a witch."[87]

As for the townspeople in Springfield it seems they were convinced that Mary Parsons had killed her child. Henry Burt, the Clerk of the Writs, entered into the "town records of deaths" that "Josua Parsons, the sonn of Hugh Parsons, was kild by Mary Parsons his wife, the 4 day of ye 4 month 1651." While this entry does not prove she was guilty of killing her child "it establishes that it was regarded as sufficiently proved to be made a matter of official record."[88]

## *The Hugh Parsons Trial*

Hugh Parsons' trial was put off for a year, "probably from the difficulty of bringing witnesses to Boston." At this time written statements could only be entered into evidence if the "witness had died or was unavoidably absent." Therefore it was critical witnesses appear in court otherwise the defendant would not be able to exercise the "common law right of direct confrontation between the accused and those who testified against them."[89]

Hugh was being held in prison and on "October 24, 1651–It is ordered on the second Tuesday in the 3d month next, there shall be a Court of Assistants held at Boston for the trial of those in prison accused of witchcraft, and that the most material witnesses at Springfield be summoned to the Court of Assistants, to give in their evidence against them accordingly."[90] As noted previously, there were no others named but it is suggested they were probably Bessy Sewall and Goodwife Merrick based on Mary Parsons' "conversation with Thomas Cooper."[91]

Hugh Parsons was tried at a Court of Assistants on May 12, 1652 "being reduced by the instigation of the divill in March 1650 and divers times before and since, at Springfeild as was concieved, had familiar and wicked converse with the divill, and used diverse and divillish practizes, or witchcrafts, to the hurt of diverse [persons], as severall witnesses and circumstances appeared, was left by the grand jury for the further triall of his life."[92]

Besides calling witnesses upon certain facts, the prosecution used the written testimony of most of the Springfield witnesses, testimony forwarded by Mr. Pynchon along with testimony taken by Henry Smith, son-in-law of William Pynchon in Boston who, on May 20, 1651, had been given judicial authority in Springfield.[93]

The testimony was used in the Court of Assistants Trial. The additional testimony taken by Henry Smith included evidence from Symon Beamon, a Pynchon servant concerning a runaway horse whose actions he attributed to "mischief" on the part of Hugh Parsons. In a second statement he said the summer before he refused to have his horse carry a sack of meal for Hugh Parsons. Parsons was offended by his refusal. After leaving Parsons, Beamon had a series of mishaps on the road. His normally gentle horse acted up throwing him and the grain sack off the horse a number of times.[94]

Other testimony heard at the trial came from Joanna Lumbard, who swore her husband had lost a trowel. When he was looking for it later, Hugh Parsons was at the house and picked up the trowel from the "door sill" even though the husband said "it was formerly not there."

Alexander Edwards testified his cow had given less milk and that it was "yellowish & somewht Blooddy as if it was festered." This happened after his wife had denied Hugh Parsons milk. Richard Excell testified to the story and said he heard Hugh Parsons ask Sarah Edwards for the milk. She told him she could not spare it and she would pay him what she owned him in some other way. He would rather have "wht was due him in milke." When he next saw the milk from that cow it was "verry yellow and unfit for any to eate."[95]

The court heard the accusations of the persons who claimed they were bewitched and Mary Parsons' confession implicating her husband.[96]

The jury's verdict was as follows and gives us a more complete sense of the witnesses and testimony used against Hugh Parsons:

> The Jurie of Life and Death findes against Hugh Parsons, by ye Testemony of such as apearde in Corte, soe much as gives them Grounde not to cleare him, but cosidered with ye Testimonys of divers y[e]t are at Springfield, whose Testimonys were onely

sent in Writeinge, as also ye Confession of Mary Parsons, and ye Impeachment of some of ye bewitched Persons of ye said Hew Parsons, which, if ye General Corte make ye Confession of Mary Parsons and ye impechment of ye bewitched Persons or other of them, and ye Testemonys y[e]t are in Writeinge, but appeared not in Person authentike Testimonys acordinge to Law, then ye Jurie findes ye saide Hugh Parfons Giltie of ye sin of Wichcrafte.

Edward Hutchinson, Foreman,
   with ye Consent of ye rest of ye Jurie.[97]

The jury was swayed by the testimony of those who appeared in court. The jury seemed to believe Hugh was practicing witchcraft on his neighbors but to a lesser extent than what his wife had accused him of and he did not bewitch his son to death because his wife had already confessed to murdering him. The jury found some of the bewitched persons not worthy of belief: they were suspicious of the written testimony from Springfield because they said some of it and the confession of Mary Parsons may not be lawful.

The Magistrates refused to accept the guilty verdict and remanded the case to the highest court, the General Court. The General Court contained the three officers mentioned previously plus Deputies. It had the power to review all civil and criminal actions. It heard cases when the magistrates on the Court of Assistants refused to accept a jury verdict. This was the case with the Hugh Parsons trial for witchcraft.[98]

After reviewing the case the General Court reversed the verdict and acquitted Parsons. Although the grounds for their action are not enumerated, they can be "inferred from the verdict. The introduction of the depositions of absent witnesses, the hearsay evidence of the wife's confession and the ravings of the afflicted was too gross a violation of the prisoner's rights to be overlooked" by the court which concluded after the perusal of the evidence brought in against Hugh Parsons "for witchcraft, doe judge that he is not legally guilty of witchcraft & so not to dye by the Law."[99]

Hugh Parsons never returned to Springfield. John Pynchon sold his lands and effects and sent him the proceeds. He moved to Watertown, married and later died there.[100]

For our purposes the examination and trial of Hugh and Mary Parsons is of interest because it is one of the few pieces of recorded evidence available from this period of what kinds of crimes witches were accused of by their neighbors in the Connecticut River Valley during this early period, the interesting view of a marriage in a tailspin where witchcraft accusations become paramount, and we get a sense of the magistrates' examination proceedings concerning witchcraft. In addition a close reading of the transcript gives us an insight into the common witchcraft beliefs in the Valley and the resulting trials were actively discussed in the river towns leading to what could euphemistically be described as "commotion in the Valley."

# 8

# "The Devill will have you quick"

## The Lethal Years, 1651–1654

The years from 1651 to 1654 were lethal for those accused of witchcraft in Connecticut. John and Joanne Carrington of Wethersfield, Goody Bassett of Stratford, Goodwife Knapp of Fairfield and Lydia Gilbert of Windsor were tried and executed for the crime of witchcraft. They were the deadliest years in the Connecticut colonies prior to the Hartford witch panic in 1662/63.[1]

Witch trials seemed to occur during a time of great turmoil when the central authorities appeared weak and the fears of the community overwhelmed the better judgment of local authorities. The political and social situation throughout Connecticut was especially traumatic during these years.

Besides the trial of Mary Johnson of Wethersfield in 1648 the next deadly trial for witchcraft was that of two other Wethersfield residents, John and Joanne Carrington. John Carrington arrived with his first wife, Mary, on the *Susan and Ellen* in 1635. Mary likely died and he subsequently married Joanne. He settled in Wethersfield prior to 1643 and was, according to his indictment for witchcraft, by trade a carpenter.[2]

John Carrington may have originated in Derbyshire, in northwest England. The people from the northwest generally held "nonorthodox beliefs" (many Quakers would hail from the same region). They believed "true conversion was sudden and could be discerned immediately, not discerned later as the orthodox preferred." They emphasized the "indwelling of the Holy Spirit ... something Orthodox Puritans would naturally resent because it "minimized human volition and left the hard work to God. If it were not popery, they thought it must be satanism." The people of the northwest were "stubborn and opinionated," and showed a "lack of deference and discontent ... when mingling in puritan towns." They "distrusted courts" and chose to "settle conflicts by taking the law into their own hands." They could be "spiritually

149

restless and troublesome. The more eccentric … could be the victims of witch-craft proceedings."[3]

We know little of John and Joanne Carrington. However, the *Records of the Particular Court* in Hartford suggested John distrusted the court. Shortly after his arrival in Wethersfield on June 6, 1644, he was a defendant in an unspecified action. On October 24, 1644, the court issued a warning that if he did not appear at court the "Governor shall call for him"; likely he had not appeared in court previously and was in some measure uncooperative. On October 29, 1646, he and a partner were in court again and ordered to pay 30 shillings to an Administrator for their "bargain of Corne." On March 7, 1649/50, he was fined 10 pounds for "Bartering of a Gunn with an Indian." This was a serious crime and the punishment of ten pounds was an extraordinary amount of money for a poor person to pay the court. The fine demonstrated how seriously the colonists took the trading of guns, shot and gunpowder because for the colonists the control of guns was central to the survival of the colonies.[4]

As noted previously, the colonists' fear of Indians was both temporal and spiritual. The clergy were certain the devil was incensed about the Christians inhabiting his land filled with his servants. Ministers had preached for years Satan and his Indian followers would try to tempt and convert as many souls in New England to the devil's cause before the expected Second Coming. Carrington had not just sold a gun to an Indian but likely betrayed his fellow colonists and in bartering with the Indian had made a pact with Satan too.

In addition, the townspeople had probably noted his seemingly independent manner, frequent court appearances and general uncooperativeness. Finally, as a carpenter he and Joanne probably associated with the carpenters, John Youngs and Thomas Bassett and their wives. They probably met in Hartford with other carpenters. (On the unusual role of carpenters and masons in apotropaic counter magic see later in this chapter.) The gossip surrounding their activities and association with the latter (especially the Youngs) would likely have confirmed the town's suspicions and contributed to their fear they might be witches.[5]

On February 20, 1650/51, nearly a year following his conviction for selling a gun to an Indian, the two were tried for the crime of witchcraft in Hartford. The jury brought forth the following indictment on March 6, 1650/51, for both. They had "done workes above the Course of nature for which both … deservest to dye."[6]

Although there is no record of the actual charges brought against the two for their crimes the accusations and trial was a topic of heated discussion in the Valley as we learned from the Hugh Parsons examination in Springfield.

There is no official record of their execution, Matthew Grant recorded in his *Diary*, "mar. 19.50. carington and his wife war Hange[d]."[7] In March 1652/53 the inventory of John Carrington's estate was "filed but not recorded." It was valued at 23 pounds and 11 shillings. The estate was indebted for 13 pounds, 1 shilling and 6 pence.[8]

## Unrest in the Connecticut Colonies

After Charles I was executed in England in 1649, the Commonwealth of England, Scotland and Ireland were founded in 1653. Oliver Cromwell served as Lord Protector of the newly formed Commonwealth from 1653 to 1658. When war broke out between England and Holland in October 1652 it was expected to spread to America, especially among the "Dutch possession of New Amsterdam, afterwards New York, and the New England colonies."[9] This combined with fear of an Indian uprising "spread a general alarm throughout the New England colonies."[10] It soon became evident to the colonists that under Cromwell, the colonies were going to continue to be left to their own military defense.

In May 1653, the Commissioners of the United Colonies ordered a draft of men in the United Colonies (Massachusetts, Plymouth, Connecticut and New Haven.) Connecticut had to raise sixty-five men for service "to be prepared forthwith, to be a day's warning with provisions suitable." Fairfield was responsible for providing eight men and Stratford six men. Although seemingly only a few men, the draft took away "one in twelve of the men" leaving the remainder as a "home guard" for self-defense. The distress resulting from this situation was reflected in an order by the General Court on June 25, 1653, to the Massachusetts Bay. The Commissioners of the United Colonies were meeting there, concerning the "distresses, fears and dangers that the English bordering upon the Dutch, both the Main [land] and Long Island are in."[11]

The situation worsened for the inhabitants of Connecticut and New Haven when they received word Massachusetts refused to participate in any war against the Dutch. The Court of New Haven met on October 12, 1653, and the Court of Connecticut met on November 25, 1653. Both agreed the "Court of Massachusetts had willfully violated the articles of the union. The people of Stamford and Fairfield became much agitated."[12]

The Dutch waited for reinforcements from Holland to attack the English colonies while the English "were in constant expectation" of an attack by the Dutch. They also feared when the signal was given "from the Dutch ships, the Indians would rise ... [and] ... fire the English buildings." Fortunately for the colonists the Dutch fleet was defeated at sea and the Indians remained friendly to the English settlers. If these events had not occurred it is likely the plantations of Stratford, Fairfield and Derby would have suffered greatly because "except east of New London," the highest number of Indians resided near these settlements.[13]

During the turmoil Stamford and Fairfield decided "to prosecute the war" against the Dutch. The adventurism on the part of Fairfield led the town to appoint Roger Ludlow (who had moved from Windsor in 1639 to found Fairfield) as the commander-in-chief. Following his unauthorized appointment as commander-in-chief Ludlow sent a letter to Governor Eaton of the New Haven Colony. During the preparations for war with the Dutch, Ludlow was appointed a commissioner and sent to Boston. He was "zealous and active for the war. Ludlow argued his town was "in imminent danger unless the Dutch could be removed from the neighborhood." Later he learned the Massachusetts Bay refused to participate in this war effort.[14]

Earlier the New Haven Court had been prepared to go to war and criticized the Massachusetts Bay for not joining "in the war." However, after the New Haven Court discussed the letter Ludlow sent to the governor, the Court was more cautious and weighed its options. It noted winter was near, that they did not have sufficient boats, and that they did not want to go it alone against the Dutch. The Court wanted to hear from the Colony of Connecticut but for the present "they see not themselves called to vote for a present war."[15]

Ludlow was disliked by the New Haven Colony because he had settled Fairfield under the auspices of its rival the Connecticut Colony. The New Haven authorities believed Fairfield was more geographically suitable to be under its jurisdiction, they did not appreciate Ludlow's more liberal civil and religious views and resented his "hot debates with makers of public opinion in the rival colonies."[16]

Ludlow was criticized for accepting the appointment as commander-in-chief in Fairfield without proper authorization, and for prosecuting the war against the Dutch. However, the most damning accusation connected him with a conspiracy using the laws of England as an excuse "to shake of the yoake of govermt they have bine under in this jurisdiction [New Haven]."[17] While Ludlow was commander two of his subordinates "attempted to foment insurrections, and without instructions from the authority, to raise volunteers for an expedition against the Netherlands."[18]

Ludlow and his subordinates were blamed for taking matters into their own hands even though the proper authorities seemed to have acted against the interests of the settlers by not actively protecting the plantations. Still his actions lost him credibility in the colony. He believed he would have to make "humiliating concessions" because he could not "escape public censure" for what he had done. The government of Connecticut saw his actions "as not just a matter of insubordination if not of open revolt, proceeded to deal with the principle movers in the affair as fomenters of insurrection."[19]

As a result, Ludlow sailed for Ireland in April of 1654. He later received a high office commission in Ireland from Oliver Cromwell.[20]

Nevertheless, tensions continued to run high among the settlers in the plantations. Following the Dutch and Indian threat, in September 1654, the Commissioners in Connecticut and New Haven decided to go to war against the Indian chief Ninigret of the Narragansett Indian nation. He had continued to make war noises and threatened to go to war against the Indians in Connecticut allied with colonists. The proposed war "awakened fear of a rising or at least a hostile conduct of the Indians" still in large numbers near Stratford. Although the Commissioners did not go to war, as we saw earlier, it was not uncommon for "individuals and families to have some difficulty with the Indians," a concern specifically articulated in Ludlow's Connecticut Code of 1650.[21]

The potential Indian uprising, the threatening Dutch fleet and accusations of insurrection caused "commotion" among the planters at Stratford and Fairfield in 1653. In the midst of all this Roger Ludlow was actively involved in one witch trial in Fairfield in 1653 and provided the accusations and written testimony for a "witchcraft" and "lying" slander trial in 1654. By now Ludlow had left the colony so the 1654 trial was prosecuted by his attorney. He accused his neighbor Mary Staples (of Fairfield) of being a witch and a liar, both serious crimes in colonial New England. Mary Staples' husband sued Ludlow for slandering his wife in 1654 in the New Haven Court (on this, see the following chapter).

Ironically, it is in the testimony at this trial we learned of the fate of two other women, Goody Bassett (originally from Windsor and in 1651 living in Stratford), accused of witchcraft, and her acquaintance Goodwife Knapp (of Fairfield), also accused of witchcraft in 1653. The irony was probably not lost on Ludlow that being accused of "fomenting insurrection" or rebellion was in political terms at that time comparable to the actions of a "witch." Granted, it was the English clergy and supporters of divine right of the king who preached "Rebellion is as the sinne of Witchcraft etc," the latter taken from the biblical verse in 1 Samuel 15:23. For royalist clergy there was a definite link: "rebellion and witchcraft both came from the devil."[22] But even so, the authorities in New Haven and Connecticut probably considered his act of rebellion not just a political act but one malefic in nature.[23]

In addition to the political and social discontent generated by Roger Ludlow and his associates there were a number of other underlying causes that contributed to the unrest and tension that fueled the witch trials in Fairfield. The first may have been environmental and the second probably more terrifying to the settlers concerned the Dutch and the Indians.

From the beginning of the first settlements in New England the climate was extremely harsh and unusually cold. Although things began to moderate in 1650, records indicate the springs beginning in 1647 were unusually wet and cold while summers saw severe droughts. This was the case throughout most of the 1650s. By 1652 famine conditions were present in Connecticut. Severe or unusual weather and witchcraft were commonly associated with each other. This was especially true during the "little ice age" in Europe when extreme weather was more common, cold and snowy winters, wet and cool springs and cool summers. Shortened growing seasons contributed to smaller yields. This seems to have occurred in the New England colonies and may have been a contributing factor but not a sole cause to increased witchcraft suspicions in the colonies. Due to these extreme conditions that led to a scarcity of provisions the Connecticut Colony passed an ordinance "no person in any of the plantations of Connecticut should ship or allow to be conveyed out of the colony, beef, pork, bacon, butter, cheese, wheat, rye or Indian corn … without a license from an appointed committee, under penalty of double the value of the article exported."[24]

While the colony was suffering from famine conditions a rumor circulated following a Dutch victory over the English on December 9, 1652, that the Dutch Governor Peter Stuyvesant was reviving old Dutch claims over land in Connecticut that would have put the Dutch only four miles from Stamford. There was "great alarm" in Fairfield and other towns to the east because of a report "the Dutch governor had entered into a conspiracy with the Indians to massacre the English."[25]

## The Witchcraft Trial of Goody Bassett in 1651

Following the examination of Hugh and Mary Parsons in Springfield the inhabitants of the Connecticut River Valley "were in a great Commotion by Witchcraft," as this outbreak had now come to Stratford, Connecticut.

In May 1651, following the Carrington's trial, Connecticut Governor John Haynes, with magistrates Captain John Cullick and Henry Clark, were sent by the Particular Court in Hartford to Stratford to try Goodwife Bassett for witchcraft. "That governor Haynes, Mr. Cullick and Mr. Clarke are desired to goe downe to Stratford to keepe Courte uppon the tryall of Goody Bassett for her life."[26]

Goody Bassett was married to Thomas Bassett, formerly of Windsor, who had arrived in Windsor in 1634/35 on the ship the *Christian de London* as an apprentice with the Stiles party. Thomas was made a freeman in 1640. He appears to have sold his lot in Windsor in 1640 and was living in Stratford, Connecticut, at the time of his wife's trial for witchcraft.[27]

There are few records of other early witch accusations and witchcraft trials in Connecticut. However, the Court did complain "many charged with capital crimes had fled to Rhode Island to escape prosecution; it is probable there were other witchcraft trials during this period for which no record survives."[28] Although there are no records on the Bassett trial there are a number of references to the trial that confirm goodwife Bassett was tried for witchcraft and executed in Stratford in 1651. A deposition by Luce Pell (wife of Dr. Thomas Pell of Fairfield) in another trial referred directly to goodwife Bassett:

> goodwife Basset, when she was condemned, said there was another witch in Fairefeild that held her head full high, and then the said goodwife Knapp stepped a litle aside, and told her, this deponent, goodwife Basset ment not her.[29]

Later, "Elizabeth bid her doe as the witch ... [Bassett] ... at the other towne did, that is, discover all she knew to be witches."[30] The Reverend Hale of Beverly, Massachusetts, wrote in 1702, "I have also heard of a Girl at New Haven or Stratford that confesseth her guilt." His "brief sentence undoubtedly refers to her [goodwife Bassett], for there is no record of any witch at New Haven ever confessing and she is the only Stratford witch of whom we have an account. Confession was a rare occurrence among Connecticut witches, and this helps to make identification more certain."[31]

The place of Goody Bassett's execution is noted by tradition in Stratford. "Gallows Brook" and "Gallows Swamp" are named as such in early land records in Stratford. The brook dried up or had been "diverted" when a railroad was built in the vicinity between 1846 and 1853 at the corner of King Street and Linden Avenue. A stone bridge crossed the stream where the former Old Mill Road and the railroad had intersected. It was here, tradition said, Goodwife Bassett was hanged as a witch.[32]

In one town history of Stratford, the author tells of some old traditions around the trial of Goody Bassett and begins by citing the Ludlow Code of 1642 which read: "If any man or woman be a witch ... they shall be put to death." Tradition noted the trial probably took place in the meeting house at Sandy Hollow with the

> Governor and his assistants, comprising the Court, seated at a long desk; to the right stands the haggard form of poor Goody Bassett between two officers of the court her woe-begone expression indicating perhaps too well that she knew what her fate was to be. Standing beside her, with head resting upon the shoulder of the unfortunate woman, was a female form whom tradition says, was the only friend Goody Bassett had in that bitter hour, and who clung to her in the belief of her innocence even to the very end.[33] In front are the witnesses, with upright hands as the oath is being administered by one of the Governor's Assistants; while the meeting-house, filled to capacity by the town folks, who had crowded in to witness the down fall of the witch who had been the terror of their lives. Perhaps on the faces of some we should see faint signs of sympathy for the prisoner, but more bearing expressions suggestive of the cruel tauntings which the place forbade them to utter.[34]

Goody Bassett was the fourth witch executed in Connecticut and the first in Fairfield County.

## Goodwife Knapp's Witchcraft Trial in 1653

Meanwhile, rumors continued to reach Hartford of more witches in Fairfield. From the evidence presented by Goody Bassett, even if Goodwife Knapp was not named as a prime suspect, she was under suspicion. Roger Ludlow inserted himself into this case "fastening the crime of witchcraft upon a poor townswoman of Fairfield named Knapp." Ludlow may have seen this as an opportunity to shift blame for the tensions in Fairfield from himself to an "inner enemy" part of a conspiracy that mirrored the conspiracy he was being charged with for his attempt to create an independent colony in Fairfield. This was likely not a difficult decision for him because of his earlier experience and training in England and the milieu noted earlier, he believed in witches and they had undoubtedly contributed to his failure in obtaining his objectives in Fairfield.

In addition, based on the participants and the depositions referred to in the trial a group of witches were suspected of being active in Fairfield and they were connected to the Indians. The testimony showed these views were shared by other elites in the community. Ludlow knew of the condemned witch Bassett's accusation in May of 1651 (everyone in town seemed to be aware of the accusation) of a witch in Fairfield. There was also an association between Knapp and Bassett. Likely, Bassett had lived at one time in Fairfield before moving to Stratford.[35]

Ludlow desired a scapegoat that would remove some of the onus of his actions and possibly get him back into the good graces of the authorities in both the New Haven and Connecticut colonies. Also, the prevailing gossip that there was a witch in Fairfield found its way to Hartford in the fall of 1653.[36] The result was that the General Court held in Hartford on October 19, 1653, ordered Mr. Ludlow, Mr. Wells, Mr. Westwood, and Mr. Hull to "keepe a particular courte at Fairfield, before winter, to execute justice there as cause shall require."[37] This was the court sent to Fairfield to try Goodwife Knapp.[38]

Our knowledge of the Knapp trial for witchcraft held in Fairfield, Connecticut, in 1653 is based on the record of the Thomas Staples-Roger Ludlow slander trial held on May 29, 1654, in New Haven. Thomas Staples took Roger Ludlow to court, accusing Ludlow of defaming his wife, Mary Staples, by saying she was a witch and "she made a trade of lying." Mary Staples witnessed the trial and hanging of Goodwife Knapp. Her unusual actions at the Knapp trial and execution aroused the suspicion that she was the other suspected witch in Fairfield alluded to by Bassett. When Mrs. Jones, the wife of the Fairfield minister, John Jones, asked Goodwife Knapp if "ther were any other that were witches, because Goodwife Basset, when she was condemned ... said there was another witch in Fairefeild ... [Knapp told her] ... goodwife Bassett ment not her."[39] In making the case for Mary Staples' guilt because of her actions during the Knapp trial, the depositions Ludlow and his lawyer gathered shed light on the Knapp witchcraft trial.[40]

Roger Knapp, Goodwife Knapp's husband, settled in New Haven before 1638 but later gave up his right to land purchased from the Indians by New Haven colonists and "took an oath of fidelity to the New Haven Colony in 1644." He later settled in Fairfield with his wife, two sons and a daughter. In 1653 his wife was "suspicioned" of being a witch.[41] It seems most likely Roger Knapp married his wife in England before 1637. He is often referred to as a "poor man" although this may be an incorrect designation.[42]

Roger Ludlow founded Fairfield in 1639 but by 1653 he was under suspicion by the New Haven and Connecticut colonies for involvement in "a Malignant pty wch hee hoped would rise, to overthrow churches and comonwealthes."[43] It was in this heated atmosphere the witch trial of Goodwife Knapp was conducted.

## The Goodwife Knapp Trial

The depositions taken for the Ludlow-Staples slander trial give us a rare insight into the earlier Knapp trial and into the following issues: how was a witch in colonial New England treated by the community, who was involved, what occurred at trial, the treatment of a condemned witch in confinement, the execution, and here the unusual post-execution treatment of Knapp's corpse.

## The Pre-Trial

As part of the initial examination, Goodwife Knapp was taken to the "prison house" where she was kept and probably watched not unlike the technique used by Matthew Hopkins in England and incorporated into Massachusetts law in 1648. One of her jailers, Thomas Lyon of Fairfield, testified he was ordered by the authorities "to watch with Knapp's wife." His brother, Richard Lyon, shared the same responsibility.[44]

Goodwife Knapp was searched and witches' teats were found on her. Luce Pell, wife of the town doctor, Thomas Pell, volunteered that she was one of the women who "was requested by the court to search Knapp before she was condemned." Goodwife Odell was the midwife called in as a specialist "for she had bine upon her oath when she found the teates." As we saw earlier, midwifes were the only female specialists called into court that could take an oath as expert witnesses.[45]

## The Trial

The trial took place in the autumn of 1653, before a jury and several "godly magistrates" (the same probably that are named in the order of the General Court), and doubtless lasted several days. There were many witnesses but the indictment and the substance of the greater part of the testimony are wanting. We know that a strong and decisive point against the accused was the evidence Mrs. Lucy Pell, the doctor's wife, and Goody Odell, the midwife found. Under the direction of the Court they examined the body of the prisoner. They "testified to finding upon it certain witch marks (probably witches' teats; see below) which were regarded as proof positive of intimacies" with familiars and a league with the devil. Mrs. Jones, the wife of the Fairfield minister [John Jones], was also "present at this examination, but whether as a spectator or as one of the examiners is not clearly stated."[46]

"The Jury brought in a verdict of guilty, and Knapp was sentenced to death. After her condemnation she was visited by a number of the townspeople, who constantly urged her to confess herself a witch and betray her accomplices on the grounds it would be for the benefit of her soul." They argued that "while there might have been some reason for her silence before the trial, since a confession then might have prejudiced her case, there could be none now, for the reason she was sure to die in any event."[47]

## Post-Trial

Goodwife Knapp was heavily interrogated prior to the trial and following her conviction. When questioned by a committee of women after her conviction her jailer, Thomas Lyon, rebuked Knapp for mentioning Mary Staples by name. Knapp replied, "Lyon hold yor tongue, you know not what I know, I have ground for what I say, I have been fished wthall [as well] in private more then you are aware of."[48]

There seems to have been some misunderstanding among the townspeople as to whether Knapp had confessed to being a witch. Goodwife Gould [Gold] stated Knapp had confessed she was a witch and "had familiarity with the Devill." But the day following her conviction, a committee of women led by Mrs. Pell came to speak to Knapp. Their purpose was "to have her confess for that wch she was condemned and if she knew any other to be a witch."[49]

Knapp had been convicted but had not confessed. There were many witnesses against her. No doubt they gave a long litany of sick cows, a sharp tongue, accusations of lying and cursing with mischief following, and evidence of familiars. The latter, confirmed by the evidence presented in court, that she had witches' teats, sure evidence of suckling a demon, and that a pact had been made with the devil. She was "cast by the jury and godly magistrats having found her guilty, and that the last evidence [it is implied below that it was Mary Staple's testimony that] cast the cause."

On the day Knapp was condemned Goodwife Sherwood went to see her in the "prison house." Midwife Odell was there. Mrs. Pell and her two daughters, Elizabeth and Mary, and Goody Lockwood and Goodwife Purdy arrived to interrogate Knapp. This was not a simple women's committee; Mrs. Pell said "she was sent to speake to her … to have her confess that for wch she was condemned and if she knowing any other to be a witch to discover them." She was no doubt sent by the court to obtain more information; the court and the community, under the external threat of war and fearing the threat of supernatural forces, needed to know if there was a conspiracy of witches that would attempt to undermine them internally while they were being threatened by actual external forces. The Bassett woman had previously confessed to being a witch. She said there was a witch in Fairfield. Knapp said she was not the witch. The committee, fueled by gossip and the authority of the court, visited Knapp in her confinement to get answers.

The women tried a different tactic to get Knapp to confess. Luce Pell told Knapp before she was convicted that confessing and naming the other witch in Fairfield would have gotten her condemned and would have been a "meanes to take away her life … but now she must dye and therefore she should discover all." Mrs. Pell said her family had "brought in nothing against her," and as she said, there were plenty of witnesses at the trial who spoke against her that had convinced the jury of her guilt. Nevertheless, Knapp must have been surprised at this comment because Mrs. Pell had headed the committee to search her for the witch's teats that had been instrumental in her conviction.[50]

The committee of women visited her again on the following day. After some questioning it was implied that Mary Staples' testimony had convicted her. Goodwife Knapp replied that she understood that Mary Staples may have done her "wrong in her testimony" but Goodwife Knapp did not take the bait. She said, "but I must not render evill for evill."

Goodwife Sherwood asked Knapp to talk with the jury because Mary Staples had not said anything more than what others had said about Knapp. She believed the jury would "informe her that the last evidenc did not cast ye cause." Knapp replied she had been told this within the past half-hour. This was probably an attempt by Sherwood to prevent Knapp from naming

Mary Staples as a witch out of spite in the event she believed it was Mary's testimony that had led to her conviction.[51]

Sherwood returned the following day "to see the witch with other neighbors" including Mrs. Jones, Mrs. Pell, her two daughters, Mrs. Ward and Lockwood. Mrs. Pell asked Knapp to admit to everything to clear her conscience and "make way" for the minister, Mr. Jones, "to doe her good." Elizabeth, Mrs. Pell's daughter, was more direct and said for her to do like the other witch (Bassett) at the other town did "that is, discover all she knew to be witches." Knapp replied she could not say anything that was not true, she would not wrong anyone and what had been said to her "in private, before she went out of the world when she was upon the ladder, she would reveale to Mr. Ludlow or ye minister." Elizabeth, Mrs. Pell's daughter, replied, no doubt with malice, that if she waited until she was on the ladder [about to be hanged] the "Devill will have you quick" before you can reveal what she knew. Knapp, perhaps showing some of the tartness and threat in her voice that got her in to trouble, replied, "Good ... take heed the devile have not you, for she could not tell how soone she might be her companyon" and added, "the truth is you would hve me say that goodwife Staplyes is a witch, but I have sinns enough to answer for already, and I hope I shall not add to my condemnation." Knapp's mention of Mary Staples provided an opening for Lockwood, who turned to jailer Thomas Lyon and asked him if he heard them mention "goodwife Staplyes name since we came here." Lyon cautioned Knapp not to "breed differenc betwixt neighbours after she was gone."[52]

Lyon testified when he cautioned Knapp not to make trouble among her neighbours. Knapp told him to hold his tongue, "you know not so much as I doe, you know not what hath bine said to me in private." Thomas Lyon added that after the women had gone Knapp volunteered "she knew nothing against goodwife Stapyles of being a witch."[53]

Finally, Martha Gould, wife of one of the leading citizens of the town of Fairfield, Nathan Go[u]ld, testified she and Goodwife Sherwood went to see the witch. She said someone in town had been making "suspicious words" about a witch in the town. A few days earlier, Thomas Staples had visited Goodwife Knapp and threatened her because she had "told some thing of his wife that would bring his wives name in question." Goodwife Gould asked her to take her advice and "not sow malicious seed to do hurt when she was dead." She continued that she was going to die soon so she "should deal truly." In response Knapp burst out "weeping" and asked Gould to pray for her and said she did not know how she was tempted but said "pray, pray for me."

According to Martha Gould, the minister Mr. Jones told her after Knapp was condemned that she had "cleered one in ye towne, ... you know who I meane sister Staplyes."[54]

## The Execution of Goodwife Knapp

The execution of Goodwife Knapp was a community event. Both young and old attended. For example, Bethia Brundage, sixteen, and her friend Deborah Lockwood, seventeen, were both present. Sarah Cable was also present but we do not know her age. Rebekah Hull, daughter of the minister Mr. Jones, related when Knapp was going to her execution she was taken from the prison and accompanied by Mr. Ludlow and Mr. Jones to the gallows. Along the way the two pressed Knapp "to confess that she was a witch." They walked past the "Tryes and mill" on the way to the place of execution.[55] Witnesses said Mary Staples continued to profess Knapp's innocence. Before Knapp was hanged she came down from the ladder and, according to Ludlow, "named goodwife Staples as the witch." After she was dead she was cut down and her corpse was "carried to a graveside." Then a most extraordinary event occurred.

## The Mishandling of the Corpse of Goodwife Knapp

Following the execution it seems the curiosity factor got the better of some women who wanted to see the witches' "teats" on her body. Mr. Davenport and his wife said Ludlow referred to Mary Staples as a "foolish woman … she tumbled the corpes of the witch up and downe after her death, before sundrie women, and spake to this effect, if these be the markes of a witch I am one, or I have such markes."[56]

Other witnesses described Mary's unusual actions following Knapp's execution. Elizabeth Brewster said Mary Staples went to the witch's graveside with some other women to search Knapp for witches' teats. Staples "handled her verey much" and called to Lockwood, "these were no witches teates, but such as she herself had, and other women might have the same, wringing her hands and taking ye Lord's name in her mouth, and said will you say these were witches teates … and called upon goodwife Lockwood to come and see them." She called on Odell because she had found them under oath. Odell would not come at first, so Staples asked Lockwood again, "will you say these are witches teates, I, … have such myselfe, and so have you if you search yorselfe." Clearly, Lockwood knew she was in dangerous territory if she agreed with Staples and replied, "if I had such, [I] … would be hanged; would you, says Staplies. Yes, … and deserve it." Staples "handeled the said teates very much, and pulled them wth her fingers." Odell told Staples no honest woman had such marks "and then the other women rebuked her and said they were witches teates, then the said Staplies yeilded it." Mary Brewster corroborated the same story and added Staples "pulled them as though she would have pulled them off."[57]

Lockwood testified Staples "looked after the teates that the women spake of appointed by the magistrate." Staples persisted, and called out "three or foure times" to have Lockwood come and look. Elizabeth Brewster testified, Staples said the so called witches' teats were "no more teates than I myself have." Lockwood replied if she had them herself then she should be hanged. Staples continued to handle Knapp's corpse. Then several women "cryed her down and said they were teates." Staples yielded, and said very likely they might be teats.[58]

Goodwife Whitlocke of Fairfield, a friend and neighbor of the Staples, described the events that occurred in the following way. When they were placing her body in the grave (probably more like throwing it, as she was a witch) several women were looking for the marks (not just Mary Staples), and several of these women said "they could finde none" and neither could Goodwife Whitlocke nor Mary Staplies. Then a woman came (probably the midwife, Odell) who had searched the witch and showed them the marks on the witch. Then she heard Staples say, "she never saw such in all her life, and that she was pswaded that no honest woman had such things as those were." The corpse was put in the grave and the women left the place of execution and returned to the town.

Goodwife Barlow corroborated Goodwife Whitlocke's testimony. Goodwife Thompson of Fairfield said Goodwife Whitlocke, Goodwife Staples, and herself "were at the grave and desired to see the "markes of the witch that was hanged." They could not see the marks at first; "then the midwife came and showed them."[59]

Cleary, Mary Staples had spoken out against evidence the court had produced to convict Knapp. She continued to defend her innocence even after her conviction. She handled the corpse in a disrespectful manner (even for a witch's corpse) and she publically questioned the court's verdict and by implication the biblical injunction "to not suffer a witch to live." She was already suspected of being a witch herself. By publically questioning the lawful conviction of Goodwife Knapp and questioning important evidence she left herself open to further suspicion of witchcraft. The magistrate Roger Ludlow had served on the Knapp trial and undoubtedly sought a conviction. Later he let it be known it was Mary Staples who Goodwife Knapp named on the gallows as the other witch in Fairfield. As we will see in the next chapter, gossip about this had gotten out into the community and Thomas Staples realized he would have to take Ludlow to court and sue him for defamation to prevent someone from bringing his wife to court on a charge of witchcraft.[60]

## Summary of the Knapp Trial

This trial raises a number of points that permit us to examine the events more closely. Mr. Thomas Wells, one of the other magistrates besides Roger Ludlow, served at the earlier trial on March 6, 1650/1, that led to the conviction and execution of the Carringtons for witchcraft. He was also active on the Knapp trial in taking depositions together with Roger Ludlow.[61] Since we have no information on the direct evidence presented at the trial I can only conclude (based on the emphasis on the "witches' teats" found on her) that the legal manual used was probably Dalton and not "Grounds for Examination of a Witch" found in the *Wyllys Papers Supplement*.[62] Both Perkins and Dalton describe a number of the same factors that raised suspicions for a magistrate when examining a witch. For example, both refer to the testimony of other witches. This was likely a factor here because Goody Bassett's statement there was "another witch in Fairfield" suggested she knew Goodwife Knapp. After all, she and her husband, Thomas Bassett, previously lived in Windsor, Fairfield and Stratford. They undoubtedly knew Alice Youngs when they lived in Windsor and the Knapps when they lived in Fairfield.[63]

Goodwife Knapp would have been suspected as a witch, according to both Dalton and Perkins.[64] By the common report of Knapp's neighbors, she was lied about by a convicted witch and she was likely a friend or neighbor when she lived in Fairfield. There are three other categories but it is not known if these were used as evidence: cursing with death following; after quarreling if mischief follows (mischief in the seventeenth century meant a more serious transgression than it does today); and the witch continually contradicting herself. All of the above are found in both Dalton and Perkins. It is on the matter of the decisive evidence needed for conviction that the two differ. For the Knapp trial the "witches' teats" are singled out for conviction and it is Dalton (based on Ludlow's local minister back in England, Bernard) who is quoted extensively in Dalton's legal manual. Bernard gave priority to witches' marks for conviction because they represented proof the witch had made a pact with the devil, the witch had a demon or familiar and finding these marks was irrefutable proof that the suspect was a witch.[65]

1. These witches have ordinarily a familiar or spirit...
2. Their said familiar hath some big or little teat upon their body, & some secret place, where hee sucketh them.[66]

According to the testimony it was the witches' teats that must have been the evidence for conviction and not devil's marks. Perkins does not refer to witches' teats in the examination portion of his book but only to devil's marks. These represent further cause for examination in the original. In the

Connecticut document *Grounds for Examination of a Witch* the line referencing devil's marks is shortened: "If ye pty suspected have ye devils mark for t'is thought wn ye devil maketh his covent with y he alwayess leaves his mark behind him to know y for his owne yt is, if noe evident reason in [unintelligble] can be given for such mark." The original sentence in Perkins reads, "If no evident reason in nature can be given for such a mark, the Magistrate in this case may cause such to be examined, or take the matter into his owne hand, that truth may appeare."[67]

For Perkins the devil's marks are not enough for conviction and they are not to be confused with witches' teats, which showed visual evidence of suckling familiars. The belief was the familiar sucked the blood of a witch. The blood was thought to "be the carrier of the spirit; in sucking blood the Devil was feeding on the witches' soul."[68]

Knapp was watched. We do not know if she was swum, walked, sleep deprived, made to say the Lord's Prayer or touch the person she may have afflicted. The testimony does not give any indication of this.[69] She was strip-searched and "witch's teats" were found. Most likely, for the conviction of Knapp the legal manual by Dalton was used with the reference to the witches' teats that proved the witch had a "familiar and had made a pact with the devil."[70]

## The Last Windsor Witch

In the fall of 1651 the Windsor trainband or town militia was drilling when eighteen year old Thomas Allyn's musket accidently fired and mortally wounded the older Henry Stiles, who subsequently died. A Grand jury inquest was held in December 1651. Thomas was indicted by the Hartford Court on the following counts: "This Jury finds that the peece that was in the hands of Thomas Allyn, going of, was the Cause of the death of Henry Stiiles of Wyndsor."

### The Inditement of Thomas Allyn

Thomas Allyn thou art indited by the name of Thomas Allyn not having that due feare of God before thine eyes for the preservation of the life of thy neighbor, didst suddenly, negligently, Carelessly Cock thy peece and Carry the peece Just behind thy neighbor ... to the great dishonor of God, breach of the peace, and loss of a member of this Comonwealth, what siast thou, art thou guilty or not guilty?

Thomas Allyn confessed to the charges and the court asked the jury to consider if it was a case of "man Slaughter or Homicide by misadventure." The jury found him guilty of homicide by misadventure; today this would be called accidental death. Thomas was ordered to pay a fine of 20 pounds for his "sinful neglect and Carless Carriages in the premises and that hee shall bee bound to his good behavior for a 12 month, and that hee shall not beare Armes for the same terme." His father, Matthew, took responsibility for his son and paid 10 pounds to the court to assure his son's good behavior.

Henry Stiles, the victim, was the oldest of the four Stiles brothers who came to Windsor in 1635 as part of the "Warwick Patent" party and was a "carpenter by trade" and a bachelor by inclination. He was killed on October 3, 1651, at the age of 58 years by the accidental discharge of a gun in the hands of Thomas Allyn.[71]

The estate of Henry Stiles was administered by his brother John Stiles. The estate was divided among the surviving three brothers, John, Francis and a brother living in England. If that brother were found to be dead then the estate was to be equally divided between the two surviving brothers.[72]

Henry Stiles was close to Francis and both were "master carpenters." Francis had led the group from London to establish the settlement for the "Warwick Patent" in Windsor in 1635. Francis Stiles left Windsor and sold a "small piece of land to Thomas Gilbert" in January 1644/45. He later sold the remainder of his property on September 12, 1647, "in the tenure of Thomas Gilbert and John Bancroft."[73]

Henry remained in Windsor and, being a bachelor, boarded with Thomas Gilbert. The two appeared to have a joint partnership of the farm. The last agreement made between the two men prior to Henry's death was on March 25, 1649, to pay Gilbert "three shillings per week for diet." Other charges included building a cow shed for Henry (suggesting Gilbert also had carpentry skills) as well as one-half the services and half the diet of Stile's hired man since April 1651, and food for "harvesting hands" for "two harvest seasons." In addition, Gilbert was living in a house which he had bought from Francis Stiles in 1647. His lot was approximately 18 rods or 297 feet from Henry's lot.[74]

Upon his death, Henry left an estate of 181 pounds and 7 shillings.[75] Thomas Gilbert claimed additional debts owed him. In short the business relationship between the two men had been close.[76]

The controversy surrounding the trial and execution of Lydia Gilbert for witchcraft has puzzled historians because Lydia Gilbert was not directly involved in the accidental death of the victim.[77] She was accused of bewitching Thomas Allyn and was brought to trial three years after the event occurred. There is no evidence of any specific malevolence yet she was linked to the accidental death of Henry Stiles. It is likely Lydia Gilbert had taken some offense with her boarder and "this was known to the neighbors to bring her under suspicion of having invoked witchcraft" to cause Henry's death.[78]

## Who Was Lydia Gilbert and Why Was She Accused of Witchcraft?

The question of who was Lydia Gilbert was raised by Stiles in his *History and Genealogies of Ancient Windsor*. Was she Gilbert's wife, daughter or a sister? Recent research has shown Lydia Gilbert was his wife and that in the past, Thomas Gilbert, Sr. (father), and Thomas Gilbert, Jr. (son), had been confused in various accounts. Thomas Gilbert, Sr., was living in Braintree, Massachusetts, until 1646 and later moved to Glastonbury, Connecticut. Thomas Gilbert, Jr., was in Windsor, Connecticut, as early as 1642/43, and "in bad company." On March 2, 1642/43, the Particular Court in Hartford ordered William Ruscoe to take into custody James Hallett, Thomas Gilbert, Lydia Bliss and George Gibbs. They were ordered to be shackled and given "a couse dyet hard worke sharpe correction."[79]

The evidence the three were from Windsor can be found in the court record of September 1644. James Hallett was convicted for stealing (this suggests the other two were involved in this enterprise as well). He was ordered to compensate four times the value of what he had stolen and be branded on the hand during the next training day at Windsor.[80]

Thomas Gilbert, Jr.'s, first wife was Mary James, who he married in West Bromwich, Stafford, England. There is no information on his wife's death. Sometime after his incarceration he married his second wife Lydia Bliss, his co-defendant on theft charges. She clearly had an unsavory reputation prior to the formal charges of witchcraft in 1653/54. After Lydia Gilbert was hanged, he married again in 1655 in Springfield and died there in 1662.[81]

The records do not show the specific accusations against Lydia Gilbert for witchcraft. However, on October 3, 1654, the court remitted the "twenty-five pound fine that had been levied against Thomas Allyn." Then on November 28, 1654, Lydia Gilbert was accused of using Satan's help in killing the "Body of Henry Styles besides other witchcrafts for which according to the law of god ... thou deservest to Dye." The jury found her guilty of witchcraft.[82] It is presumed she was hanged although there is no record of her execution. However, as noted previously, Thomas Gilbert, Jr., married again in 1655 so it is likely Lydia was executed or at least died shortly thereafter.[83]

It is obvious Lydia (Bliss) Gilbert had a bad reputation documented in her incarceration and punishment with Thomas Gilbert and James Halleck. The community would have held her in the same low opinion. We saw the similar example of Margaret Jones when her neighbors linked her witchcraft to accusations of stealing some years ago.[84]

The court did not just find Lydia guilty of the death of Henry Stiles but of "other witchcrafts" as well. Demos imagined these other witchcrafts "spoiled food, the loss of cattle, illness and injury to several of her neighbors but Henry Stiles death is the clincher.... The bullet that took his [Henry's] life was not simply a random mischance; to the contrary its course was purposefully guided." It was the actions of a "spiteful witch which has used a young man's carelessness to murder another who she hated."[85]

The gossip and innuendo would likely have included her association with other suspicioned women in Windsor, Alice Youngs, Goody Bassett and Mrs. Marshfield. The gossip would have increased dramatically after the conviction and death for witchcraft of Alice Youngs and Goody Bassett and the continued suspicion Mrs. Marshfield was a witch. After all, who else but women with a reputation as low as hers would Lydia have been able to consort with in Windsor?

It is unlikely, except for Mrs. Marshfield, that any of her close associates were covenanted members of the Windsor Church. In addition she married another ex-felon, Thomas Gilbert. Thomas and Lydia were in a business partnership and lived with an outsider one of the original "Warwick Patentees," Henry Stiles. Finally, like the husbands of the other convicted witches Henry was a carpenter and Thomas had carpentry skills too.

Although some have seen Lydia as a convenient scapegoat to remove the guilt from Thomas Allyn by his father Matthew, it was likely gossip and other evidence of witchcraft including her association with the convicted witch Alice Youngs that put a target on her back long ago.[86]

If the court proceeded like the other trials that resulted in a death sentence, Lydia was watched and searched. The evidence presented was highly circumstantial but convincing to the jury. Lydia did not have to be at the scene to convince the jury of her guilt. It was likely argued she sent her familiar or her specter to do the deed. The Henry Stiles accident was merely a final opportunity to remove the last suspected witch and presumed troublemaker Lydia Gilbert permanently from the community.

Demos uses the Gilbert trial to illustrate an imagined pastor in the Windsor Church devoting his sermon to answer the question on his parishioners minds why did the "scourge of witchcraft" come to their "little community." He argued the pastor would have partially blamed the Windsor community and say it was due to their own failings and they needed "to mend their ways."[87]

While the former was likely true, in reality pastor Warham and his congregation also breathed a sigh of relief. They knew they were not wholly guilty themselves. The witches discovered in Windsor had spread their witchcraft to the communities of Stafford and Fairfield. They had been discovered and hanged. They likely believed, although Mrs. Marshfield had not been tried for a witch, that she had caused the commotion in Springfield that led to the witchcraft accusations resulting in the discovery of other witches.

However, for Windsor, the last witch, Lydia Gilbert, had finally been brought to trial and hanged. There would be no more witches discovered in Windsor following her execution.

## Apotropaic Counter Magic

Besides the theme that many of these witches and their husbands were known to each other there is also the fact most of these early victims were either carpenters or married to carpenters. Why were these carpenters and possibly masons and their wives suspected of witchcraft? Certainly this was not the case for all carpenters and masons. Carolyn Langdon first made the suggestion of guilt by association of a group of carpenters in the Connecticut Valley resulting from their acquaintance with the convicted witch Alice Youngs, whose husband was a carpenter. She posited Goody Bassett had lived in Windsor and knew Alice Youngs before she moved to Stratford, Connecticut, with her husband. Thomas Bassett was a carpenter, as was John Carrington. Likely, Hugh Parsons may have known John Carrington and this explained his reluctance to accuse him of witchcraft. Finally, another Windsor resident accused of witchcraft was Lydia Gilbert, "who with her husband cared for Henry Stiles, still another carpenter, with whom Bassett had come from England." The connection was probably made in "Hartford where artisans from both towns gathered." I would add they probably came together from more than just the two towns Langdon mentioned.[88]

Why might some carpenters and masons come under suspicion of witchcraft in early New England? The attack on the houses and bodies of those in fifteenth and sixteenth century England and colonial New England was considered "a central feature of witchcraft." As demons and spirits entered the bodies of people so they entered into the house a metaphor for the body. They entered through the orifices of the body so to the orifices in the house, the door representing the mouth, the windows representing the eyes, the chimney or hearth (the heart) and through cracks and keyholes.[89]

"Spirits attacked the same orifices where disease and sin collect, and they were as worrisome to carpenters and yeoman farmers as to ministers and magistrates."[90] In East Anglia, England, builders used a variety of means to protect their houses "and carried out small and obscure evidences of ceremony ... by the owner or his surrogates, the carpenters." This was done to prevent ill luck, in its most "aggressive form of evil spirits and witches." Witches were human but not subject to ordinary physical limitations, so therefore it was necessary that the chimney as well as the door should be protected against a witch's entry." The "hearth and the threshold" received special attention to prevent evil influences from entering the house.[91]

In the left top panel, demons are trying to enter the house through the chimneys. In the panel below a witch is attempting to gain entrance to the house through a window. From Joseph Glanvill, *Saducismus Triumphatus*, London, 1681 (courtesy Kislak Center for Special Collections, Rare Books and Manuscripts, University of Pennsylvania).

Iron was thought to have special protective powers, and included iron horse shoes and iron tridents. They were placed on framing timbers and chimneys. Boots and shoes were placed behind walls to confound and trap the devil and evil spirits as they tried to enter the house. Other apotropaic objects and symbols included witches' bottles and the corpses of cats and sundry animals. Finally, colonists from "England's northern and western counties may have carved their chimney parts with designs that would have prevented a witch from crossing the threshold, made their chimneys with salt glazed bricks ... because they believed salt could ward of demons."[92]

It could be argued the carpenters and masons, by placing objects in the foundations and walls of the houses they built or making "witches' marks" or "demon traps" on the beams, chimneys and doors to act as counter-charms, performed an important but acceptable role in a newly emerged Protestant society that "forced its adherents into the intolerable position of asserting the reality of witchcraft, yet denying the existence of an effective and legitimate form of protection or cure."[93] In seventeenth century New England there simultaneously existed both "popular and theological beliefs within the symbolic framework of witchcraft ... to assert the priorities of one belief system was to create a crisis for the other." The problem was ministers, by virtue of their own beliefs and teachings, lacked any power to defend their flock from "malefic powers." Strong theological directives would have "upset the balance of mystical forces that helped to stabilize the popular usage." The resolution was that the clergy stopped just shy of the complete "repudiation of witchcraft belief to effectively contain its popular expression, and the common folk only barely escaped ecclesiastical censure in their search for protection against mystical harm."[94]

There was a delicate balance between the folk beliefs and the antimagical views found in both England and New England that allowed the continued use of counter-charms by carpenters and masons in the newly built homes of seventeenth century New England without censure from the clergy. For those New England colonists dependent on these carpenters and masons accused of witchcraft or acquainted with convicted witches this was a serious matter. The townspeople in Connecticut and Massachusetts depended on them to install the counter-charms to protect their homes and families from witches and evil spirits. To alienate these men (like Hugh Parsons) was probably foolhardy and could have real consequences (as the example of the Reverend Mr. Moxon and his two possessed girls demonstrated).[95]

Ironically, in the Connecticut River Valley, most of the accused witches were associated with carpenters (or were themselves carpenters.) It is unlikely this was just a coincidence. Perhaps the colonists came to fear their charms to protect their homes might work against their families someday. The unease and fear that they might be at the mercy of witches and demons in their

Image of apotropaic marks, also called witch marks or demon traps, to ward off evil. The apotropaic marks can be seen on the fireplace mantel in the Isaac Winslow House in Marshfield, Massachusetts, 1699 (image by Christine Ross, courtesy Historic Winslow House Association, Marshfield, Massachusetts).

homes may have been an additional contributory fear fueling paranoia in the Valley. The only solution was to remove the witch and those connected with the witch from the community. We saw instances of this previously with the trials of either carpenters and masons or their wives. After Alice Youngs was executed, her husband and family later moved out of Windsor. John and Joanne Carrington were both hanged. Mary Parsons died in prison and Hugh Parsons never returned to Springfield. Goody Bassett, the wife of a carpenter, was hanged. Lydia Gilbert was connected to Henry Stiles, a carpenter, and her husband, Thomas Gilbert, she was hanged.

# 9

# A More Compassionate
# Magistracy

## The Trials of Elizabeth Godman

At least two trials involving witchcraft accusations were held in southern Connecticut in 1653, reflecting the unsettled times and tensions in the Colony of New Haven and Colony of Connecticut. The first trial of Elizabeth Godman was held in New Haven on August 4, 1653.

On the subject of witches, Elizabeth Godman had appeared suspiciously sympathetic to them and refused to denounce them. She may even have condemned the execution of Goody Bassett earlier that year.[1] As a result, dangerous gossip began to circulate about her and she brought a number of neighbors to court for defamation.[2]

Elizabeth Godman was probably a "widow or spinster with no household of her own." She was called Mrs. and mistress at different times, and when she died, she left an estate of £200. She lived in the household of Stephen Goodyeare, the Deputy Governor of New Haven. The Goodyeare household included his wife and two daughters by his wife's first marriage. She did not live alone because the New Haven Colony required all single persons to live in a household so "their behavior could be monitored."

Mrs. Godman likely thought this was a good arrangement because at the time the size of her estate would have distinguished her as a person of quality in New England. Instead, the record demonstrated the two families lived in an on-going antagonistic relationship. The two daughters spied on Mrs. Godman regularly and Mrs. Goodyeare finally accused Godman of sorcery. The ongoing conflict may have been the result of Elizabeth Godman expecting more deference than she received from the Goodyeare family.

Elizabeth Godman had tried to stop the gossip and rumors before taking her neighbors to court. She brought Goodwife Larremore before the governor of the New Haven Colony for saying "she thought of a witch in ye Bay when she see Mrs. Godman." The governor asked Goodwife Larremore if she thought "Mrs. Godman was a witch, and she answered no."[3]

The gossip and rumors continued. Mrs. Godman brought a complaint to the authorities on May 21, 1653, because the situation had become intolerable, not just the conflict in the household but especially gossip from her neighbors implying she was a witch. When Elizabeth brought the complaint she was examined by the magistrates on May 21, 1653, and a second time on May 23.

What is unusual about the Godman case and seems to reflect the uncertainty was it involved not only her neighbors but a number of New Haven elites and their household members, to an extent not seen in earlier cases in New England. This supports the idea witchcraft accusations came to the surface in New Haven as the elites in the community may have contemplated their current situation. These concerns are articulated in a letter sent to Oliver Cromwell in November 1653 by the Reverend William Hooke, teacher at New Haven from 1644 to 1656 in the Reverend John Davenport's church (Hooke was one of Godman's chief accusers) and later one of Cromwell's chaplains at Whitehall. The letter was sent on behalf of the General Court held at New Haven on October 12, 1653.[4]

Hooke wrote the Massachusetts Bay refused to support New Haven in a military expedition against the Dutch and more recently the Indians "from whom we have received much injury and contempt." This lack of support was unfortunate because the Bay was "nearly in greatness to the other three" plantations.[5] In addition, there is "a language of mutiny and sedition heard among us and of renouncing present authority ... we are endangered as well from within as from our selves and greater fractures and disjunctions are threatened and the changes hastening upon us where of Mr. Cotton spake on his death-bed, upon occasion of the comet which shined many nights during his sickness and extinguished about the time of his dissolution."[6] Also, trade was "obstructed" and there was a lack of clothing. He continued, "the intelligent among us understand that our cure is desperate," the Dutch and French must be removed for their future expansion; that they were under threat from the natives because the Dutch and French have traded "multitudes of guns, with powder, shott, and weapons which the English have alwais refused to do, that they might reserve the advantage of weapons to themselves, which (until of late) hath been a terrour to the heathen."[7] On this topic he concluded that because of this the natives were armed and ready to use those weapons against the English.

Hooke finished by imploring Cromwell to either send "two or three friggots" to clear the coast of the Dutch and this would put to rest our "intestine discontents" or demand "quietness" among the colonies but order "assistance" by the Bay to the other three colonies in the event of war with the Dutch.

This would "heal our breaches and present distempers" and do a "singular service to many churches of Christ" and Cromwell as God's instrument would affect "greate things in these four colonies ... as God has used you to accomplish greate matters in three Kingdoms."[8]

Hooke does not mention the Godman witchcraft case for which he had given much testimony during both examinations, but his reference to being "endangered from within" may refer to the witchcraft trials in New Haven and Fairfield. His letter shows a distinct and documented paranoia among the elites in New Haven who were nervous about the security of their own positions and feared the palpable threat of the Dutch, the Indians and an internal insurrection not only as a threat to themselves but to the great project of establishing Christ's kingdom in New England. For these people the internal threat was obviously the devil in collaboration with his followers (witches) and his agents, the Indians, who were intentionally undermining the New England colonies.

His reference to the comet of 1652 was significant as a portent of ill-starred change. The Reverend John Cotton was one of the most prominent clergymen in New England. His death was linked with the comet a "long blaze dim also to the east. And was quicke in motion. And every night it was less and less till the 22 of the same month and then it did no more appeare, it being the night before our Reverend Teacher mr. John Cotton Died, the Greatest starr in the Churches of Christ."[9] New England clergy paid close attention to many "wonders" but "phenomena such as comets and eclipses warned sinners of divine displeasure and urged them to spiritual reawakening."[10]

Comets were traditionally seen as portents of "disaster," "civil disorder" and the fall of kingdoms. Writers who described the "coming of Christ's kingdom referred to comets and eclipses as presaging the Apocalypse." As Hooke knew during this time, "Satan raged incessantly against God's kingdom leading many into sin and tormenting godly seekers after truth."[11]

Between the Minister Mr. Davenport who spoke of witches in his sermons and his partner the Reverend Mr. Hooke who believed in witches too, it was no wonder some people began to identify Elizabeth Godman as a witch. She had odd ideas and acted strangely. As a result, she was gossiped about as a witch, proof to her neighbors Satan was indeed working in their midst.

Given the previous description about the current troubles of New Haven one can imagine these events were interpreted as Satan raging against their colony. Many of the defendants in the Godman slander case represented elites in New Haven and some had only recently experienced great personal and financial tragedy.

For example, prior to 1646, New Haven merchants wanted to have ships that could sail directly from their port to England by avoiding Massachusetts' ports. The leading men of the town formed a company to purchase a large ship likely constructed in Rhode Island that could carry 150 tons of cargo. The governor, Mr. Eaton, the deputy governor, Mr. Goodyeare and other leading men of the colony formed a second company to hire the ship "to make a trading voyage to England." Everyone in the town supported the venture and contributed what they could to the cargo from "silver plates and spoons" to hides, lumber and beaver skins because "if the voyage was successful" everyone would "make a handsome profit." At the same time, because so much was invested in this venture "if it was a failure, the loss would be ruinous."

"The Great Shippe" sailed out of New Haven in January 1646 (winter is not the best time to sail across the Atlantic). As the months passed nothing was heard of the missing ship. That summer ships from England arrived but provided no news. By fall anxieties began to increase and turned to "despair" with the realization "The Great Shippe" had likely been lost at sea. The loss of so much "valuable property destroyed all hopes" of future commercial success in the colony.[12] This adversely affected the fortunes of the Goodyeare and Lamberton families. Likely they and other elites were resented by the poorer colonists who had invested everything in this enterprise with the advice of the leading men of New Haven. They had lost everything in this bold venture. Perhaps, the Goodyeare family was looking for an opportunity to deflect criticism from their families and saw Elizabeth Godman (the Goodyeare tenant) with her peculiar ways as an opportunity to blame someone for the colony's past and present troubles.

At the same time, not only was regular cargo lost but the most "precious of the cargo, the passengers," many of them from leading families in the colony. Mr. Stephen Goodyeare, merchant, deputy governor and planter in New Haven lost his first wife. Goodyeare's second wife, Margaret Lamberton lost her famous sea captain husband, George Lamberton, in the same tragic shipwreck. Hannah and Elizabeth Lamberton lost their father. The colony also lost Mr. Gregson, who was in charge of the cargo and responsible for obtaining a charter for the colony. The loss of so many lives almost "crushed the spirit of the new colony" and nearly caused the colony's demise.[13]

Naturally the colonists wanted to know what happened to the ship and began praying for a sign. The following summer shortly after a passing storm the people witnessed an unusual sight "The Great Shippe" came "sailing in a cloud through the air into the mouth of the harbor." The ship was whole and recognizable. The colonists swore they saw Captain Lamberton himself on the ship. As the ship approached close to the shore the rigging began to collapse, the hull capsized and "disappeared in the mist and cloud."[14]

John Davenport declared this was a sign their prayers had been answered. The ship was since called the "Phantom Ship." Cotton Mather referred to the incident in his book *Magnalia Christi Americana* (1702) and Longfellow immortalized the incident in his poem *The Phantom Ship*.[15]

## The First Examination of Elizabeth Godman, May 21, 1653

The defendants in the August 4, 1653, Elizabeth Godman slander trial were named by her in her first examination before the magistrate and included Stephen Goodyeare, deputy governor of the colony, Margaret Goodyeare, the Reverend William Hooke, Mrs. Jane Hooke (the sister of Edward Whalley, one of the judges who signed the order to behead Charles I and a cousin of Oliver Cromwell), Mrs. Mary Bishop (the sister of Captain George Lamberton), Mrs. Atwater, wife of Joshua Atwater (the treasurer of New Haven Colony) and her maid Mary Miles.[16]

Save the maid, these individuals were leading members of the New Haven Colony and it was these people who Elizabeth Godman said suspected her of being a witch. In order to forestall a serious charge of witchcraft Mrs. Godman summoned them to court, saying these several persons had said things that "made people think she was a witch." In court she said Mrs. Atwater was the "cause of it all" and asked that her prior examination on May 21, 1653, be read before the court. In the examination she complained against the previously mentioned individuals saying they all "suspected her for a witch."[17]

Elizabeth Godman may not have been aware nor have read the deposition because for whatever reason she asked to have it admitted. Here a lawyer would probably have served her well because it was damning to her case. Given her reputation and the status of those she was suing to forestall witchcraft charges, it is not unlikely that after the preliminary examination information was added later by other witnesses to the record of which she was not aware. Secondly, one of the defendants, Stephen Goodyeare, was one of the magistrates seated as a member of the Court.[18]

The first complaint was against the Reverend Mr. Hooke and his wife. Elizabeth Godman was asked what she had against them. She said she heard they had something against her about their son. "Mr. Hooke said hee was not wthout feares, and hee had reasons for it; first he said it wrought suspition in his minde because shee was shut out at Mr. Atwaters upon suspicion, and hee was troubled in his sleepe aboute witches when his boye, was sicke." In addition, she often spoke about witches and "she said why doe they provoake them, [and seemed to be baiting Reverend Hooke] why doe they not let them come into the church." Mr. Hooke was "horrified of such laxity of sentiment and by such disloyalty to the laws of Moses."[19] At other times she spoke for no reason about witches and said "if they accused her for a witch she would have them to the governor, she would trounce them. Another time she was saying she had some thoughts, what if the Devill should come to sucke her, and she resolved he should not sucke her."[20]

Hooke said she had foreknowledge of what was done in Church meetings even though she was not there. The magistrate had even interviewed Mr. Hooke's Indian servant, Time, who said, "in church meeting time she would goe out and come in againe and tell them what was done at meeting." Time asked her who told her what went on, and "she answered plainly she would not tell, then Time said did not ye Devill tell you." She was also accused of "talking and muttering to herself." Time said "she heard her one time talking to herselfe" and asked her "who talke you too…. Time said you talke to ye Devill, but she made nothing of it."[21]

Mr. Hooke accused her of not being able to stay away from his sick boy: "they [witches] are addicted that way" and cannot easily be kept away from houses "where they do mischief." He said,

when his boy was sicke, she would not be kept away from him, nor gott away when she was there, and one time Mris. Hooke bid her goe away, and thrust her from ye boye, but she turned againe and said she would looke on him.
    Mris. Goodyeare said that one time she questioned wth Elizabeth Godmand aboute ye boyes sickness, and said what thinke you of him, is he not strangly handled, she replyed, what, doe you thinke hee is bewitched; Mris. Goodyeare said nay I will keepe my thoughts to myselfe, but in time God will discouer.[22]

Mr. Hooke added that when Mr. Bishop was married (to Mary Lamberton, Captain Lamberton's sister and Margaret Goodyear's former sister-in-law), Mrs. Godman came to Hooke very upset. He suspected she had "some affection to him, [Mr. Bishop] and he asked her, she said yes; now it is suspitious that so soone as they were contracted Mris. Byshop fell into verey strang fitts wch hath continewed at times ever since, and much suspition there is that she hath bine the cause of the loss of Mris. Byshops chilldren, for she could tell when Mris. Bishop was to be brought to bedd, and hath giuen out that she kills her chilldren wth longing, because she longs for every thing she sees, wch Mris. Bishop denies." When queried on this by Mrs. Hooke, Elizabeth Godman replied Mrs. Bishop "longed for some pease … [and] … was much given to longing, and that was the reason she lost her children."[23]

Elizabeth Godman also came under suspicion because she "could tell Mris. Atwater had figgs in her pocket when she saw none of them; to that she answered she smelt them, and could smell figgs if she came in the roome, nere them that had them; yet at this time Mris. Atwater had figgs in her pocket and came neere her, yet she smelt them not." Mrs. Atwater also said Mrs. Godman could tell one time they had pease porridge, "when they could none of them tell how she came to know, and beeing asked she saith she see ym on the table, and another time she saith she was there in ye morning when the maide set them on."

Mrs. Atwater also accused Mrs. Godman of bewitching Betty Brewster, and said when Mrs. Godman was at their house, "she cutt a sopp [bread] and put in pann; Betty Brewster called the maide to tell her" what she was doing. The maid likely aware of Mrs. Atwater's accusations and filled in on town gossip said Mrs. Godman "was aboute her workes of darkness, and was sus-pitious of Mris. Godman." That night Betty Brewster was "in a most misser-able case, heareing a most dreadfull noise wch put her in great feare and trembling, wch put her into such a sweate as she was all on a water when Mary Miles came to goe to bed."[24]

Mrs. Atwater told Mrs. Godman of the suspicious things she had done and told her not to come around to her house. Mrs. Godman said she would have her in court and the next day Mrs. Godman came around to her house for beer.

Mrs. Godman accused Mr. Goodyeare of "calling her down" when Mrs. Bishop was ill, and said "hee feared she was a witch." Mr. Goodyeare denied she was a witch. "Mrs. Godman was exceeding angrie and would have the servants called to witnes, and bid George the Scochman goe aske his master who bewitched her for she was not well." Stephen Goodyeare's stepdaughter, Hannah Lamberton, who was in the room, "fell into a verey sore fitt in a verey strang maner."[25]

The deposition continued with additional accusations that Mrs. God-man had bewitched Mrs. Bishop and Hannah Lamberton. Concerning Mrs. Bishop, Mrs. Goodyeare asked Mrs. Godman whether someone had bewitched a "poor weak woman" like Mrs. Bishop. "She laughed and said alass who should bewitch her, she had a cousin was so." Mrs. Goodyeare said if there were such people, "God would finde them out.... I never knew a witch to dye in their bed." Mrs. Godman replied, "you mistake for a great many dye and goe to the grave in an orderly way."

Mrs. Goodyeare also said to her, "what do you think about my daughters illness? She answered, doe you thinke I have bewitched her; Mris. Goodyeare said if you be the ptie looke to it, for they intend to have such as is suspected before the magistrate."[26] Coming from the wife of the Deputy Governor of New Haven this may have been the final threat motivating Elizabeth Godman to take her accusers to court.

Mrs. Godman charged that Hannah Lamberton implied she had a famil-iar, a serious charge because it was a sure sign of a pact with the devil, espe-cially if witch marks or witches' teats were found on her body where the familiar presumably sucked. Hannah said she and her sister observed Eliza-beth Godman lay down for somewhat to sucke her, when she came in hott one day and put of some cloathes and lay upon the bed in her chamber. Hanah said she and her sister Elizabeth went up into the garret above her roome, and looked downe & said, looke how she lies, she lyes as if som bodey was sucking her, & upon that she arose and said, yes, yes, so there is; after said Hanah, she hath something there, for so there seemed as if something was under the cloathes; Elizabeth said what have you there, she said nothing but the cloathes.

After the two sisters accused her of having a familiar Godman threatened Hannah. Two days after the incident, Hannah began to have fits. One night Hannah had an especially "dreadfull fitt, and was pinched, and heard a hedious noise, and was in a strang manner sweating and burning, and some time cold and full of paine yt she shriked out." Next, Mrs. Goodyeare said one time the children came down and heard Mrs. Godman talking to herself. They were scared and they heard her talking softly and saying, "will you fetch me some beare, will you goe, will you goe, and ye like" to the girls, obviously talking to her familiar. "One morning aboute breake of day [one] Henry Boutele ... [another witness] ... said he heard her talke to herselfe, as if some body had laine wth her" (presumably the devil).[27]

## The Second Examination of Elizabeth Godman, May 24, 1653

A second examination was held on May 24, 1653. The minister Mr. Davenport was present. The subject matter under discussion was whether Mrs. Godman had said Mrs. Bishop was "given to longing [envying] and that was the reason she lost her children." Witnesses who confirmed this included Hannah Lamberton and Mrs. Bishop. Mrs. Bishop said another woman in the town had heard her say the same thing. Godman was asked why she inquired often after Mrs. Bishop's delivery time to know it, and why she said Mrs. Bishop's longing was a "meanes to lose her children when it was not so." Godman could "give no reason" and was told the latter "was a high slander upon Mrs. Bishop."

Next, "Mrs. Goodyeare said when Mr. Atwaters kinswoman was married Mrs. Bishop was there, and the roome being hott she was something fainte, vpon that Mris. Godman said she would have many of these fainting fitts after she was married, but she saith she remembers it not."

Finally, Goodwife Thorp made a complaint against Elizabeth Godman on June 16, 1653. She said Mrs. Godman came to her house and asked to buy some chickens. Because she had none to sell, Mrs. Godman muttered to herself and walked away. Mrs. Thorpe said she thought if this woman was as everyone suspected, she will "smite my chickens, and quickly after one chicken dyed, and she remembred she had heard if they were bewitched they would consume wthin, and she opened it and it was consumed in ye gisard to water & wormes, and divers others of them droped, and now they are missing and it is likely dead, and she never saw either hen or chicken that was so consumed wthin wth wormes." Goodwife Thorp thought her own experience, along with some other things told to her by Mrs. Godman, were important enough to "be considered wth other things" as part of Mrs. Godman's second examination.[28]

## Elizabeth Godman, Plaintiff, Trial for Slander, August 4, 1653

At the August 4, 1653, trial in New Haven, Elizabeth Godman accused the Goodyeares and her neighbors of slander. She said Goodwife Larremore called her a witch when she entered Goodman Whitnels' home. Goodwife Larremore admitted she had told the Reverend Hooke Mrs. Godman was a witch because "Mr. Davenport aboute that time had occasion in his ministry to speake of witches, and showed that a froward discontented frame of spirit was a subject fitt for ye Devill to worke upon in that way, and she looked upon Mrs. Godman to be of such a frame of spirit."[29] However, she denied saying this at Goodman Whitnels. Mrs. Godman asked for the maid to be sent for to corroborate her story. The maid testified she thought she heard Goodwife Larremore say "she thought of a witch in ye Bay when she see Mrs. Godman." Goodwife Larremore said when she was called before the governor previously she denied Mrs. Godman was a witch.

Mrs. Godman was told by the court that she had called many persons before the court and was asked "what she had to charge them with." She said they made speeches that "made folks think she was a witch." She charged Mrs. Atwater was the cause of it all and was in court with the written testimony "taken in way of examination before ye magistrate" (see above). She said the court would find many things about Mrs. Atwater which would be specified in this trial.

She said Mrs. Atwater called her a witch and "Hobbamocke was her husband." This reference would have been shocking because the townspeople lived in fear of an Indian uprising and linking her with the Indians and their chief god or the devil would give credence to the witch accusation. The colonists understood the Indians worshiped "another power ... whom they call Hobbamocke ... as fare as we can conceive is the Devill" who of course was trying his best to undermine their godly colony.[30] This would have been highly slanderous. However, Mrs. Godman had no witnesses to prove Mrs. Atwater said it.

**Mistrefs Godman's Trial**

"The Trial of Elizabeth Godman," wood engraving from sketch by Irving E. Hurlburt. in *The New Haven Almanack*, 1911, no. 20 (courtesy William L Clements Library, University of Michigan).

Nevertheless, after hearing the "passages" from the magistrates' examination the court moved toward the view she may be a witch. She was asked if these passages "did not give just ground of suspition to all that heard them that she was a witch." She confessed they did but said that when she spoke of "such things ... she was not herself." She was told she used the same excuse before the governor when she said "she was not in a right mind." Mrs. Hooke testified Mrs. Godman was lying and "she spake in a deliberate way, as she ordinarily did at other times."

The final testimony in court concerned Mr. Goodyeare. According to the testimony he was in his home explaining a scriptural passage he had just read. Mrs. Godman was there and thought the passage was "against her." As soon as Mr. Goodyear finished, she "flung out of the roome in a discontented way and cast a fierce looke ... [an evil eye] ... upon Mr. Goodyeare as she went out." Mr. Goodyeare fell immediately into a "swond"(faint). The trial transcript noted, "beside her notorious lying in this buisnes" [a sure sign of witchery], when she was asked how she knew what happened there, she said she was present at the time. The Goodyears and their daughters "all affirme she was not in ye roome but gone up into the chamber."[31]

The court concluded Mrs. Godman had "unjustly" brought the defendants to court. She could offer no proof against them. Her habitual conduct and behavior "doth render her suspitious of witchcraft." By bringing her slander accusations against these people, Mrs. Godman had not been successful in forestalling a witchcraft accusation. Instead, she caused the court to accuse her of witchcraft. The court said she "herself in so many words" confessed to witchcraft. Fortunately for her, the court was compassionate and she was sentenced to looking after her conduct and demeanor in the future. If there was further proof of witchcraft the court would revisit the depositions. It charged "her not to goe in an offensive way to folkes houses in a rayling manner ... but she keep her place" and mind her own business.[32]

The historian Charles Levermore wrote that "after a summer full of stories of ague-stricken girls, bedeviled chickens, and swooning magistrates this verdict was admirably sane." Theophilus Eaton, the governor, was simply too "judicious to play the part of [Samuel] Sewall [of Salem fame] ... to mistake a cross-grained temper on the one side and a frenzy of gossip on the other for evidence of a literal compact with Satan. There was no trial by jury in the New Haven Colony. If there had been and based on the outcome of other trials in the Connecticut Colony she likely would have run a greater risk of judicial murder."[33]

Levermore was arguing in favor of "the theocratic system of New Haven [that he thought] proved to be safer [for witches] than the democracy of Connecticut or the aristocracy of Massachusetts." However, a deeper look at who participated in the accusations indicates both ministers believed in witches (Davenport's sermon quoted by Mrs. Larremore) and Hooke's evidence Mrs. Godman had probably bewitched his son do not demonstrate theological skepticism.

Woodward has argued that the outcome of the Godman trial may have been heavily influenced by John Winthrop, Jr., based on an interpretation of one of three surviving letters from Nicholas Auger, the physician attending the Lamberton girls. Auger suspected witchcraft but Winthrop offered alternative natural explanations for their illnesses raising some doubt as to whether witchcraft was involved. He argued Winthrop (who would become Governor of Connecticut in 1657), when it came to witches, "refused to let a witch die, but he was not at all averse to coercing a witch to conform to social conventions." But with the provision if they did not adhere to the expected behavior they would be brought back to court and the original charges would be revisited with dire consequences. It was more important the accused be found "not completely innocent, but, not exactly guilty." This outcome "validated the grounds for the public suspicion … of the witchcraft charges, without empowering the accusers … defusing some of the fear and anger that underlay the charges." An outcome evident in the Godman trial and an approach found in a number of trials under his later governorship in Connecticut.[34]

The court's decision in New Haven may also have been based on a practical businessman's suspicion that she was being exploited by Goodyeare and others. But in order to pacify the public, who believed she was a witch, some recognition of her guilt and punishment was necessary, including if she continued her ways she could be brought back into court and the previous depositions and trial would be used against her in a second trial.[35]

## The Second Trial of Elizabeth Godman, New Haven, August 7, 1655

Mrs. Godman was brought back for a second trial in 1655. There appeared to be a financial involvement between Mrs. Godman and Mr. Goodyeare. I would suggest that from the first Governor Eaton suspected financial motivations for the rumors that brought her to the court in the first place and landed her on trial for witchcraft for a second time in 1655. For example, when Stephen Goodyeare died in London in 1658, Mrs. Godman was his fifth highest creditor out of fifty-six creditors in the amount of 152 pounds.[36]

In August 1655, Elizabeth was before the General Court of New Haven (also called the Town Meeting or Particular Court composed of the magistrates of the town government) for witchcraft. She had continued to live in Goodyeare's home since her first conviction. Her activities aroused suspicion "for witchcraft, as she knows the grounds of which she was examined in the former Court." The passages from the former Court were read. She knew them to be "just grounds for suspicion," and additional passages were read with more added.

The Court record gives the following account. There was an epidemic sickness in New Haven at the time. A private prayer meeting had been arranged by Mr. Goodyeare to "seeke God." Elizabeth Godman wished to attend the meeting but was told "she was under suspicion, and it would be offensive." She explained she was

> exercised wth many temptations, and saw strange appearitions, and lights aboute her bed, and strange sights wch affrighted her; some of his family said if she was affraide they would worke wth her in the day and lye with her in the night, but she refused and was angry and said she would have none to be wth her for she had her spirituall armour aboute her.

When asked why she would not take the help offered to her she said she would "have none lye wth her because her bed was weake; she was told that might have been mended." However, she knew if anyone became sick she would have been blamed as "the cause." About three weeks after, Goodyeare told Mrs. Godman she had to find another place to live. That night there was a great noise in the house and something came into the girls' room and "jumbled" the trunk, their shoes and the headboard. The clothes were pulled off the bed more than once even though the girls held on to them. Elizabeth Godman said she heard nothing but the noise and was frightened. With all the commotion she thought the house might be on fire. The next morning she said she did not know what was going on until Mr. Goodyeare came to her room that evening. Mr. Goodyeare asked her why

> she went downe staires after she was gon up to bed, she said to light a candell to looke for two grapes she had lost in the flore and feared the mice [her familiars?] would play wth them in the night and disturbe ye family.

On this matter the "Courts apprehension renders her more suspitious." Other testimony included that of Goodwife Thorpe. The earlier incident about the chickens was read into the record and new accusations from Thorpe included that Elizabeth Godman caused one of her cows to become sick; it recovered, but its milk dried up and the cow became sterile. She bought another cow that was also infertile. She bought a third cow. It remained healthy for two weeks but then began to pine away, its milk dried up and it began to sweat profusely. She began to think her cows were bewitched. Later she admitted after prayer her last cow was delivered of the evil that had befallen it.

A week later Thorpe went by the Goodyeare house and saw Elizabeth Godman in the road. Godman had not lost her sharp tongue and said to Thorpe: "I am behoulden to Goody Thorpe above all the weomen in the Towne: she would have me to the gallows for a few chickens; and gnashed and grinned wth her teeth in a strang maner." Elizabeth admitted she had done this but said in her defense she "owned nothing aboute ye cowes."

The Court heard from her neighbor, Allen Ball, who claimed Godman had bewitched his pigs and "all but one dyed" and one of his calves acted most strangely then died. Another neighbor, Mr. Yale, told the Court after words with Elizabeth Godman, things were "throwne aboute the house in a strange manner." One time while he was at Goodman Thorpe's there were words over "weaving some clothe." Mrs. Godman was "discontented" and "that night they had a great noise in ther house, wch much affrighted them, but they know not what it was."

The court ordered,

> These things being declared the Court told Elizabeth Godman that they have considered them, wth her former miscarriages, and see cause to order that she be

comitted to prison, ther to abide the Courts pleasure, but because the matter is of weight, and the crime whereof she is suspected capitall, therefore she is to answer it at the Court of Magistrates [the General Court of the Jurisdiction of New Haven responsible for capital cases] in October next.[37]

On September 4, 1655, Elizabeth Godman was called before the General Court. The Court noted she had been a prisoner since the last Court. However, she was released from prison because of her poor health. She was ordered to attend the Court of Magistrates on the third Wednesday of October and to go live with the Thomas Johnson family because they were willing to take her in. Again the Court said she could remain with the Johnsons as long as she did not bother the neighbors and give offense. She was, however, to be shunned from fully participating in the Church because she was forbidden to come to the "contribution, as she formerly had done," that is, the "offering for the support of the ministry made in a formal manner every Sunday by going up to the table before the pulpit." And as customary, she was ordered to pay the marshal for "the charge and trouble ... during ye time of her imprisonment."[38]

On October 17, 1655, Elizabeth Godman came before the Magistrates Court and was informed "upon grounds formerly declared wch stand upon record, she by her owne confession remains under suspition for witchcraft." Another charge that she had spoiled beer more than once at Mr. Hookes' house was added. The Court gave her the opportunity to clear herself. She brought several persons to help clear her and "much time was spent in hearing ym, but to little purpose, the grounds of suspition remaining full as strong as before and she found full of lying."[39]

The court ordered, "though the evidenc is not sufficient as yet to take away her life, yet the suspitions are cleere and many, wch she cannot by all the meanes she hath used, free herselfe from." She was again ordered not to go from house to house giving offense, to act in an orderly manner with whatever family she was with or she would have to go back to prison and she had to give to her primary accuser Mr. Goodyeare before the court "fifty pound of her estate ... for her good behavior, wch is further to be cleered next court, when Mr. Goodyeare is at home."[40]

She was ordered to live with the family of Thomas Johnson where she continued till her death on October 9, 1660. After meeting the estate debts she left the remainder of her estate to the Johnson family. The Court questioned the authenticity of her will because Thomas Johnson had written her will and the primary witnesses were his family members.

Questions concerning the estate came before the court on November 6, 1660, December 4, 1660, February 5, 1660/61, and April 2, 1661.[41] At the April 2 Court "Thomas Johnson was told the writing presented for the will of Mrs. Godman was so darke & difficult, & indeed such as her never was presented, that it hath occasioned these delays, & must yet be delayed that further advice may be taken about it."[42] As for the final settlement of the estate it is not known but on October 21, 1663, there was entered in the Court of Magistrates at New Haven the following:

> James Bishop, (attornie for Mrs. Lucie Farneden,) having made claim upon the estate of Mrs. Elizabeth Godman, (deceased), now in the hands of Thomas Johnson, desired of the court right in the case, & for that end presented a letter of attornie from Mrs. Farneden aforesd. Wth a certificate under the hand of a justice of the peace [from England] that shee was the onely naturall sister of Mrs.[43]

Here the record stops and there are two blank pages. Mrs. Godman, even with all her troubles in life, left an estate of nearly 200 pounds, a considerable amount at that time for a woman. Perhaps she never invested in "The Great Shippe" that caused so much financial ruin for others in the colony and caused some to be jealous of what they considered her "underserved good fortune." Whatever the reason, there were those in the colony, whether in life or death, willing to take advantage of the woman for their own benefit.

Elizabeth Godman was essentially told to go about and mind her own business but if there were new suspicions of witchcraft the Court would not have forgotten the original charges. In 1655 new suspicions arose and Godman was back in court again. This time she was "almost but not quite guilty of witchcraft." Winthrop was living in New Haven as a "short term resident" and according to the historian Woodward, undoubtedly had an informal influence over this decision. Woodward explained that New Haven had been trying to attract Winthrop as a businessman to open an ironworks, to practice medicine and support John Davenport's efforts to establish a college.[44] His "knowledge and opinions" and "medical abilities" would have carried great weight in New Haven. Winthrop's strategy of "coercing suspected witches into social conformity," if not "banishment," was a strategy he used in both New Haven and later in the Connecticut Colony.[45] Although Godman was not able to avoid jail, thanks to Winthrop's influence, she was at least able to avoid being hanged for a witch.

## The Nicholas Bayley Trial in New Haven in 1655

Nicholas Bayley and his wife were accused of witchcraft and brought to trial in New Haven in 1655 as well. His wife was more "suspitious in point of witchcraft." The Court did not intend to proceed with the witchcraft charge at that time. The Court charged the two with "impudent and notorious lying," causing discord among their neighbors and "filthy and unclean speeches uttered by her." She had confessed to some charges privately to the governor and now confessed them in court. The court's decision was that the two were "not fit to live amonge such neighbors" and between now and the next court they were to "remove themselves to some other place." The two appeared in court in August 1655 and asked they be given more time to remove themselves. They appeared again in the New Haven Court on September 4, 1655. Bayley's wife was given the opportunity to clear herself but could not. The suspicion of "witchcraft was a strong as before" and they were further accused of entertaining suspicious persons at their house." At the next court on October 2, 1655, only Nicholas appeared. He claimed his wife and child were sick. He offered to give surety if he and his family could remain until the spring. The court refused to hear any more excuses and the family left New Haven a few days later. Woodward has concluded although Winthrop probably did not participate in the case he most likely had some influence because removal or banishment was "a strategy of conflict resolution Winthrop frequently resorted to in future witchcraft cases."[46]

## The Roger Ludlow vs. the Staples Trials in New Haven in 1654

Bad blood appears to have existed between Roger Ludlow and Thomas Staples and his wife Mary prior to the trial in New Haven in 1654. They were neighbors in Fairfield and seemed to be continually feuding. On July 8, 1650, Roger Ludlow had sued Thomas Staples for slander and defamation in the Particular Court at Hartford.[47] The court found in favor of Roger Ludlow for 200 pounds but eventually only awarded him ten shillings and court costs. Thomas Staples attempted to have Roger Ludlow arrested after word got out that he was accusing his wife of being a witch and a liar. Then on May 16, 1654, Roger Ludlow took Thomas Staples to court in an action of "ffalse imprisonment to the damage of 200 pounds." Ludlow did not appear in court and his attorney refused to prosecute the case. The court ordered the plaintiff to pay Staples "reasonable Cost: which they Judg to bee 25s [shillings]."[48]

On May 29, 1654, Thomas Staples accused Roger Ludlow of defaming his wife, Mary Staples. This case was tried in the New Haven Court and presided over by Governor Eaton. The attorney for Thomas Staples was John Banks of Fairfield; the attorney for Roger Ludlow (who was out of the country) was Ensign Alexander Bryan of Milford. John Banks opened the case by declaring that Mr. Ludlow had defamed Thomas Staples' wife when he told the minister in New Haven, Mr. Davenport, and his wife that Mrs. Staples "had laid herselfe under a new suspicion of being a witch" because she had "caused Knapps wife to be new searched after she was hanged, and when she saw the teates, said if they were the markes of a witch, then she was one, or she had such markes; secondly, Mr. Ludlow said Knapps wife told him that goodwife Staplies was a witch, thirdly, that Mr. Ludlow hath slandered goodwife Staplies by calling her a liar."[49]

Following a discussion over whether Mr. Davenport should take an oath to proceed, he recounted one evening he, his wife and Mr. Ludlow were sitting in his home when Mr. Ludlow began to discuss the witch Knapp's execution. He said Knapp came down from the ladder and asked to speak with him alone. She told Ludlow the suspected witch was Goodwife Staples. Davenport said he could not believe it. Ludlow then told him "how she tumbled the corpes of the witch up and downe after her death, before sundrie women and spake to this effect, if these be the markes of a witch I am one, or I have such markes."[50] Davenport said he "disliked" this talk and had heard nothing like it from anyone else. He did not remember that Ludlow asked for secrecy on the matter because Ludlow told him "some did overheare what the witch said to him ... he is careful not to make unlawful promises, and when he hath made a lawful promise, ... careful to keepe it." Mrs. Davenport confirmed his testimony.[51]

That Goodwife Staples doubted Knapp was a witch, her "tumbling" of the corpse and questioning the evidence of the witches' teats has been previously discussed. We saw each side give their version of what occurred. However, there were also some charges not directly related to Goodwife Knapp that were specific to Goodwife Staples contained in the testimony. For example, Mary Staples was accused of notorious lying by Roger Ludlow. One witness, Goodwife Sherwood, said she heard Mr. Ludlow call her a liar several times.[52] "All witches were presumed to lie," and it was their relationship with the devil, "The Prince of Liars," that provided "sufficient evidence of the fact." Not only was lying a serious sin in the seventeenth century, it was also a crime "legally punishable by the courts" but was left to be decided in the following year because the court wanted more evidence.[53]

Roger Ludlow also thought Mary Staples (as a woman in a Puritan man's world) likely suffered from the sin of pride for calling into question his judgment in the earlier Knapp conviction. Also, according to Goodwife Gould's testimony, "that in a debate in ye church wth Mr. Ludlow, goodwife Staples desired him to show her wherein she had told one lye, but Mr. Ludlow said she need not mention pticulars, for she gon on in a tract of lying." There is no documentation about what the two argued about, but their feuding appeared later in the depositions in the Particular Court in Hartford and the New Haven Court. Ludlow suspected Mary Staples was a witch because of her intemperate nature and was confirmed when Goodwife Knapp named her on the gallows as the other Fairfield witch. Also, because she caused contention with him in the church, a place considered a haven that represented a "garden amidt the wilderness" and a sanctuary from the devil and all his works, this was sign of the devil's influence over her.[54] He and others in Fairfield had their suspicions about Goodwife Staples. Shortly after the argument in the Fairfield church, Roger Ludlow informed John Davenport of Knapp's gallows confession that Mary Staples was the other witch in Fairfield.[55]

One statement appears in the testimony that seems unusual until one considers the specific circumstances of a feared Indian uprising at the time: the accusation Mary Staples was consorting with an Indian and receiving talismans of Indian gods. The day after Goodwife Knapp was condemned, Hester Ward gave the following testimony concerning Mary Staples, verified by Luce Pell and Mrs. Jones. Knapp said Goodwife Staples had told her that "an Indian Brought unto her ... two litle things brighter than the light of day, and told ... goodwife Staplyes they were Indian gods, as the Indians called ym; and the Indian told her ... if she would keepe them, she should be so big rich, all one god, and ... Staplyes ... said ... she gave them ... to the Indian." But Goodwife Knapp seemed to raise some doubt as to whether Mary Staples had returned the objects and said she "could not tell whether she did so or no."[56]

The following day Goodwife Sherwood recounted that when she arrived to visit Goodwife Knapp, Goodwife Baldwin told her Knapp said "a woman in ye towne was a witch and would be hanged wthin a twelve moneth." Baldwin asked Knapp "how she knew she was a witch." Knapp said she was told she had "received Indian gods of an Indian, wch are shining things wch shine lighter than the day." Goodwife Baldwin had probably heard the rumor and immediately suspected Knapp was speaking about Mary Staples. When questioned Knapp denied she said this, only that there was an "Indian at a womans house and offered her a coople of shining things; but the woman never told her she took them, but was a afraid and ran away; and she knows not if the woman ever took them." Thomas Sherrington, a guard at the prison house with Knapp, when asked did not remember her speaking about a suspected witch that "would be hanged" but he did remember her speaking of "shining things."[57]

Attempting to connect suspected witches with Indians and their demon gods does not seem to be unusual in the popular imagination at the time. In the Godman trial, for example, one accuser said "she thought ... [Godman] ... was a witch and Hobbamocke was her husband." Relating the witch to Indian gods (who were seen as demons and followers of Satan) in 1653 was a significantly dangerous accusation because the threat of an Indian conspiracy with the Dutch was real as well as the rumor the Indians were going to kill all the English in that part of the colony. The colonists understood the battle against Satan was being waged on two fronts, the invisible world of the witches and the visible world of his agents, the Indians. This explains why Thomas Staples visited Goodwife Knapp and threatened her for telling stories that would "bring his wives name in question." Not only was she being accused of being a witch but by implication also of conspiring with the Indians. By accepting the Indian gods (conspiring with Satan) she would selfishly become "big rich" at the expense of the community. We do not know what Mr. Staples threatened Knapp with after all she was condemned to die as a witch, but it seemed to work as Knapp modified her original story and made it less damning.[58]

Ironically, the only truly supernatural accusation in the testimonies against Mary Staples occurred when Mary's sister, Martha, told Goodwife Knapp of a strange incident that happened in her house prior to her trial. Knapp recounted the incident while in prison awaiting her execution. Martha said Mary stood "by the fire in there house." She called out, "sister, sister, and she would not answer ... but she [Martha] struck at her and then she [Mary] went away, and ye next day she asked her sister and she said she was not there." Two witnesses verified Knapp had told this story about Goodwife Staples.

It is likely that in court the story would have suggested more than a simple incident to be ignored. The reason this event was included in the court testimony in support of Roger Ludlow was because he understood the impact it might have on a jury. The story was originally related by Mary's sister and indicated a specter or demon was at the hearth or heart of the house (as it was understood this is where demons or witches might enter the home through the chimney if unprotected). In England, in East Anglia, for example, "under the hearthstone was the spot most frequently chosen to bury a witch bottle, a device to act as a repellant against witches." New England narratives suggest the doors, and windows, etc., were attacked by witches but it was the chimneys and hearths that were the most vulnerable to them. The setting of Martha's story would have suggested supernatural activities. The jury would have understood the importance of the setting in the home and what this symbolized. Again, from Ludlow's viewpoint it only confirmed his worst suspicions that Mary Staples was a witch.[59]

Martha struck at her sister and she "ran away." Mary Staples fled from the house. When Martha confronted Mary about what happened she said she was "not there." This would have suggested to the jury that it was not Mary Staples (but a specter or spirit in Mary's likeness) sent by Mary Staples the witch. The jurymen and magistrates would have known as the ministers explained to their congregants, "specters were demons who assumed human form on instruction from Satan: when witches signed a covenant with him, the Devil agreed to send demons on request to torment their enemies." In addition, "witches had no occult power of their own; demons acted on their behalf, taking on the appearance of witches for whom they acted." The magistrates and the jurors would have also known witch's had familiars that could appear as "spirits" in the shape of a "man, woman or boy" or a variety of animals.[60]

However, a "matter of debate in the seventeenth century" was whether the devil could impersonate an innocent person. Most Protestant authorities agreed he could assume a "pleasing shape." It is likely in mid–seventeenth century New England, with limited experience in witch hunting, the more likely suspicion was that the devil took on the likeness of a guilty person (the witch). The question of the innocent impersonated by the devil as evidence in the Connecticut Courts as we will see later was resolved by the report of a committee of ministers in 1669. It rose to the crisis level in Massachusetts during the Salem witch trials. Cotton Mather was disposed to write because of the multitude of accusations, "the devils have obtain'd the power, to take on them the likeness of harmless people and in that likeness to afflict other people."[61]

The New Haven court concluded it had listened to both sides of the argument and it was not satisfied with the evidence presented by the attorney for Roger Ludlow, Mr. Ensign Bryan, and yet were not fully convinced of the testimony on the side of the plaintiff either. From the beginning the plaintiff's lawyer was concerned about the unorthodox way the testimony was gathered by Mr. Ludlow and Mr. Wells. He objected to the fact the testimony was written down by Mr. Ludlow and the witnesses were given an oath administered by Mr. Ludlow. Nevertheless, the court "caused ym to be read that they might make such use of them as they should se cause." However, the court eventually concluded Roger Ludlow had defamed Mary Staples. Yet, the court also noted it was more inclined "to more favour then possibly they should doe if Mr. Ludlow was here." The court determined "they see no cause to lay any blemish of a witch upon goodwife Staplyes, but must judg that Mr. Ludlow hath done her wrong, and therefore is by this court ordered to pay Thomas Staplyes, by way of fine for reparation of his wives name, tenn pounds, and for his trouble … five pounds more."[62]

The case was not finished because there was a third charge the "tract of lying." The court required more evidence. Attorney Bryan was told to answer the third charge at the next court of magistrates held on October 18, 1654. The court laid out the charge, Mr. Bryan, attorney for Mr. Ludlow, was ordered to prepare proof for the trial. Mr. Ludlow had charged Mr. Staples' wife of having gone in "a tract of lying." The three earlier testimonies of Goodwife Sherwood, John Thompson and Mrs. Gould were introduced. Attorney Bryan was asked if he had any evidence to present that Mary Staples had lied. He said that "he had nothing to say on the case at the present."

Curiously, the court concluded "considering the nature of the charge, her relation to the church at Fairfeild [she must have been a full member able to take communion and undoubtedly this carried much weight with the court], and the censure such a tract proved might have brought upon her, by way of sentence ordered, that Mr. Ludlow paye to Thomas Staplyes, towards ye repairing his wives name so defamed ... the some of tenn pounds."[63]

It should be noted Thomas Staples had brought Roger Ludlow to court as a "back stop" action to prevent his wife from being tried as a witch. In a case of slander, an attorney was permitted. If there was evidence she was a witch she would have been tried again under a felony statute and would not have been permitted to have an attorney. It also appears that the court indulged Roger Ludlow, even allowing his own handwritten and sworn testimonies taken by him and Mr. Wells into the proceeding over the objections of the plaintiff's lawyer. However, in the end, the court sided with the plaintiff and fined Roger Ludlow for defaming Mary Staples. Roger had left Fairfield for Virginia. He was later invited back to England by Oliver Cromwell and took up a post in Ireland. He died in 1664. He never returned to Connecticut.[64]

Although the court had cleared Mary Staples of the suspicion of being a witch the court had been somewhat ambiguous as to how it came to the decision and admitted if Roger Ludlow had been there the court might have come to another conclusion. The testimonies presented in court—all the neighbors suspected her of being a witch—and her actions may not have convinced the court but they fueled the gossip that remained with her throughout the remainder of her life.

As a result of this ambiguity, the damage to her reputation had been done. An acquittal for witchcraft did not necessarily assuage public opinion that the accused was not a witch.[65] For example, the suspicion of witchcraft followed Mary Staples and not surprisingly the female members of her family the remainder of her life.[66]

As late as 1692 Mary Staples, her daughter, Mary Harvey, and granddaughter, Hannah Harvey, were named as witches by Katherine Branch, a maid servant in Stamford who said they appeared as specters to her along with two other women.[67] On February 7, 1692, they were indicted on suspicion of witchcraft.[68]

A later grand jury recognized there was little evidence against Mary Staples, her daughter and granddaughter.[69] The evidence included hearsay and an incident with Mary Staples concerning a trip on horseback in which a witness reported an odd incident that had occurred thirty years ago.[70] Final testimony was given by Esther Grumman, who recounted "she saw the shapes [specters] of the Widow Stapells and Marcy Disborah sitting upon her floor and then dancing at the foot of her bed when she was sick."[71]

The irony here is the only supernatural testimony in the Mary Staples "slander case" in 1654 was the report of a "specter" by her sister Martha as told to a witness by the convicted witch Elizabeth Knapp. In 1692 the primary accusations by the maid servant Katherine Branch and Esther Grumman were the report of specters in the likeness of Mary Staples. As noted, in Connecticut the evidence for witchcraft had changed. The magistrates determined they could not legally convict on spectral evidence in a court of law because it now required a "plurality of witnesses" to "testify to one and the same individuall ffact" and the witnesses did not provide evidence of a simultaneous sighting. Mary Staples, Mary Harvey and Hannah Harvey were set free on September 16, 1692.[72]

# 10

# "A world of sin was doubtlessly committed"

*"From the Fires of the Altars there issued thunderings and lightnings and earthquakes through the colony."*
—Cotton Mather

During the Salem witch trials in 1692 one of the more important aspects of the eventual accusations that arose from the economic and social conflict in Salem village was played out in the religious strife within the village meeting house that served as the Church. In the case of Salem this strife was at first limited to Salem village and spread outward from there.

In Hartford the acrimonious conflict over doctrine and authority began in the First Congregational Church and came to affect the New England colonies. The church at Hartford was one of the "largest and most eminent in New England." The actual beginning of the controversy that led to such heated confrontations and the rending of a community is obscured by a lack of documents.[1]

While Thomas Hooker was minister there was no serious conflict in the Hartford Church. Hooker, like other first generation clergy, established a unique bond of authority with his congregation, and Hooker himself supported the basic doctrines of Independent Congregationalism including the "ruling authority" of the "brethren." In truth the congregation often "deferred to his wisdom and expertise" on important questions of church government.

Samuel Stone, the teacher, believed the "brethren" had too much authority in the governance of the Church and was determined to make "doctrine and discipline ministerial concerns, allowing the brethren a voice only in admission and censure."[2]

Puritans believed religious strife was an "old stratagem of Satan, with which he vexes the church ... by sowing the seeds of error in the hearts of some that was of very good esteem."[3] For example, representatives of the Churches in Massachusetts in 1656 admonished the First Church in Hartford on the strife in the church, "ye scandalls of ye best men afford materialls for ye most dangerously ensnaring traps of Sathan."[4] The Ministers in Massachusetts addressed their criticism of this ongoing conflict in the harshest of terms:

> You are a city whose fame hath sett you upon a hill, therefore you cannot be hid.... Ye evil report thereof will be published in pts beyond.... A world of evill is herein, in yt scandals cannot be kept from ye world; woe be to ye world because of offences.[5]

The background to this conflict and its effect on the "visible saints" and brethren in Hartford was an underlying cause of the discontent and conflict in Hartford that later led to the witchcraft accusations in 1662. The quarrel involved the minister of the First Church of Hartford, Samuel Stone, the major antagonist in the religious strife in Hartford who later played a critical role in the Hartford witchcraft trials in 1662. Stone's involvement in that "great horror of the period to which belongs alike in Old England and New- the delusion of Witchcraft" was the most "distinct instance of the contact with the Hartford Church."[6] This religious conflict shook the foundations of colonial society in Connecticut and affected the Massachusetts colony. It gave rise to "an aging and embittered man, whose authority and prestige had been severely threatened" and encouraged "accusations of witchcraft against those who opposed him or the authority of the church." A descendant of an accused witch during the Hartford witch trials wrote, "It cannot be denied that he [Stone] was largely responsible" for the witchcraft trials.[7]

The years 1653 to 1659 in New England was a time of religious, political and economic ferment. The clergy and people began to see themselves under assault. The quarrel in the Hartford Church was symptomatic of this assault mentality, and the quarrel was "of such virulence, contagiousness, and publicity, that it attracted the attention of all the churches in New England, and occupies a large place in every history of early ecclesiastical affairs in the Colony."[8]

The intensity of the conflict was remembered in 1659 when a day of Thanksgiving was celebrated throughout the Massachusetts Colony. The prayers offered were for a "comfortable harvest," "the health of the country," "preservation from the destructive desires of the persistent company of the Quakers," and for the "healing of the great breach at Hartford."[9] Cotton Mather later wrote the quarrel had colony-wide repercussions because, "Where will the Devil shew most malice; but where he is hateth and hatest most ... [and] casts his Net, but where is the best Prey. Those he cannot damn, he will do his worst to trouble."[10]

Early historians attributed the conflict over acceptance of the "half-way covenant" in the church.[11] According to Trumbull, the particular "act" by Mr. Stone or the church which gave elder Goodwin, Mr. Stone's antagonist in this

drama, "disgust and began the dissension" does not appear anywhere. It originated in Mr. Stone's views on "congregationalism" that seemed to border on
"Presbyterianism" rather than the idea of an independent church, the basis
of congregationalism and the view of the first ministers in the New England
settlements."[12]

The conflict likely began around 1650 when Samuel Stone attempted to
change the requirements for church membership to a more simple profession
of faith "combined with evidence of good character." The congregation immediately divided and thus began a conflict that lasted nine years and led Cotton
Mather to comment there was "such a monstrous enchantment upon the
minds of the Christians and Brethren" in all the surrounding towns people
chose sides and "the factions insinuated themselves into the smallest as well
as the greatest affairs of the towns.... A world of sin was doubtlessly committed, even by pious men on this occasion, while they permitted so many
things contrary to the laws of charity."[13]

Following the initial quarrel the two groups were at an impasse until
the conflict was reignited in 1652 or 1653 when Michael Wigglesworth
preached at Hartford in hopes of being appointed pastor.[14] Congregational
churches were organized with a pastor who "exhorted" and a teacher who
taught doctrine. The elders tended to the daily concerns of the church and
pastorate. Stone was the teacher but not the pastor.[15] He was accused of interfering with the church's vote on whether to accept Wigglesworth. Stone said
it was his right to "hinder the church from putting forth" Wigglesworth. He
was accused of asserting a prerogative he did not have. A series of "stormy
meetings followed." After debating the issues Stone was acquitted. However,
some members of the church continued to challenge Stone.[16] Stone resigned
his position sometime prior to June 1656. However, he continued to perform
some of his duties and advised on the choice of moderator. The latter generated more opposition in the church.

Stone's authority to confront Goodwin was based on his belief church
government was a "speaking Aristocracy in the face of a silent Democracy,"
an idea elder Goodwin and others in the church could not abide. To the elders
it smacked of Presbyterianism, anathema to the independent church government beliefs of the brethren in the Hartford Church.[17]

Before we proceed to the climax to this controversy we offer some background on Stone's experiences with religious overtones prior to and in the
midst of the Hartford Church conflict. They include his conversion of Mary
Johnson, convicted of witchcraft in Hartford in 1648, his involvement in the
alleged adulterous affair between Elder William Goodwin and Mrs. Hooker
in 1654, Stone's debate with two Quakers in Hartford in 1658 and Stone and
his allies' failed attempt to introduce moderate congregationalism in Connecticut during the 1650s.

## Samuel Stones' Mentor Thomas Hooker's Involvement with Spiritual Cures or "Protestant Exorcisms"

Samuel Stone had earlier attempted to enhance his pastoral reputation as Hooker had famously done in England. Hooker had undertaken "spiritual cures" described as bordering on "exorcisms" while in England. Like Hooker, Stone successfully confronted the devil in 1648 in the person of the convicted Wethersfield witch Mary Johnson.[18]

Thomas Hooker's most famous spiritual cure was the case of Mrs. Joan Drake, who "untill the time shee revealed the Devil's counsell, shee was contented to live and use the meanes of having any hope of being saved."[19] Joan Drake was attended by a number of ministers for her "melancholia" and confronted them as if possessed by the devil.[20] The ministers fasted and prayed with Mrs. Drake with no success. One minister was so upset he would not accompany her fearing the "ground would open up and swallow them up." Later he said, "under the Law the blasphemer was to die ... he would ... bear witnesse against her, and provide faggots to burn her."[21] Joan asked her maidservant, Susannah Garbrand, the future Mrs. Hooker, why did he "complain about me, and provide faggots to burne me." Susannah replied, "Mistress, you have spoken some strange untoward things."[22]

The English clergyman John Dod was called in to "comfort the melancholic woman." It was reported that when Dod came to the house Mrs. Drake fled from him before she was introduced.[23] When he attempted to advise her he decided "the Devills rhetoricke taught her against herself." Her husband asked Dod to invite Thomas Hooker to help his wife, hoping Hooker could protect her "from falling under Satan's spell.[24] Hooker, newly ordained, came to the Drake residence "with a new answering method" and managed Mrs. Drake's spirit "especially Satan's windings and turnings" even though "Satan delighted still in raising new uproars in her."[25] Hooker used "prayer, catechizing, especially reading of the word and singing psalms."[26] After two years Mrs. Drake's "mind improved." Hooker married Susannah Garbrand on April 3, 1621, and left the Drake residence. He obtained a position as a minister in Essex, England.[27]

Samuel Stone also had a famous success confronting the devil following the indictment and conviction of Mary Johnson in Hartford on December 7, 1648. Under the guidance of Stone she confessed to familiarity with the devil.[28] Cotton Mather wrote after Mary Johnson's conviction for witchcraft "in the time of her imprisonment the *famous* Mr. Stone took great pains to promote her Conversion unto God and represent unto her both her misery and remedy of which was very desirable." He exercised pastoral care for the sake of her soul. She was "judged very Penitent both before and at her execution.... And she died in a Frame extremely to the Satisfaction of them that were Spectators of it." He enjoyed considerable success for this action.[29]

When persons were executed in New England the "drama lay in whether someone would confess or not, and if so, in judging whether the confession was heartfelt." Stone had been successful getting Mary to confess. From the minister's view the land was cleansed, the righteousness of the law upheld and most importantly the "healing power of the Gospel" was confirmed. In Stone's case the crowd was satisfied the spiritual and lawful needs of the community were met by her righteous and correct execution.[30] For Stone, like his mentor Thomas Hooker, preaching was important but a "spiritual cure" would likely establish and consolidate a minister's clerical reputation.[31]

Stone likely believed he had gained the credibility among his congregation for making the changes he contemplated in the Hartford Church and this would also hold him in good stead to later successfully confront the devil during the Hartford witch panic in 1662/63.

## Adultery Accusations in Hartford

A major distraction in Hartford during a quiet period in the church quarrel was the court case involving Stone's primary antagonist, William Goodwin, and Mrs. Susannah Hooker, widow of Thomas Hooker. The two were accused of adultery by Walter Gray, a servant in Mrs. Hooker's household. Goodwin was married and Mrs. Hooker was a widow. They were all neighbors and were leading members of the church and the community in Hartford. They served as "actors in the drama of adultery and the later epic of the troubled church" followed by the exodus of the "withdrawers" from Hartford.[32]

This adultery case should be seen as a backdrop and a significant but not sole factor to the conflict and essential breakdown of the "puritan covenant" in Hartford that led to the "withdrawal" of many prominent residents in Hartford and precipitated the final fury of the Hartford witch hunt in 1662/63. Between the gossip and accusations of adultery and the conflict in the Hartford Church that involved these same neighbors and their families "one can only wonder of the thoughts" of the other members of this bedeviled community during the ongoing strife in the 1650s in Hartford.[33]

Adultery was a capital offence in Connecticut although the death penalty was never imposed. There is one instance of the death penalty carried out in Massachusetts for adultery on James Britton and Mary Latham, who were hanged in 1643. Nevertheless, the penalty in Connecticut could be harsh. For example, in 1666, Hannah Hackleton was tried and convicted of adultery and blasphemy. The jury sentenced her to death. The jury's verdict was overturned by the recently formed Court of Assistants. Nevertheless, she was sentenced to be whipped with thirty lashes, made to climb the ladder to the gallows and place a rope around her neck for one hour.[34]

However, one of the more famous cases that may have had some bearing in Hartford was the adultery case of Captain John Underhill, a hero of the Pequot War. He confessed to the sin of adultery before the General Court in Massachusetts. The court could not pardon him but lifted his banishment. The law had changed in Massachusetts concerning adultery and the court could not "touch his life." He had to confess before the church to be accepted as a member. His confession was somewhat odd and suggests that he was not wholly repentant. He stated "she withstood him for six months against all his solicitations (which he thought no woman could resist) before he overcame her chastity but being once overcome, she was wholly at his will." He later went to the husband in the presence of some elders and "confessed the wrong he had done him."[35]

Walter Gray, who started the gossip that William Goodwin and Susannah Hooker had engaged in an adulterous relationship, was no stranger to the Hartford Court. He appeared in court ten years earlier in 1644 for "laboring to inveagle the affections of Mrs. Hookers mayde." He was ordered to be "publiquely corrected the next lecture day."[36] Gray likely behaved himself afterward because on May 18, 1654, he was made a "free man of Hartford."[37] However, following the Wigglesworth uproar in the church he accused elder William Goodwin and Susannah Hooker of adultery.[38] Gray's charge, if true, had the potential to undermine the authority of its church leaders who were the most prominent families in Hartford.

Gray undoubtedly nursed a grudge against the Hookers but why was Goodwin the correspondent in this affair? How had he cleverly come up with the adultery ploy? Had he done this to get his revenge on Mrs. Hooker and at the same time rid the church of the troublesome Elder Goodwin to the benefit of Mr. Stone and the community? Or perhaps the adultery charge was true and was he paid off to change his story?

Gray may have sensed the struggle between the two neighbors, Stone and Goodwin, and cleverly plotted his revenge on the Hookers by accusing his mistress of adultery with William Goodwin, Stone's chief antagonist.[39] Goodwin was a figure of authority in the Church. As the senior elder, Goodwin's role was to assist the pastor and teacher. He called and dismissed meetings, "and, in the absence of Pastor and Teacher" preached."[40] Over the years Goodwin had "magnified his office of Ruling Elder." He was by virtue of his office, the natural Moderator at church meetings. It was his duty to prepare business for the action of the church" and perhaps most pointedly with regard to Gray's earlier immoral actions and a reflection on his own he was responsible for "the conduct of its members." Gray may have especially disliked Goodwin. Goodwin may have insulted him on a number of occasions as he was known "in the heat of argument" to use "unreverend speech."[41]

If it was idle gossip, then the adultery accusation may have been inspired by Captain Underhill's time in Hartford. He arrived in Hartford on June 27, 1653. He "seised this house, the Hope with all the…. Duch goods, belonging to the West Indian Company of Amsterdam."[42] His visit may have reminded Walter Gray about the adultery charge against Underhill and how effective it could be in undermining the reputation of an individual whether it was true or not. He waited for his opportunity. Underhill stayed in Hartford nearly three months in 1653 at John Webster's house. He was supported by other prominent inhabitants of Hartford who were neighbors of Mrs. Hooker, the Goodwins and Stones. Captain Underhill had gotten under an obligation regarding a "frolic" that forced him to remain longer than he had anticipated. The servants in the prominent households of Hartford must have heard much gossip and learned much about Captain Underhill during his ongoing visits to the various houses.[43]

Walter Gray's accusations of adultery between Mrs. Hooker and Elder Goodwin quickly reached beyond the small group he told about the affair he witnessed.[44] He was brought before the court on December 7, 1654, for slandering William Goodwin and Mrs. Hooker. Mr. Stone and Mr. Webster (who sided with Goodwin in the church dispute and later served as the Governor of Connecticut from 1656 to 1657) interrogated Gray and recorded his confession prior to Gray's court appearance.

Given the conflict between Stone and Goodwin, Stone's involvement would appear to be unusual. However, adultery was a sin as well as being unlawful and was a matter for the church. Adulterers would be required to publically confess their sins and seek forgiveness in the church. Secondly, as much as Stone may have seen Goodwin as an antagonist and wished him to go away, the idea that this accusation involved Mrs. Hooker and Elder Goodwin struck at the heart of the founders of the church in Hartford and likely considered "visible saints." This would have been another factor damaging the reputation of the Hartford Church and given rise to the further suspicion of Satan's influence in causing strife in the church by sowing the seeds of discord.[45]

The adultery accusation was especially pertinent in this case because Thomas Hooker had preached against adultery in Chelmsford, England, and likely repeated his sermons in Hartford. For him, adultery was one of three sins he found especially detestable. They included drunkenness, adultery and "unjust business dealings." For Hooker and his ardent followers this sin would cast suspicion on Goodwin and Mrs. Hooker's personal morality, lowered their status in the community and the church and called into question their leadership roles in the church as covenanted members. According to Thomas Hooker even throwing doubt on their likely "elect" status, "what a miserable accursed damnable estate are those men, they will not leave and forsake their lewd practices, and therefore they cannot will grace, and if they cannot will it, then we may certainly conclude, they shall never obtain it."

There was much to lose physically and spiritually if the accusation was proven true.[46] Some historians have hinted Gray's confession was "the first great payoff—to protect Mrs. Hooker ... and the Elder William Goodwin from scandal."[47] I would argue that Stone immediately recognized it was more important to protect the integrity of the church from suspicion of satanic influence by the corruption of "two visible saints" rather than merely saving the reputations of Goodwin and Mrs. Hooker. (The irony that Mrs. Hooker had been a maid and already married when she married Thomas Hooker was probably not lost on some. That Walter Gray had been convicted of seducing the Hookers' maid likely created interesting gossip.)

If Gray's testimony was in fact paid off to protect them they did not get off completely free. Embarrassing testimony was placed in the record. Whether it was true or not Mrs. Hooker and Mr. Goodwin must have been "dismayed and shocked" when they learned this gossip had gone into the public record. The court named the individuals to whom Gray related his "false report" and included the following:

> Walter confesseth yt he hath done Mr. Goodwine & Mrs. Hooker wrong in that false & Slanderous report ... yt Mr. Goodwine & shee being togeather late in the night in her parlour yt *Mr. Goodwine stood Between her & did the same Act with her which a man doth with his wife.*[48]

Gray was sentenced "for his gross abuse & evil in Slaundering Mr. Will Goodwyn & Mrs. Hooker in Charging them with the Act of Adultery ... to be whipt this day publiquely & next Lecture day in Hartford ... [and] ... be whipt againe, as also stand in the pillory, & find sureties for his good Behavior."[49]

Finally in the *Petition of Walter Gray to the Courte* we learn a little more about Gray. He could not read because he signed his name with an x, and his petition dated December 9, 1654, "was writ" by William Edwards (later involved in the Hartford witchcraft accusations and not a Stone supporter) from Walter Gray's "one mouth."[50] His petition contained a full measure of contriteness:

> I have most unjustly & sinfully Raised & Published [made public] a most grievous & false report uppon Mr. Goodwine & my Mis home ... I ... freely doe confess [that I have most falsely] *slandered them in that particular charge saying that they were uncleane together* or anything ... most humbly beg yor worships to pitty mee & grant what marcy you can with Justice & so hoping to find so shall rest yor poore & sinful prisoner."[51]

Walter Gray's petition to the court differs somewhat from the original confession. He admits to slandering the two victims but the graphic description of the "act" is removed and replaced with the more common legal expression at the time: "they were unclean together." However, it was important Gray go through what Hall has called the "ritual of confession." The guilty party was expected to explain what he did, condemn himself, ask for forgiveness and accept his punishment. This would normally satisfy the church and the court in punishments meted out for a multitude of crimes. In the case of Walter Gray, there is no record of a church punishment for his transgression; however, it appeared he accepted the punishment meted out by the court. Ironically, Winthrop's example of when this "ritual confession" was not sincere was in regard to a case that included adultery.[52]

On December 27, 1654, Walter Gray was "bound in bond for 100 pounds to the deputy Governor Thomas Wells." William Phillips, a relative of the Hookers through marriage, and Nathaniel Ruscoe, the jailer, were appointed guarantors for Walter Gray's good behavior.[53] Walter Gray essentially faded into obscurity appearing one more time in court for a small debt. Gray remained in Hartford and died in 1684 leaving a small estate and no family.[54]

Due to the graphic nature of Gray's original description of what he had seen between Mrs. Hooker and Mr. Goodwin he was probably telling the truth. Gray was probably taken to court to stop the gossip and prevent the further undermining of Church leadership. Stone and Webster likely colluded to protect the Church even in the midst of a temporal power struggle because the spiritual consequences would have had longer term consequences for the Church and cast suspicion on the moral leadership of the entire community.

## Samuel Stone Confronts Quakers

The 1650s was a period of religious ferment in New England and there were many who were attracted to a number of new religious sects. The authorities in the Massachusetts Bay especially feared the newly arrived Quakers in Boston in 1657, who they suspected were witches. For the Puritans, Quaker tenets (guidance by a divine internal light and the objection to the organized structure of the church) put them in the category of "suspicious persons prone to practice witchcraft."[55] In addition, they were "uncivil in behavior, showing no respect to any, ready to censure and condemn all" and were disruptive of the churches and politics of the colony. Both the civil and church authorities were intolerant of these "seducers." For example, when the first two Quaker women, Mary Fisher and Anne Austin, were arrested in Boston in 1656 they "were suspected ... for Witches; whereupon they took upon to appoint women to search them ... [for witches' marks] ... took men along to restrain them ... stript stark naked not missing head nor feet, searching betwixt their toes and among their hair ... abusing their bodies more than modesty can maintain."[56]

Hull wrote, the Quakers who arrived the previous summer and had been deported returned in the summer of 1657 and "they knew the law against any such seducers ... and where severely whipped in the House of Correction."[57] The New England clergy saw the early Quakers and their teachings as threat to the orderly discipline of the churches of New England. Samuel Stone was in Boston during the summer of 1657 and undoubtedly saw their ideas might be a significant threat to his conflicted church. It may explain why he was one of the few ministers in New England to publically confront the two Quakers, John Rous and John Copeland, in a public disputation. In addition he may have thought his successful defense would give him additional local support in the ongoing conflict in the Hartford Church.

In the spring of 1658 John Copeland and John Rous held their public disputation with Samuel Stone in Hartford. If, as Rous' narration makes clear, Stone was not able to successfully defend his faith then it suggests if there were doubters in the community this would have given them opportunity to find an alternative religious expression outside the church, offering them a third way, an idea anathema to Stone and other like-minded clergy. For the New England clergy this was not out of the realm of possibility. For example, in 1662 in Dover, New Hampshire, the townspeople were perplexed by the teachings of the recently arrived Quakers and demanded their minister, the Reverend John Reyner, answer them. The minister was not able to answer the Quakers to his flock's satisfaction and fled in a "rage." As a result of being deserted by their minister and his inability to answer the Quakers to their satisfaction "many were convinced of the truth that day."[58]

There is no direct evidence the Quakers were successful in converting individuals in Hartford but it is not out of the realm of possibility that some members of this church in conflict were beginning like the Quakers as well as other religious sects to question the role of the clergy and the churches.[59] Nevertheless, for the true Puritans, the choice was either the less democratic congregationalism of Stone or the original congregationalism of the true believers who later become the "withdrawers." It is likely the unresolved religious tensions of the time in Hartford were significant factors contributing to the later flare-up of the "witch hunt" in Hartford in 1662/63.

The dispute in Hartford with Samuel Stone was written by the Quaker John Rous. If accurate it suggests there were many in attendance and Samuel Stone did not acquit himself with distinction in this dispute. Rous wrote:

> What manner of spirits the New England Priests are, I shall give you a brief account of what passed between my beloved brother, John Copeland, and a high Priest we met at Hartford ... we being at the Ordinary were sent for by the Governor [John

Winthrop Jr.] to come to his house ... the Governour, a moderate man and some of
the Magistrates ... and their Priest called Samuel Stone.

Samuel Stone and the Quaker John Copeland argued over the nature of
God. Copeland accused Stone of knowing more about logic than of God and
not being able to answer questions with scripture. Stone "was much puzzled"
because he could not answer a specific question in front of "so many hearers
that were present." He was so confused the Governor had to intercede to help
him. "After this he raised another lying Argument, which was this; None are
saved without a promise, you have no promise in the Scripture, and therefore
are not saved ... we replied, the Promise is, *I will give him for a Covenant, a*
*light, that he may be my Salvation to the ends of the earth, to as many as beleeve*
*in him;* we beleeve in him, and are in the ends of the earth, and therefore are
saved by him; to which he objected nothing." Rous concluded he had given
"an account of some of the Doctrines of one of the highest of the New-
England Pharisees, who is accounted the greatest disputant in all the Land,
(as one of his Hearers told us) but it hath so pleased the Father, by babes to
confound and stop the mouths of such wise ones." Following the disputation
a magistrate informed the Quakers that according to the law they could not
remain in the Colony.[60]

## The Conflict in the Hartford Church Reignited

The struggle over the Hartford Church from the Puritan perspective
was seen as both temporal and metaphysical, caused by the machinations of
the devil who wanted the Puritan enterprise to fail in New England. One
minister wrote Stone's "example in this and the consequences of it is like to
have a destructive influence upon all the Churches in New England."[61] For
our purposes a brief outline of the strife is only necessary as a detailed telling
is beyond the scope of this book. The conflict involved the courts, local ministers, and the elders of the churches, and because the brethren in conflict
believed the local churches were prejudiced, the courts requested elders from
the Massachusetts Bay to help arbitrate the conflict.

The issue over Stone's infringement of the church members and their
prerogatives, especially choosing Wigglesworth as a potential pastor for the
church, were reignited in the spring of 1656. Stone acknowledged he had put
forward his opposition to Wigglesworth and he would leave the church if the
members wanted him to out.

The situation became so heated at one church meeting in the spring of
1656, Stone threatened, "he would lay down his place and office power" and
take his leave of the congregation. He had gone to Boston to seek the advice

of church elders there: "He clearly saw that his work was done in this place and that he had the Advice of the Ablest Elders in the Bay for what he did."[62]

Once Stone resigned for practical reasons, Goodwin was removed "from the Ruling Eldership–and consequently from the official headship of the Church." A new "moderator" was chosen for the Church "in accordance with the advice of Mr. Stone to lead the Church in his place." Stone was accused of interfering in church governance in the selection of a moderator. The minority immediately withdrew from "communion" with the Church. They argued Stone had resigned but continued to act as an officer of the Church by sending to them letters objecting to their actions along with other "brethren" of the Church.[63] Stone admitted he only "advised on it."[64]

On March 12, 1656, the minority called for a "mutually chosen" Council to consider their case. If this was not to be granted, then they asked to be released.[65] On March 20, the dissenting brethren asked that a Council comprised of representatives from the Connecticut and New Haven colonies be called. If this was not possible they asked for a second time to be released from the Hartford Church.[66] The Church approved the council composed of Elders from the Connecticut and New Haven Colonies. It met in Hartford on June 11, 1656. The Council substantially vindicated the position of the minority, and found the procedures of Mr. Stone and the church arbitrary.[67] Mr. Stone and his supporters "refused to submit to the decision of this Council." Later in May 1658 Stone told the Court as far as he was concerned its decisions were "canciled and of no force" and when the dissenters withdrew it was a "sin exceeding scandalous & dreadful."[68]

Mr. Stone was in Boston in August of 1656 and received support from five ministers who wrote a strongly worded letter to the dissenters. Inviting the dissenters to come to confer in Boston, "You are not ignorant of Satan's devices" and "the Church is under assault not by outsiders" but by "home bred contention."[69]

In September 1656 the dissenters received another letter from several churches in Massachusetts asking them for a second meeting, not to withdraw and said "the scandals of the best men afford materials" for Satan's best traps to ensnare them, perhaps, a reminder of Elder Goodwin's adultery scandal. "Other congregations, though diseased among us have been cured ... [do not let it be said] ... that you were the first which proved incurable."[70]

Although the Hartford Church accepted the suggestion for a second Council the issue had become so volatile it came before the General Court. In February 1656/57 the Court requested the Council held the previous June meet with the elders of the Bay in their proposed visit to Hartford. Captain Cullick, Mr. Steele, and Governor Webster (all withdrawers) and members of the General Court opposed the action. They withheld their vote and asked why the "Church at Hartford could not submit to the advice given, [in the first Council] ... as the dissenting brethren had done."[71] As for the response to the letter the "withdrawers" also declined.[72]

The quarrel continued unabated and included the churches in Boston. A second Council composed of ministers from Boston met in Hartford on April 6, 1657. All the documents in the case were put forward and included the findings of the Council of 1656, Mr. Stone's "refusal to let the Church take a vote on Mr. Wigglesworth's candidacy; his resignation of office; choice of moderator," etc.[73]

On May 6, 1657, the minister John Norton who had attended the Council reported the "lord had ... wrought the church at Hartford to a reunion."[74]

In June 1657 Stone attended a Synod in Massachusetts that lasted from June into August. The Synod approved the doctrine of the halfway covenant.[75] Perhaps the decision of the Synod in support of the halfway covenant and recent events in Boston gave Stone the fortitude to move forward on his original thinking on his role in the church. Although Stone accepted and supported the more liberal interpretation of the Synod for church membership (most of his church members did as well) he was strictly congregational concerning the independence of the churches. He believed no court, council or synod should interfere in what was a purely "internal matter" within his church. Stone and his supporters "proceeded to apply congregational discipline to the refractory members who wished to secede."[76]

On August 2, 1657, Stone sent an inflammatory letter from Boston with four propositions: the church must submit to every doctrine advocated by the teacher, no new officers without Stones assent, Stone could choose his own assistant and a physician be "procured" for Hartford.[77]

The letter acted as a "firebrand in the rubbish of the old quarrel." The minority denounced "Mr. Stones breaking of our pacification."[78] The flare-up reached Boston. Hull recorded in his diary, the breach at Hartford renewed, God leaving Mr. Stone, their officer, to some indiscretion, "as to neglect ... the celebration of the Lord's supper, and to ... discipline ... the formerly dissenting brethren; and Satan ... [by] ... Mr. Stone's absence some weeks ... to look unto their newly set bones and joints, they easily brake again. The dissenting brethren removed from the church."[79] After Stone's return from Boston there were "angry words" and one of the more serious complaints arising from this was Mr. Stone had refused to "administer the sacrament."[80] The tensions spread out into the surrounding communities. The dissenters issued a letter on November 11, 1657, to the churches in the Connecticut Colony explaining their reasons for their withdrawal and asked for their support.[81]

The majority in the church accused the dissenters of defaming Mr. Stone and the church at Hartford. They petitioned the General Court for relief and requested "help, and direction."[82] They addressed the court because they claimed the "brethren doe deny any relation to the Church" and the civil authorities were responsible for "peace, ordinances and rules of Christ in every Ch: within this jurisdiction."[83]

The dissenters applied to the Wethersfield Church for admission to the church. The ministers John Higginson of Guilford and John Davenport of the Colony of New Haven supported the acts of the dissenters up to the "act of withdrawing." Davenport recommended the dissenters "appeal to the old Council of Elders of 1656" to be received by the Wethersfield Church. He could see no reason why there should be any consequences for the dissenters "for separating from the Hartford Church."[84]

Tensions arising from this conflict had spread into other communities affecting other churches. On March 11, 1658, the court issued a notice stating "no ministry or church" be established when there is a "settled and approved Minister of the place."[85] The court ordered the Church of Hartford to stop persecuting the dissenters and the dissenters stop attempting to join the Wethersfield Church or any other churches until the court could determine how to resolve the issue. The court proposed to meet with church Elders on March 24, 1658, in Hartford to receive advice about the current troubles of the church at Hartford.[86]

Meanwhile, Stone now reached a level of arrogance the withdrawers could not abide. On May 20, 1658, Stone petitioned the court with six overly hostile and threatening propositions and concluded the controversy "between the Church of Christ at Hartford and the withdrawing persons" is an internal matter and should not be determined by any other church.[87]

Meanwhile, William Goodwin and Captain Cullick were in Boston petitioning the General Court of Massachusetts "with several others of the colony of Connecticut … [to] … remove themselves and their families" to Massachusetts. On May 25, 1658, the Massachusetts Court gave them permission to leave.[88]

On August 18, 1658, the Connecticut Court ordered a hearing to resolve the differences between the two groups. The parties were ordered to meet in Hartford on September 17, 1658.[89] No Council met in the fall or spring. On March 9, 1659, the court recognized the "troubles and distance twixt the Church at Hartford and the withdrawn party … ordered … a Council to be called."[90]

None of the churches in Massachusetts contacted by the court supported the interference on its part. The churches at Boston and Roxbury wrote because neither party from the Hartford Church had contacted them, and we do not see how the council would have "any decisive power in the Lord."[91]

There was no Council meeting in June 1659. There was a Council called in Massachusetts and held from June 15, 1659, to August 19, 1659, composed of ministers from nine Massachusetts churches and attended by both parties. The parties received the sentence of the Council on September 26, 1659. Stone was "mildly censured" for his "non-administration of the Lord's Supper." It said he had been unreasonable for his quick "Dismission ... after the pacification" and it found much evidence of his "rigid handling of divers Brethren." Church members who supported Stone were found to share some blame as well.[92]

The Council found the withdrawers guilty of "breaking the pacification" and attempting to tear themselves away from the church in Hartford by creating a schism. It softened the finding however, saying they were led down this path due to a mistake originating from an act by the Council at Hartford held in June 1656 "enabling them." Finally the Council declared the withdrawers were still members of the Hartford Church and could either remove themselves to another location or to another church. However, those remaining in Hartford had to remain in the church and could not establish another church there.[93]

What probably led to the "pacification" and ready acceptance of the recommendations of the Council in Massachusetts in 1659 was the fact the withdrawers on April 18, 1659, had already signed an Act of Engagement to remove themselves from Connecticut to Massachusetts. Five men were selected to go to the "foresaid plantation" and lay out home lots in what would become Hadley, Massachusetts. Their leaders, William Goodwin and John Webster, quickly moved to Hadley after the Council along with a significant number of prominent earlier settlers of Hartford.[94]

The most "baffling" aspect of the controversy was undoubtedly the "personal element." Stone "held high views of the prerogatives of his office" and his conception of ministerial authority belonged to an earlier period in his education in England. It is difficult to assess who was more correct in this conflict. Walker concluded the "general weight of right and justice was with the defeated and emigrating minority."[95] Nevertheless, according to one historian, the actions of the court on March 11, 1657–58, that enjoined the "withdrawers from joining with any other Church" left the "withdrawers in a predicament" that for our purposes drove some of the best men from Hartford.[96]

Following what appeared to be a "pacification" in Hartford, Hull wrote in his diary the Council had settled the matter of the Hartford Church "to the very good satisfaction unto both parties" but no sooner had "God blessed us with this sweet peace, but he tried us with other troubles. Sundry Quakers came into town, boldly and presumptuously resolving to outvie the authority of the country." Another contemporary wrote by 1659 Quaker opinions were being "vented up and down the Country" disturbing the peace and spreading heretical ideas.[97]

But there was also another religious conflict coming to a resolution with moderate congregationalism, which advocated more open baptism, a more authoritative clergy and less stringent rules for admitting members, a conflict that had brewed in the Hartford Church for nearly ten years. This conflict between the traditionalist or conservative Congregationalists and moderates was also leading to anti-clericalism in the community. The court as we saw attempted to remedy the situation and support the moderates by "forbidding dissident laymen from withdrawing from church fellowship." However, there was great opposition to this court interference and the moderates like Samuel Stone "were blocked at every turn."[98] The result of this Congregationalist conflict coupled with the rising tide of Presbyterianism was likely another factor in the willingness of three Congregationalist ministers, Samuel Stone, John Whiting and Samuel Hooker, to actively participate in the coming witch hunt in Hartford.

Following the resolution in 1659 various members of the community now looked for a cause for not only the discord that had come to their community but the continuing forces that jeopardized its peace and welfare. The conflict between the moderate Congregationalists the conservative Congregationalists and the rising power of the Presbyterians led to more conflict in the Connecticut River Valley. For example, the founding of the Second Congregational Church in Hartford in 1669 six years after Stone's death was led by Stone's minister, the Reverend John Whiting, by now a more conservative Congregationalist. The new church was founded in opposition to the Presbyterian influence of Joseph Haynes, who took Samuel Stone's place in the Hartford Church in 1663.[99]

The discord both local and that emanating from the England had continued to haunt the New England colonies throughout the 1650s. Stone's insistence on independent (but a more moderate) congregationalism was likely because he and other ministers saw themselves and their churches under new assaults. "[Massachusetts] had just escaped from disruption at the hands of Presbyterian malcontents, [now] … it was threatened by a horde of Quakers" and would soon be threatened by "Anglicanism." What was seen as a final blow in Connecticut was the return of Charles II to the English throne. The Connecticut and New Haven colonies were now threatened with questions concerning the legal ownership and rights to land, the unwanted thrust toward religious diversity (except Catholicism), the consequences for the New England clergy of the Act of Uniformity and the King restored to power with a new threat to the Connecticut colonies for harboring his father's killers.[100]

# 11

# "The Glory is departed, & Evill come upon the people of God"

## Governance and Property Rights Questioned in the Connecticut Colonies

Although the Connecticut towns of Hartford, Windsor, Farmington, Wethersfield and New Haven would appear to have been isolated at the time, they were not and received regular news from England. Events occurring in England had a critical impact on the general climate of opinion and unease contributed to a renewal of witchcraft accusations, trials and executions. The witchcraft hysteria broke out in Wethersfield, Farmington, and Hartford.

Contributing factors to the general anxiety and unease in the Connecticut colonies included the restoration of Charles II in 1660 to the English throne. With the death of Cromwell in 1658 and the restoration of Charles II "most New Englanders were distressed by this turn of events." The ministers and elites in New England expected Cromwell to usher in a new and more "godly age" in the three kingdoms and the colonies.[1] In addition, under Cromwell the colonies had been left to govern themselves. With the ascension of Charles II the elites in Connecticut realized they had settled lands without royal authority and no official charters. The only document Connecticut colonists could point to was the Warwick Patent but "it was not clear if the charter permitted more settlement of the land" and it was highly doubted if it could "provide the basis for the creation of laws and operations of independent government."[2] Only Massachusetts held a royal patent. In effect, the colonists of New Haven, Connecticut, and Rhode Island, in the eyes of royal officials, were squatters and their "title to self-government highly suspect." John Winthrop, Jr., who had been elected governor of Connecticut in 1657 wanted to obtain "a settled constitutional government, political sovereignty and royal recognition for Connecticut."[3]

The Connecticut General Court proclaimed its allegiance to Charles II on May 14, 1661, and authorized Winthrop to go England to obtain a royal charter. Winthrop was empowered to petition for a charter that would incorporate Rhode Island, New Haven and the Dutch New Netherlands [specifically Long Island] into the Connecticut Colony.[4] Winthrop set off for England in July 1661 and reached London in September 1661. He found Charles II "willing to make large territorial grants in America and charter colony governments as long as he did not have to pay for their upkeep."[5]

Winthrop received the charter for Connecticut on May 10, 1662. It granted the Connecticut Colony "self-government and continued the existing political structure" while Connecticut officials had to "swear allegiance to the King and Connecticut law must to conform to English law." But it was the matter of the boundaries laid out in the charter where tensions arose, especially between the colonies of New Haven and Connecticut. The Connecticut magistrates received the charter in September 1662. They saw a charter that laid claim to half of Rhode Island, New Haven and Long Island. Meanwhile, in England, the Rhode Island Agent Dr. John Clarke forced a reexamination of the charter. This required Winthrop to remain in England for another year.[6]

The charter caused a bitter struggle between the New Haven Colony and the Connecticut Colony. In England, Winthrop attempted to block any efforts by New Haven agents to "petition for a separate royal charter." When he returned to Hartford he found "strong arm tactics" had been used by some towns to leave New Haven jurisdiction and join the Connecticut Colony.[7]

It was not only Connecticut officials who wanted a union with New Haven, but there were those under the jurisdiction of New Haven who wanted to get out from under its strict religious governance. Over the years this issue had led entire communities to rebel against its jurisdiction. The conservative New Haven Colony did not allow non-church members to vote. This rankled less strict settlers in outlying towns who believed as Englishmen they had the same rights as they had in England. For example, when John Brown was brought into court for drunkenness he and his father challenged the authority of the New Haven Court as not coming from "Charles the Seacond." Another example concerned Bray Rossiter and his son John Rossiter of Guilford, who were brought before the New Haven Court for refusing to pay rates and making offensive speeches against the laws and churches of New Haven Colony.[8] The contempt for authority was a common complaint in the New Haven courts.[9]

The resulting anxieties were felt not only in New Haven but in the Connecticut Colony as well and by the "end of 1663 the two colonies were nearly at war with each other."[10]

Although the Hartford witch hysteria had subsided by January of 1662/63 there is no doubt the time spent trying to obtain the charter then the controversies over the land and boundaries of the two colonies continued unresolved tensions between the two colonies and acted as an additional contributing factor to the anxiety in Hartford resulting from over a decade of internal church conflict.

## The Tale of the Regicides

A second factor contributing to the tensions not only in New Haven but in Hartford, too, was the arrival of the former regicide Judges Edward Whalley, with his son-in-law, Major-General William Goffe, two men who had "a hand in the execrable murder of the late King."[11] The two fugitives escaped to North America and landed at Boston on July 27, 1660. Information did not reach the Massachusetts Bay until November 1660 that Whalley and Goffe were not among those pardoned by parliament. Colonial leaders debated what was to be done with the two men. On February 22, 1661, the two men left Massachusetts.

The two wanted men arrived in New Haven on March 7, 1661, and stayed with John Davenport. News of the orders for their arrest arrived in New Haven shortly afterward. Whalley and Goffe remained in the New Haven area until May 1664. They finally settled in Hadley, Massachusetts, where they remained for the rest of their lives.[12]

The tension raised by hiding the two regicides in New Haven spilled over into the Connecticut Colony because the king's men were searching for them in all the colonies. A notice was received dated September 5, 1661, stating that a "diligent search hath been made for the said persons [Whalley and Goffe] in the several colonies." The notice warned the settlers if they did not comply they would be considered "enemies to public peace and welfare of the United Colonies" and be punished accordingly.[13]

When the two regicides fled to New Haven they sought refuge with Governor William Leete of New Haven. When the arrest orders arrived in New Haven this put the governor in an awkward position, especially as Winthrop was preparing to sail to England to obtain a charter from the king. It was in this context that Davenport wrote Winthrop to request New Haven's interests be well represented in England. Nevertheless, before Winthrop sailed in July to England, New Haven still had not acknowledged Charles II as sovereign and did not do so until August 21, 1661.[14]

The Royal Commissioners noted "his majesty's probable resentment" at the lack of cooperation of the "magistrates of New Haven" and that they "knew all the time where the colonels were." The lack of support did not go well back in England. Letters were later sent by Governor Leete and John Davenport offering excuses as to why the two colonels were not arrested in

New Haven.[15] The king's agents reported Whalley and Goffe were "harboured in the house of one Davenport, a minister of New Haven" and Governor Leete "knew as much."[16]

Governor Leete could hardly expect favorable treatment from Charles II for the New Haven Colony. The Colony was punished, as the new Charter incorporated New Haven into the Connecticut Colony. The union was much opposed by the followers of Davenport.[17]

While the New Haven Colony had resisted the king's agents when they arrived in Hartford on May 10, 1661, they met with Governor Winthrop, who was highly cooperative, and "promised a diligent search should be made after them which was afterward performed." Winthrop realized to obtain a charter from Charles II that resistance on this matter of such great importance to the king would only stiffen the king's resistance to Winthrop's goal of obtaining a charter with the terms outlined previously for Connecticut.[18] His actions should have been clear to Davenport and Leete. In February 1661/2, Winthrop wrote to Davenport about Goffe and Whalley, "There is noe more speech of those things that I can heere of."[19]

When Winthrop arrived in England in September 1661 there was good reason for residual resentment toward the Puritans and their supporters in New England. This resentment was tainted not only by New England's support of the two regicides but also the trial of Thomas Venner, a cooper and rebel who tried to lead a coup against Charles II in January 1661.

Venner moved to New England in 1637 and lived there for 22 years. He returned to England in 1657 and became the leader of a radical religious group, the Fifth Monarchists, in October 1660. On January 6, 1661, Venner led a rebellion in London on the anniversary of the "day the Regicides at Westminster passed their ordinance for the Trial of ... King Charles I." He led a second attempt on January 9, 1661, the anniversary of the date the king's trial was proclaimed. Venner was arrested along with his co-conspirators. More than 22 of the "king's men were slain and as many rebels." The rebels were indicted for high treason and murder. Thomas Venner was the first one called to the docket and when he was asked whether he was or was not guilty he gave a rambling discourse about "New England" which according to the account "made Old England smart having been the nursery and receptacle of sedition too long.... Gough [Goffe] and Whalley are there alive."[20]

Venner and a companion were both found guilty. For their punishment the two men were drawn and quartered, their quarters "set upon the four gates of the City, by the late executed Regicides, whose quarrel and revenge they had undertaken in this their fanatic attempt. Their heads were also set upon poles, next to some of the other regicides on London Bridge."[21] If the remains were not still on display the story of the trial and execution of these rebels with the connection to the regicides would have been told to Winthrop.

The situation concerning the regicides in the New England colonies was serious business in London. It undoubtedly had the same unsettling effect in the Connecticut Colony as the New Haven Colony. Given the deference shown in New Haven toward the "regicides," it is clear why Winthrop recognized New Haven had little chance of obtaining a charter for itself.

## Religious Turmoil in New England 1650s and Early 1660s

The religious turmoil in New England in the later 1650s and early 1660s can be attributed to decisions made in England, the Quaker invasion of New England and the Act of Uniformity passed in Parliament on May 19, 1662.[22] By the late 1650s New England was witnessing an invasion by Quakers who were confronting the ministers and elites throughout New England by challenging their religious authority. Unfortunately for the New England elites the Quakers at first appeared to be gaining some influence with Charles II.

Although the Act of Uniformity was not imposed in New England it affected thousands of ministers in England and there was great anxiety it might be imposed in New England as more controls over the government of New England were increasingly considered by the Council for Foreign Plantations.

It is understandable the Act of Uniformity and its possible imposition in New England, when coupled with the ongoing invasion of Quakers, was viewed by the clergy and the elites as another assault on all they held dear and all they had built. The people in New England saw the new king appearing to side with these Quakers, who to the "godly" in New England were "heretics" if not "witches."

## The Quaker Invasion in New England Threatens the Political and Clerical Elites

The height of the Quaker invasion in New England began in 1657 and led the authorities in Massachusetts, New Haven and Connecticut to pass harsh measures against them. To the authorities in New England, Quakers acted beyond all propriety and "showed no respect" for the civil or church authorities.[23] In Boston, Quakers who had arrived the previous year and were banished returned in the summer of 1657. John Hull, a Massachusetts colonial official, wrote, "they knew the law against any such seducers … and were severely whipped in the House of Correction."[24] Hull condemned Quakers as "uncivil in behavior, showing no respect to any, ready to censure and condemn all" and that they were disruptive of the churches and politics of the colony. Both the civil and church authorities were intolerant of these "seducers."

The authorities in Massachusetts at this time were so incensed by their actions and beliefs they believed they crossed the heresy boundary by actively inciting rebellion and what is more initially suspected them of being witches. This was not misguided on their part because in England during the 1650s accusations were "legion" that Quakers used "the power of witches to seduce others to their heresies."[25] However, afterward there is no evidence Quakers were considered witches in New England.

The first two Quaker women, Mary Fisher and Anne Austin, arrived in Boston and were seized by the authorities because according to Scripture, "rebellion is the sin of witchcraft." This was written in the Geneva Bible, Samuel 15:23, and therefore it was only logical to seize these two females not only as "cursed as heretics, Adamites, Blasphemers" but to look for an even more serious transgression and one that could be more harshly punished perhaps with less criticism from their co-religionists in England by suspecting them of being witches. Indeed the authorities in Massachusetts believed they were witches. And searched them for witches' marks.[26] The New England authorities rightly feared Quakers because initially they were not the "pacifistic, respectable, well educated, and contemplative" sect that "would later emerge ... behind the charismatic leadership of George Fox." This was at the beginning of the Quaker movement when it was "unorganized, enthusiastic, and millennial" comparable to the Diggers and Ranters in England.[27]

The threat was so fearsome that Massachusetts established a series of anti–Quaker laws in 1656, 1658 and 1659 while anti–Quaker laws were quickly enacted in Plymouth Colony, the New Haven Colony and the Connecticut Colony.[28] There was initially a uniformity of anti–Quaker laws as a result of the recommendation of the Commissioners of the United Colonies, who at their September session in 1656 on the suggestion of the "Governor and Magistrates of the Massachusetts Colony" recommended "all Quakers, Ranters and other notorious heretics be prohibited from coming into the Colonies" and if they do, they be "secured and removed out of all the jurisdictions."

The General Court held at Hartford on October 2, 1656, ordered no Quakers, Ranters, Adamites and other heretics be allowed in any of the jurisdictions in Connecticut. Magistrates and assistants were give the power "to send them to prison, for the securing of them until they can be conveniently sent out of their Jurisdiction" and no "Master of any vessel shall land such a Heretics but if they doe they shall be compelled to transport them again out of the Collony."[29] As a supplement to the law of October 2, 1656, the General

Court ordered on October 1, 1657, that no person within its jurisdiction shall "kepe Quaker books or manuscripts containing their errors, except teaching Elders" or they would incur a 10 shilling fine.[30]

The treatment of these early Quaker proselytizers was severe and harsh. Early Quaker writings show a range of punishment from banishment, imprisonment, starvation, whippings, disfigurement and death.[31] For example in the more religiously conservative colony of New Haven, John Rous, a Quaker, was imprisoned in June 1658. He wrote the New Haven court passed an "unjust sentence." He and a fellow Quaker were brought to the stocks where after the two prayed and "saluted each other in public" they told the executioner they would take the clothes off their own backs and they would give their backs to be "smitten." The executioner gave them "thirty-eight strips."[32]

At the same time it seemed in some places the Quakers relished the opportunity to challenge these "high priests" of New England. Humphrey Norton wrote that these priests only come to see these Quakers when they are "called before the Court." Those who dealt with them were the jailers, hangmen, governors and deputy governors but not their pastors or teachers.[33] However, it should be noted Quakers, unlike the Antinomians and Baptists, were not permitted to freely debate at "church meetings, in a synod or in a Court" because the other heretics were at least "residents, citizens and Church members." Quakers were strangers and "roaming vagrants." Their obnoxious behavior and insane ideas were "simply to exasperating for the Puritans who were simply unwilling to descend to their level of discussion." Where the Quakers believed their message was divinely inspired the Puritans saw it as pure blasphemy. However, in their overwrought preaching against the fervent proselytizers who appeared so earnest not unlike the other emotional religious expression of other dissenter groups, some out of "curiosity and interest in it ... became disciples" out of those very flocks where the most ardent anti–Quaker preaching was taking place.[34]

As we saw earlier, not everyone was afraid to take the Quakers on. Stone was willing to dispute two Quakers in the spring of 1658 even in the midst of his deeply divided Hartford Church. However, his failure to win the public dispute may have been a final straw for his enemies in the church as the withdrawers were negotiating and scouting for land in Hadley, Massachusetts, in the spring of 1658. This may have added to an already underlying tension contributing to the later flare-up of the "witch hysteria" in Hartford in 1662.[35]

One can readily imagine at the same time with Stone's troubled parishioners the sentiments of some of them similar to an event that happened a few years later in New Hampshire. A group of Quakers arrived at an Inn near Dover, New Hampshire, in 1662. The people there attempted to dispute with these Quakers. They could not seem to confound them so they ran to their minister and wanted him to dispute the Quakers. The minister's wife asked them, "Which do you like best, my Husband or the Quakers?" One of them said, "We shall tell you that after your Husband have been with them." This was of course what the authorities and ministers in the 1650s feared.[36]

Quakers were generally not permitted to debate freely with ministers, but the highly charged sermons against the Quakers in contrast to the earnestness of these itinerant preachers attracted followers, for they were not unlike some of the other radical religious groups that had been making inroads among others dissatisfied with the strictness of the congregational church messages coming from the pulpits of New England.[37]

Connecticut did not follow the lead of Massachusetts' harsher anti–Quaker laws in 1658 that included the death penalty. Additionally, the treatment of Quakers in Hartford continued to be less harsh than in the New Haven Colony.[38]

Nevertheless, Quakers coming to Hartford were not given free license to preach. Following Copeland and Rous' visit in 1658, two Quaker women, Sarah Gibbons and Dorothy Waugh, were "called to Hartford." They were "imprisoned in jail for several days" and some of their clothes were sold to pay their jail fees. They were released and told to leave.[39] Even by 1676 Quakers and Baptists were still unwelcome persons in Connecticut. One Quaker who came first to New London described how when he tried to meet with some Baptists, the "Constable and other officers" forcibly broke up the meeting, "abusing them," but suggested there was some sympathy among the common people for them and wrote, the "sober people were offended at them." When he arrived in Hartford he delivered a message in the first Congregational Church (Samuel Stone's old church) and "afterward many people stayed and I had good service among them." However, in the newly established and more conservative Second Congregational Church he was arrested and eventually released but he had set the "town talking of Religion."[40]

The antipathy of the more established religious groups like the Congregationalists and Presbyterians toward even the more moderate Baptists was demonstrated by a conversation the Quaker William Edmundson had with the Baptist minister John Rogers, who led a flock in New London. He had been called to Hartford because his father-in-law, Mathew Griswold of Lyme, Connecticut, a devout "Presbyterian" and elder, wanted his daughter Elizabeth to be divorced from Rogers since he had become a Baptist—even though he and Elizabeth had two sons. The General Assembly granted the divorce on October 21, 1676.[41]

By 1660 the threat and antagonism of the Quakers to the authority of the Congregationalist ministers and civil authorities reached its peak. The Quakers appeared to be launching an assault on Massachusetts. The time had come to put into practice the new death penalty law in Massachusetts.

Hull wrote in 1656 that the crime of Mary Fisher and Ann Austin, the two Quakers from Barbados, was their "opposing the ministry" and their "breeding contempt in the people for the Magistracy because they were uncivil in their behavior." Following the first two Quakers, soon after eight more followed and were forced to leave. While this Quaker invasion was going on, the breach in the Hartford Church was a colony wide concern. It seemed to the authorities in the colonies they were under assault. By the spring of 1657 it appeared reconciliation in the Hartford Church had occurred. But in 1659 the more conservative church members withdrew from the Church in Hartford, settling the matter. However, following what appeared to be a return to peace in the colonies, several Quakers came into Boston to "compete with the authority of the country." Three of these Quakers had previously been banished not to return "on pain of death": William Robinson, Marmaduke Stevenson and Mary Dyer (the friend of the now deceased Anne Hutchinson) who had become a Quaker. The three were tried by the General Court of Massachusetts and the sentence was death. Hull wrote, "And well they deserved it." On October 27, 1659, the two men were executed. Mary Dyer as a result of a petition of her friends was reprieved providing she left the jurisdiction within two days.[42]

On December 8, 1659, a day of thanksgiving was proclaimed. It is interesting that the day was marked by the colony in thanks for a good harvest, the general health of the country and specifically "the preservation from the destructive desires of that pestilential company the Quakers" and following that the "healing of the great breach at Hartford."[43] However, this more peaceful state of affairs did not last long because ships from England in 1659–60 (January to March) did not bring good news. There were reports Quakers were increasing in numbers in England and there were "all manner of heresies." Parliament was in an unsettled state (Parliament had been dissolved) and there were many "insurrections and discontents in the people … as if the reformation by so much war and blood should be given up again to heretics and Papists."[44]

Meanwhile, Mary Dyer, who had been reprieved, returned to Boston in May 1660 and was seized and hanged on June 1, 1660. These executions did not stop the Quaker invasion the colonial authorities feared. By early 1661 two Quakers were under the sentence of death and twenty-seven others were awaiting trial. However, with the re-establishment of the Stuart monarchy there was no longer a sympathetic Puritan ruler in England or a civil war to distract the authorities. England had a new monarch, Charles II, son of the beheaded Charles I, who expected the colonies to abide by English law. An English Bay Colony Quaker, Samuel Shattuck was sent to the Massachusetts Bay Colony to stop the "persecution and torture" of the Quakers and to allow those Quakers in prison to return to England.

In June 1661, John Davenport wrote there is "noe sect soe much favored as the quakers."[45] Indeed, petitions concerning the laws passed in Massachusetts and the treatment of the Quakers were turned over to the Council for Foreign Plantations. On September 9, 1661, the king ordered Governor Endecott of Massachusetts and all the governors of the other colonies to return to England any imprisoned Quakers under a variety of penalties including death "to send said persons whether condemned or imprisoned to England ... to the end such course may be taken with them here as shall be agreeable to our laws and their demerits."[46]

The clergy and officials in New England were mindful of the treatment of their co-religionists in England and feared if they continued to abuse and execute the Quakers the new government would punish them. Aware of government interest in the disposition of the colonies, the Massachusetts Bay replied in a cautious and diplomatic manner they wished "to enjoy the same liberties and privileges in civil and ecclesiastical matters as they have enjoyed for thirty years past." On November 27, 1661, they received the following reply, "that his majesty be the least not offended, it is ordered that the execution of the laws in force against the Quakers so far as they respect corporal punishment or death, be suspended until further order."[47]

Soon after the king changed his mind concerning the Quakers and wrote their principles were "basically incompatible with the existence of any kind of State." Even in England he had found it "necessary to make sharp laws against them." In Massachusetts the execution of Quakers was stopped but in its place the authorities passed the Cart and Whip Act of 1662. Now Quakers could be tied to a cart and whipped out of town.[48]

In 1664 the king sent a Royal Commission to re-establish greater control of the colonies. The colonial authorities realized in order to keep some semblance of autonomy they had to tread lightly on what they considered their local prerogatives, including their persecution of Quakers.

In 1663 the "spiritual leader of the persecution of the Quakers" in Massachusetts, the minister John Norton, died. Two years later Governor John Endicott, the most active government official in the persecution of the Quakers, died. However, as we saw in the example in Hartford in 1676, we are reminded for officials and clergy anti–Quakerism was not dormant and could rear its ugly head whenever Quakers attempted to proselytize and criticize the congregational ministers and the local authorities.

## The Act of Uniformity

The Act of Uniformity was an Act of the Parliament that prescribed the form of public prayers, administration of sacraments, and other rites of the

Established Church of England. Adherence to this act was required in order to hold any office in government or the church. Over 2,000 clergymen in England refused to take the oath and were expelled from the Church of England.[49] The ministers who refused to support this act had no means of support and were under threat of arrest. On October 8, 1662, John Davenport received the following news in a letter from a minister in England: "These are sad ths: soe that all Publicke Assemblies are utterly broken, & those who meete in private are watched & many of them haled off to prison, & how soon I know not."[50] On their income, "Hundreds of able ministers with their Wives and Children had neither House nor Bread."[51] Davenport also reported in August 1662: "Sad newes ex England, all good ministrs put out, & and the heighth of wickedness in church & state broken in."[52] On November 22, 1661, concerning non-conformists it was ordered "all ministers holding unlawful assemblies on the pretence of religion and the neglecting of the Divine service, as thereby a bloody and horrible design has been contrived for the subversion of the government."[53]

Davenport was concerned the same order might be applied in New England. And as for his friends in England, they had great doubt as to what to do and were "much in the dark whether to ffly or stand & abide the issue." He suspected there might be changes in the government and affairs at Connecticut and they might not "escape the same."[54] In July 1662 he wrote to Goffe, "There are great thoughts of heart (among the Godly) about us, what imposicions wilbe laid upon N[ew] E[ngland]."[55] There was fear a new governor, Sir Robert Carr, would be appointed ("a ranck Papist)" and the godly thought there would be impositions placed on New England that would include an Episcopal Government (the Act of Uniformity) proclaimed by Parliament and high taxes. Davenport concluded, "The King is engaged to the utmost to promote Episcopacy."[56]

Davenport was not the only one questioning what conditions the "godly" would find in New England. John Winthrop, Jr., received the following plea in a letter: "congregational men ... rendered odeus to the generality of the nation.... I entreat your advice ... concerning friends here ... if tymes press them to transport their families to New England."[57]

Davenport communicated regularly with other members of the New England elite on the news from England. On April 14, 1662, he wrote, "You will also receive from me ... bookes of the newes which when you have perused ... they may be sent to Mr. Stone or Mr. Willis [Wyllys] for freindes there to see."[58] A letter from Mr. Davenport dated June 2, 1662, contained the following: "A briefe Relation of some newes ffrom England: 1: That many of the people of god are imprissoned, very sad times feared to be approaching...."[59]

Davenport summed up the attitude of many of the "godly" in New England and added other issues that caused considerable anxiety during the few years leading up to the witchcraft hysteria in Hartford. He wrote of his English friends, "the Glory is departed, & evill come upon the people of God, to the utmost. The rage of the Enemie, & the sufferings of the Saints increase mor and more." And of the problems in Connecticut:

> And beside the Devisions in the churches here, with there strange Degeneratings From the pure wais of the Lord, either through feare, coldness of hart, or Luke-warmnes, bewitchings of the world, or other weaknesses, or through wicked designes of some; which things I say threaten the like missery heere.[60]

The invasion of the Quakers and Royal sympathy toward them, when coupled with the Act of Uniformity in 1662 and its consequences, undoubtedly contributed to more unease among the clergy and "godly" in New Haven and Hartford. They saw the likelihood of all they had achieved being dismantled by the return of Charles II to the throne and his policies undermining their religious independence and authority.

The clergy in the Connecticut river towns may have seen the rising tide of witch hysteria as an opportunity to reassert their spiritual authority in a community that had spent nearly a decade questioning that authority and now a community, if not a colony, under the threat of royal interference both from civil and ecclesiastical authorities in England. These threats might lead people to ask who was behind this constant turmoil and what had they done to deserve this?

If the colonial authorities over the years had to tread lightly in their persecution of heretics there was still one acceptable group they were able blame and persecute for all their troubles during this time. It was a group they could identify from within and who, according to the laws of England and the colonies, had no protection and if identified could be tried and if convicted of witchcraft hanged.

The witch hysteria in Hartford was based on a number of domestic and foreign activities that produced much anxiety in the community. Witchcraft accusations had never gone away during the 1650s and, as we saw in the Connecticut Colony witchcraft trials, led to a series of executions. Witch accusations also occurred in the New Haven Colony but due to the indirect influence of Winthrop, the witchcraft trials there did not end in the execution of the accused.

## Elizabeth Garlick and Goody Davis

John Winthrop, Jr., was elected governor of the Connecticut Colony in May 1657. Once in office he was in a position to directly influence the outcome of any witch trials that came before him.[61]

His first witch trial as governor occurred in the following year and concerned Elizabeth Garlick of East Hampton, Long Island. The East Hampton settlers were originally a group of nine settlers from Maidstone, ten miles from the port of Kent, England. The group first settled in Lynn, Massachusetts.[62] From there they moved to the south fork of Long Island in 1648. East Hampton was one of three villages settled in the 1640s: South Hampton, Southold and the last, and most isolated, was East Hampton. They did not have a patent or a royal charter and purchased their land from the local native population.[63]

The government was local and minimal. The towns needed protection from the Dutch. South Hampton had earlier joined the Connecticut Colony and Southold the New Haven Colony. East Hampton held out until 1658 and accepted the jurisdiction of the Connecticut Colony. In 1658 there were about 20 families in East Hampton with a population of less than 200 persons.

The most important person in East Hampton was Lion Gardiner. He was also known and respected in Connecticut. Originally hired by the Connecticut Company in 1635 to oversee construction of fortifications in the new colony, he was also a hero of the Pequot War, during which he commanded the fort at Saybrook at the mouth of the Connecticut River (1636–1637). East Hampton likely joined with the Connecticut Colony because of Gardiner's respect for the newly elected governor, John Winthrop, Jr., as a man he could do business with. Another settler had been impressed with Winthrop's medical skills.[64]

A second reason for joining with the Connecticut Colony had to do with concern over the town's legal jurisdiction in deciding a capital case. The town was bitterly divided over the behavior of Elizabeth Garlick, accused of witchcraft. There were those in East Hampton who thought her guilty while others believed her innocent. Because witchcraft was a capital offense town leaders did not think they had the authority to try a witchcraft case. They "turned to the Connecticut courts and brought Elizabeth Garlick to Hartford along with the witnesses against her."[65]

Suspicions of witchcraft occurred soon after Goodwife Garlick moved to Gardiner's Island where she lived prior to her move to East Hampton. The island was located in the Long Island Sound and first settled by Lion Gardiner and his family, it became known as Gardiner's Island. In 1653 Gardiner moved his family from the island to East Hampton.[66]

One woman, Goody Davis, one of Goody Garlick's chief accusers, said when she heard Elizabeth Garlick was planning to move to East Hampton she was concerned the town "would repent it as well as they had done at the Iland" because of events that occurred there. First there was a child's death, Lion Gardiner's ox broke its leg, a black child died "in a strange manner," a man died and a seemingly healthy sow after giving birth to a litter of pigs died. To determine if the pig was bewitched and who the witch was, "they Did burne yt sowes stale and presently Goody Garlicke did come in." This confirmed their suspicions that Goody Garlick was a witch.[67]

Goody Burdsill recounted that Goody Simons and Goody Davis were at Goody Davis' home waiting for Goody Bishop to return with "dock weed" from Goody Garlick to calm Goody Simon's fits. Goody Garlick, later that day, came into the Davis house and saw how "pretty" her child looked. After she had spoken she said, "the child is not well for it groaneth." Goody Davis took her child from Garlick. Garlick said she "saw death in the face of it and her child sickned … and lay 5 daies and 5 nights and never opened the eyes nor cried until it died."[68]

Goody Garlick was obviously a local healer who the townspeople resorted to when they were ill. It seems Goody Simon was suspicious of Garlick's herbal medicines and she would later play a pivotal accusatory role in attempting to provide evidence of Garlick's involvement in the bewitchment and death of Elizabeth Howell. All the women involved had formerly lived on Gardiner's Island and carried their suspicions about Goody Garlick with them to East Hampton.[69]

In addition, Goody Davis said Goody Stratton had earlier received a request for breast milk from Elizabeth Garlick. Goody Stratton's milk dried up and her child died. Goody Davis said Garlick asked her for breast milk too; afterward her breast milk dried up and her child died. She wished that hers and Goody Stratton's [child] both "were not bewicht for they were taken both much alike."[70]

Goody Davis was convinced Goody Garlick killed her infant child by use of the evil eye. Goody Davis was no stranger to bad luck. She was widowed twice and her current husband, Fulke Davis, was a womanizer. In addition, in June 1654 he and three other men were accused of public "masturbation." After an extended examination, serious debate and consultation with their Saybrook Connecticut neighbors, the Townsmen, it was determined the offence was not worthy of loss of life or limb. Fulke Davis was ordered to "be placed in a Pillory and receive corporal punishment" while the others were whipped.[71]

However, Davis's accusation that Garlick had killed her child was contradicted by Goodman Jeremiah Vaile and his wife, who testified they heard from Gardiner on the Island "that Goody Davis should speake as if her child were bewicht…. Goody Davis had taken an Indian child to nurse and for lucre of A little wompon had merely starved her owne child."[72] Lion Gardiner doubted the truthfulness of Davis' accusations and his secondhand testimony may have cast doubt on her other accusations. The jury later learned why she remained friendly with Garlick after all her suspicions. She said "she were as good please the Devill as anger him" and of Goody Garlick "she was a wich if there were any in New England."[73]

Perhaps if the evidence in the town had only been gossip Goody Garlick would not have been taken to court. However, the townsmen found themselves in a situation forcing them to take action because of the bewitchment and death of Elizabeth Howell, the recently married sixteen-year-old daughter of Lion Gardiner.

## The Bewitching to Death of Elizabeth Howell

On February 4, 1648, Samuel Parsons came to visit his friend Arthur Howell. He found Elizabeth Howell, his wife, at home alone. She complained to Samuel of a chill and invited Samuel to warm himself by the fire. He soon left and returned later. He found Elizabeth in worse condition. Her husband arrived home with William Russell, a friend. She complained about a fever. Arthur Howell convinced her to first suckle their infant child then to go to sleep.

After the child was removed she cried out, "a witch a witch you have come to torter me because I spoke 2 or 3 words against you." Arthur and his friends were all "afrighted at her being taken sudenly in soe strange a maner." They sent for Mr. Gardiner, hoping Betty was not bewitched. After Gardiner arrived she continued to cry out about a witch but did not name her tormentor. She was asked what the witch did and said there was "a black thinge at the beddes fete" and tried "to strike at it."[74]

The next morning Lion Gardiner went to his daughter and saw her condition had worsened. Mrs. Gardiner, sick herself, asked her husband about Betty's condition. Lion told her she had a fever and went to visit her again. His wife, after a few attempts to raise herself from her sickbed, was finally able to get to her daughter's bedside. Betty told her mother, "I am bewicht." Her mother suggested she might have been dreaming. She replied she was not dreaming. Her mother asked her who she saw. She said, "Goodie Garlicke in ye further corner and a black thing [familiar] at ye hither corner both at feete of ye bedd." Her mother "charged her yt she should not tell her husband nor noe liveinge soule and ... [she] said your husband will tell. [Crossed out in the original]."[75]

Goodie Garlick was the specter and Elizabeth was the only one in the room that saw her. It was Garlick who bewitched her. Goodwife Simons, no friend of Goodie Garlick, was called to attend Betty Howell day and night. She slept in the bed with her. Her deposition provided evidence confirmed by Arthur Howell and Goodwife Birdsill.[76] The three stood by the bed while Elizabeth asked three times to send for Joshua and Goody Garlick. She said she could tear Goody Garlick to pieces. Simons asked her why she wanted Garlick. Elizabeth said when her husband had worked at Joshua Garlick's during threshing time and she went to fetch him home, Garlick had laughed and "jeered" at her and said, "Oh you are a prettie one," the latter suggesting she believed Garlick had given her the evil eye. Elizabeth then cried out she was a "duble tounged woman ... did you not see her last night stand by the bedside readie to pull me in peeces and she prickt me with pins she prickt with pins and soe a 3rd time."[77]

Other strange occurrences were related by those attending Betty. The first evening while Goody Simons and Betty Howell were asleep Arthur Howell and his friend Samuel Parsons sat in the room keeping watch. The two men heard scratching noises, lit a candle, and were puzzled because the two women appeared to be fast asleep. On the immediate Sabbath after Elizabeth's illness, Arthur Howell and William Russell reported a "Doleful noyse"

A bewitched woman vomiting. Note the pins and other objects. The image is from *The History of Witches and Wizards: Giving a True Account of All Their Tryals in England, Scotland, Swedeland, France, and New England*, T. Norris, London, 1720 (courtesy Wellcome Library, London).

like a large stone being thrown on smaller stones coming from the fireplace. They were both "affrighted by the noyse."[78] (As we have seen, the English were suspicious of the fireplace in the house as an entry way for witches and demons.)[79]

Finally the jurors in Hartford would have heard the testimony of Goody Birdsill and Goody Edwards, who brought up the matter of the strange pin that appeared in Elizabeth's mouth. Goody Edwards said she saw a pin pulled out of Mrs. Howell's mouth and to her best remembrance Mary Gardiner said there was "noe such pin in the house." A few moments before the pin was taken out and given to Goody Simons, Goody Edwards attempted to use counter-magic to help Mrs. Howell. She "did put the handle of a knife into her mouth and gave her "solitt [salt] oyle and sugar and did loke into her mouth and she Did not see nor diserne any pin there."[80]

The removal of the strange pin did not help. Betty died that Sabbath evening having named Goody Garlick as the witch who had tormented and bewitched her. Her family, friends and neighbors had not only witnessed strange and otherworldly events casting suspicion on Goody Garlick but remembered past events that confirmed her guilt in their eyes, including that she kept a black cat, an obvious familiar in their eyes.[81]

It would have been common, according to John Demos, for "the family to have kept a vigil by her bedside; while neighbors come and go." The minister would have come to "lead prayers for her soul." Important in her case as she was dying under suspicious circumstances and unfortunately for her family, the Puritan view was that in order for her to have been bewitched she had to have been open to bewitchment so suspicion fell on Betty. In short, it was her own fault. She undoubtedly struggled through the evening and died later that night. There would have been a "short funeral, and burial the following day."[82]

Given the strange events that had transpired and Garlick's reputation, Arthur, his neighbors and friends were sure Betty had died from "unnatural" causes and were prepared to seek redress. Meanwhile, on March 16, 1657/58, Joshua Garlick attempted to defend his wife and entered an "Action of Defamation upon the case against the wife of fulk Davis." Undoubtedly, he was attempting to keep the charges in the local East Hampton Court to more easily clear his wife's name as defamation was not a felony and hardly carried the death penalty. However, Arthur Howell and his neighbors were not about to let Goody Garlick get away with her crime of bewitching and killing Arthur's wife on a lesser and unrelated charge. On March 19, 1657/58, the townsmen agreed to send representatives to bring the town under the government of Connecticut and "to carie upp Goodwife Garlick yt she may be delivered up unto the Authoritie there for the triall of the cause witchcraft which she is suspected for."[83]

## The Trial of Elizabeth Garlick in Hartford on May 5, 1658

The Court of Magistrates of Hartford took up the Garlick case on May 5, 1658. The magistrates of the court included Governor John Winthrop, Jr., deputy governor John Welles, Mr. John Webster, Mr. John Cullick, Mr. Henry Clark, Mr. Samuel Wyllys and John Talcott. Four of the magistrates had been involved in other witch trials that ended in execution. Henry Clark had participated in the Bassett trial in Stratford.[84] Looking at the following indictment and knowing the contents of the depositions previously discussed it would appear that things looked bleak for Goodwife Garlick and that she would likely be found guilty and hanged, given the previous decisions of the court on more slender evidence and the common belief that for someone to "rid the community of persons who were believed to hold conversation with familiar spirits and to be under the direct influence of the devil, was regarded as a righteous act, according to the Law of Moses."[85]

The indictment for Goodwife Garlick read:

> Elizabeth Garlick the wife of Joshua Garlick of East Hampton, that not having the feare of God before thine eyes thou hast entertained familiarity with Sathan the great enemy of God and mankind and by his helpe since the yeare 1650 hath done works above the course of nature to the losse of lives of severall persons (wjth severall other sorceries) and in perticular the wife of Arthur Howell of East Hampton, for which both according to the lawes of God and the established law of this Comon wealth thou deserves to dye.

However, the jury did not find Elizabeth guilty according to the indictment. Instead Joshua Garlick and Elizabeth were ordered by the court to pay thirty pounds as surety for their good behavior toward all people in the Connecticut Colony jurisdiction and to appear later in East Hampton Court September or October to ensure their good behavior.[86]

Woodward has noted that the reason Elizabeth Garlick was not convicted and hanged was because of the influence of John Winthrop. In witchcraft cases the "influence of magistrates was paramount, even though a separate jury rendered the actual verdict. The magistrates collected evidence, conducted the prosecution, interrogated witnesses, poked holes in testimony, and generally used their privileged position to shape the jury's understanding of the case. If the jury subsequently returned a verdict with which the magistrates disagreed, they could even overturn it."[87]

Winthrop was skeptical about "witchcraft accusations." His understanding of the occult was different from the other magistrates because he studied it. As governor he had the opportunity to "set the direction for the magistrates to follow." Besides, having been long courted by the colony he was engaged in a "honeymoon period" and "enjoyed both extraordinary influence and immunity from criticism." As chief magistrate he could use his knowledge of the occult and question the witnesses to subvert their testimony and diminish their credibility in front of the jury.[88]

In addition to the esteem in which Winthrop was held and apropos of the trial Winthrop had personal dealings with Lion Gardiner. He had used the services of Joshua Garlick a number of times to carry messages and goods between Gardiner and Winthrop.[89] In addition, Goody Garlick, although not one of Winthrop's distributor of potions, was a healer in her own right and provided the dock weed to help Goody Simons overcome her fits.[90]

Later, Winthrop wrote to the authorities in East Hampton and praised them for "searching into that case, according to such just suspicion as appeared" of Elizabeth Garlick but after a legal trial there was "not sufficient evidence to find her guilty." He advised the town authorities, according to the court, that they should "cary neighbourly and peaceably, without just offence, to Jos. Garlick and his wife … they should do like to you." Joshua Garlick was ordered to pay for his wife's upkeep, and the town was ordered to bear the cost of any charges at home, travel, transportation and messengers for the trial. The cost of the trial itself was borne by the Connecticut Colony.[91]

Witch trials, as well as other trials during the 17th century, were public spectacles. A witch trial and hanging was even more exciting for the audience because it had the added *frisson* of confirming the reality of Satan in the lives of the community and confirming their belief system. For the common people proof was offered of the malicious acts and bad luck experienced that stemmed from a neighbor who they were certain was a witch. If this evil person could be eliminated then all would be well again in their lives. In the past things had gone well in the Court at Hartford: when a suspected witch was accused the legal system worked for them. Previously, Governor Haynes had made known the need for the "harsh treatment of witches" and had probably like Winthrop used his influence in "earlier witchcraft proceedings" but to obtain a conviction instead of a not guilty but suspicious like Winthrop.[92]

However, this most recent witch trial had been anything but satisfying, especially to true believers. They heard the testimony of various witnesses. The young victim, Elizabeth "Betty" Howell, cried out that her tormentor was Garlick. Garlick had a familiar. When Betty saw Garlick's specter in her room she "turned a psalme and screked out severall times together very grievously and uppon yt cried out a witch a witch: now you come to torter mee." Young Betty had cried out this and other things with such "vehemencie" and named Goody Garlick as her tormentor before she died. There could be no doubt Garlick was a witch. But their new governor, a healer and alchemist (suspicious practices), had influenced the jury. What this meant to some was it would be difficult to bring a case against a neighbor suspected of witchcraft while Winthrop was in office and worse to obtain a conviction that would permanently eliminate the threat from the community.

Some older colonists and ministers like Stone and Warham would have remembered the English government's earlier campaign to inhibit witch accusations and trials in the 1630s, prior to the English Civil War. The common people would have resented their inability to rid themselves of malicious and evil neighbors ready to do them harm while some elites and ministers would have resented this interference in rooting out Satan's agents in these especially dire times in the Connecticut Colony.

Doubtless there were many in the community confused as to why a woman with so much evidence against her was not convicted and executed as a witch. Instead Goody Garlick was to be treated in a neighborly manner and she for her part should "conform to community expectations" or there would be consequences.[93]

## Nicholas and Margaret Jennings, Suspected Witches, September 5, 1661

In another witchcraft case on September 5, 1661 (shortly after Winthrop left for England), Nicholas and Margaret Jennings were accused of witchcraft. The indictment accused them of causing the deaths of several people, especially the death of Reynold Marvin's wife and the child of Balthazar de Wolf, as well as other sorceries. The jury stated the majority found Nicholas guilty and the rest "strongly suspect it that he is guilty" and likewise for Margaret: some of the jury found her guilty and the rest "strongly suspect her to be Guilty." They were not convicted nor were they completely cleared. They returned to the community still under suspicion. The accusers were doubtlessly frustrated with the outcome, believing the two were a danger to the community. They were also declared unfit parents because both their sons were taken away and apprenticed out. The two eventually fled the colony for Rhode Island. For a second time a decision had been made that did not fully resolve the community's suspicions of individuals under suspicion of witchcraft and these unresolved accusations of witchcraft exacerbated the tension and unease in Hartford.[94]

Although Winthrop's influence here might appear to be a more humane approach to handling these cases I believe in a community like Hartford under such external pressures as described above and additional local tensions this moderate and humane approach to dealing with witches contributed to the later explosive situation that occurred in 1662, leading to the Hartford Witch hysteria. After all, the adversaries of the witches "lodged their complaints out of a firm conviction that their neighbors were practicing *maleficium* and were therefore a serious menace to them, their families and their society."[95] Hartford by 1662 was a tinderbox and only needed a spark to set off a firestorm. That spark was initiated later that year by the suspicious death of an eight-year-old girl who claimed to be bewitched by her neighbor.

# 12

# Demonic Possession and the Witch Hysteria in Hartford

During the early 1660s Hartford was insecure and facing an uncertain future. Perched on the edge of the wilderness it was surrounded by hostile Indians and wolves and other wild animals. It suffered from a recent flood, disease, and threats from abroad. This "fragmented and dispirited society" was prepared to believe only "satanic forces" could be responsible for the hard times experienced by their godly community. After all, these people believed "religious confusion was synonymous with the devil" and he was clearly the root cause of their troubles. Torn by bitter dissension and abandoned by many of its leaders in 1659, by the spring of 1662 the colony was in a deep crisis.

Undoubtedly there had been a variety of whisperings and accusations concerning witchcraft in Hartford and likely in the church itself. However, there had not been any executions for witchcraft in the Connecticut Colony since 1655.

## A Family in Free Fall Strikes Out

On March 23, 1662, returning from a church service accompanied by one of her neighbors, eight-year-old Elizabeth Kelly became ill. She accused her neighbor Judith Ayres of bewitching her. Her accusations and death initiated the Hartford Witch Panic of 1662/63 that led to eleven people being accused of witchcraft and four people convicted and hanged with additional charges and trials extended to 1665 and beyond.

In some respects it was not unusual the Hartford witch panic began in the family of Elizabeth Kelly. Elizabeth was the granddaughter of Samuel

Wakeman, an original Hartford proprietor who held a variety of offices in a number of New England towns. His family was one of high status in the community. However, in the summer of 1641 on a voyage to buy cotton, he was killed "by a shot from the Spanish fort at Providence in the Bahamas."[1]

Samuel had four children by his wife, Elizabeth, a son, Ezbon, and three daughters, Elizabeth, Grace (Bethia) and Joanna (Hannah). Nathaniel Willett of Hartford married his widow Elizabeth on June 3, 1643.[2] The Wakeman estate was acquired by Nathaniel Willett in December 1645 under the condition he had to pay Ezbon 40 pounds when he reached 21. The three daughters were to receive twenty pounds each when they turned eighteen.[3] There was some suspicion that it required a court settlement by the children to obtain their share of the estate because based on court records not all of the daughters received their inheritances at the age of eighteen. For example, Bethia finally received hers in 1663 at the age of 24.[4]

Elizabeth (Wakeman) Willett probably died shortly after the Hartford witch uproar because her husband, Nathaniel Willett, married Hannah Adams in 1665. Willett played an important role in the Wakeman family line as a witness at the autopsy of his stepgranddaughter Elizabeth Kelly and taking care of Hannah and her children later when she got into a series of legal difficulties.[5]

His two youngest stepdaughters, Bethia and Hannah, married below their previous status. Bethia was approximately 16 when she married the 52-year-old "Irishman" John Kelly on March 2, 1655 (the child Elizabeth was eight in 1662).[6] The family was poor. Kelly did not own any land and on his death he left an estate of just 14 pounds, 11 shillings and 9 pence.[7] Kelly had a drinking problem. On June 14, 1661, he was convicted of "drunkenness" and was "to set in the stocks 2 hours on yt next Lecture day."[8]

Elizabeth's aunt, Hannah Wakeman, married Francis Hackleton, a brick maker from Northampton, Massachusetts, in 1658. They resided in Hartford although it appears Francis spent part of 1659/60 in Springfield, leaving his wife in Hartford. Beginning in 1659 he was litigating in the courts of Hartford, Springfield and North Hampton. A variety of lawsuits culminated on March 25, 1662, just when the accusations and interrogations concerning his wife's niece Elizabeth Kelly were under way in Hartford. Samuel Marshfield of Springfield (ironically the son of the suspected witch Goody Marshfield) sued Francis in the North Hampton court for six pounds due on a debt. Francis disappeared, leaving some land and his estate to Samuel.[9]

Hannah had two children, a son born in 1658 and a daughter born in 1661. There is no record as to what Francis had done with Hannah's inheritance but one writer has suggested she may have taken up with a Henry Fraesser as revenge because when her husband was away she became pregnant by him in 1663 and delivered after seven months a sickly infant that died.

Hannah was returned to Hartford in March 1664 from Fairfield on charges of being "gilty of hevy crimes." While in the Hartford jail Hannah managed to send evidence to the Connecticut Council of Safety that the jailer, Daniel Garrett's son, was an "accessory to a scurrilous paper." The evidence was "presented to the Councill from Hana Hackleton which is stuffed with reproachful passages against the Governour and Magistrates."[10]

In 1664 Hannah was charged with murder of her infant child and adultery. Outspoken, she was also charged with blasphemy for saying such things as "God made poor bastards on purpose to damn them" and "there was as much mercy in the devil as in God."[11] In 1666, the Court of Assistants overturned the lower court's conviction of death for adultery and blasphemy (she was not convicted of murder by the lower court).[12]

She later admitted to a court in Kingston, New York, in 1670 that while in Oyster Bay, New York, her husband "secretly buried" the child after threatening her. She "let it lay for two days" without feeding him. He died two days later.[13]

Hannah had been in Hartford during the Hartford witch panic and had likely been caught up in it.[14] She had a "natural weapon her tongue—and used it." In 1673 while living in New York a neighbor complained Hannah (now married to Edward Whittaker) was "a Woman reputed to be a Witch." On June 12, 1673, the Executive Council of the Province of New York determined "ye woman has been in great Trouble about it already" and because the council thought the charges were simply "idle stories" it ordered "The woman [Hannah Hackleton Whittaker] to bee declared innocent."[15]

Based on her background and subsequent activities I have outlined it is highly likely Hannah was intimately involved in the family dynamics concerning Elizabeth's bewitchment and subsequent gossip concerning Judith Ayres and the other accused women. Hannah was a force to be reckoned with. Oddly, the records show when John Kelly died shortly after June 10, 1663, "the townsmen in September 1665 offered his widow's next husband, David Phillips of Milford Connecticut," 10 pounds to get "Bethia Kelly his wife out of town." It is likely Hannah and Bethia goaded John Kelly on with his obsession proving Judith Ayres had bewitched his daughter and killed her.[16]

The low status marriages of the two younger sisters placed them in a position where they may have envied their more successful neighbors, may have gossiped about it and attributed their low stations in life to more than bad luck. They might even have had prior suspicions about their neighbor Judith Ayres as to whether she was a witch and discussed this with John Kelly while the impressionable Elizabeth was present. All three would have remembered the shocking statements from the Elizabeth Garlick trial in 1658 and undoubtedly repeated some of the testimony before the child as she seemed to have echoed "the reported deathbed cries of Betty Howell in East Hampton four years earlier."[17]

It was likely in the face of the communitarian Puritan values and expectations the ongoing financial success of William Ayres, Judith's husband, must have promoted envy and jealousy among the less prosperous townspeople like the Kellys and Hackletons. Ayres successfully bought and sold land in Hartford. Ayres had owned ten acres of woodland and sold it before 1649/50. His second lot was on the "north side of Hartford" and included his house sold in 1659. The third piece of property was a four acre parcel he bought from Andrew Sanford and sold to Nathaniel Greensmith (both their wives would be accused of being witches) about "1659/60." He was also a partial owner of another lot in Hartford of five acres or more.[18]

But paradoxically he was constantly in court charged with misdemeanors, theft and slander throughout the 1650s. In December 1656 he was fined for "stealing a hogg"; the next year he was back in court in an action "about a Boy."[19] On January 23, 1661/62, Ayres gave to the widow Abigail Olcott a red cow "as security for a debt due her."[20]

Judith Ayres was probably not a church member. She and her husband appeared before the court in June 1655 and were bound by the court to ensure their good behavior until the following September.[21] Undoubtedly suspicions were raised about her because of her time in London. For example, she told Goody Burr and her son, Samuel, she had met the devil:

> then came a fine young gentlleman a suting to her and when they were discoursing together; the young gentlleman made her promis him to meete him at that place another tyme [she said she would] but looking downward upon his foote: she perseived it was the devil: then she would not meet as she promised him.[22]

In addition, her relationship with eight-year-old Elizabeth Kelly appears unusual based on the little evidence we have. She seemed to be close with her but her parents and even Elizabeth resented what seems to be her obsessive behavior with her. It is possible the following event was the basis for her later unusual behavior. As we will see even Goody Whaples admonished Elizabeth that Goody Ayres came to see "her out of love."

Her behavior might have originated in the manner of the death of her second child. Shortly after December 1659, John Winthrop, Jr., wrote in his medical records:

> Aires William his wife in Labour & great paines but cannot be delivered ... sent for Willia[m] Clerke his wife [uncertain words] the mid wif was forced [uncertain words] Child whereby it was cut in the head & died next day but saved the woman.[23]

This tragic event must have unsettled Goody Ayres mind to know her child had to be destroyed to save her life. The mental anguish of losing a child in this especially horrible manner is something she likely carried with her over the years and may have affected her mentally. This was not unusual or unique. For example, Nathaniel Mather wrote the following to his brother Increase Mather concerning witchcraft:

> of Lake's wife, of Dorchester, whom I have heard, the devil drew in by appearing to her in the likeness, & acting the part of a child of hers then lately dead, on whom her heart was much set: as also another of Connecticut [Mary Johnson] judged to dye a reall convert, tho she dyed for the same crime.[24]

Ayres' mental anguish and guilt might explain her later behavior that included making inappropriate comments concerning her meeting with the devil and her apparent obsession with the Kelly child.

## The Bewitchment of Elizabeth Kelly

With the family dynamics discussed and John Kelly's suspicions (see below) on the morning of March 23, 1662, healthy eight-year-old Elizabeth Kelly had gone to her grandmother's house and from there she attended the morning service at 9:00 a.m. During the afternoon break she returned home accompanied by her neighbor, Judith Ayres.[25]

On May 23, 1662, John

whereby they rid aire, and accom their desires. S there be anie chil baptised, or not with the signe crosse, or orison the witches may catch them fro mothers sides night, or out ( cradles, or otherv them with their nies; and, after steale them out graves, and seet in a caldron, untill their flesh be made potak the thickest whereof they make ointments, v

they ride in the aire; thinner potion they r flaggons, whereof wh drinketh, observing ( ceremonies, immediat commeth a maister, or a mistresse in that and facultie.'

But there were otl broths used by witches may see by the accomp illustration from Molitor's 'Die Hexen' (148 which a cock and serpent form part of the

Judith Ayres had told the story that when she was living in London, "then came a fine young gentlleman a suting to her and when they were discoursing together; the young gentlleman made her promis to meete him at that place another tyme [she said she would] but looking downward upon his foote: she perseived it was the devil." The top picture shows the devil consorting with a woman, and below, two witches making weather. The image is from *The Devil in Britain and America*, John Ashton, London, 1896; original is found in Ulrich Molitor's *Buch De laniis et phitonicis mulieribus*, 1489 (courtesy Wellcome Library, London).

Kelly and his wife testified about their daughter's sickness, the accusations she was bewitched by Goodwife Ayres and about her death. They recounted when Judith Ayres and Elizabeth returned to the Kelly house, Ayres "going to eate did take broth hot of the boyling pott and did immediately eate thereof and did require our said child to eate with her of the same, which wee did Forbidd Telling her it was hott for her." Elizabeth ate the broth from the same "vessel" as Ayres and began to "complaine of Paine at her stomache." John Kelly said he "gave her a small dose of the powder of Angellica roote which gave her Some present ease."

The parents added they "wondered their child shoulde eate broth so hot" as she had never done this before and added "we did nott then suspect the Sd: Ayres."

The latter is unlikely, as John Kelly suspected something because he gave his daughter the angelica powder. His wife stated later she did not know he had given her the powder. Angelica powder was not usually given for the symptoms Elizabeth showed. However, according to the seventeenth century English herbalist, John Gerard, "it is reported that the roote is available against witchcraft and enchantments."[26]

John Kelly was likely hedging his bets and may have gotten the powder from someone in the neighborhood who knew of such things, especially when the plant was not normally harvested in a garden until July or August, according to Gerard.[27] Nevertheless, he was probably trying to affect a physical and spiritual cure for his daughter by using the herbal remedy.

Elizabeth returned to the church Sunday afternoon and did not complain much when she returned home. Three hours into the night she was in bed with her father "asleepe" and suddenly awoke "holding upp her hands cried Ffather Ffather help mee help mee Goodwife Ayres is upon mee, Shee choakes mee, Shee kneels on my belly, Shee will breake my bowels, Shee will make me black and blew, Oh Ffather will you not help mee." She continued with "other expressions of like nature to my greate griefe and astonishment."

Kelly told his daughter to be quiet and "not disturb her mother." She quieted down but soon cried out against Ayres. On Monday she continued to cry out against Ayres with "great violence" and said, "Goody Ayres torments mee! Shee pricks mee with pins, Shee will kill mee, Oh Ffather sett on the great furnance and scald her, get a broad axe and cut of her head, if you cannot get a broad axe get the narrow and chopp off her head." She continued with similar violent expressions. The parents thought and the neighbors said they could not "conceive" her "malady was natural."

Elizabeth continued in this condition until Tuesday. Bethia Kelly testified while she was in the house with the wife of Thomas Whaples and Nathaniel Greensmith her daughter was in "great misery." Goodwife Ayres came into the house. The girl said to her, "Why doo you torment mee and prick mee."

Image of the "Testimony of John Kelly and Bethia Kelly his wife concerning the sickness and death of his daughter Elizabeth Kelly aged 8 yrs. and upwards" (courtesy Samuel Wyllys Papers, Ms. Wyllys, Brown University Library).

Goodwife Whaples said to Elizabeth, "you must not speak against G:Ayres. Shee comes in Love to see you." While Ayres was there the girl "seemed indifferent … and fell asleepe." Ayres said, "Shee will bee well againe I hope."

That night Elizabeth told her parents Goody Ayres had threatened her. She told them Ayres said, "why doo you speake soo much against mee I will bee even with you for it before *you* die, but if you will say noo more of mee I will give you a fine lace for your dressing."[28]

A neighbor, Joseph Marsh, said on Tuesday morning he heard Elizabeth say, "father bring hether the brad axe or el ye naro axe hur mother being by, hur asked hur what to doe & she answered to cut of goody arss head." However, he did not hear Goody Ayres threaten Elizabeth but said "their sat goody ares upon the bed wher betty kely lay … saying if she would bee quiet & hold hur tong & lye still & goe to sleep & say no mor to hur father about hur shee would com to moro morning & bring hur … lase to set upon hur dresin … [Elizabeth] replye saying will you & [Ayres} sayed yes/ indeed i will & if I livf."[29]

On the same day the child said, "Ffather why do you not goe to the maigstratets and get them to punish G:Ayres pray Ffather goe to the maigstratets and if I could goe myself I would complain to them of her how she misuses mee: in this plight she continued till Wednesday night and then dyed her last words she Spake was Goodwife Ayres choakes mee and then Speechless."[30]

## Committee of Inquest into Elizabeth Kelly's Death

Following the death of Elizabeth a Committee of Inquest was called to try to determine if Goodwife Ayres, or possibly Goodwife Whaples, was responsible for Elizabeth's death by supernatural causes. The committee reported what was a "bier right" in the following manner, "Wee whose names are under written, were called forth and desired to take notes, of the dead child of John Kelly, doe hereby testifie, what wee saw as followeth: the child was brought forth and layd upon aforme, by the good wife Aeres and good wife waples, and the face of it beinge uncovered good wife Aeires was desired, by John Kelly to come up to it and to handle it."[31]

The members of the committee included Thomas Bull; Thomas Catlinge; Sergeant Joseph Nash; Gregory Wilterton, a tanner; George Graves, a weaver; Thomas Catlin, a Hartford official; and Nathaniel Willett, Elizabeth's step-grandfather.[32] They were there to serve as witnesses. Goodwife Whaples and Goodwife Ayres were brought in as suspects because they had direct contact with the child.

Dalton's *The Countrey Justice* listed seven evidentiary examples of witchcraft, including that a dead body will bleed upon the witches touch. This was justified because as the author of the manual noted, magistrates "may not always expect direct evidence" because the works of witches "are the works of darkness, and no witness present with them to accuse them."[33]

The bier right, *cruentation,* or "bleeding corpse," was common in the Middle Ages was used in Europe. It was used in unnatural homicides, including death by witchcraft.[34] The idea was a murdered person's corpse would bleed either in the presence of the murderer or when touched. King James I had famously written, "if the deade carcase be at any time thereafter handled by the murtherer, it wilgush bloud as if the blud were crying to heaven for revenge of the murtherer." It was especially used "for tryall of ... unnatural crime."[35]

It was likely from Dalton the magistrates obtained their justification for the inquest committee to perform the bier right, especially because the two women involved were brought into the room to handle the child's corpse. It is unlikely the family would have wanted the women suspected of their child's death there unless they were looking for proof of their involvement by this particular ordeal.

Once the child's body was presented to the two women "the child havinge purged alittle at the mouth the goodwife Aeires wiped the corner of the childs mouth with acloth, and then shee was desired to turn up the sleeve of the arme and shee did indeavour to doe it, but the sleeve beinge some what straight, shee could not well doe it." Ayres, probably out of respect, wiped the child's mouth but Kelly wanted her to handle the body to see if the child would bleed. Clearly, she was being respectful of the dead child. Kelly took charge and "ripped up both the sleeves of the armes ... and upon the back side of both the armes, from the elbow to the top of the shoulders were black and blew, as if they had bin bruised or beaten, after this the child was turned over upon the right side and set upon the belly, and then there came such a sent from the corps, as that it caused some to depart the roome, as Gregorie wolterton, and George Grave."[36]

Kelly seems to have been in a rage manhandling the child's body. The blood in her body had pooled due to gravity (liver mortis) as the child lay on her back. She had begun to bloat, giving off a putrefying odor sending two of the men from the room. That the body was in this state confirms the "blood-tinged flow or purge" from the nose and mouth was not blood. The inexperienced will frequently misinterpret this as blood.[37] In the seventeenth century this was a likely outcome because the purge fluid is mistaken for blood and flows readily from a wound or the body's orifices.

John Kelly was not finished: "then the child being turned again, and layd into the coffin John Kelly desired them to come into the roome againe, to see the childs face, and then wee saw upon the right cheeke, of the childs face, a reddish tawny great spott, which covered agreat parte of the cheeke, it beinge on the side next to goodwife Aeires where shee stoode, this spot or bloach was not seene before the child was turned and the armes of the child did apeare to be vere limber, in the handlinge of them."[38]

John Kelly did not get a copious "blood" flow but in his eyes did obtain evidence the girl had been bewitched because a great spot had appeared on the child's cheek (under the skin) near where Goodwife Ayres had stood. This could have been the result of decomposing capillaries expedited by the handling of the body. There was an expectation there would be bleeding at the "mouth or nose or both" if the person suffered from an "unbloody death." However, it could be argued at the time by medical officials and magistrates that preternaturally where the "blood fixeth" as in the cheek of the child it was "set afloat by the Discordant Effluvia's emitted from the body of the neer approaching or touching murtherer" or more likely in John Kelly's mind and of the clergy, "this was a miracle to sustain God's justice" in this case for him, a witch had bewitched his daughter to death.[39]

Undoubtedly the handling of the body had caused purge fluid to pool in her cheek. Today we recognize the limbs of the child were limber not for any preternatural reason but because *rigor mortis* had passed.

The results of the Committee of Inquest had likely generated gossip throughout Hartford and the other river towns. The magistrates were faced with a difficult decision. John Kelly would not allow his daughter's body to be buried until something more was done about the accusations and the evidence. He believed she had been bewitched to death. In order to determine more thoroughly the cause of death the magistrates took the unusual course for seventeenth century New England and ordered an autopsy. The magistrates called on the services of Bray or Bryan Rossiter, a physician residing in Guilford, Connecticut. Hartford had no physician at the time. The autopsy was the second in New England and the first in Connecticut. It was unusual because it was an attempt to determine the cause of death of Elizabeth Kelly by witchcraft.[40] In Germany as early as 1600 family members, if they suspected poisoning or witchcraft, asked for an autopsy. It was held in the home with "Family members of the deceased crowded around the table to watch the dissection" and offering their observations.[41] However, an autopsy for evidence of witchcraft was not common in England or New England.

Bray Rossiter came from a distinguished family in England. His family was from Combs St. Nicholas in Somerset. He arrived on the ship the *Mary and John* with the other Windsor worthies. He was said to be educated as a physician in England but there is no information on his training. Nevertheless, after settling in Windsor he was "admitted to practice by the General Court of Connecticut." He was examined by Mr. Hooker, Mr. Stone of Hartford and Mr. Smith of Wethersfield, who formed the court. Stiles noted, "it was customary in those early days for the medical examining committee to be composed wholly, or in part of clergymen, who were always more or less skilled in medical lore."

## The Autopsy

The autopsy of Elizabeth Kelly took place on March 31, 1662, five days after her death. Bray Rossiter was assisted by William Pitkin, prosecutor for the General Court, who made notes of the procedure. Rossiter and Pitkin attested the following before Daniel Clark, magistrate, on the General Court:

All thyse 6 perticulars underwritten I judge preternaturale uppon the opening of John Kellyes child at the grave I observed.

1. The whole body, the musculous pts, nerves, the joints were all pliable, without stiffness, or contraction. The gullott only excepted: experience of dead bodyes renders such symptoms unusual:
2. From the Costal ribs to the bottom of the belly in the whole latitude of the wome; both the scarfe skinne and the whole skinn with the enveloping or covering flesh had a deep blew tincture, in the inward pt thereof, was fresh and bowels under it in true order, without any discoverable peccancy, to cause such an effect or symptome.
3. Noe quantity or appearance of blood was in eyther Venter or Cavity as belly or brest, but in the throat only at the swallow, where was a large quantity, as that part would contayne, both fresh fluid, and no way congealed or clodded. As it comes from a vein opened so that I stoke it out with my finger as water.
4. There was the appearance of pure fresh blood on the backside of the arme, affecting the skinn or blood itself without bruising, or congealing.
5. The bladder of gall was all broken, and curded, without any tincture in adjacent pts.
6. The gullet or swallow was contracted like a hard fish bone so that hardly a pease could be forced through. Br. Rosseter[42]

Other historians have looked at Rossiter's description and conclusion that the six particulars he judged as preternatural were blood pooling and the effects of gravity on the blood in the body and the cessation of *rigor mortis*. However, what he took for uncongealed blood was the purge fluid mentioned in the Kelly inquest. That he did not recognize these symptoms as normal "seemed to reflect a quite limited empirical understanding of anatomy" by Rossiter.[43]

As for the cause of Elizabeth's death it was suggested in an article in the

**"Testified upon Oath before the Magistrates by Mr. Rossiter and Mr. Pitkin, Attests, Daniel Clark Secretary," the testimony of Dr. Rossiter on the death of Kelly's child (courtesy Samuel Wyllys Papers, Ms. Wyllys, Brown University Library).**

*Lancet* early in the twentieth century she had "broncho-pneumonia" and more recently an "upper air way obstruction probably caused by diphtheria epiglottis."[44] The latter may be closer to the actual cause of Elizabeth's death as Cotton Mather wrote about a disease called "bladders in the windpipe," later described as diphtheria that in December 1659 "invaded and removed many children."[45]

However, it was Charles J. Hoadley's description and comments on the autopsy that suggested it was Rossiter's conclusion that the particulars were preternatural that acted as a catalyst for the witch hunt that followed:

> Rossiter evidently was predisposed to attribute the death of Elizabeth Kelly to preternatural causes. Had he been skeptical on the subject of witchcraft he might have attributed some of the appearances in his report to incipient decomposition. The child died on March 26th and the dissection was made on Monday, March 31st.[46]

## *Natural, Preternatural and Supernatural*

Rossiter has been criticized for not recognizing decomposition after death and diagnosing her remains as preternatural thus supporting the witchcraft beliefs of the Kellys and possibly other members of the community. In the seventeenth century the three categories were specifically defined. The "natural was natures habitual custom or things that could be explained by natures inviolable laws," the preternatural was associated with "dubious and possible demonic activities of magic" and the supernatural "reserved for God alone."[47]

Essentially, preternatural as a category of knowledge increased dramatically in the late sixteenth and well into the end of the seventeenth century. It was a twilight area between "nature and the supernatural," a category that "defied tidy attempts to divide it in half down the line of natural versus supernatural causes."[48]

If the question is, was the death of Elizabeth natural or supernatural the question at this time is "wrongly put. Seventeenth century medicine left considerable room for natural, preternatural and supernatural causes for death and illness." After all it was known, the devil could employ a "wide-ranging mastery over naturalistic processes: he could instruct a witch in the use of poison or make use of natural processes himself to cause misfortune."[49]

Essentially Rossiter's use of the term preternatural for an atypical death with suspected witchcraft would not have been unusual for its time. Many doctors in Europe would have made a similar diagnosis if they could not rule out a demonic cause or witchcraft for an illness or death.[50] For Rossiter the evidence was unusual, therefore her death was "occult" or "hidden" and in seventeenth century medical terms his diagnosis had to be preternatural because looking at the evidence he could not rule out witchcraft and call it a natural death.

The pronouncement that Elizabeth's death was from preternatural causes suggested witchcraft, which the Kellys suspected. Gossip and the fear their worst suspicions were confirmed about a group of people in town, yet unnamed, except that the Ayreses had been working for years to cause the destruction of their church and community. It even endangered the colony, the ultimate goal of the devil, a view held by many ministers in New England. Now there was an opportunity to bring these witches to heel. The "true believers" had been recently thwarted by John Winthrop, Jr., in the Garlick and the Jennings trials. These suspected witches had been sent back into the community which undoubtedly bred much resentment. It was probably a contributing factor to the fury unleashed in the Hartford witch panic. With Winthrop in England during the panic, the true believers were able to use his absence as an opportunity to take revenge on those they suspected of witchcraft in Hartford and the surrounding towns. This was their opportunity to rid themselves of these devil's servants. As further evidence of their obsession with these suspected witches some of those not originally convicted during their first trial during the panic were brought to trial more than once over the next few years. Others, like William and Judith Ayres, fled from the Hartford court's jurisdiction with the accusations following them to their new homes.

## William and Judith Ayres

William and Judith Ayres present an interesting account of a couple who were able to flee Hartford and avoid a trial and likely death sentence. The Ayreses were examined by the magistrates and jailed. Prior to his arrest, William Ayres sued Nathaniel Greensmith for "slander respecting his wife." The case was heard on the same day as the Elizabeth Kelly inquest. Greensmith probably accused Judith Ayres of witchcraft. Aside from Goody Whaples, Rebecca Greensmith was the only other female neighbor mentioned who was in the Kelly house during the child's sickness. The accusation by Nathaniel was likely an attempt to direct suspicion away from his own wife as she had probably by now come under suspicion too.[51]

Goodwife Ayres was "implicated early in a deposition by Joseph Marsh" and in the "testimony of sundry persons respecting Goody Ayres killing Kelly's daughter."[52] According to testimony in the trial of the accused witch Elizabeth Seager on January 16, 1662/3, Goody Ayres, on hearing some testimony given in court, said, "this will take away my liffe."[53]

It is thought Goody Ayres and her husband were given the "water test" for witches. According to Increase Mather there were some in Hartford who wanted to know if the stories about witches "not being able to sink under water, were true." The two had their "hands and feet tyed, and so were cast into the water and they both apparently swam after the manner of a buoy, part under, part above the water." A bystander who seemed skeptical and thought anyone bound up in such a manner would float "offered himself for trial, but being in the like manner gently laid in the water, he immediately sunk right down." Mather wrote the practice was not "considered legal evidence against suspected persons; nor were they proceeded against on any such account."[54]

Swimming was a relic from trial by ordeal. Swimming the witch had been popularized by Matthew Hopkins, and although it had been forbidden in England after 1645, "ordinary people" continued to believe in the "efficacy of the ordeal."[55] However, even with the understanding of a lack of legal evidence for swimming, strangely it seems the "test" was addressed by the court (perhaps a carryover from Hopkins' influence in earlier New England witch trials) or else why would Elizabeth Seager have been "spoken to about trial by Swimming"; and in her defense about not undergoing the ordeal, skeptically answered, "the divill that caused me to com heare can keep me up."[56]

The Ayreses were broken out of jail by friends and the two fled to Rhode Island. The consequences of their action were that it saved their lives but left their two sons, John and Thomas, behind. John was ordered to be apprenticed to James Ensigne to be instructed as a cooper until the age of twenty-one. Thomas is not mentioned in the record. On December 30, 1662, the Court ordered the Ayres estate and bond confiscated. On March 3, 1675/76, John Ayres appeared in court and "acknowledged his full satisfaction."[57]

When the Ayreses fled to Rhode Island they initially fled to the house of John Smith, who was an official of the Rhode Island Colony. He had his residence in Connecticut. Connecticut officials requested Rhode Island issue a warrant for "Goody Ayres for breaking prison." The Ayreses were apparently tipped off and escaped from the Smith residence.[58]

The gossip and accusations had been flowing freely in Hartford and old suspicions of the "witchcraft" activities of some of the inhabitants led to the arrest of Judith Varlett, the daughter of Dutchman Casper Varlett, probably sometime after March 13, 1662. On June 6, 1662, a grand jury was convened and indicted Andrew and Mary Sanford of Hartford for entertaining familiarity with Satan and having "acted in a preternatural way beyond the Course of nature." When the jury returned it could not agree because some found the indictment to be true and others only suspected. Andrew Sanford was not convicted. His wife was indicted on the same charge and with the additional charge of help from Satan in obtaining "knowledge of secrets in a preternatural way." (Perhaps she told fortunes like another woman under suspicion, Katherine Harrison.) Mary Sanford was found guilty and sentenced to death. She was likely hanged because her husband, Andrew, "moved to Milford, Connecticut in 1667 and remarried there and had seven children."[59]

## The Demonic Possession of Ann Cole

Perhaps the excitement of the witch hunt would have subsided. However, it was to be reignited with the demonic possession of Ann Cole, the daughter of a "godly man" John Cole. We are fortunate to have a description of her possession and other aspects of the Hartford witch hunt provided in a letter written in 1684 to Increase Mather by a participant in the events, the Reverend John Whiting, then minister in the Second Church of Hartford.

His description included the activities of the four ministers involved in the Hartford witch hunt. The elderly Mr. Stone, and three young ministers: the minister at Farmington, Mr. Sam Hooker (son of Thomas Hooker); minister Joseph Haynes, son of the former Governor John Haynes and minister in Wethersfield, who would succeed Samuel Stone in the Hartford Church in 1664; and John Whiting the "relator," minister in the Hartford Church with Stone who wrote down what Ann Cole said while possessed.

Whiting and Hooker were Congregationalists and Haynes, Presbyterian. The Congregationalist ministers were under special pressure from the measures discussed in the previous chapter against their co-religionists in England. The threat was not an illusion in 1666. Whiting was confronted by individuals who wanted to become members of the Hartford Church. Their only rationale was they were in full communion with the Church of England. This was unacceptable to Whiting and he refused them membership. Both this and the rising Presbyterianism in Connecticut were seen as threats to the purity of the original Congregational doctrine concerning baptism, church membership and governance.

In 1662 the perceived satanic threat united these ministers under the leadership of the Reverend Samuel Stone. Stone was "an eager participant in attempting to identify the witches." He had a reputation for bringing a witch, Mary Johnson, in 1648 to "repentance" prior to her execution. To the ministers at this time, as we will see in Willard's sermon (see below), possession was not easily distinguishable from a mere act. To the Protestant clergy it was a "preternatural" sign from God and the actions of the possessed were so extreme and beyond the natural world the devil had to be involved. In this case, God had decided to warn the people of Hartford and the other river towns of the ongoing danger of the devil by Ann's possession. It also suggested to these communities and their ministers they held a special place in God's plan concerning the Second Coming. Stone likely saw this as an opportunity to confront the devil and reconfirm his ministry in the eyes of his contentious congregation. He and the other ministers likely believed the witches Ann named were a satanic danger to their communities. In order to ensure the full prosecution, conviction and execution in the Hartford Court of these witches rather than releasing them back into the community (as

Winthrop advocated) Stone and the other ministers acted as "a prosecutorial tribunal, gathering evidence, recording notes and vigorously interrogating witnesses" to ensure a conviction.[60]

Ann Cole was the daughter of John Cole, a carpenter, who was a "neighbor to the man and woman that afterward suffered for witch craft" [Nathaniel and Rebecca Greensmith]. She had for some time lived in fear of "her spirituall estate." Two of her brothers were lame. As for her possession and her utterances, she said "she knew nothing of those things that were spoken by her, but that her tongue was improved to express what was never in her mind, which was a matter of great affliction to her." She lived at home and was taken by "strange fits, wherein she (or rather the Devill, as 'tis judged, making use of her lips) held a discourse for a considerable time." Whiting wrote, "a company of familiars of the evill one, (who were named in the discourse that passed from her) were contriving how to carry out mischievous designes, against some and especially against her" and saying how they would do this by afflicting "her body, spoile her name, hinder her marriage, &c., wherein the general answer made among them was, She runs to her Rock." This went on for some "howers." The demons decided to confound her listeners with "unintelligible mutterings, the discourse passed into a Dutch tone" (there was a Dutch family living in town at the time). She followed this with the account of various afflictions that had befallen a young woman, her neighbor and the sister of the minister John Whiting. Whiting's sister could barely speak and had recently met with "great sorrow, as pinchings of her armes in the dark, &c." She had previously told her brother of her affliction. Ann, in a "Dutch-toned discourse," gave "plain intimations ... by whom and for what cause such a course had been taken with her."

The ministers were astounded by Ann's possession. Mr. Stone declared it impossible "one not familiarly acquainted with the Dutch (which Anne had not been) should so exactly imitate the Dutch tone in the pronunciation of English: Sundry times such kind of discourse was uttered by her, which was very awful and amazing to the hearers."

In addition, the minister wrote she had many "Extreamely violent bodily motions ... even to the hazard of her life in the aprehensions of those who saw them." Additionally, Ann had public outbursts in the Church causing "two other women" to have "strange fits."[61]

## The Idea of Demonic Possession

The idea of demonic possession was commonplace in the seventeenth century in Europe. It was not "abandoned by a substantial portion of the literate classes of Europe, including the medical profession, until beyond the seventeenth century" and for the common people it was not especially "disturbing."[62] As to the cause of possession, the early English exorcist John Darrell wrote, "it would be no more then to be sick of a fever as to have the palsy, or some other disease."[63]

The difference in thinking of this "wonder" before the modern period was "demons were said to be the cause of madness and not madness the cause of demons."[64] From a religious viewpoint, demonic possession was seen as a sign of the coming end times and was anchored in theology and especially in the book of Revelation. To seventeenth century Protestant theologians, history was rooted in three defeats for Satan: his being cast out of heaven, the New Testament and the final judgment. It was in the final days Satan would unleash his "wrath" on "mankind" in a raging fury mirrored in the struggle of the possessed—"storming," "raving," "roaring" and in the frenzied paroxysms of possession. Christ and the devil had come into direct confrontation in the New Testament "and on both occasions demoniacs were, in effect the battleground."[65]

Although we do not have information on what sermons were given in the Hartford Church we do know the gossip about witches, and the meaning of this outbreak must have been the subject of sermons in the church on at least two occasions as we have mention of the outbursts of two unidentified women and Ann Cole during public worship. Possession was also seen as preternatural, that is, either the "demon mingling with merely natural causes or effecting their own." Even if there were those like Elizabeth Seager, who were skeptical of Ann's outbursts and witch naming, there were too many others who would not question it and saw it as a result of the "devil's own doing."[66]

There is some direct evidence as to how the clergy in New England understood the issue of possession at that time. A few years following the Ann Cole possession, Samuel Willard, minister in Groton, Massachusetts, confronted the public possession of Elizabeth Knapp in 1671. In 1673 he published two sermons and introduced them in a manner suggesting it had been a public occasion and it had been God's judgment to proceed in this way:

> Sermons to the inhabitants of Groton, Massachusetts in regard to the Touching the occasion of them I need not advertise you, you may well enough call to minde, the loud voice of speaking providences.... The sad hand of God which was upon the poor possessed creature ... but you were eyewitnesses of it ... that you may be prepared for shaking times.[67]

Willard warned some judgments are more extraordinary "such as possession by Devils." Natural causes can bring "awful judgments" but preternatural causes are when "God goes out of the ordinary path, here is a more awakening Call." It is not "suspect for God to give Satan such liberty and power, to rack and to torture so to harry and perplex poor creatures ... something is special to be learned by us." For clergy especially, "God's judgments are documents ... there are doctrinal conclusions to be drawn for our instruction."[68]

The possessed were to be read as signs and to awaken the community to God's warning to his people. The actions of the possessed were an opportunity for the clergy and the community to take stock of themselves for their sins and to study the Devil. It also gave physical evidence of the value of the minister and the proof of God's existence.

Protestant clergy did not believe in exorcisms like Catholics but engaged in prayer, vigils and fasts. The underlying theme was the bedeviled had done something to open themselves to possession. So we find a public fast day and prayer session held at the Wyllys mansion where Ann is put on public display and where she named other witches in Hartford and surrounding towns.

What of those named as witches by the possessed? Why would the devil expose his followers? Perkins wrote that the devil, after he has ensnared his witches, uses "all means possible to disclose them." The cause of "his malice towards all men, in so high a degree, that he cannot endure they should enjoy the world or benefits of this life." The second, "his insatiable desire of the present and full possession of them, whom he has got within the bonds of the covenant."[69]

Cotton Mather, during the Salem witch trials, wrote to one of the judges, John Richards, on the same subject and gives an insight into the thinking of the time on this issue. He wrote: "When you are satisfyed or have good plaine legale Evidence that the Daemons which molest our poor neighbours, do indeed represent such and such people to the sufferes ... yet I suppose you will not reckon it a conviction that the people so reprsented are witches to be imediately Exterminated ... divells have sometimes reprsented the shapes of persons not onley innocent but also vertuous." Mather countered this with the advice God "provides a way to prove their innocence."[70]

## A Special Day of Fasting and Prayer

A special "day of prayer" was held for Ann and two other women afflicted with "strange fits." It was a public event held at the Wyllys mansion most likely in the late fall.[71] The "motion and noise of the afflicted was so terrible that a godly person fainted under the appearance of it." Ann Cole appears to have been the center of attention and named other people as witches.[72] Goodwife Watson testified she told Elizabeth Seager that at the fast to pray for the healing of Ann Cole "in her fitts she mentioneth many, but no more you than others."[73]

Ann Cole was prominently mentioned by the jailer, Daniel Garrett, and Margaret Garrett, his wife, in testimony concerning the accused witch Elizabeth Seager. They said, "there was a day Kept at Mr. Wyllys in reference to An: Coale … at the Fast at Mr. Wyllys [she] cryed out against … Goodwife Seager.… Goodwife Seager [later] said Mr. Haines had ritt a great deal of hodg podg that An: Coale had said she was under suspicion for a witch." As a result, Elizabeth Seager was "in such agony" she sent her daughter with a gift of parsnips to Goodwife Hosmer (a neighbor of Ann Cole's). Goodwife Hosmer was at the fast; her husband refused the gift of the parsnips and told her to send her father to him to learn the reason they were refused. Seager's husband went to question Goodman Hosmer and was told "An: Coale at the fast at Mr. Wylly's Cryed out against his wife as being a witch: and he would not receive the parsnips, lest he should, be brought in heraft as a testimony against his wife."[74]

Elizabeth Seager also attempted to defend herself, quoting Scripture against Ann Cole's demon and the statements taken down by the Reverend Stone and his clerical collaborators. On being told she was under suspicion of being a witch by Ann Cole on the day of prayer, witnesses said Seager said, "she had sent Satan to tell them she was no witch." On being confronted by what she said, Seager replied, "you do not speak of the whole you say nothing of what I brought to prove that Satan knew I was no witch, I brought that place in Acts, about the sons that spake to the evil spirits in the name of Jesus whom Paul preacheth I have forgot their names."[75] The passage Seager was referring to is as follows:

> Vagabond Jews, exorcists took in hand to name over them which had evil spirits, the Name of the Lord Jesus, saying, We abjure you of Jesus whom Paul preacheth … (and there were certain sons of Sceva, a Jew, the Priest, about seven which did this) … [They were charlatans imitating Paul.] … and the evil spirit answered, and said, Jesus I acknowledge, and Paul I know, but who are ye?[76]

She also said the demon naming the witches could not be trusted and Stone and the other clergy had no power to confront the demon or expel the demon from Ann. As traditionally taught by Protestant theologians, the age of miracles and the exorcism of demons had ended with the Apostles.

## Was Ann Cole Influenced by Her Family?

Ann Cole was the daughter of John Cole, a prominent member of the conservative Congregationalist minority in the Hartford Church and an enemy of Samuel Stone's progressive policies. He supported the minister John Whiting in a number of instances during the 1660s that led to the founding of the more traditionalist Second Church of Christ in Hartford in 1669.

John Cole and others who played an important role in Ann's life "opposed the methods of church government and management adopted by Mr. Stone. They regarded Mr. Stone's views as opposite ... to Mr. Hooker."[77] In 1660, in order to quiet the dissenters, Stone hired John Whiting, a "moderate Congregationalist" to replace Hooker. After Stone's death in 1663 his replacement was Joseph Haynes, a Presbyterian that involved the church in controversies that continued until 1669 with the founding of the new church.[78]

During the period under discussion the public law of 1658 forbade the establishment of a church outside the jurisdiction of the original church, forcing John Cole and like-minded congregants "to attend worship with those whom they differed in fundamental doctrine under penalty of fine."[79]

Ann was a girl of sixteen and had grown up in a church and home beset by inordinate tensions and likely heard many discussions about the state of the Church, Satan's influence in the Church and gossip about neighbors who appeared to be successful yet led dissolute lives, cheated their neighbors, appeared constantly in court either suing or being sued, or in some cases with rumors of having dabbled in the occult or been responsible for the death of their neighbors. Cotton Mather much later wrote of a group of people who seemed to fit this category earlier in Hartford:

> I do suspect ... persons who have too much indulged themselves in Malignant, Envious, malicious Ebullitions of their soules may unhappily expose themselves to Judgment of being represented by Divells, of whom they never had any vision, and with whom they have much less written any Covenant.[80]

Examples of this group included gossip surrounding the Aryeses and Greensmiths, rumors about Elizabeth Seager's unfaithfulness and gossip about Goodwife Palmer, who it was claimed had bewitched and killed Hannah Robbins. The most serious gossip concerned Katherine Harrison, who, it was rumored in the 1650s when she was a servant in Captain Cullick's house, used magic and told fortunes. She was also suspected in causing the death of Hannah Robbins by bewitching her.[81]

Although Ann and her family were likely frustrated by their minority status in the Church, economically, John Cole until recently had been successful in acquiring land. The family lived on the south side of Hartford, even sharing a "section of land dominated by the Wyllys mansion."

They were neighbors of the Hosmers and the Greensmiths. However, even with his extensive holdings had come some bad luck. In addition to Ann, who had been "afflicted and in some fears for her spirituall estate," two of the men in the family were "very lame," one whose "knee-joint of one leg had no motion."[82]

For the Coles, the crippling of two family members must have been subconsciously attributed to bewitchment. Family and neighbors likely influenced Ann's fragile psyche. John Cole believed in witches as noted in the following testimony: "Eliazer kimmerly ... upon some discourse about master Robins his death" said "in the presence of sondry persons when yur father m [aste r Robins was killed ... that Goodman Cole of Hartford hearinge the words aforesaide it tooke deepe impression upon his spirit as suspitious of murther" through witchcraft by Katherine Harrison.[83]

The frustration level of the Cole family and the other members of the minority in the Church likely hit a fever pitch when witchcraft accusations began in Hartford. Ann was unconsciously influenced by gossip and a series of events including her fear of not being able to marry (a fear announced in one of her seizures) because the devil's familiars would "afflict her body, spoile her name, hinder her marriage."[84]

Her marriage prospects were probably reduced because of the recent migration of many of the more conservative congregational families in the Church to Hadley, Massachusetts, limiting the number of suitable partners in the Church that shared her family's strict congregational views. Ann did marry a suitable partner many years after her possession, a widower, Andrew Benton at the unusually older age for a first marriage for a female of 32. However, Ann's crisis over her marriage prospects may have been a contributing factor but not the sole factor for Ann's possession.[85]

Strangely enough there was a connection between the Coles of Hartford and the Elizabeth Godman witchcraft case in New Haven in 1653. Elizabeth Lamberton and her sister Hannah Lamberton, the two daughters of Captain Lamberton of New Haven phantom ship fame, lived in their stepfather Stephen Goodyeare's house with Elizabeth Godman. The girls accused Elizabeth Godman of being a witch; they spied on her and gave evidence in court. In addition Hannah "swooned" and had fits as if bewitched by Goodwife Godman.[86] According to Nicholas Auger, a physician in New Haven, Hannah Lamberton, Elizabeth Lamberton and two other women were cured of their fits when Elizabeth Godman was called "bee fore the magistrate for some suspition ... and after Examination, theire fits left them and they Never weare troubled with them since."[87]

Abigail Cole (the daughter of James Cole, John Cole's sister and Ann's aunt) was married to Daniel Sillivant (Sullivane) and lived in New Haven during the Godman trial in 1653. Abigail was alive in November 1653 when her father's will was probated.[88] I would suggest a fairly close relationship between the Sillivant and the Goodyeare (Lamberton) families because following Abigail's death, likely sometime in 1654, Daniel Sillivant quickly married one of the principle Godman accusers, Elizabeth Lamberton. The marriage occurred in 1654 or otherwise before Daniel's death in the summer of 1655.[89] John Cole was in contact with Elizabeth, his former brother-in-law's widow, and purchased land from her in Hartford in October 1655. What gossip may have passed among these family members concerning witchcraft and the bewitched will never be known but it is possible some of the conversation may have later influenced Ann as she began to question her faith and her prospects.

In 1662, John Cole and his supporters were aware Ann could not accuse other church members of witchcraft because it would raise too many questions in the Church. By law they were forced to worship with their fellow congregants, of which many in the majority were full members, and there was the chance witchcraft accusations in the Church might permanently tear the religious fabric of the town and the Church apart. There was a group that would lend credibility to their charges that Satan was trying to undo their settlement in Hartford and the surrounding towns—and at the same time not destroy their Church. Ann could focus her accusations on those who many in the community believed held non-Puritan values, were constantly before the courts, and preternaturally successful, likely with the help of the devil.

It appears Ann was supported by a core of men that later followed John Whiting to found the conservative Second Congregational Church of Christ in 1669. The role these men played in the church was extremely prominent. The minority likely acquired more authority due to Ann's accusations and the elimination of a number of suspected witches in Hartford, of which four were hanged and the rest fled, the death of Samuel Stone in July 1663, and the leadership of the church by John Whiting, who supported the minority Congregationalists. This core group included Andrew Benton, John Cole and two other members present with John Whiting on November 22, 1666 "at Mr. Wylly's house" when William Pitkin and others "came to speak with Mr. Whiting" to demand "full communion with the Hartford Church on the grounds of their English church membership," a demand Whiting boldly refused.[90]

Also, in 1667 John Cole, Andrew Benton and William Edwards (John Cole's half-brother) were delegated to "correct any disorder they shall discover in the time of public worship."[91]

The Presbyterian Joseph Haynes was hired in 1663 to take Samuel Stone's place. Even with a strengthened minority, new controversies erupted in the Hartford Church. Haynes attempted "to introduce innovations in baptism" unacceptable to Whiting, Cole, Benton and Stocking (Benton's father-in-law).[92]

The ongoing controversies between the minority traditionalist Congregationalists and the Presbyterians, or, according to Davenport, the "looser and worser party," led to the founding of the new church in 1669.[93]

Ann was admitted to the new church in full communion in 1670. Other new members included her father, John Cole, her future husband, Andrew Benton, and his father-in-law, George Stocking. Additional members included people mentioned in the court testimony as accusers or witnesses: Thomas Whaples, Margaret Watson and Stephen Hosmer. One of the primary accusers of Elizabeth Seager named by Ann was her step-uncle, John Cole's half-brother, William Edwards, who in accusing Seager said, "Seager did fly." He is not listed as a member of the Second Congregational Church and may have died prior to the founding of the second church.[94]

Ann Cole married Andrew Benton following his wife's death in 1672. Benton was originally from Milford, Connecticut. He settled with his first wife, Hannah Stocking, the daughter of George Stocking, in 1649. They moved to Hartford in 1660. The Stocking and Benton families were part of the minority in the Hartford Church and supported John Cole and his stepbrother, William Edwards. Andrew Benton from the beginning "stood steadily with the minority in the First Church of the old doctrine."[95]

Andrew married Ann Cole sometime before 1678. They had four children. The oldest son, Ebenezer, was "feeble minded"; the two daughters grew to adulthood and married; a second son died in infancy.[96]

Andrew was a creditor to Nathaniel Greensmith. He acquired the Greensmith homestead from the court on May 14, 1668. It was recorded to him March 11, 1671. Andrew lived there with Hannah, who died in the old Greensmith house. He and his second wife, Ann Cole Benton, also lived there. Andrew died in the house in 1683. Ann died there on April 4, 1686. Because of Ebenezer's "impotence," he lived with Ann until her death.[97]

## The Confession of Rebecca Greensmith

Little is known about Nathaniel Greensmith prior to his settling in Hartford in 1655.[98] He was described as a "small wiry and quarrelsome man."[99] He was the third husband of Rebecca Mudge. The couple were like the Ayreses, successful in acquiring property but as a couple had an unsavory reputation with the more respectable inhabitants of the town. The inventory of Nathaniel's property "filed in the Hartford Probate Office, January 25, 1662/3, after his execution carried an appraisal" of just over 137 pounds, a considerable amount of property for that time.[100] He was by this account a "well to do farmer" but during the prior ten years had been convicted of petty thievery, assault and battery and lying to the court.[101] Rebecca would later confess even she was afraid of him before their marriage because she had heard "so much of him" before she married him.[102]

Rebecca Greensmith developed her own poor reputation. She married her first husband, Abraham Elson, in 1645. They lived in Wethersfield where they had two daughters. Abraham died in 1649, when his daughters were three and one and a half years old. Then Rebecca married Jarvis Mudge. The welfare of Rebecca's two girls was of concern to her neighbors. Shortly after marrying Javis, the court saw fit to "sequester" part of the Elson estate for the benefit of the girls. Jarvis, Rebecca and the girls moved to Pequot (New London). Jarvis died in 1652. Rebecca and her daughters returned to Wethersfield. Rebecca was in court on June 2, 1653. The court granted "Liberty" to sell land belonging to the "widdow Mudge" in Pequot "for the paing of debts & Bettering the Childrens portyons." Not only was her ability to look after her daughters' welfare in question but her morality was questionable as well. The same court fined John Nott for "miscariedg with the widow Mudge." It was also highly unusual for a woman in the seventeenth century to bury two husbands in so short a time; this would likely have thrown more suspicion on her character.[103]

Rebecca married Nathaniel Greensmith sometime after 1655. New to Hartford, Nathaniel acquired "a lot of about twenty acres, with a house and barn" on the south side of town near John Cole "in the point of land between Wethersfield Lane and the highway to Farmington." He also had other holdings "neer Podunk."[104] The Coles and Greensmiths were neighbors. Like the Greensmiths, John Cole was new to Hartford, having settled in 1655.[105]

Rebecca was not named immediately as a suspect after Elizabeth Kelly died. However, I suspect she was gossiped about as she had attended the child with Judith Ayres and Goodwife Whaples. On the same day the inquest concerning the Kelly child was held, May 13, 1662, Nathaniel Greensmith brought a suit against William Ayres "in an action of slander respecting his wife." William Ayres had probably accused Rebecca of witchcraft before the upcoming inquest to forestall an accusation against his wife, Judith. The action did not go forward because William and Judith Ayres fled to Rhode Island. However, it is likely the gossip and accusation that appeared in court that day against Rebecca reached the ears of Ann Cole, her neighbor, and was incorporated into her ravings along with the names of other suspects.[106]

When Ann Cole made her accusations against Rebecca and others, probably in late October or early November, Rebecca was already "a prisoner upon suspicion of witchcraft." Whiting referred to Rebecca as "A lewd, ignorant considerably aged woman." However, Rebecca Greensmith was probably in her late thirties or early forties based on the average age at first marriage and the ages of her two daughters from her first husband's death in 1649.[107]

According to Whiting, Rebecca Greensmith on December 30, 1662, admitted to witchcraft while in prison before her trial. The day after the trial she was questioned further about her confession and told the court she was "resolved to deny her guilt (as she had done before)."[108] However, Whiting might have had this wrong. She must have previously implicated her husband because the two were indicted on December 30, 1662, for "familiarity with Satan the Grand Enemy of God and mankind and by his help hast acted things in a preternatural way beyond humane abilities in a naturall course."[109]

The court sent for "Mr. Haines and myselfe [Whiting] to read what we had written," presumably, Ann Cole's utterances during her various states of possession and possibly other things Rebecca said in prison. Rebecca was present in court. When Haynes finished reading Ann's hysterical ramblings Rebecca "forthwith and freely confessed those things to be, that she [and other persons named in the discourse] had familiarity with the devill." When she was asked if she had made a specific "covenant with him, she answered she had not, onely as she promised to goe with him when he called (which she had accordingly done sundry times)."[110]

Rebecca was asked if she had signed a pact or covenant with the devil. She replied she had not yet signed a covenant. But the devil said to her "at Christmass they would have a merry meeting, and then the covenant should be drawn and subscribed." Mr. Stone, who was in court, rose "with much weight and earnestness laid forth the exceeding heinousnes and hazard of that dreadful sin." The covenant with the devil was seen as mirroring the covenant Puritans were expected to sign when they were accepted for full communion into the church. Among the Protestant clergy signing a covenant with the devil was enough to invoke the death sentence. On this, the Westminster Assembly following the English Civil War decreed, "Some have thought witches should not die unless they had taken away the life of mankind, but they are mistaken.... Though no hurt ensue in this contract at all, the witch deserves present and certain death for the contract itself."[111] The heinousness of this act which Stone wished to point out to the court was that it was a full commitment to Satan and a complete turning away from God.

To underscore the gravity of the act Stone "solemnly took notice (upon the occasion given) of the devill's Loving Christmass." Massachusetts had just banned Christmas in 1659. Rebecca's mention of Christmas as the day she would sign the covenant with the devil no doubt horrified the staunch Puritans in the courtroom and confirmed their worst suspicions. Puritans abhorred the traditional English celebrations associated with Christmas and saw the day as purely a pagan holiday. Increase Mather wrote the celebrations on Christmas consisted of gaming, reveling, drinking wine to excess and engaging in "mad mirth." Instead of "Christmass" it should be called "the Devil's Mass rather than to have the Holy name of Christ put upon it."[112]

Whiting wrote, "a person ... [magistrate?] ... at the same time present being desired, the next day more particularly to inquire of her about her guilt." The inquiry took place the following day and Rebecca said when "Mr. Haines began to read, she could have torn him to pieces ... yet after he read awhile, she was as if her fflesh had been pulled from her bones (such was her expression) and so could not deny any longer."

Rebecca had confessed "the devill first appeared to her in the forme of a deer or faune, skipping about her, wherewith she was not much affrighted ... their meetings were frequently at such a place (neare her own house). That some of the company came in one shape, some in another, and one in particular in the shape of a crow came flying to them. Amongst other things she owed that the devill had frequent use of her body with much seeming (but indeed horrible hellish) delight to her...."[113]

Rebecca's confession included some continental ideas newly introduced into England as a result of the Lancashire trials in 1612 and the Hopkins witch hunting trials in the 1640s. The witch rather than strictly committing *maleficium* or doing harm was now also a devil worshiper, attended a sabbat with other witches (suggesting a conspiracy of witches) and had carnal knowledge of the devil.

Rebecca does not explain what caused the devil to appear to her in the first place but does suggest her meeting was innocent at first. She is introduced to other witches and their familiars at a number of meetings or sabbats held near her house. She finally admitted the devil had sexual intercourse with her. Since the Lancashire witch trials, a new type of real life story was given as legal evidence that "witches congregated at secret locations to hold their sabbats." It is possible that some of her confession was helped along by an aggressive magistracy and clergy to obtain evidence that sabbats were held and to obtain the names of who else was there. Demos observed "these modest revels were far from 'the horrible plots against mankind' of which the clergymen wrote and spoke so fervently."[114] This was because the sabbats in England were derived from the "traditional merry-making" of the poor, "feasting, drinking, dancing and courtship (including pre-marital sex)." When the godly and pious began to frown on them, "the restraint these men tried to enforce explain why tales of public devil-worship included harmless recreations made heinous, and why so many private encounters with Satan were said to involve sexual intercourse."[115]

In general, because torture was not used as it was on the continent, it was difficult for magistrates to obtain the names of additional witches even though a conspiracy of witches was suspected. However, in two instances Mary Parsons of Springfield and Rebecca Greensmith of Hartford admitted attending meetings with other witches and their familiars. Unlike the clergy who were more concerned with the activities that occurred at these meetings (see, especially, continental descriptions of the sabbats), in this case, the New England magistrates were probably more interested in obtaining the names of other suspected witches.

On January 8, 1662/63, Rebecca in court expanded on her confession about

Rebecca Greensmith confessed, "there we danced, & had a bottle of Sack: it was in ye night, & something like a catt cald me out to ye meeting." This woodcut, ca. 1700–1720, shows a circle of witches dancing around the devil (courtesy Wellcome Library, London).

her attendance at these meetings. The court had its conspiracy of witches that Ann Cole had uncovered in her utterings. A description of what they did there and the names of other witches who attended these meetings was given by Rebecca:

> I allsoe Testify that I Being in ye woods at a meeting there was with me Goody Seager Goodwife Sanford and Goodwife Ayres: that at another time there was a meeting under a tree in ye Green By our house & there was there James Wakeley, Peter Grants wife Goodwife Ayres & Henry Palmers wife of Wethersfield & goody Seager & there we danced, & hada bottle of Sack: it was in ye night, & something like a catt cald me

out to ye meeting & I was in Wakeley orchard with.... Judith Varlett & shee told me
that she much troubled with Marshall Jonah:Gilbert.... She said if it lay in her power
she would do him a mischief, or what hurt she could;
    Taken upon oath in Court.

Rebecca's second confession implicated a number of people named by
Ann Cole earlier. She said they had attended two meetings (sabbats) in the
South Green near her house in Hartford at night under a tree where the rev-
elers drank sack (a fortified wine or sherry) and danced. Rebecca introduced
a familiar (something like a cat), which suggests this is more than a friendly
get-together—a band of witches meeting who had met before. The cat called
her to meet in one of the witches orchards. There she meets Judith Varlett,
who is being troubled by the town marshal. Rebecca says Judith said if she
could she would try to harm him.[116]

Rebecca Greensmith testified in court January 8, 1662/63, against her
husband. The confession was probably made earlier because, as noted before,
Nathaniel was indicted and found guilty on December 30, 1662. The following
is the evidence brought against her husband and was provided by Rebecca.

She said when her husband visited her in prison he told her now that
she had confessed against herself, "let me alone and say nothing of me and
I will be good unto thy children." She then gave examples of her husband's
unusual strength. She said, "when my husband hath told me of his great
travail and labour I wondered at how he did it this before I was married and
when I was married I asked him how he did it and he answered he had help
yt I knew not of." Further, "I have seen logs my husband hath brought home
in his cart that I wonder ... he could get them into the Cart being a man of
little body and weake to my apprehension and ye logs were such that I thought
two men such as he could not have done it."

She also spoke of strange creatures that appeared around her husband
at various times that would have been understood as familiars:

About three years agoe as I think it: My husband and I were in the woods ... several
miles from home.... I saw ... a red creature following my husband.... I asked him
what it was ... and he told me it was a fox. Another time.... I saw two creatures like
dogs and one a little blacker than ye other they came after my husband pretty close
to him and one did seem to me to touch him. I asked him what they were he told
me he thought they were foxes. I was still afraid when I saw anything, because I
heard so much of him before I married him.

Rebecca finished her confession about her husband with the following:
"I speak all of this out of love to my husbands soule and it is much against
my will that I am now necessitated to speak against my husband. I desire that
ye Lord would open his hart to owne and speak the truth."[117]

There is no evidence Rebecca was searched for witch marks or swum,
although it is possible she was watched and sleep deprived. We know from

previous cases like that of Goodwife Knapp that the prisoner was visited by various interested parties, including the clergy of the town, with the object of getting the suspected witch to confess and to name other witches. In Rebecca's case this badgering seems to have finally broken her down with the final impetus being her husband's visit in which he bargained with her that he would take care of her girls if she did not implicate him.

For the court Rebecca's self-confession was critical to the legal justification for her conviction of witchcraft and sentence of death. According to Dalton, a witch's confession "exceeds all other evidence" and written in the *Grounds for Examination of a Witch* is the following: "ye voluntary confession of ye pty suspected adjudged sufficient proofe by both divines & lawyers."[118]

As for Nathaniel he did not confess to witchcraft but Rebecca as a witch "gave testimony" her husband "isa witch," and moreover, he seemed to have "entertained a familiar" and "invocated ye devil for his help." Although there were no other witnesses mentioned in the documents the fact Rebecca had heard stories that frightened her prior to her marriage suggests other witnesses may have come forward with their accounts, but their depositions are not available.[119]

Finally, it is interesting that the members of the Greensmith jury included Nathaniel Willett and John Cowles (Cole), certainly not two disinterested parties in the conviction of the Greensmiths.[120]

On January 6, 1662/63, Mary Barnes of Farmington, the wife of Sergeant Thomas Barnes, was indicted on the same charges as the Greensmiths. She pleaded not guilty. The jury returned a guilty verdict and Mary was sentenced to death. There is little known about Mary and what she had done to be sentenced to death for witchcraft. Elizabeth Seager was also indicted on the same day. She was more fortunate and was found not guilty by the jury.[121]

Goffe, the regicide judge, in his diary under the date of January 20, 1662, wrote "three witches were condemned at Hartford; and afterwards,—February 24, the maids were well after one of the witches was hanged."[122] According to Taylor, Nathaniel and Rebecca Greensmith and Mary Barnes were hanged on Gallows Hill, on a bluff a little north of where Trinity College now stands, "a logical location" as it afforded an excellent view of the execution to the "large crowd ... a hanging being then a popular spectacle and entertainment."[123]

Unfortunately, Taylor does not cite his source. It is unlikely for a variety of reasons the three witches were hanged on Gallows Hill in 1662/63. At the time the area was virtually inaccessible, and as we saw earlier, the colony already had places of execution. The witches were likely hanged outside of the town boundaries "on the road from the Cow Pasture into the county ... on the highway leading out of Hartford town to Symsbury" probably near Albany Avenue. Many came out to see the execution. Hanging the witch was both crowd entertainment and a moral lesson for old and young alike.[124]

The inventory of the Greensmith estate was 137 pounds, 14 shillings, and 1 penny. On February 11, 1662–3, additional inventory raised its value to over 181 pounds for the two claimants, Hannah and Sarah Elson. Further, the court ordered the Marshal and two others "to preserve the estate from Waste and to take account of Debts, and to discharge any just debts, and to pay fourty pounds to ye Treasurer for the County ... until the March quarter court."[125]

In the Particular Court held March 5, 1662/63, the court allowed the jailer Daniel Garrett for maintaining the Greensmiths "six shillings a week for keeping Nathaniel Greensmith and his wife besides their fees wch is to be paid out of the Greensmith estate." The same court also disposed of the debt for "keeping Goodwife Barnes 3 weeks 21 shillings besides her fees wch Goodman Barnes is to see discharged."[126]

Whiting wrote that based on the evidence the Greensmiths were put to death "as the devill's familiars, and most of the others persons mentioned" in Ann's "discourse made their escape into another part of the Country." Following the executions and escapes "the good woman had an abatement of her sorrows."[127] No doubt Whiting was partial to Ann's "goodness and piety" as she had been one of the first to follow him to the Second Congregational Church in Hartford. He did not write about a troubling incident concerning a revisit of her demons in April 1664. As Increase Mather described it, when Ann Cole's brother, Matthew Cole, was at a prayer in a meeting at the home of his father-in-law, Henry Condliff, in Northampton forty miles away, "there came a ball of lightening in at the roof of the house.... Matthew Cole ... was struck stone dead." There were twelve people in the room and no one else "received any harm." Ann's demons "intimated their concurrence in that terrible accident."[128]

## The Fate of the Remaining Witches Named by Rebecca Greensmith

When Winthrop returned to the Connecticut Colony in June 1663 he found a town in disarray. Of the accused witches two had been declared not guilty: Andrew Sanford and Thomas Barnes. Elizabeth Seager (tried on the same day as Mary Barnes) on January 6, 1662/63, was declared "not guilty of the indictment." Elizabeth Seager would be brought into court in July shortly after Winthrop's return, accused of witchcraft, blasphemy and adultery. This was not Elizabeth Seager's last court appearance.[129]

Mary Sanford, Mary Barnes, Rebecca and Nathaniel Greensmith were hanged. The remaining accused witches were not executed; however, the suspicion of witchcraft followed them for the remainder of their lives. Some,

*Above and opposite:* "Testimony of Rebecca Greensmith in Court, January 8," 1662/63 (courtesy Samuel Wyllys Papers, Ms. Wyllys, Brown University Library).

I have seen logs that my husband hath brought home in his Cart that I wondered at it that he could get them onto y Cart being a man of little body and weake to my apprehension and y logs were such that I thought that when further he could not have done it

I speak all this out of love to my husbands soule and it is much against my will that I am now necessitate to speake against my husband I desire that y lord would open his heart to owne and speak y truth

I allso Testify that I being in y woods at a meeting there was w me Goody Seager Goodwife Sanford & Goodwife Ayres: y at another time there was a meeting under a Tree in y greene by y house & there was there James Walkely peter Grants wife Goodwife Ayres & Henry palmers wife of wethersfeild & Goody Seager, & there we danced, & had a botle of Sack: it was in y night, & something like a catt Cald me out to y meeting & I was in m Varletts orchard w mis Judith varlett & shee Tould me that shee was much Troubled w y Marshall Jonath: Gillett: & y it lay in her power shee would doe him a mischeif, or what shee could

—Taken upon oath in Court

like Elizabeth Seager, were tried multiple times for witchcraft until she finally left Connecticut. Some fled immediately like the Ayreses of Hartford and James Wakely of Wethersfield. Katherine Harrison of Wethersfield was convicted of witchcraft then pardoned by a higher court. She continued to live under suspicion and finally fled Connecticut. Judith Varlett, imprisoned on a "pretend accusation of witchery," was saved by her brother-in-law, Governor Peter Stuyvesant of New Netherlands, when her brother, Captain Nicholas Varlett, arrived with a letter on October 13, 1662, stating because of her excellent education "life, conversation and profession of faith" she could not be guilty of witchcraft. The intercession was a success and Judith left for New Netherlands.[130]

Some of the accused fled to Rhode Island and others to New York. Even in their new locations they continued to be suspected by their new neighbors and some were forced to move more than once.[131] The fear they inspired continued to be felt in Connecticut. On May 4, 1668, the town of Stonington, Connecticut, petitioned the General Court at Hartford, making numerous moral complaints of the people in Westerly Rhode Island that "they take in new comers contrarie to orders.... Goodwife Seager, James Waklie and the [William Ayres] tinker."[132]

Later changes in the administration of the Connecticut courts after 1666 and the stricter evidence necessary to convict a witch made the conviction and execution of a witch more difficult. Public opinion was not necessarily assuaged by the more progressive approach of the magistracy toward convicted witches. The case of Elizabeth Seager provides an introduction into the changes Winthrop and others began to introduce into the court system following the Hartford witch hunt that led to the three-way tension among the magistracy, the community and the "convicted" witch found guilty by a jury and then the verdict being later overturned by a "progressive" magistracy.

# 13

# "They seeke my inocent blood"

## *The Witchcraft Trials of Elizabeth Seager*

The reactionary or "true believers" had succeeded in getting some of the accused witches brought to trial. Others escaped their clutches before trial and fled to Rhode Island. One of the chief witches, based on Ann Cole's accusations and Rebecca Greensmith's confession in court, was Elizabeth Seager. She had not fled (perhaps she had been imprisoned earlier). She was first indicted for witchcraft along with Mary Barnes on January 6, 1662/63. Following her indictment for entertaining familiarity with Satan she pleaded not guilty and "referreth her self to trial by the Jury."[1]

In her first case the jury received testimony from neighbors who heard Ann Cole name Elizabeth in a public meeting as a witch. Rebecca Greensmith, under oath, confessed in court to being a witch and told the jury she saw Elizabeth Seager at two meetings. At the second meeting, she said, "we danced, and had a bottle of Sack: it was in the night." To suggest it was a diabolical meeting rather than a "merry meeting," she added, "something like a catt ... [a familiar] ... called me out of the meeting."[2]

Another neighbor, Robert Sterne, said he "saw Goodwife Seager in the woods with three more women and with them I saw two black creatures like two Indians but taller [.] I saw likewise a kettle there over a fire [.] I saw the women dance round the black creatures and whiles I looked upon them one of the women Goodwife Greensmith said look ayonder and then ran away up the hill ... the black things came towards me.... I knew the persons by their habit or clothes."[3]

In short, Robert Sterne testified to seeing a diabolical "sabbat" under way. As noted previously, many earlier witchcraft accusations linked a suspected witch with Indians, so by implication, they were Satan's demons. Elizabeth is associated again with Goody Greensmith. The kettle over a fire in the woods suggested to the jury something diabolical was being brewed that evening.

Despite the passion and heat of the witch hunt, in Elizabeth's case, wiser heads prevailed. The jury found the prisoner "Not guilty of ye Inditement." The decision by the jury caused an uproar in Hartford because the foreman of the jury, Lt. Walter Fyler, was forced to explain the jury's decision. His rationale suggests the jury may have been following the advice of the document known as the *Grounds for Examination of a Witch* as the following testimony suggests.

Fyler wrote Goody Seager was nearly convicted, however, her conviction was not unanimous. The jurors disagreed, but many were nearly convinced of her guilt. Part of this was by her own making. First, it seemed that by "legal evidence" she was associated with two convicted witches, Goody Sanford and Goody Ayres.

Second, she previously said the witnesses were prejudiced, but in court she denied it. She said, she was no more intimate with them than the witnesses themselves and said, "they belie me." The magistrate, John Allen, asked if one of the women had not taught her to knit. She at first said no. Pressed, she replied, "nay I will hould what I have if I must die." Under further questioning she confessed she had "much intimacy with one of them as that they did change worke one with another."

Third, she first said she hated Goody Ayres, but assisted her when Goody Ayres said in court, "this will take away my liffe, Goody Seger shuffed her with her hand and said hould your tongue." John Allen was witness to the incident and after he spoke Elizabeth Seager said, "they seeke my inocent blood ... the magistrate replied, Who. She said everybody."

Fourth, "being spoken to about triall by swimming; she sayd the divill that caused me to com heare can keep me up! About the business of fli ing the most part brought it was not legally proved." Finally, since the woman and Robert Sterne took an oath, their testimony was considered legal. Some in the jury doubted Robert Sterne's first statement because he said, "I saw these women and as I take it Goody Seger was there ... after that he said he saw her there." He also said he saw her kettle but was too far to have seen it clearly. Some members of the jury "doubted that these things did not only weaken and blemish testimony, but also in a great measure disable it for standing to take away liffe."[4]

Although the deposition indicated she had associated with convicted witches, Elizabeth Seager tried to protect Goody Ayres in court. She lied about knowing the suspected witches, and she blasphemed when she said the devil would hold her up during the swimming trial because he had brought her to this court. However none of this was proof enough to convict her in court. There was also no proof she could fly or had flown. The jury doubted the testimony of Robert Sterne because at first he was not sure it was Goody Seager in the woods with the other women and the Indians. Second, he

claimed to have recognized her kettle but was too far away to have known it was her kettle. In the end there was not sufficient evidence to convict her of witchcraft.

The accusation by Rebecca Greensmith and the other testimony was enough to suspect her of witchcraft but according to the *Grounds for Examination of a Witch*, not sufficient evidence to convict her and take away her life. The only sufficient proof is a "voluntary confession ... adjudged sufficient proof by both divines & lawyers." The other is the "testimony of 2 witnesses of good and honest reporting avouching things in theire knowledge before ye magistrate" that the accused has "made league with the devil" or "practiced witchcraft." The witnesses have to be able to prove the suspected witch "called on the devil for his help," "entertained a familiar," or if they can take an oath affirming the suspected party has done work that "inferreth a ct [contract] wth ye devil."[5]

## Winthrop Returns with the New Charter

When Governor Winthrop returned in June 1663 he must have been disappointed to find four individuals had been hanged as witches, three had been acquitted and others under suspicion had fled the colony. Although Elizabeth Seager had been acquitted in January she was again under indictment, and a second trial was scheduled for July. The old Particular Court was soon to be superseded by the Court of Assistants as a result of the new charter Winthrop had received from the king. The new charter also gave the governor and deputy governor the authority to overturn convictions in the court.[6] Winthrop, who was an alchemist and healer and thus had an understanding of the occult, was likely skeptical of the powers of witches and not convinced they could have compacted with the devil that made it necessary to put them to death.[7]

His leniency may also have been reinforced by some guilt on the part of Winthrop Jr., for having been on the Court in Massachusetts that condemned Margaret Jones, a healer, to death as a witch in 1648. His leniency was not without danger. It could have placed him in an even more precarious position because he was a known alchemist. Many considered that alchemists engaged in occult practices. When Winthrop pardoned convicted witches, he and his supporters had to concern themselves with public opinion. To stop the execution of convicted witches and evaluate the reliability of the evidence used to accuse and convict witches was the struggle Winthrop and his supporters engaged in for the next few years with accused witches Elizabeth Seager and Katherine Harrison, previously accused witches from the Hartford witch hunt.

## The Subsequent Trials of Elizabeth Seager

The first witch trial Winthrop confronted on his return to the Connecticut Colony was the second trial of the recently acquitted Elizabeth Seager. The indictment read she had acted in a "preternatural way," had "committed adultery," and "spoke blasphemy against God." The penalty for each of these crimes was death. The only surviving deposition given in May, likely in 1663 for this trial, was that of Mrs. Mygatt. We find the following information inscribed on the document "tests: [testimonies] concerning Wich craft G: Seager 1663" and "greensmith test to it."

Rebecca Greensmith's testimony from her prior trial was likely introduced into court again along with the new testimony of Goodwife Mygatt. She provided what was thought to be damning testimony of witchcraft and blasphemy. Although she recounted that Goodwife Seager said "god was Naught, god was Naught, it was very good to be a witch and desired her to be one, she should not need fear, going to hell, for she should not burne in ye fire."

Although she did not accuse Seager of adultery, she told a most curious story about Seager visiting her bedroom as an apparition and suggests she represented a threat to her marriage bed. She said Seager appeared in her bedroom, "took her by the hand and struck her on the face as she was in bed with her husband." She could not wake her husband, Goodwife Seager left and Mrs. Mygatt said she "darst not Looke out after her."[8] Seager was not charged with blasphemy or witchcraft. There must have been other credible witnesses to Elizabeth's adultery because the jury found her guilty of that crime only.[9]

## Quarter Sessions Trial of Elizabeth Seager, June 26, 1665

The true believers were not finished with Elizabeth Seager and were convinced they could convict her and others on witchcraft charges even with the lack of support on the part of Governor John Winthrop, Jr. Perhaps the recent successful witchcraft trial in England at Bury St. Edmunds in the first quarter of 1662 in which two women had been hanged as witches provided the basis for the accusers to go forward hoping for a similar result. There is no doubt that many of the elites as well as clergy and the common folk knew of the Bury St. Edmunds witchcraft trial, the evidence presented and the satisfactory outcome.

The Bury St. Edmunds trial "attracted widespread interest throughout

England and especially East Anglia [the counties of origin of many of these New Englanders] and was attended by local clergymen, some of whom would shortly be ejected from their living" due to the newly enacted Act of Uniformity. For the general populace witchcraft trials were of great interest and generated much talk and discussion. Many residents of New England, especially in the Massachusetts Bay and the Connecticut Colony, had relatives in Suffolk County, England, where Bury St. Edmunds was located. John Winthrop migrated from Suffolk County, and his son John Winthrop, Jr., had gone to grammar school in Bury St. Edmunds. William Goodrich from Wethersfield served as a juryman in a number of cases on the old Particular Court in Connecticut and was originally from Bury St. Edmonds.[10]

News of this trial undoubtedly spread quickly across the sea to New England by oral if not written communication among family members and friends. In addition, we know the non-conformist clergymen were in direct communication with their brethren in New England and the results of the trial would have been communicated to their fellows there.[11]

What made the Bury St. Edmunds trial especially important was the outstanding legal reputation of the presiding judge, Sir Matthew Hale, Lord Chief Baron of the Exchequer. However, even with his outstanding legal reputation, he seems to have not doubted the existence of witches: "the Scriptures affirmed it, and all nations provided laws against such persons."[12] With a "different charge to the jury [he] could as easily have made the current of judicial decisions run in favor of accused witches all over England." Unfortunately, he did not and his name was successfully invoked in the direction of "the witch-triers for a half-century to come."[13] This trial and his name attached to it were important because it set the tone for a newly reinvigorated series of witchcraft trials in England and was referenced later in the Salem witch trials.[14]

By the time Elizabeth Seager came to trial Winthrop had managed to reform the court system. She was tried before the new *Quarter Sessions* in June of 1665 specifically on the charge of witchcraft, having "entertained familiarity with Satan … and hast practiced witchcraft formerly and continuest to practice witchcraft for which, according to ye law of God and established law of this corporation, thou deservest to die."[15]

Her enemies marshaled their resources and reached back to her first trial to provide testimony of her crimes. This included evidence from Ann Cole's possession, as well as Elizabeth's intemperate comments and other evidence that pointed toward her guilt. This also included the testimony taken on June 17, 1662, for her first trial (in which she was acquitted) about her skepticism of Ann Cole's possession and calling the ministers' written testimony "hodge podge."

Elizabeth's sharp tongue was noted by the jailer, Daniel Garrett, and his wife, Margaret. They testified when Ann Cole said Elizabeth was under suspicion as a witch, Elizabeth "went to prayer, and did adventure to bid Satan to tell them, she was no witch." When asked why she did not ask God "to tell them she was no witch," Elizabeth answered, "because Satan knew she was no witch."

After recounting Goodwife Garrett's testimony as to why Elizabeth Seager sent Satan, three witnesses confirmed Goodwife Garrett's testimony. Elizabeth Seager agreed and said "the reason why she sent Satan was because he knew she was no witch, and to prove that she brought that place in ye 19 act.14."[16]

Three witnesses also swore when Goodwife Garrett testified in front of Elizabeth, she said, "Dame you can remember part of what I said, you do not speak of the whole you say nothing of what I brought to prove Satan knew I was no witch, I brought that place in the Acts, about the sons that spake to the evil spirits in the name of Jesus whom Paul preacheth I have forgot their names."[17] Elizabeth's accusers were shocked she called on Satan to prove her innocence, perhaps suggesting to them Satan had a signed covenant with Elizabeth asking the Prince of Lies to lie for her.

Elizabeth's defense was to use a somewhat ambiguous biblical passage to show that those who thought they could speak to demons and write down what they said could not speak to them because demons only recognized Jesus and St. Paul, not the charlatans who claimed to be able to understand them and cast them out of the possessed.

The court had Rebecca Greensmith's confession used in Seager's second trial and Mrs. Mygatt's deposition in which she said Seager admitted she was a witch. Goodwife Watson also gave testimony on June 17, 1665, and said when Elizabeth heard Ann Cole had spoken out against her, she told Elizabeth, "in her fitts she mentioneth many, but you no more than others" and no more about you than any others. Elizabeth said, "they missed their mark: they aimed at me ... [suggesting a conspiracy against her] ... why do they not lay hold ... [arrest?] ... of others as well as me, why do they lay hold of the chief actor ... [suggesting a head witch yet undiscovered]" because Goodwife Watson said to her, "if you know others to be chief why do you not discover them." Elizabeth said she "would in du time." Elizabeth confirmed her words before Deacon Stebbins and three other witnesses. She never revealed any other witches.[18]

Elizabeth's accusers were also willing to swear to occult events and *maleficia* attributed to her. William Edwards (step-uncle of Ann Cole) brought up her flying for a second time. In a deposition on June 17, 1665, Goodwife Garrett stated that William Edwards said "that she did fly, then Goodwife Garrett said then you own you did fly." Goodwife Seager turned the accusation back on Edwards and said, "if I did fly William Edwards made me fly."

Goodwife Garrett, in the same deposition, said she had made an "extraordinary cheese," and when Elizabeth was husking Indian corn in the Garrett barn she asked her husband to get the cheese which "she had marked with several notches." When he brought her the cheese, one side was "full of maggots" and the other side was fine. She "cut out the maggoty side ... and flung it into the fire." As a demonstration of inadvertent counter-magic (at least on her part as so not to be accused of practicing magic herself) and confirming her worst suspicions for the court, she said, "Goodwife Seager cried out exceedingly in the barn" because she heard her in the house, "and after a short time Goodwife Seager came into the house, cried out she was full of Paine, and sat wringing of her body and crying out." As everyone knew, Seager's actions "indicated witchcraft had been the source of the maggot infestation."[19]

This time the jury found Elizabeth Seager "Guilty of familiarity with Satan."[20] Elizabeth spent about a year in prison while Winthrop, who had not participated in the trial, attempted to "challenge the decision." He first called together a meeting of his officials and magistrates to inform them he would not "enforce" the jury's verdict. He deferred a decision until the Quarter Court in September 1665. There was no decision given in September. Meanwhile, he waited until he could make the reforms in the court system based on the new charter obtained from Charles II. The new charter gave the governor, the deputy governor and magistrates the right to "impose, alter, change or annul any penalty, and to punish, release or pardon any offender."[21]

When the newly appointed Court of Assistants met on May 18, 1666, it rendered the following verdict on Elizabeth Seager: "Respecting Elizabeth Seager, this Court considers the Verdict of ye Jury, and finding that it doth not legally answer the Inditement, doe therefore discharge and set her free from further suffering or imprisonment."[22]

Now "for the first time in Connecticut's history, a convicted witch did not die."[23] The overturning of this verdict did not mean the matter was settled. After all, Elizabeth Seager had been brought to court three times on the same charge. The manner in which she had been acquitted by overturning the finding of the jury did not allay suspicion. As we have seen, memories were long, and once suspected of being a witch, the suspicion lasted a lifetime. Not only did it last the lifetime of the accused but it was also intergenerational. Elizabeth was free in the eyes of the law but found returning to the community impossible because suspicions continued. Even after she and her husband moved to Westerly, Rhode Island, the people of Stonington, Connecticut, still complained of Elizabeth and others who sought refuge from persecution in Connecticut.[24]

Elizabeth Seager's trial concluded the witch-hunting that originated in 1647 in the Connecticut River Valley and led to the execution of convicted witches. Elizabeth was finally found guilty of witchcraft but her conviction was set aside and she did not face execution. However, she did eventually face self-exile as did others who were accused and escaped to Rhode Island or New York.

## Epilogue

The outbreak of witch hunting in the New England wilderness in 1647 can be attributed to the following events. While the English government suppressed witch trials in England from 1618 to 1642 and forbade the publication of new books on witchcraft after 1633, previous editions of books, like Dalton's legal manual the *Countrey Justice*, were still allowed to add fresh information in later editions. Unfortunately, the new passages concerning witchcraft contained the latest demonological thinking on witches, greatly expanded witchcraft material, and provided a prosecutorial guide for conducting a trial. It was the updated legal manual (with added material, especially after the 1633 edition) on the prosecution of witches which served as the intellectual and legal foundation for witchcraft prosecutions from the 1640s on and was used in New England courts during the period under discussion.

A new witch hysteria was unleashed during the English Civil War. The Parliamentarians and Royalists used witches on both sides in their propaganda war to overcome their enemies. The witch hysteria was fanned further when Hopkins and Stearne took advantage of the breakdown in the central government and the courts by using new techniques to find and prosecute witches. They raised the witch hysteria to new heights in England.

It was as only a short time later before the hysteria crossed the Atlantic and fell on fertile soil in New England. A population sensitized to witchcraft beliefs, a ministry and elite steeped in Protestant demonology, in the belief the devil was actively working against them to force them out of New England, fear of the native populations, epidemic disease, famine and the generally harsh environment converged with a legal manual that provided prosecutorial guidance to the deeply religious but untrained in the law magistrates in the Connecticut River Valley. The combination unleashed the first wave of trials and executions starting in 1647. Once the precedent of witchcraft prosecutions was set in the Connecticut River Valley, witchcraft accusations began to emerge as an option to eliminate undesirables in the community. The accusation of witchcraft was likely used when other less extreme options failed. Magistrates in the Connecticut Colony and the New Haven Colony during the 1650s, as well as some jurists, saw the accusation being a little too freely used and the evidence not serious enough to take away a person's life. The magistrates tried to prevent accused witches from being convicted of witchcraft and receiving the death penalty. In this they were successful until the witch hysteria returned, especially in Hartford, due to religious, political and economic conflict. The situation was so volatile that the suspicious death of a young girl while Governor Winthrop was abroad trying to obtain a charter for the colony unleashed accusations of witchcraft and demonic possession leading to the conviction and execution of four persons for witchcraft in 1662/63.

On Winthrop's return with a new charter he was in a legal position to use his influence in the courts to prevent future witchcraft executions. Under Winthrop's leadership in the Connecticut Colony there were no more executions for witchcraft. Indictments were limited, and in one case, "the magistrates rejected what they considered an unwarranted witchcraft accusation." However, like in England, undoing the fears of the populace through fiat from above was no easy task. In England at various times the population took matters into their own hands when they realized they could not get a conviction. The "lynching of alleged witches remained a sporadic feature of English rural life until later in the nineteenth century."[25] Similarly, there was abuse to near death of an acquitted witch in Hadley, Massachusetts in 1685.

The inability to obtain a witchcraft conviction for Katherine Harrison, whose trial goes beyond this study, was a critical turning point in the prosecution of witchcraft in Connecticut. Katherine was a healer but accused of causing illness and deaths, of admitting to know astrology, and appearing as a specter. At her first trial the jury could not agree on a verdict. She was imprisoned until the next court held in October 1669. Released before October, she returned to her home in Wethersfield. Her accusers had been gathering more depositions for the October trial. They were furious she had been released. Over thirty-eight residents from Wethersfield, Hartford and even Hadley, Massachusetts, including two ministers, signed a petition against her release. They believed the magistracy, especially Winthrop, favored Katherine. There was considerable and serious unrest in Wethersfield. Throughout the community there was likely gossip about Winthrop's favoritism toward witches and his alchemical or occult experiments.

On October 12, 1669, Katherine was convicted of witchcraft, but before passing sentence, Winthrop asked a group of ministers led by Gersholm Bulkeley, minister in the Wethersfield Church (who was also a physician and alchemist), for advice on four evidentiary matters. First, concerning witchcraft acts, did it require two witnesses viewing the same act or two witnesses viewing two separate acts? In summary the ministers said there needed to be "a plurality of witnesses, to testify to one and ye same individuall ffact; and without such a plurality, there can be no legall evidence of it."

On the second question of spectral evidence the ministers said that the "most high" would not make an "undistinguishable representation of any innocent person, in a way of doing mischief before a plurality of witnesses."[26]

"The Answer of Some Ministers to the Questions Propounded to them by the Honored Magistrates, October 20, 1669" (courtesy Samuel Wyllys Papers, Ms. Wyllys, Brown University Library).

On the third and fourth questions the ministers combined them and wrote having knowledge of future events that could only have been obtained from the devil were grounds "to argue familiarity with the Devill, inasmuch as such a person doth thereby declare his receiving of the Devills testimony, and yield up himself as the Devills instrument to communicate the same to others."[27]

The court did not want to execute Katherine Harrison. The local population had revolted against Winthrop and his manipulation of the court. Winthrop could not allow Katherine to return to Wethersfield. The court turned to a third option: Katherine was to be banished. She was to remove herself from Wethersfield "which ... will be the most to her own safety and contentment of the people who are her neighbors."[28]

As a result of the ministers' evidentiary standards for the next 22 years there were no more witchcraft cases in Connecticut until 1692.[29] When charges did occur some familiar names like Mary Staples resurfaced, accused of witchcraft. However, while the judges in Salem were convicting and hanging witches the Connecticut magistrates "displayed a remarkable reluctance to exact punishment on the suspects."[30]

On a contemporary note, although the State of Connecticut has not issued posthumous pardons, on February 6, 2017, the Town of Windsor, Connecticut, passed a resolution. This resolution declared Alse Young and Lydia Gilbert's "good names restored in the Town of Windsor so that they may rest in peace."

# Appendix
## *Grounds for Examination of a Witch*

The undated document *Grounds for Examination of a Witch* is held in the Connecticut State Library. The handwriting of the document has been attributed by John M. Taylor to William Jones, deputy governor of the Connecticut Colony from 1692 to 1698.

Tomlinson wrote for some the *Grounds for Examination of a Witch* has been attributed to William Jones and "if he did create the document it is based on earlier English law such as *Dalton's Countrey Justice*." Woodward believes the "internal evidence suggests it dates from the end of the century, rather than the middle." There is no reason why the content of this document could not have been used earlier in Connecticut and this surviving document a copy taken from an earlier record.[1]

The document is an abridgement of William Perkins' *A Discourse on the Damned Art of Witchcraft* (1608), pages 200–219. This book would have been familiar to the Protestant clergy in the colonies. The authorities may have used it in their examination of suspected witches from the beginning. As we have seen some of the most important proofs for witchcraft included "witch marks … [also called devil's marks] … association with other suspected witches, self-confession and, sometimes, the controversial water test." No doubt Ludlow, who was involved in writing the laws of Connecticut, would have had some familiarity with Perkins' work and he and others likely worked together with the clergy to provide guidelines to the magistrates for examining a witch. Although not as guarded as the Perkins original, it still suggests there should be wariness on the part of the magistrate.

I have provided the Perkins text as given. The text in italics are the words from Perkins used in *The Grounds for the Examination of a Witch*. The original text from *The Grounds for the Examination of a Witch* is in parenthesis.

## The Text

The first in order is this: If any person, man, or woman, be notoriously defamed for such a partie. *Notoriously defamed, is a common report of the* greater

277

*The Grounds for Examination of a Witch,* held in the Connecticut State Library Archives (courtesy Samuel Wyllys Papers, Ms. Wyllys, Brown University Library).

sort of *people,* with whome the partie suspected dwelleth, that he or she is a Witch, This yeeldeth a strong *suspition.* Yet the Magistrate must be warie in receieving such a report. For it falls out oftentimes, that the innocent may be suspected, and some of the better sort notoriously defamed. Therfore the wise and prudent judge ought carefully to looke that the report be made by men of honestie and credit: which if it be, he may then proceede to make further inquirie of the fact.

[1. Notorious defamacon by ye common report of the people a ground of suspicion.]

The *second* is, *if a fellow-witch* or Magician *give testimonie* of any *person* to be *a Witch,* either voluntarily, or at *his* or her *examination, or* at his or her *death. This is not sufficient for conviction, or condemnation,* but onely a fit presumption to cause strict examination of the partie to be made.

[2. Second ground for strict examinacon is if a fellow witch gave testimony on his examinacon or death yt such a pson is a witch, but this is not suffi- cient for conviccon or condemnacon.]

Thirdly, *if after cursing there followeth death, or at least some mischiefe.* For Witches are wont to practice their mischievous acts by cursing and banning. This also is a sufficient matter of Examination, not of Conviction.

[3. If after cursing, there follow death or at least mischief to ye party.]

Fourthly, *if after* enmitie, *quarreling, or threatening, a present mischiefe doth follow. For parties devillishly disposed , after cursing doe use threatnings; and that also is a great presumption.*

[4. If after quarreling or threatening a prsent mischiefe doth follow for ptye's devilishly disposed after cursings doe use threatnings, & yt alsoe is a grt prsumcon agt y.]

Fifthly, *if the partie suspected be the sonne or daughter,* the manservant or maidservant, the *familiar friend, neere neighbor, or old copanion of a known* and *convicted Witch. This* may be likewise *a presumption. For Witchcraft is an art that may be learned and conveied from man to man, and often it falleth out, that a Witch dying leaveth some of the* forenamed, *heires of her Witchcraft.*

[5. If ye pty suspected be ye son or daughter, the serv't or familiar friend, neer neighbors or old companion of a knowne or convicted witch this alsoe is a prsumcon, for witchcraft is an art yt may be larned & covayed from man to man & oft it falleth out yt a witch dying leaveth som of ye aforesd heires of her witchcraft.]

Sixthly, some doe add this for a presumption; *If the partie suspected* be found to *have the devills marke; for it is* commonly *thought, when the devill maketh his covenant with them, he alwaies leaveth his marke behinde him,* whereby he *knowes them for his owne.* Now if by some casual meanes, such a marke be descried [dis- covered] on the bodie of the partie suspected, *whereof no eveident reason in* nature *can be given*, the Magistrate in this case may cause such to be examined, or take the matter into his owne hand, that truth may appeare.

[If ye pty suspected have ye devills mark for t'is thought wn ye devill maketh his covent with y he alwayess leaves his mark behind him to know y for his owne yt is, if noe evident reason in _____ (the illegible word in the original document is nature) can be given for such mark.]

*Lastly, if the partie examined be unconstant,* or *contrarie to himselfe in his* deliberate *answers*, it argueth a guiltie minde and conscience which stoppeth the freedome of speech and utterance, and may give just occasion to the Magistrate to make further enquirie. I say not if he or thee be timorous and fearefull: for a good man may be fearefull in a good cause, sometimes by nature, sometimes in regard of the presence of the Judge, and the greatnes of the audience. Againe, some may be sodenly taken, and others naturally want the libertie of speech, which other men have. And these are the causes of feare & astonishment, which may befall the good, as well as the bad.

[7. Lastly if ye pty examined be unconstant & contrary to himselfe in his answers.]

Touching the manner of *Examination*, there be two kinds of proceedings; either by a single *question*, or by some *Torture*. A single question is, when the Magistrate himslefe onely maketh enquirie, what was done or not done, by bare and naked interrogations. A torture is, when besides the enquirie in words, he useth also the racke, or some other violent meanes to urge confession. This course has beene taken in some countries, and may no doubt lawfully and with good conscience be used, howbeit not in every case, but only *upon strong and great presumptions* going before, and when the party is obstinate, And thus much for Examination: now followeth Conviction.[2]

[Thus much for examinacon wch usually is by Q. & some tymes by torture upon strong & grt presumscon.]

*Conviction,* is an action of the Magistrate, after just examination, discovering the Witch. This action must proceed from *just & sufficient proofes*, and not from bare presumptions. For though presumptions give occasion to examine, yet they are no sufficient causes of conviction. Now in *general the proofes* used *for conviction are two sorts, some be lesse sufficient, some be more sufficient.*

[For conviccon it must be grounded on just and sufficient proofes. The proofes for conviccon of 2 sorts, 1, Some be less sufficient, some more sufficient.]

The *lesse sufficient* proofes are these. First *in former ages*, the partie suspected of Witchcraft was brought before the Magistrate, who caused *red hoat iron, and scalding water* to be brought, and *commanded the partie to put his hand in the one, or to take up* … iron in his bare hand without burning, or endured the water without scalding hereby he was *cleared*, and judged free, but if hee did burne or scalde, he was then *convicted, and condemned for a Witch.* But this manner of conviction, hath long agone beene *condemned* for wicked and diabolical, as in truth it is, considering that thereby many times, an innocent man may bee condemned, and a rancke Witch scape unpunished.

[Less sufficient used in formr ages by red hot iron and scalding water. Ye pty to put in his hand in one or take up ye othr, if not hurt ye pty cleered, if hurt convicted for a witch, but this was utterly condemned.]

Againe, our owne times have afforded instances of such weake and insufficient proofes. As first Scratching of the Suspected partie, and present recoverie thereupon. Secondly, burning of the thing bewitched, if it be not a man, as a hogge, or oxe, or such like creature, is imagined to be forcible meanes to cause the Witch to discover her selfe. Thirdly, burning of the thatch of the suspected parties house, which is thought to be able to cure the partie bewitched, and to make the Witch to betray her selfe.

Besides these, in other *countries* they have a further *proofe justified by some* that be *learned*. The partie is taken, and bound hand and foote, and cast cross wais into water, *if she sincke*, she is *counted innocent*, and escapeth, if shee float on the water, and sincke not, she is taken for a Witch, convicted, and accordingly punished.

[In som countryes anothr proofe justified by some of ye learned by casting ye pty bound into water, if she sanck counted inocent, if she sunk not yn guilty, but all those tryalls the author counts supstitious and unwarrantable and worse.]

All these proofes are so farre from being sufficient, that some of them, if not all, are after a sort practices of Witchcraft, having in them no power or vertue to detect a Sorcerer, either by God's ordinance in the creation, or by any speciall appointment since. For what vertue can Scratching of a Witch have to cure a hurt? Where doe we finde it in any part of the word of God, that scratching should be used? Or what promise of recoverie upon use thereof.

But how then comes it to passe, that helpe is often procured by these & such like meanes? Ans. It is the sleight and subtiltie of the devill upon scratching the Witch, to remoove such hurts, as himselfe hath inflicted, that thereby he may inure men to the practise of wicked and superstitious meanes. And what I say of scratching, the same maybe enlarged to all other proofes of this kind before named. God hath imprinted no such vertue in their natures to these purposes, or added the same unto them by speciall and extraordinarie assignment. That therefore which is brought to passe by them when they are used commeth from the devill.

And yet to justifie the *casting* of a Witch into Water, it is alledged, that *having made a covenant with the devill, shee hath renounced her Baptisme,* and hereupon there growes an *Antipathie betweene her, and water.* Ans. This allegation serves to no purpose: for all water is not the water of Baptisme, but that onely which is used in the very act of Baptisme, and not before nor after. The element out of the use of the Sacrament, is no Sacrament, but returnes again to his common use.

[Although casting into ye water is by some justified for ye witch having mad a ct wth ye devil she hath renounced her baptm & hence ye antipathy between her & water, but this he makes nothing off.]

To goe yet further, in other *insufficient* proofe, *is the testimonie of some wizzard.* It hathe been the oridnarie custome of some men, when they have had any thing ill at ease, presently to go or send to some wise man, or wise woman, by whome they have beene informed, that the thing is bewitched, and to winne credit, to their answer, some of them have offered *to shew* the *Witches face in a glasse*: whereof the partie having taken notice, returnes home, and detecteth the man or woman of witchcraft. This I graunt may be a good presumption to cause strict examination: but a sufficient proofe of conviction it cannot be. For put the case the grand Jurie at the Assises goeth on a partie suspected, and in their consultation the Devill comes in the likeness of some knowne man & tells them the person in question is indeed a Witch, and offers with all to confirme the same by othe [oath]; should the Inquest receive his othe or accusation to condemne the man? Asuredly no; and yet that is as much as the testimonie of another wizzard, who onely by the devills helpe revealeth the Witch. If this should be taken for a sufficient proofe; the devill would not leave one good man alive in the world.

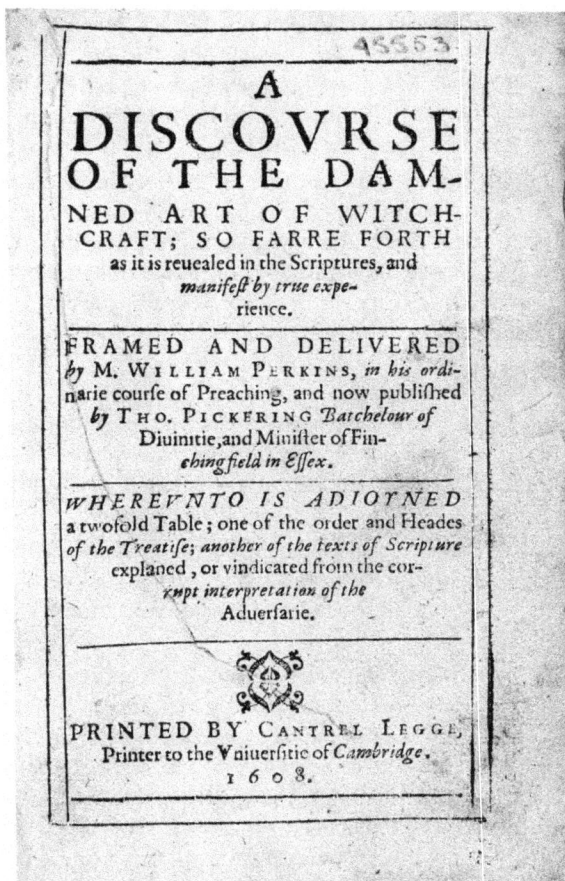

The title page of William Perkins' influential demonological tract *A Discourse of the Damned Art of Witchcraft*, London, published posthumously in 1608. He died in 1602 (courtesy Wellcome Library, London).

[Another insufficient testimony of a witch is ye testimony of a wizard, who prtends to show ye face of ye witch to ye party afflicted in a glass, but this he counts diabolicall & dangerous, ye devill may represent a pson innocent.]

Againe, all other presumptions commonly used, are insufficient, though they may minister occasion of trial, for example; If a man in open court should affirme before the judge; Such a one fell out with me, and cursed me, giving me threatening words, that I should smart for it, and some mischiefe should light upon my person or goods, ere it were long. Upon these *curses and threats*, presently such and such evills befell me, and I suffered these and these losses. The magistrate thus informed may safely proceed to inquire into the matter, but he hath not from hence any sure ground of conviction. For it pleaseth God many times to lay his hand upon mens persons and goods, without the procurement of Witches. And yet experience shewes, that ignorant people who carie a rage against them, wil make strong proofes of such presumptions, whereupon sometimes Jurers doe give their Verdict against parties innocent.

Lastly, if a man being dangerously *sicke, and like to die,* upon susption will *take it on his death,* that *such a one hath bewitched him,* it is an allegation of the same nature, which may moove the judge to examine the partie, but it is of no moment for *conviction.* The reason is because it was but the suspition of one man, and a man's owne worde for himselfe, though in time of extremite, when it is likely he will speake nothing but the truth, is of no more force then another mans word against him.

[Nay if after curses & threats mischiefe follow or if a sick pson like to dy take it on his death such a one has bewitched him, there are strong grounds of suspicon for strict examinacon but not sufficient for conviccon.]

And these are the proofes, which men in place and time have ordinarily used, for detecting of such ungodly persons: but the best that may saide of them is, that they be all either false or uncertaine signes, and unavailable for the condemnation of any man whatsoever.

Now follow the *true proofes, and sufficient meanes of conviction,* all which may be reduced to two heads.

The first, is the free and *voluntarie confession* of the crime, made by the *partie suspected,* and accused after examination. This hath beene thought generally of all men both *Divines, and Lawyers* a *proofe sufficient.* For what needs more witnes, or further enquirie, when a man from the touch of his own conscience acknowledgeth the fault.

[But ye truer proofes sufficient for conviction are ye voluntary confession of ye pty suspected adjudged sufficient proofe by both divines & lawyers.]

And yet the patrons and advocates of Witches except against it, and object in this manner: That a man or woman may confess against themselves an untruth, beeing urged thereto either by feare or threatening, or by a desire, upon some grief conceived, to be out of the world; or at least, being in trouble, and persuaded it is the best course to save their lives, and obtaine libertie, they may upon simplicitie be induced to confesse that, which they never did, even against themselves. Ans. I say not, that a bare confession is sufficient, but a confession after due examination taken upon pregnant presumptions. For if a man examined without any ground or presumptions, should openly acknowledge the crime, his act may be justly suspected, as grounded upon by respects; but when proceeding is made against him at the first, upon good probabilities, and hereupon he be drawn to a free confession, that which he hath manifested thereby, cannot but be a truth. Other points of exception urged by them, are of small moment, and may easily be answered out of the grounds before delivered, and therefore I omit them.

Now if the partie held in suspition, be examined, and will not confesse, but obstinately persist in denial, as commonly it falleth out; then there is another course to be taken by a second sufficient means of conviction: which is the *testimonie of two witnesses, of good and honest report, avouching before the Magistrate* upon *their* owne *knowledge*, these two things: Either that *the partie accused, hath made a league with the devill; or hath* done *some knowne practices of Witchcraft*. And all arguments that doe necessarily proove either of these, beeing brought by two sufficient witnesses, are of force fully to convince the partie suspected. For example.

[Or 2 the testimony of 2 witnesses of good and honest report avouching things in theire knowledge before ye magistrate 1 wither yt ye party accused hath made a league with ye devil or 2d or hath ben some knowne practices of witchcraft.]

First if they can proove that the *partie* suspected, *hath invocated and called upon the devill, or desired his helpe*. For this is a branch of that worshippe, which Satan bindeth his instruments to give unto him. And it is pregnant proofe of a league formerly made betweene them.

[Argumts to prove either must be as 1 if they can pve ye pty hath invocated ye devill for his help this pt of yt ye devill binds withes to.]

Secondly, if they can give evidence that the partie *hath intertained a familiar spirit,* and had conference with it, in former or likeness of a *mouse, catte, or some other visible creature.*

[Or 2 if ye pty hath entertained a familiar spt in any forme mouse cat or othr visible creature.]

Thirdly, *if they affirme upon oath* that the suspected person *hath done any action or worke,* which necessarily *inferreth a covenant* made, as that he hath *shewed the face of a man* suspected, being absent, *in a glasse; or used Inchantment, or such like feats.* In a word, if they both can avouch upon their owne proper knowledge, that such a man or woman suspected, have put in practise any other actions of Witchcraft, as to have *divined of things* afore they came to passe, and that peremptorily; to have *raised tempests, to have caused the forme of a dead man to appeare, or the like,* standing either in divination or operation, it *prooveth sufficiently* that he or shee is *a Witch.*

[Or 3 if they affirm upon oath ye pty hath done any accon or work wch inferreth a ct wth ye devill, as to shew ye face of a man in a glass, or used inchantmts or such feates, divineing of things to come, raising tempests, or causing ye forme of a dead man to appare or ye like it sufficiently pvs a witch.]

But some may say, if these be the onley strong proofes for the conviction of a Sorcerer, it will be then impossible to put any one to death, because the league with Satan is closely made, and the practices of Sorcerie are also very secret, and hardly can a man be brought, which upon his owne knowledge, can averre such things.

I answer, howsoever both the ground and practise be secret, and to many unknowne, yet there is a way to come to the knowledge thereof. *For it is usual with Satan to promise any thing, till the league be ratified:* but when it is once made, and the partie intangled in societie with him, then he *indeavoureth nothing more,* than his or her *discoverie,* and useth all meanes possible to disclose them. So that what end soever the Witch propoundeth to her selfe in the league, he *intendeth nothing els, but her utter confusion.* Therefore in the just judgment of God, it often falleth out, that these which are true Witches indeede, *that either by confession discover themselves, or by true testimonie be* convicted. The causes which moove the devill not onely to effect, but to hasten this discoverie are two principally.

[But altho those things are difficult to prove yet yr are wayes to come to the knowledg of y, for tis usuall with Satan to pmise anything till ye league be ratified, & then he (endeavoreth) ... nothing (more than) ... ye discovery of y, for wtever witches intend the devill intends nothing but theire utter confusion, therefore in ye just judgmt of God it soe oft falls out yt some witches shall by confession discour ys, or by true testimonies be convicted.]

*The first is, his malice towards all men,* in so high a degree, that he cannot indure they should enjoy the world, or the benefits of this life (if it were possible) so much as one houre. Though therefore by vertue of the precontract, he be cocksure of his instrument, yet his malice is not hierwith satisfied, till the partie be brought to light, and condemned to death. Which may be a caveat to all ill disposed persons, that they beware of yielding themselves unto him.

[And ye reasons why ye devill would discover y is 1 his malice toward all men....]

The second, is this *insatiable desire* of the present and full possession of them, whom he hath got within the bonds of the covenant. For though he have good hope of them, yet is he not certan of their continuence. The reason is, because some united with him in confederacie; have through the great mercie of God, by careful usage of holy meanes and faith in Christ been reclaimed and delivered out of his bondage, and so at length freed from his covenant, so as he hath eternally left them. Hence it is, that he labours by might and maine, to keepe them in ignorance, and to present the usage of meanes effectuall to ther conversion, by laying a plot for their discoverie. But how then comes it to passe, that all such persons are not speedily detected, but some live long and others die without any mans privirie [knowledge]?

[... 2 his insatiable desire to have ye witches not sure enough of y till yn.]

First, because ___ one or more of them may belong to Gods election and therefore albeit for causes best knowne to himselfe, he may suffer them for a time to be holden in the snares of Satan, yet at length in mercie he claims them, and in the meane time suffereth not the devill to exercise the depth of his malice in discovering them to their confusion. Againe for others, the Lord may in justice and anger suffer them not to be disclosed that living under the meanes, where they might be reclaimed, and willfully contemning the same; they may live to fill up the measure of their iniquities, and thereby be made finally inexcusable, that they may receive their utter condemnation.

Secondly, the devill suffereth some to live long undisclosed, that they may exercise the greater measure of his malice in the world; specially if they be parties malitiously bent to doe hurt to men and other creatures.

Thirdly, some Witches doe warily agree with the devil, for a certaine tearme of yeares, during which time he bindeth himselfe not to hurt them, but to be at their command. And Satan is careful, specially in case of his owne advantage, to keepe touch with them that they may the more strongly cleave unto him on their parts. But if the case so stand, that neither the parties suspected confesseth, nor yet sufficient witnesses can be produced, which are able to convict him or her, either of these two wais: we have no warrant out of the word either in general, or in special, to put such a one to death. For though presumptions be never so strong, yet they are not proofes sufficient for conviction, but onley for examination.

I would therefore wish and advise all Jurers, who give their Verdict upon life and death in courts of Assises, to take good hedde, that as they be diligent in zeale of Gods glorie, and the good of his Church, in detecting of Witches, by all sufficient and lawful meanes; so likewise they would be carefull what they doe, and *not to condemn* any party *suspected* upon *bare presumptions without* sound and *sufficient proofes,* that they be not guiltie through their own rashnesse of shedding innocent blood.

[And ye authors warne jurors &c not to condemn suspected psons on bare prsumtions wthout good & sufficient proofes.]

## The Final Sentence

The following is not part of the original advice given by Perkins in this section of chapter 7 in his *Discourse on the Damned Art of Witchcraft.* It was added by the individual who did the original extraction from his book or used a previously written document titled "The Examination of a Witch." However, throughout Perkins' book he advocated death for convicted witches. Therefore, this final sentence would undoubtedly be a fitting conclusion. It was in the same spirit of his discussion of Mosaic Law in regard to witchcraft. The concluding sentence in the *Examination of a Witch* is of course in reference to Exodus 22:18, and this reference is also found in the early laws of Connecticut.

[But if convicted of yt horrid crime to be put to death, for God hath said thou shalt not suffer a witch to live.][3]

# Chapter Notes

## Preface

1. John Ashton, *The Devil in Britain and America* (London: Ward and Downey, 1896), 317.
2. L. P. Hartley, *The Go-Between* (London: H. Hamilton, 1953), 1.

## Introduction

1. Malcolm Gaskill, "Witches and Witnesses in Old and New England," in Stuart Clark, ed., *Languages of Witchcraft: Narrative, Ideology, and Meaning in Early Modern Culture* (New York: Palgrave Macmillan, 2001), 57. With regard to the interconnections and influence of England on the early New England "plantations" see David Grayson Allen, *In English Ways: The Movement of Societies and their Transferal of English Local Law and Custom to the Massachusetts Bay in the Seventeenth Century* (Chapel Hill: University of North Carolina Press, 1981); David Cressy, *Coming Over: Migration and Communication between England and New England in the Seventeenth Century* (New York: Cambridge University Press, 1987); Francis J. Bremer, *Puritan Crisis New England and the English Civil Wars, 1630–1670* (New York: Garland Press, 1989); Carla Gardina Pestana, *The English Atlantic in an Age of Revolution 1640–1661* (Cambridge, MA: Harvard University Press, 2004); and Alison Games, *Migration and the Origins of the English Atlantic World* (Cambridge, MA: Harvard University Press, 1999).
2. Joseph Hall, *Susurrium cum Deo soliloques, or Holy Self-Conferences of the Devout Soul Upon Sundry Choice Occasions* (London: Will. Hunt, 1651), 51–53.
3. Malcolm Gaskill, "Witchcraft, Emotion and Imagination in the English Civil War," in John Newton and Jo Bath, ed., *Witchcraft and the Act of 1604* (Boston, MA: Brill, 2008), 163;

R. Trevor Davies, *Four Centuries of Witch Beliefs* (London: Methuen, 1947), 90–93; and C. L'Estrange Ewen, *Witch Hunting and Witch Trials* (London: Kegan and Paul, 1929), 100.
4. For Salem see Paul Boyer and Stephen Nissenbaum, *Salem Possessed: The Social Origins of Witchcraft* (Cambridge, MA: Harvard University Press, 1974); Emerson Baker and James Kences, "Maine, Indian Land Speculation, and the Essex County Witchcraft Outbreak of 1692," *Maine History* 40 (2001): 159–89; Carol F. Karlsen, *The Devil in the Shape of a Woman: Witchcraft in Colonial New England* (New York: Norton, 1987); and Mary Beth Norton, *In the Devil's Snare: The Salem Witchcraft Crisis of 1692* (New York: Alfred A. Knopf, 2003).
5. Bremer, 347.
6. Ibid., 246–247; John Eliot, *The Christian Commonwealth* (London: 1659); John Cotton, "A Sermon upon the Day of Publique Thanksgiving, from Rev. 15:13," 10 January 1651, mss. in *Massachusetts Historical Society*, 14–20; Bremer, 247; see also Francis J. Bremer, "In Defense of Regicide," *William and Mary Quarterly*, 3rd series, XXXVII, no. 1 (1980): 103–124.
7. James Sharpe, *Instruments of Darkness Witchcraft in Early Modern England* (Philadelphia, PA: University of Pennsylvania, 1996), 140–141.
8. Frederick C. Drake, "Witchcraft in the American Colonies, 1647¬-1662," *American Quarterly* 20 (Winter 1968): 712.
9. Michael Dalton, *The Countrey Justice* (London: 1618) and Richard Bernard *A Guide to the Grand-Jury Men* (London: 1627). On the 1630 edition of *The Countrey Justice,* Dalton incorporated additional material on witches based on Barnard's *Guide to Grand-Jury Men,* 277.
10. Douglas H. Shepard, *The Wolcott Shorthand Notebook Transcribed* (State University of Iowa, Dissertation, 1957), 176.

11. During the 1640's the conversion of the Indians to Christianity was begun and served two purposes: fewer followers for Satan's nefarious purposes and during the economic slump in the 1640's in New England, funds from the charitable societies in England to support the conversion of the Indians added additional income to the cash starved New England plantations.

12. For a discussion of the question of "Continental" ideas infecting English witchcraft beliefs as a consequence of Matthew Hopkins influence in the East Anglian witchcraft trials, 1645–1647, see *Sharpe*, 130–131.

13. For pre-Salem witchcraft activities in New England see Demos, *Entertaining Satan* (New York: Oxford University Press, 1982); Karlsen; Drake, 694–725; and David D. Hall, ed., *Witch Hunting in Seventeenth Century New England* (Boston, MA: Northeastern University Press, 1991). For Springfield, Massachusetts, see Samuel G. Drake, *Annals of Witchcraft in New England, and Elsewhere in the United States from Their First Settlement* (Boston, MA: Woodward, 1869), 219–258. For Connecticut see John M. Taylor, *The Witchcraft Delusion in Colonial Connecticut* (New York: Grafton, 1908); Hall; Richard G. Tomlinson, *Witchcraft Trials of Connecticut* (Hartford, CT: Bond Press, 1978); Richard G. Tomlinson, *Witchcraft Prosecution: Chasing the Devil in Connecticut* (Rockland, ME: Picton Press, 2012); and Cynthia Wolfe Boynton, *Connecticut Witch Trials: The First Panic in the New World* (Charleston, SC: History Press, 2014).

14. Cressy, viii; Allen, 6.

15. Cressy, viii. For Connecticut see The Wyllys Papers, "Correspondence and Documents Chiefly of the Descendants of Gov. George Wyllys of Connecticut 1590–1796," *Collections of the Connecticut Historical Society* 21 (Hartford, CT: Published for the Society, 1924).

16. John Winthrop, *John Winthrop Journal: History of New England* 2, J. Kendall Hosmer, ed., (New York: C. Scribner and Sons, 1908), 99, 178–179.

17. Bremer, 104–105; Cressy, viii–ix.

18. Gaskill, 167.

19. Diane Purkiss, *The English Civil War* (New York: Basic Books, 2006), 377.

20. Sharpe, 129.

21. Benjamin Hubbard, *Sermo Secularis or A Sermon to Bring to Rememberance the Dealings of Jehovah…* (London: R.L., 1648), 19.

# Chapter 1

1. *Signes and Wonders from Heaven* (London: 1645), 2; Purkiss, 375–376.

2. *Observations Upon Prince Rupert's White Dogge Called Boye* (London: 1642), 1; Purkiss, 377–378.

3. *Observations*, 7.

4. *A Dog's Elergy or Ruperts Tears, For the Late Defeat Given Him at Marston Moor Near York* (London: 1644), 1; See Malcolm Gaskill, ed., *English Witchcraft 1560–1736* 3 (London: Pickering & Chatto, 2003), 401–402.

5. *Ibid.*

6. For a discussion of this event and the purpose for this unusual action see the explanation by Davies, 158.

7. Tessa Watt, *Cheap Print and Popular Piety 1550–1640* (New York: Cambridge University Press, 1991), 124; for an example of a ballad telling the story of the witches of Lincolnshire, see "Damnable Practices of the Three Lincolnshire Witches" (London: 1619) in Samuel Pepys, *A Pepysian Garland: Black-letter Broadside Ballads of the Years 1595–1639…*," (Cambridge, England: Cambridge University Press, 1922), 97–103.

8. *Signes and Wonders*, 2; "While every one of the forty counties of England was represented in the great Puritan exodus the East Anglian countries contributed to it far more than the rest"; John Fiske, *The Beginnings of New England: Or, the Puritan Theocracy in Its Relations to Civil and Religious Liberty* (New York: Houghton, Mifflin and Co., 1889), 63; and John Algeo, ed., *Cambridge History of the English Language: English in North America* 6 (New York: Cambridge University Press, 2001), 63. However, those in the Connecticut Valley who initiated the witch hunts were from the West Country. See Frank Thistlethwaite, *The Story of West County Pilgrims Who Went to New England in the 17th Century* (London: Barrie & Jenkins, 1989); Henry R. Stiles, *The History and Genealogies of Ancient Windsor Connecticut* (Hartford: Case, Lockwood and Brainard, 1891); and Linda A. Bissel, *Family, Friends and Neighbors: Social Interaction in Seventeenth-Century Windsor, Connecticut* (Waltham, MA: Brandeis University, Dissertation, 1973).

9. Demos, 12; C. L. Ewen, *Witchcraft and Demonianism* (London: 1913); Wallace Notestein, *A History of Witchcraft in England from 1558–1718* (Washington, DC: 1911), Appendix C.

10. Sharpe, 128–129.

11. Gaskill, xiii–xiv.

12. Richard Weismann, *Witchcraft, Magic, and Religion in 17th Century Massachusetts* (Amherst, MA: University of Massachusetts Press, 1984), 13.

13. Gaskill, xiv–xvi.

14. Davies, 126

15. *Ibid.*, 117.
16. *Ibid.*, 97 and 126
17. *A True and Exact Relation of the several Informations, Examinations, and Confessions of the Late Witches ... the 29th of July, 1645*; Davies, 126; and Malcolm Gaskill, *Witchfinders A Seventeenth-Century English Tragedy* (Cambridge, MA: Cambridge University Press, 2005), 136.
18. Gaskill, 136; Henry Peacham, *The worth of a peny ... and also what honest courses men in want may take to live* (London: 1641), 21.
19. Hall, *Susurrium...*, 50–51.
20. *Mercurius Britannicus,* no. 95 (August 25, to September 1, 1645): 850–851.
21. John Downame, *Annotations upon all the books of the Old and New Testament* (London: 1652), Exodus XXII, verse 18.
22. Samuel Clarke, *The Lives of Sundry Eminent Persons in this Later Age* (London: 1683), 172.
23. Clarke, 172; Gaskill, 152.
24. Clarke, 172.
25. Gaskill, 156.
26. Clarke, 172.
27. Gaskill, 157–158.
28. *Ibid.*, 158
29. *A True Relation of the Araignment of Eighteene Witches ... St. Edmunds-bury in Suffolke* (London: 1645), 5; Gaskill, *English Witchcraft 1560–1736*, 47; Notestein, 179; and for a contemporary mention that took a skeptical look at these proceedings "we received this day from Bury 200 indictments" for witchcraft. The writer found it incredible the Devil only appeared to "silly women." *Moderate Intelligencer*, no. 28. (September 4, to September 11, 1645): 217.
30. Notestein, 361.
31. Dalton, 251.
32. Gaskill, *Witchfinder*, 32.
33. *Ibid.*, 32–33.
34. See the dedication of his book to the judges at the Taunton *Azzises* in 1626, Bernard, 3–4; Notestein, 234–236; Davies, 136–137; T. Wright, *Narratives of Sorcery and Magic* (New York: Redfield, 1852), 298–300; and Ewen, *Witchcraft and Demonianism* (London: Muller, 1933), 452.
35. Bernard, 218; Davies, 98.
36. Davies, 100.
37. *Ibid.*,105.
38. Dalton, 277; Davies, 106–107
39. S. F. Davies, Matthew Hopkins, John Stearne, eds., *The Discovery of Witches and Witchcraft: The Writings of the Witchfinders* (Brighton, England: Puckrel, 2007), xvii; Hutchinson, *The Witchcraft Delusion of 1692*, ed., William Frederick Poole (Boston, MA: Privately Printed, 1870), 16; and for the period in colonial Massachusetts before 1650, see "William Pynchon to John Winthrop," March 9, 1646/47, "as Dalton in his *Countrey Justice* sheweth" in the *Winthrop Papers 1645–1649* 5 (Boston, MA: Massachusetts Historical Society, 1947), 135.
40. George L. Kittredge, *Witchcraft in Old and New England* (Cambridge, MA: Harvard University Press, 1929), 273. A facsimile of Stearne's book is available in Gaskill, *English Witchcraft 1560–1736* 3, 333–399; see also F. Davies, Matthew Hopkins, John Stearne, eds., *The Discovery of Witches and Witchcraft...*, 9–50. In a more contemporary assessment F. Davies concluded "Stearne's text is indispensable for the study of witchcraft in the seventeenth century," xxiii.
41. Peter Charles Hoffer, *Law and People in Colonial America* (Baltimore, MD: Johns Hopkins University Press, 1992), 7; G.L. Burr, *Narratives of the Witchcraft Cases 1648–1706* (New York: C. Scribner's Sons, 1914); with reference to Connecticut see Taylor, *The Witchcraft Delusion in Colonial Connecticut*, 43; and for an early use of Dalton by Governor Winthrop, Jr., see Hugh King and Loretta Orion, "It Were As Well to Please the Devil As Anger Him," in Tom Twomey, ed., *Awakening the Past: The East Hampton 350th Anniversary Lecture Series 1998* (New York: Newmarket Press, 1999), 199 and 121.
42. John Gaule, *Select Cases of Conscience Touching Witches and Witchcrafts* (London: W. Wilson, 1646), 78–79.
43. Hopkins, *The Discovery of Witches*, 1–2.
44. *Ibid.*, 3.
45. *Ibid.*, 5.
46. *Ibid.*, 6–9.
47. *Ibid.*, 9–10.
48. S. F. Davies, xxi.
49. Nathaniel B. Shurtleff, ed., *Records of the Governor and Company of the Massachusetts Bay in New England 1642–1649* 3 (Boston, MA: William White, 1853), 126 and v. 2, 242.
50. Winthrop, v. 2, 344–345.
51. *Ibid.*; and for confirmation, "14 June 48 Marg. Jones was executed at Boston for witchcraft," in Samuel Danforth, *An Almanac for the Year of our Lord 1648* (Cambridge, MA: 1648), 11.
52. For a good discussion of this problem see Godbeer, 14–20.
53. Simon Walker, *The Witches of Hertfordshire* (Stroud, Gloucestershire: Tempus, 2004), 41. For a discussion of witchcraft beliefs and traditions carried over from England to New England see Kittredge, 22–32; David D. Hall, *Worlds of Wonder Days of Judgment* (Cambridge, MA: Harvard University Press, 1989), Chapter 2; Godbeer, Introduction; and Weismann, Chapters 3–5.

54. Davies, 117.

55. Drake, 711–712, and for the number of witches executed see Sharpe, 129; Stearne estimated there "...being about 200 in number," 336; even the imprisoned Royalist James Howell was suspicious of such a high number and wrote on February 3, 1646, "we saw likewise a multitude of witches among us, for in Essex and Suffolk there were above two hundred indicted these two years, and above the one half executed..." and concluded England had never seen anything like it "since the Creation"; James Howell, *Epistolæ Ho-Elianæ: the Familiar Letters of James Howell* 2 (Boston, MA: Houghton Mifflin, 1908), 309.

56. Drake, 711.

57. Kittredge, 363.

58. Sally Smith Booth, *The Witches of Early America* (New York: Hastings House, 1975), 142–43; John Cotton, *An Abstract of the Lawes of New England As they are now established* (London: 1641), 10.

59. For the latter see Hall, *Worlds of Wonder Days...*, Chapter 2; and Richard Godbeer, *The Devil's Dominion: Magic and Religion in Early New England* (New York: Cambridge University Press, 1992).

60. John Hart, D.D., *Trodden down Strength by the God of Strength or Mrs. Drake Revived...*, (London: 1646), 127–129; Thomas Shepard, "Memoirs of My Life" in Alexander Young, ed., *Chronicles of the First Planters of the Colony of Massachusetts Bay, 1623–1636* (Boston, MA: Little and J. Brown, 1846), 528.

61. *Winthrop's Journal*, vol. 1, 268, and vol. 2, 8.

62. Owen Davies, *Popular Magic: Cunning-folk in English History* (New York: Hambledon and London, 2003), viii, 31, 67–70.

63. *Winthrop Papers*, vol. 4, 76 and 99.

64. Philip F. Gura, *A Glimpse of Sion's Glory Puritan Radicalism in New England 1620–1660* (Middletown, CT: Wesleyan University Press, 1984), 12–13.

65. Richard Mather and Willliam Tompson, *A Modest and Brotherly Answer to Mr. Charles Herle his Book, Against the Independency of Churches* (London: 1643), 58; Bremer, 106.

66. Joseph Hall, 51–53.

67. Shurtleff, vol. 3, 126, and vol. 2, 242; Justin Winsor, ed., *The Memorial History of Boston: Including Suffolk County 1630–1680*, vol. 2, 132.

68. Cressy, 213.

69. *Ibid.*, 216.

70. *Ibid.*, 223–225; and *The Wyllys Papers...*, vol. 21, 95.

71. *Ibid.*, 232, and see *Winthrop Papers*, vol. 3, 190–191, for an example of an encrypted letter with a casement for de-coding.

72. *Ibid.*, 217.

73. Kenneth A. Lockridge, *Literacy in Colonial New England* (New York: Norton, 1974), 15.

74. Cressy, 232; Anthony Fletcher, "National and Local Awareness in the County Communities," in Howard Tomlinson ed., *Before the English Civil War* (London: MacMillan, 1983), 173.

75. Gardiner wrote to Winthrop, Jr., of a young person sent to work for him, "being ... but a yong man hapily he hath not manie books thear fore let him know what I have first the 3 books of Martters Erasmus, most of Perkins [William Perkins the protestant theologian and demonologist] Wilsons dixtionare ... [and] ... Mayo on the N[e]wtestment." "Lion Gardiner to John Winthrop Jr.," April 27, 1650, in *Winthrop Papers*, vol. 6, Malcolm Freiberg, ed., (Boston, MA: Massachusetts Historical Society, 1992), 36.

76. John Davenport, *Letters of John Davenport*, Elizabeth Calder, ed., (New Haven: Yale University Press, 1937): 137–138 and 148.

77. Cressy, 233–234; and "sent two dozen almanacs." Letter from Henry Dunster's father in Lancashire, England, to Henry Dunster, in Massachusetts, March 20, 1640, *Dunster Papers*, Massachusetts Historical Collections ser. 4, vol. 2 (1854), 191.

78. Aside from the puritans "who professed to have their thoughts glued on the endless spaces of eternity and among those who read only for information and clues to success, the reading audience sought pleasure and diversion in books, and many writers." As a result, "many of these people craved entertainment ... and sensationalism." Edwin Miller, *The Professional Writer in Elizabethan England* (Cambridge, MA: Harvard University Press, 1959), 54 and 84. Besides humor and sex this also included "the violence that pervaded narratives of witchcraft, war, death and supernatural wonders." David D. Hall, *Worlds of Wonder...*, 53.

79. Cressy, 246.

80. *Winthrop Papers*, vol. 5, 157.

81. Cressy, 247.

82. *Winthrop Papers*, vol. 5, 320.

83. *The Parliaments Post*, 29 July–5 August 1645, 2; Davies, 158.

84. *Diary or an Exact Journal ... of the Houses of Parliament*, 24–31 July 1645, 6; *The Parliaments Post*, 29 July–5 August 1645, 1; *A Perfect Diurnal*, 21–28 July 1645, 830; and *Mercurius Aulicus*, 10–17 August 1645, 1697.

85. *The Moderate Intelligencer*, 4–11 September 1645, 217.

86. Gaskill, *Witchfinders*, 158–159 and 162–163. *Moderate Intelligencer*, 217.

87. *Ibid.*, 136.

88. *Winthrop Papers*, vol. 3, 106.

89. *Winthrop Papers*, vol. 4, 491–493.

90. *Winthrop Papers*, vol. 5, 157.

91. Cressy, 52–53.

92. *Winthrop Papers*, vol. 5, 353.

93. Charles Chauncy, *God's Mercy Shewed to His People Giving Them Faithful Ministry and Schooles of Learning for the Continual Supply Therof* (Cambridge, New England: 1651), 19.

94. Edward Johnson, *Wonder-working providence of Sions Saviour in New England* 2 (London: 1654, reprint Andover, MA: W.F. Draper, 1867), 199; for criticism of Johnson's Springfield, Massachusetts, witchcraft troubles see Hutchinson, 6; and Douglas Shepard, 336.

95. *Mercurius Politicus*, 18–25 September 1651, 1091; see also Joseph H. Smith, *Colonial Justice in Western Massachusetts 1639–1702* (Cambridge, MA: Harvard University Press, 1961), 22.

96. *Mercurius Politicus*, 1091.

97. John Eliot, "To his Excellency, the Lord General Cromwel, Grace, Mercy and Peace," in John Eliot and Thomas Mayhew, *Tears of repentance: or, A further narrative of the progress of the Gospel amongst the Indians in New-England...* (London: Peter Cole, 1653), A2.

98. Bremer, 250–25.

99. *Ibid.*, 252–253.

100. *Ibid.*, 278–279.

101. *Ibid.*, 282–284.

102. See for example Richard Beale Davis, "The Devil in Virginia in the Seventeenth Century," *Virginia Magazine of History and Biography* 65 (1957):131–49 and Frederick C. Drake, "Witchcraft in the American Colonies, 1647–62," *American Quarterly* 20 (1968): 694–725. In some cases "justice" was meted out directly. On June 23, 1654, at the Proceedings of the Council of Maryland there were two depositions concerning a woman on the ship *Charity* of London purported to be a witch. The crew asked the captain to do something about her and have a trial. He refused. The "ship grew more leaky." The crew became more desperate. They attempted to hold a trial with men from other ships but the weather was too foul. Finally "two of the Seamen apprehended her without order and Searched her and found some Signal or Marke of a witch upon her." The next morning she confessed to being a witch. The crew asked the captain to put her to death. The captain refused and simply returned to his cabin. The next thing he knew she had been hanged by the crew. William Hande Brown, ed., *Proceedings of the Council of Maryland 1636–1667* (Baltimore, MD: 1885), 306–308.

# Chapter 2

1. Winsor, vol. 2, 132.

2. Gura, 127.

3. Thomas Hooker, *The Danger...*, 15.

4. Gura, 127.

5. *Ibid.*, 128.

6. *Ibid.*

7. Winsor, vol. 2, 132.

8. Cotton Mather, *Wonders of the Invisible World* (London: John Russell Smith, 1862), 195.

9. *Ibid.*, 74.

10. Gura, 128–129; see David D. Hall, ed., "Examination of Hutchinson at Newtowne," *The Antinomian controversy, 1636–1638: a documentary history* (Middletown, CT: Wesleyan University Press, 1968), 339.

11. John Winthrop, *Antinomians and Familists Condemned by the Synod of Elders in New England,* (London: Ralph Smith, 1644), 22, 31, 39, 40, and 43.

12. "A Brief Apologie in defence of the general proceedings of the Court, holden at Boston the ninth day of the fifth month, 1636 against Mr. Wheelwright, a member there, by occasion of a Sermon delivered there in the Same Congregation," in John Winthrop, *Antinomians*, 59.

13. *Ibid.*, 64.

14. *Ibid.*, 64–65.

15. Peter Bulkley, *The Gospel Covenant, or the Covenant of Grace Opened* (London: Matthew Simmons, 1646), 293.

16. John Winthrop, *Winthrop's Journal History of New England 1630–1649* 1 (New York: Charles Scribner and Sons, 1908), 267–268.

17. *Ibid.*, 268.

18. *Winthrop's Journal* 2: 8; Winthrop, *Antinomians*, 44.

19. William Perkins, *Discourse of the Damned Art of Witchcraft* (Cambridge, England: Cantrel Legge, 1608), 176.

20. John Winthrop, *The History of New England from 1630 to 1649*, J. Savage, ed., vol. 1 (Boston: Thomas B. Waite, 1825), 271.

21. Thomas Weld and John Winthrop, *A short story of the rise, reign, and ruin of the antinomians familists & libertines that infected the churches of New-England ... and the lamentable death of Ms. Hutchison* (London: Ralph Smith, 1644), preface.

22. John Josselyn, *An account of two Voyages to New-England* (London: G. Widdowes, 1674), 11 and 27–28.

23. Winthrop, *The history of New England from 1630 to 1649* 1 (1825): 271–273, (The Savage 1825 edition contains Mr. Clark's findings); see Margaret Richardson and Arthur T. Hertig, "New England's First Recorded Hydatidiform Mole," *New England Journal of Medicine* 260 (March 1959): 544–545; and Weld and Winthrop, *A short story of the rise...*, preface.

24. John Winthrop, *Winthrop's Journal: History of New England, 1630–1649* 2 (1908): 7–8.

25. Joseph Barlow Felt, *The Ecclesiastical History of New England: Comprising Not Only Religious but also Moral, and other Relations*, vol. 1 (Boston, MA: Congregational Library Association, 1855), 466.

26. Gura, 69–70; and Weld and Winthrop, *A short story of the rise...*, preface.

27. *Ibid.*, 320.

28. *Ibid.*, 304 and 309.

29. *Ibid.*, 305.

30. Smith, *Colonial Justice*, 13–15; and J. Hammond Trumbull, *The Public Records of the Colony of Connecticut*, vol. 1 (Hartford: Brown & Parsons, 1850), 11–16.

31. Perry Miller, *Errand into the Wilderness* (Cambridge, MA: Harvard University Press, 1956), 45.

32. Mason A. Green, *Springfield, 1636–1886: History of Town and City* (Springfield, MA: C.A. Nichols & Co., 1888), 54–60.

33. Simeon Eban Baldwin, *The Secession of Springfield from Connecticut* (Cambridge, MA: John Wilson and Son, 1908), 70.

34. Smith, *Colonial Justice*, 18.

35. For example in the "Articles of Confederation betwixt the Plantation under the government of the Massachusetts Bay, the Plantation under the Government of Plimouth, the plantation under the government of Connecticut, and the government of New Haven, with the Plantations in Combination therewith," in *New Haven's Settling in New-England* (London: Livewell Chapman, 1656), on witchcraft 22–23 and heresy 42.

36. Alan Macfarlane, *Witchcraft in Tudor and Stuart England; a regional and comparative study* (New York: Harper & Row, 1970), 440–441.

37. Edward Johnson, *A history of New-England. From the English planting in the yeere 1628. untill the yeere 1652* (London: 1654), 199; and Hutchinson, 6.

38. Henry M. Burt, *The First Century of the History of Springfield; the Official Records 1636–1736*, vol. 1 (Springfield, MA: Henry M. Burt, 1898), 73–74.

39. *Ibid.*, 74, 78

40. Smith, *Colonial Justice*, 24.

41. Burt, 80; and Smith, *Colonial Justice*, 26.

42. Nathaniel B. Shurtleff, ed., *Records of the Governor and Company of the Massachusetts Bay in New England, 1644–1657*, v. 4, 29 (Boston, MA: William White, 1854); Burt, 83.

43. Burt, 83–84.

44. *Ibid.*, 86.

45. *Ibid.*, 87.

46. John H. Lockwood, *History of Western Massachusetts 1636–1925*, vol. 1 (New York: Lewis Historical Publishing Co., 1926), 108.

47. Gura, 320–321.

48. *Ibid.*, 322.

49. Smith, *Colonial Justice*, 27–28; Burt, 88.

## Chapter 3

1. Thistlethwaite, 24–25.

2. *Ibid.*, 45.

3. *Ibid.*, 45–46. In the previous spring a few families of Dorchester origin had sailed on the *Lyon's Whelp* for Salem with families from Dorset and Somerset. It seems the people of Dorchester were well aware of "New England's high purpose" as preached from the pulpit because one woman "accused her parson of funneling away money for that project which ought by rights to have gone to the town poor."

4. *Ibid.*, 49–50.

5. *Ibid.*, 54.

6. *Ibid.*, 55–56 and 62.

7. Cressy, 149–150.

8. *Ibid.*, 149.

9. John White, *The Planter's Plea or the Grounds of Plantations Examined and Usual Objections Answered* (London: William Lones, 1630), 62; Thistlethwaite, 51.

10. Cressy, 146.

11. Thistlethwaite, 64; and Cressy, 148, for all the fear of sailing "of 198 recorded voyages bringing settlers to New England in the 1630's only that of the *Angel Gabriel* ended in disaster and even then most of the passengers survived."

12. Thistlethwaite, 66–67.

13. Cressy, 144, 148–150.

14. Thistlethwaite, 69; Cressy, 150, for examples on other ships.

15. Roger Clapp, "Memoirs of Roger Clapp. 1630," *Collections of the Dorchester Antiquarian and Historical Society*, No. 1 (Boston, 1844): 40–41; and for examples of religious devotions on board other ships carrying Puritan ministers who were not the sole proponents of "providentialism" see Cressy, 157–158; and Thistlethwaite, 152.

16. Thistlethwaite, 94–95.

17. *Ibid.*, 97.

18. Thistlethwaite, 97. Mr. Maverick died on March 3 that year. Mr. Warham was now "free to lead his flock westwards."

19. Bissel, 12–13.

20. Stiles, 43–44; Bissel, 13.

21. Bissel, 14.

22. *Ibid.*; see Stiles, 24–63, on settlement and land purchases see Stiles.

23. Thistlethwaite, 99.

24. *Ibid.*, 99.

25. Stiles, 45.

26. *Ibid.*, 47.

27. Stiles, 63; Thistlethwaite, 144–148.

28. Thistlethwaite, 144–145.
29. *Ibid.*, 144–145
30. *Ibid.*, 145–146.
31. *Ibid.*, 147.
32. Stiles, 151.
33. Thistlethwaite, 147–148.
34. Thomas Cooper, *The Mystery of Witchcraft* (London: N. Okes, 1617), 12–13; Kittredge, 294–295; and Davies, 54.
35. Kittredge, 291.
36. For a discussion of witchcraft at Oxford and Cambridge Universities see Kittredge, 290–297.
37. Thistlethwaite, 174.
38. Shepard, "The Wolcott Shorthand Notebook...," and Carolyn S. Langdon, "Connecticut Witchcraft-What Was It?" *Connecticut Historical Society Bulletin* 38 (January 1973): 26.
39. Notestein, 121; Phillip Almond, *The Lancashire Witches: A Chronicle of Sorcery and Death on Pendle Hill* (London: I.B. Tauris, 2012), xii.
40. Notestein, 126; and Davies, 76–95, passim.
41. Ewen, 452.
42. John Collinson and Edmund Rack, *The History and Antiquities of the County of Somerset: Collected from Authentick Records*, vol. 2 (Bath, England: R. Cruttwell, 1791), 362.
43. R. L. Tongue, *Somerset Folklore* (London: Folk-Lore Society, 1965), 65; and belief in witches in the nineteenth and twentieth centuries in the areas of Devon, Dorset and Somerset is described by Olive Knott, *Witches of Dorset* (Dorset: Dorset Pub. Co. 1974), 17: "Advertising a seven-toad cat in our regional rural newspaper is enough to bring every witch from Dorset and Somerset to your doorstep." "A Dorset doctor even testified to cases of a mysterious healing of farm animals brought about by witches."
44. See Kittredge, 80, for an early investigation of witchcraft in "Somerset, Dorset and Cornwall," in 1426; see Ewen 439–446 and 452, for an index to witchcraft cases for the western circuit 1559–1707 assembled from a variety of sources.
45. Bernard, title page.
46. Notestein, 235; Davies, 97; Jonathan Barry, *Witchcraft and Demonology in South-West England 1640–1670* (London: Palgrave MacMillan, 2012), 29–30, see especially page 47 for his connection to Reverend Richard Bernard.
47. John Collinson, vol. 2, 362.
48. Brit. Mus., MS. 36, 674, f. 189 in Ewen, *Witchcraft and Demonism*, 452.
49. Thomas Wright, *Narratives of Sorcery and Magic from the Most Authentic Sources*, vol. 2 (London: Richard Bentley, 1851), 141–143.

50. Thistlethwaite, 211.
51. "Extracts of Letters to Rev. Thomas Prince," in *Collections of the Connecticut Historical Society*, vol. 3 (Hartford, CT: Connecticut Historical Society, 1895), 277; Thistlethwaite, 211–212.
52. Peter Lake, *The Boxmakers Revenge, Orthodoxy, Heterodoxy and the Politics of the Parish in Early Stuart London* (Manchester, UK: Manchester University Press, 2001), 86.
53. "Mr. Chamberlain to Rev. Joseph Mead February 18, 1624–25," in Thomas Birch, *The Court and Time of James the First*, vol. 2 (London: Henry Colburn, 1848), 498.
54. Lake, 86.
55. "Richard Montague to Mr. John Cosin, St. Valentines Day, 1624–5" and "Richard Montague to Mr. John Cosin, February 1624–25" in G. Ormsby, ed., *The Correspondence of John Cosin*, vol. 52 (Durham, NC: Andrews and Co., 1869), Part 1, 59 and 61.
56. Lake, 87.
57. David R. Como, *Blown by the Spirit: Puritanism and the Emergence of an Antinomian Underground in Pre-Civil War England* (Stanford, CA: Stanford University Press, 2004), 78; Lake, 86.
58. Edward Elton, *Exposition of the Commandments of God* (London: 1624), 1–3.
59. Stuart Clark, *Thinking With Demons the Idea of Witchcraft in Early Modern Europe* (Oxford, UK: Oxford University Press, 1997), 496.
60. Elton, 30.
61. *Ibid.*, 56.
62. *Ibid.*, 139–140.
63. *Ibid.*, 182–183.
64. *Ibid.*, 17.
65. Sophia Coe, *Memoranda Relating to the Ancestry of Sophia Fidelia Hall* (Meriden, CT: Curtiss Way, 1902), 163.
66. Edgar J. McManus, *Law and Liberty in Early New England* (Amherst, MA: University of Massachusetts Press, 1993), 82.
67. Taylor, 43; McManus, 92; Weisman, 99.
68. John M. Taylor, *Roger Ludlow, the Colonial Lawmaker* (New York: G.P. Putnam's Sons, 1900), 74; Benjamin Trumbull, *A Complete History of Connecticut, civil and ecclesiastical, from the Emigration of its First Planters from England* (Hartford, CT: Hudson & Goodwin, 1797), 98; and Royal Hinman, *The Blue Laws of New Haven Colony Usually Called Blue Laws of Connecticut* (Hartford, CT: Case, Tiffany & Co, 1838), 102.
69. Taylor, *Robert Ludlow*, 24–26
70. *Ibid.*, 27.
71. Gaskill, *English Witchcraft*, vol. 3, 401.
72. Thistlethwaite, 101; Taylor, *Roger Ludlow*, 26.

73. Benjamin Brook, *Lives of the Puritans Containing a Biographical Account of Those Divines who Distinguished Themselves on the Cause of Liberty*, vol. 2 (London: James Black, 1813), 461–462.

74. See Barry, 26–29 and 47–49. Jonathan Barry makes a similar claim regarding Bernard's influence on Robert Hunt who like Ludlow was a trained lawyer who attended Cambridge University and the Middle Temple and who practiced law until 1642. He participated in Somerset county local government throughout the 1640's and 1650's serving as a Sheriff, Justice of the Peace and a member of the parliament. During the 1650's and 1660's Hunt became involved in witchcraft cases as a JP "in the area of east Somerset, bordering on Wiltshire and Dorset." Hunt gained a reputation as a witch hunter. Barry also makes the case Hunt was directly influenced by Bernard.

75. Richard L. Greaves, "Richard Bernard," *Oxford Dictionary of National Biography*, vol. 5 (New York: Oxford University Press, 2004), 439. Richard Bernard had dabbled in "exorcisms" as a young man and may have been skeptical of Dinham's bewitchment by the witches especially by Bull. Early in his career he claimed to have exorcised a demon.

76. "the most dangerous of all crimes."

77. Susan H. Moore, *Pilgrims New World Settlers and the Call of Home* (New Haven, CT: Yale University Press, 2007), 47; Greaves, vol. 5, 440.

78. Thistlethwaite, 101.

79. Greaves, vol. 5, 440.

80. Winthrop, *History of New England*, 331.

81. Taylor, *Roger Ludlow*, 46, and 61.

82. Charles H. Levermore, "Witchcraft in Connecticut," in Brian P. Levack, ed., *Articles on Witchcraft, Magic, and Demonology: Witchcraft in colonial America* (New York: Garland, 1992), 305.

83. McManus, 10–11.

84. *Ibid.*, 132–133.

85. Tomlinson, 26.

86. Barry, 48.

87. *The Code of 1650: Being a Compilation of the Earliest Laws and Orders, of the General Court of Connecticut* (Hartford, CT: Andrus and Judd, 1833), 28.

88. *McManus*, 133.

89. Russell Hope Robbins, *The Encyclopedia of Witchcraft and Demonology* (New York: Crown Publishers, 1959), 553; Barry, 48.

## Chapter 4

1. *Winthrop Papers*, vol. 3, 298.

2. Winthrop, *Journal*, vol. 1, 194; Stiles, 67.

3. *Records of the Colony or Jurisdiction of New Haven from May 1653 to the Union*, Charles J. Hoadley, ed., vol. 2 (Hartford, CT: Case, Lockwood and Co., 1858), 86.

4. Cotton Mather, *Magnalia Christi Americana: or, the ecclesiastical history of New-England: from its first planting in the year 1620. Unto the year of our Lord, 1698*, vol. 2 (Hartford: Silus Andrus and Son, 1853), 622–23.

5. Mary Beth Norton, *In the Devil's Snare: The Salem Witchcraft Crisis of 1692* (New York: Alfred A. Knopf, 1992).

6. Demos, 71.

7. Thomas Lechford, *New-Englands advice to Old-England* (London: 1644), 50–51.

8. *Winthrop Papers*, vol. 3, 298.

9. Charles H. Levermore, "Witchcraft in New England," *New Englander and Yale Review* 44 (1885): 793.

10. Ashton, 317.

11. *New Englands First Fruits in Respect, First of the Conversion of Some Indians* (London: 1643), 1; see pages 1–12 for examples of Indian converts and the colonists tribulations among the Indians.

12. *Winthrop Papers*, vol. 4, 76–77.

13. Stiles, 75.

14. Thistlethwaite, 212–213.

15. James Hammond Trumbull, *Notebook Kept by Thomas Lechford, Esq. Lawyer: In Boston Massachusetts Bay From June 27, 1638 to July 29, 1641* (Cambridge, MA: J. Wilson, 1885), 324.

16. *Ibid.*, 325.

17. *Ibid.*

18. "Thomas Marshfield to Samuel Wakeman, 3 June 1641," *Suffolk Deeds*, vol. 1, in Trumbull, *Notebook Kept by Thomas Lechford*, 324.

19. Thistlethwaite, 213; "Records of the Particular Court 1639–1663," *Collections of the Connecticut Historical Society*, vol. 22, 17.

20. See "Records of the Particular Court…," 17–24, 26–27, 40, 49, and 65 for a list of cases and creditors.

21. Smith, *Colonial Justice*, 219–220.

22. *Winthrop Papers*, vol. 2, 117.

23. White, *Planters Plea*, 25.

24. Thomas Morton, *New English Canaan* (Amsterdam: Jacob Frederick Stam, 1637), 24.

25. David S. Jones, *Rationalizing Epidemics: Meanings and Uses of American Indian Mortality since 1600* (Cambridge, MA: Harvard University Press, 2004), 33–34.

26. Jones, 31 and 33.

27. William Bradford, *History of Plymouth Plantation* (Boston: Privately printed, 1856), 326. As a side note, Bradford wrote the condition of the Indians was so bad those in the English house, after making sure that the disease was not infectious to them, "had compas-

tion of them, and dayley fetched them wood and water, and made them fires, got them victualls whilst they lived, and buried them when they dyad."

28. *Winthrop Papers*, vol. 3, 172 and 149.

29. *New Englands First Fruits*, 20.

30. Herbert U. Williams, "The Epidemic of the Indians of New England 1616–1620," *Johns Hopkins Hospital Bulletin* 20 (1909): 342.

31. Jones, 45.

32. Ronald Takaki, "The Tempest in the Wilderness: The Racialization of Savagery," *Journal of American History* 79, no. 3 (December 1992): 908; Thomas Mayhew, "To the Much Honored Corporation in London, Chosen to Place of Publick Trust for the Promoting of the Work of the Lord among the Indians of New England," *Massachusetts Historical Society, Collections* 3 (1833): 201.

33. William Hubbard, *A General History of New England: From the Discovery to MDCLXXX* (Boston, MA: Charles C. Little and James Brown, 1897), 531–532.

34. *Winthrop Journal*, vol. 2, 326.

35. Sherburne F. Cook, "The Significance of Disease in the Extinction of the New England Indians," in Kenneth Kiple and Stephen Beck, eds., *Biological Consequences of the European Expansion, 1480–1800* (Aldershot, UK: Hampshire, 1997), 260.

36. *Winthrop Papers*, vol. 5, 219.

37. Samuel Danforth, *An Almanac for the Year of Our Lord 1647* (Cambridge, MA: 1647); Kenneth B. Murdock, ed., *Handkerchiefs from Paul Being Pious and Consolatory verses of Puritan Massachusetts* (Cambridge, MA: Harvard University, 1927), 130–131.

38. Murdock, 131.

39. Samuel Danforth, *An Almanac for the Year of Our Lord 1649* (Cambridge: 1649). See December the tenth month.

40. "Mathew Grant Record, 1639–1681," in *Some Early Records and Documents of and Relating to the Town of Windsor Connecticut 1639–1703* (Hartford, CT: Connecticut Historical Society, 1930), 79–80.

41. "Quarter Session Records for the County of Somerset, Volume I, 1607–1627," *Somerset Record Society* 23 (London: Butler & Tanner, 1907): 96–97.

42. Bissell, 128–129.

43. Demos, 371.

44. Jon Butler, *Awash in a Sea of Faith: Christianizing the American People* (Cambridge, MA: Harvard University Press, 1990), 67.

45. Francis Higginson, "Higginson's Journal of his Voyage to New England," in Charles M. Andrews, *The Colonial Period in American History*, vol. 3 (New Haven, CT: Yale University Press, 1934–38), 231.

46. *Winthrop Papers*, vol. 4, 97–98.

47. Thistlethwaite, 51; Stiles, 44.

48. Cressy, 99–100. Examples include Robert Wright in the 1630's wanted for "clipping the King's coin," Mary Groves "a known harlot" and William Schooler "a common adulterer" who was later hanged in Massachusetts for "raping and killing a maidservant."

49. *Winthrop Journal*, vol. 2, 8.

50. Godbeer, 30.

51. "Case of witchcraft against Goodwife Harrison of Wethersfield, with testimony by John Welles, Thomas Waples and others," *Samuel Wyllys papers*, August 7, 1668, Document No. 6–17, Connecticut State Library, State Archives, *Samuel Wyllys papers*; and "Testimony of Elizabeth Smith, Regarding Fortune Telling," October 29, 1668, MS. 350, Box 1, Folder 12, Ms. Brown University Library, https://repository.library.brown.edu/studio/item/bdr:211559/; Demos, 356; Drake, 74–75.

52. David Harley, "Historians as Demonologists: The Myth of the Midwife-witch" *Social History of Medicine* 3 (April 1990): 16–18.

53. Davies, Cunning-Folk, 83.

54. Hoadley, vol. 2, 254–255; Taylor, 149–150

55. "Records of the Particular Court...," vol. 22, 34. For example Baggett Egleston of Windsor was fined 20 shillings on June 5, 1645, for "wife sale" or bequeathing his wife to a young man."

56. McManus, 132–133.

# Chapter 5

1. Green, 93.

2. Cressy, viii.

3. Davies, *Four Centuries*, 100.

4. See Kittredge, 9, for an early witchcraft case in Devon, England, in 1601 as one of pure *Maleficuim* with no attendant foreign or learned elements like a "Black man, no book to sign, no compact with Satan ... no infernal revels , no fiendish lovers"; see Barry, *Witchcraft and Demonology* ... who provides some background for cases in the 1650's but little prior to that date; for an important case regarding the treatment of a "healing woman" accused of witchcraft in this earlier period in Dorset see G. J. Davies, ed., *Touchying witchcrafte and sorcerye*, vol. 9 (Dorset, UK: Dorset Record Society, 1985), 25–32; on healing women see especially *Winthrop Journal*, vol. 1, 266–8, and vol. 2, 8; Harley, passim; on the two ministers see *Wolcott Shorthand Notebook*, passim; Langdon, 23–29.

5. Howell, 49.

6. Perkins, 3, 174, and 176.

7. Bernard, 127–137.

8. *Ibid.*, 137.

9. *Ibid.*, 154.

10. MacFarlane, 121.

11. John Melton, *Astrologaster or The Figure-Caster* (London: Barnard and Alsop, 1620), 47.

12. Davies, *Cunning Folk,* 68.

13. Melton, 21

14. Macfarlane, 125.

15. Perkins, 256–257.

16. Davies, *Touchyng…*, 28–29.

17. Bill of Complaint, June 29, 1604, Public Record Office, Star Chamber 8/149/24, dated December 2, 1604, in Davies, *Touchying…*, 26–27. This attack on Joan Guppy was not a simple scratching for blood but a furious attack on her whole person. The neighbors laid in wait as she rode to the market town of Crewkerne on June 29, 1604, to "buy provisions." They were armed with "longe pikes staves, swords, daggers and other warlike weapons, and having also provided great overgrown brambles to tear and rent the flesh of the said Johane Guppy…." They seized Joan and "did with pynnes pricke … and thrust them into the body and leggs of … Joan Guppy, and took the said overgrowne brambles and drew them athwart the face … and … rent and tear the flesh from the face of … Joan Guppy, saying that your said Subject was a witche and they came for the blood of …Joan Guppy and they would have it and her life also before they left her." Joan was able to escape to a nearby house in South Perrott where there lived a widow, Agnes Holford. The group followed her there and attacked her at the house "and did with theire hands and nayles scratch … upon the face and also tooke the said brambles and rubbed them athwart the legs and other parts of the body … whereby she was grievously wounded, rente and torne, and her face thereby cankered and blemished to the great effusion of her blood and to the great feare and terror of all the people and Inhabitants thereabouts."

18. The passing bell was rung when death was immediately expected in order "to ask for prayers from good Christians for a soul departing" and to "drive away the evil spirits that stood at the bed's foot, and about the house, ready to seize their prey, or at least to molest and terrify the soul in its passage." *Lambeth and the Vatican: Or, Anecdotes of the Church of Rome, of the Reformed Churches and of the Sects and Sectaries,* vol. 1 (London: John Knight & Henry Lacey, 1825), 221.

19. Davies, *Touchyng,* 30.

20. *Ibid.*, 26.

21. "Certificate That Joan Guppy, of South Perrott, in the County of Dorset, Was Not a Witch. 1606." *The Antiquary* 33 (July 1897): 215; Davies, 31–32.

22. *Winthrop Journal,* vol. 2, 8; Perkins, 176.

23. Margaret Jones may have brought her healing skills and use of herbs to Massachusetts but it is unlikely she would have been tolerated by the authorities if she had the immediate reputation of a "healing touch, a healing object or used biblical verses" in her practice. Initially, the people of Boston and Charlestown saw her as a healer or even a "blesser" who used herbs to cure the sick. Over time, it appears because of her "intemperate attitude" and as the reality of witches was confirmed in England (and as we will see the prior year in Connecticut) rumors of witchcraft surrounding Margaret Jones turned from suspicions to accusations. Davies, *Cunning-Folk,* 83.

24. J. G. Nichols, *Narratives of the Days of the Reformation,* vol. 77 (Westminster: Camden Society, 1859), 332.

25. William Hale, *A Series of Precedents and Proceedings in Criminal Causes, extending from the Year 1475–1640 Extracted from Act-Books of the Ecclesiastical Courts in the Diocese of London* (London: Francis and John Rivington, 1847), 219.

26. George Gifford, *A Dialogue Concerning Witches and Witchcraftes* (London: John Windet, 1593), G3.

27. Macfarlane, 129.

28. Davies, *Four Centuries,* 57.

29. Cooper, *The Mystery of Witchcraft,* 315.

30. Perkins, 206–207. Perkins admonition about using "white magic" in the detection of witches probably explains why it was not mentioned by Winthrop in his description of the trial. For cunning folk in England, traditionally their most important role was to determine if someone or an animal was bewitched, identify the witch that bewitched them and lift the curse. One method was by "burning of the thing bewitched, if it be not a man, as a hogge, or oxe, or such like creature, is imagined to be a forceable meanes to cause the Witch to discover her selfe." However, as Perkins wrote, it was "farre from being sufficient" and is simply another form of "Witchcraft" and has no power to "detect a Sorcerer…." In fact, it is a trick and "commeth from the devil." Therefore, again both the "black witch" and the "white witch" were equally guilty in his eyes. For cunning folk services offered concerning bewitchment see Davies, *Cunning-Folk,* 103–109; John Hale, *A Modest Enquiry into the Nature of Witchcraft* (Boston, MA: B. Green and J. Allen, 1702), 17.

31. Winsor, vol. 2, 133.

32. *Ibid.*, 134.

33. *Ibid.*

34. Perkins, 177–78.

35. *Ibid.*, 256.

36. Shurtleff, vol. 3, 126, and vol. 2, 242.

37. Gaule, 78–79.

38. Winthrop, vol. 2, 344.

39. *Ibid.*

40. Hale, 17; on her death see notice "14 June 48 Marg. Jones was executed at Boston for witchcraft" in Danforth, *An Almanac ... 1648*, 11.

41. Winthrop, vol. 2, 344–345; Perkins, 314.

42. Winsor, 134.

43. Taylor, *The Witchcraft*, 36; Winsor, 134.

44. *Winthrop Papers*, vol. 5, 230.

45. Drake, *Annals of Witchcraft*, 233–234.

46. *Winthrop Journal*, vol. 2, 6 and 19; Thistlethwaite, 156–157.

47. *Winthrop Journal*, vol. 2, 19; Cressy, 199; Bremer, *Puritan Crisis...*, 126–127.

48. Cressy, 42; Bremer, 97–130.

49. Shurtleff, vol. 2, 242, and vol. 3, 126.

50. Charles J. Hoadley, "Some Early Post-Mortem Examinations in New England," *Proceedings of the Connecticut Medical Society* (Bridgeport, CT: Connecticut, 1892), 210; Taylor, *The Witchcraft*, 40; Godbeer, 161; Walter W. Woodward, *Prospero's America John Winthrop, Jr., Alchemy, and the Creation of New England Culture 1606–1676* (Williamsburg, VA: Omohundro Institute of Early American History and Culture, 2010), 233; Tomlinson, *Witchcraft Prosecution*, 23–24.

51. Perkins, 200; on Roger Ludlow see Tomlinson, *Witchcraft Prosecution,* 19.

52. Dalton, 277 (1633 edition).

53. Langdon, 28.

54. "Wolcott Shorthand Notebook," 334.

55. *Ibid.*, 336.

56. *Ibid.*, 43.

57. *Ibid.*, 45–46.

58. "The Wyllys Papers Correspondence, 19.

59. *Note-Book of Thomas Lechford*, 324–325; William Blake Trask et al., *Suffolk Deeds*, vol. 1 (Boston, MA: Rockwell and Churchill Press, 1880–1906), f12.

60. "Records of the Particular Court," 17, 20, 22–23.

61. *Ibid.*, 26, 31, 40, 49, and 92.

62. *Winthrop Journal*, vol. 1, 141.

63. Royal Ralph Hinman, *A Catalogue of the First Puritan Settlers of the Colony of Connecticut* (Hartford, CT: Gleason, 1846), 52.

64. "Wolcott Shorthand Notebook," 176.

65. Hoadley, *Records of the Colony*, vol. 2, 30.

66. During the 1640's the conversion of the Indians to Christianity was begun by ministers like John Eliot. This conversion activity served two purposes: it led to fewer followers for Satan's nefarious purposes and during the economic slump of the 1640's in New England funds were made available from charitable societies in England to support the conversion of the Indians.

67. Hoadley, *Records of the Colony*, vol. 2, 30.

68. Trumbull, *A Complete History of Connecticut*, 109–111.

69. *Ibid.*, 111.

70. Hoadley, *Records of the Colony*, 1638–1649, vol. 1, 135.

71. Savage, ed., *Winthrop Journal*, vol. 1, 188–189.

72. Trumbull, *A Complete History of Connecticut*, 115.

73. Trumbull, 159–160; see *The Code of 1650*, 51–56. Written by Roger Ludlow, the laws on the Indians can be seen to be directly derived from many of the foregoing incidents described here.

74. Anonymous, *New Englands First Fruits* (London: H. Overton, 1642), 1 and 8.

75. Cotton Mather, *Wonders of the Invisible World*, 126; see "A Faithful Account of many Wonderful and Surprising Things which happened in the Town of Gloucester, in the Year, 1692," in Cotton Mather, *Decennium luctuosum An history of remarkable occurrences, in the long war, which New-England hath had with the Indian salvages, from the year, 1688. To the year 1698* (Boston, MA: B. Green and J. Allen, 1699), 104–113.

76. *New Englands First Fruits*, 20; *Winthrop Papers*, vol. 3, 149 and 172.

77. Willams, "The Epidemic...," 342.

78. Jones, *Rationalizing*, 45.

79. "The Mathew Grant Record 1639–1703," 79–82.

80. Barry S. Hewlett and Bonnie L. Hewlett, *Ebola, Culture, and Politics the Anthropology of an Emerging Disease* (Belmont, CA: Thomson Wadsworth, 2008), 117.

81. Langdon, 126.

82. John Eliot and Thomas Mayhew, *The Glorious Progress of the Gospel Amongst the Indians of New England* (London: Edward Winslow, 1649), 3. "In 1647 Thomas Mayhew recounted how he had sought to help cure an Indian of his illness." After helping him, he "sought againe unto Witches" or the Indian "Powwawes."

83. Johnson, *A History of New-England*, 76.

84. Grant, *Matthew Grant Diary*, 93, 103. http://cslib.cdmhost.com/cdm/ref/collection/p15019coll14/id/548

85. Karlsen, 147.

86. Grant, *Mathew Grant Diary*, 100.

87. Gura, 23; Winthrop, *Winthrop Papers*, vol. 4, 456; Johnson, *A History of New-England ...*, 97. Gorton and his followers were connected in the eyes of New England clergy with the earlier antinomians who they saw as heretics. For

example, these heretics saw the sacraments as
nothing more than "black magic." Besides baptism, they wished to throw out the sacrament
of the Lords Supper "for to make use of Bread,
or the juce of a silly Grape to represent the
Body and Bloud of Christ, they account it as
bad as Negromancy in the Ministers of Christ
to performe it."

88. Charles Maclean Andrews, *River Towns
of Connecticut: A Study of Wethersfield, Hartford, and Windsor* (Baltimore, MD: Johns Hopkins University, 1889), 119; Trumbull, *Memorial
History of Hartford Connecticut*, 46; Winthrop,
*Winthrop Papers*, vol. 4, 456.

89. Johnson, *A History of New-England*,
205.

90. Peter Bulkeley, *The Gospel-covenant; or
The covenant of grace opened* (London: Benjamin Allen, 1646), 104.

91. Johnson, *A History of New-England*,
93–94.

92. *Code of 1650*, 43–44.

93. Davies, *Four Centuries*, 126; the pamphlet was published on August 19, 1645, *A True
and Exact Relation of the several Informations,
Examinations, and Confessions of the Late
Witches, arraigned and executed in the county
of Essex … at Chelmsford … the 29ᵗʰ of July,
1645*, in Gaskill, *Witchfinders*, 136.

94. *Mercurius Britannicus*, no. 95, 25
August–1 September 1645, 850–851.

95. John Downame, *Annotations upon all
the books of the Old and New Testament*, Exodus XXII, verse 18; Gaskill, *Witchfinders*, 138.

96. Clarke, *The Lives of Sundry*, 172; Gaskill,
*Witchfinders*, 152.

97. Cressy, xix.

98. Shurtleff, vol. 2, 242, and vol. 3, 126.

99. Tomlinson, *Witchcraft Prosecution*, 23.

100. Smith, *Colonial Justice*, 220; Drake,
*Annals of Witchcraft*, 234.

101. Johnson, *A History of New-England*,
100.

102. Demos, 368.

## Chapter 6

1. Stiles, vol. 1, 443.
2. Stiles, vol. 1, 445; Winthrop, *Winthrop
Journal*, vol. 2, 323.
3. Stiles, vol. 1, 445; and "The first instance
of capital punishment for witchcraft, in New
England occurring in colonial history was in
this year [1648]. Margaret Jones of Charlestown
was indited [sic] for a witch, found guilty, and
executed" in Abiel Holmes, *American Annals :
Or, A Chronological History of America: From
Its…*, vol. 1 (London: Sherwood, Neely & Jones,
1813), 285, see Hutchinson, v. 1, 150.

4. Stiles, vol. 1, 447.
5. *Ibid.*
6. Marion Gibson, *Witchcraft Myths in
American Culture* (New York: Routledge, 2007),
45; and for a contemporary critical approach
to Connecticut witchcraft trials in the late
nineteenth century see Gibson, 46–47, for her
discussion of Charles H Levermore, "*Witchcraft in New England*," *New England Magazine*
12 (July 1892): 637–644.
7. Stiles, 447–448; and on Lydia's indictment
"Records of the Particular Court," vol. 22, 131.
8. Thistlethwaite, 147–149.
9. *Matthew Grant Diary*, Connecticut State
Library, http://www.cslib.org/matthewgrant.
htm#Description.
10. *Hartford Courant*, 3 December 1904,
A11–A12.
11. *Matthew Grant Diary*; Taylor, *The Witchcraft Delusion*,147.
12. *Matthew Grant's Diary*, 95a.
13. *Matthew Grant's Diary*; Taylor, *Witchcraft Delusion…*, 145–147; "Records of the Particular Court," vol. 22, 48, 92–93; and Tomlinson,
29–31.
14. Savage, ed., *Winthrop Journal*, vol. 1, 150;
Stiles, 151.
15. Stiles, 44.
16. Demos, 505.
17. Alice Youngs, "Baptism Record, March
2, 1633/34," Saint Margaret's Church, Westminster, London, England.
18. "Massachusetts, Marriages, 1695–1910,"
index, Family Search (https://familysearch.
org/pal:/MM9.1.1/FCX4-SV: accessed 10 Nov
2014), Symon Beamon and Alis Young, 15 Dec
1654; FHL microfilm 0185414, 0185415, 185416.
19. Bissell, 45. See chart compiled by Bissell
of the average age at marriage in Windsor,
Connecticut.
20. Demos, 505, n. 29.
21. Macfarlane, 170; Bernard, 210–211;
Perkins, 202–203; John Stearne, "A Confirmation and Discovery of Witchcraft," 12, in Gaskill,
*English Witchcraft…*, vol. 3, 350; Gaule, 46.
22. Thistlethwaite, 144–145; Stiles, 75.
23. Thistlethwaite, 144; and Stiles, 43–47.
24. Ephraim Huit, *Anatomy of Conscience*
(London: 1626), 327.
25. *Winthrop Papers*, vol. 6, 160–161.
26. *Ibid.*, 161.
27. John Aubrey, *Brief Lives*, vol. 1 (London:
Oxford University Press, 1898), 350.
28. Walker, 67.
29. Smith, *Colonial Justice*, 219; Gaule, E3;
Drake, *Annals of Witchcraft*, 225–227.
30. Godbeer, *The Devil's Dominion*, 171.
31. *American Genealogist*, XLIII, in Demos,
356.
32. "Testimony of Goody Burr and Samuell

Burr," No. 3, *Samuel Wyllys Papers*, Connecticut State Library, State Archives, http://cslib.cdm host.com/cdm/compoundobject/collection/ p15019coll10/id/164/rec/3.

33. *Ibid.*

34. *Ibid.*, 128–130; Clark, 465.

35. George Webbe, *The Arraignment of an Unruly Tongue* (London: John Budge, 1619), 22.

36. Jane Kamensky, "Female Speech and Other Demons: Witchcraft and Wordcraft in Early New England," in Elizabeth Reis, ed., *Spellbound Women and Witchcraft in America* (Wilmington, DE: SR Books, 1998), 27.

37. Perkins, 201–203; Kamensky, 29.

38. Kamensky, 27.

39. *Wolcott Shorthand Notebook*, 338.

40. Davies, *Touchyng*, 21.

41. Kamensky, 34.

42. *Ibid.*, 41–42.

43. Stiles, 98.

44. Thistlethwaite, 174.

45. *Wolcott Shorthand Notebook.*

46. Thistlethwaite, 174.

47. *Wolcott Shorthand Notebook*, 176 and 304.

48. *Ibid.*, 293.

49. *Ibid.*, 334.

50. *Ibid.*, 335–336.

51. *Ibid.*, 332 and 335.

52. *Ibid.*, 340.

53. *Ibid.*, 347.

54. *Ibid.*, 342–343.

55. *Ibid.*, 347–348.

56. Langdon, 26.

57. James Sharpe, *Witchcraft in Early Modern England* (London: Routledge, 2001), 56; for more examples of these charms see John Aubrey, *Miscellanies Upon Various Subjects*, 4th ed. (London: John Russell Smith, 1857), 130–141; on Catholic based charms see Owens, 36; *Diane Purkiss, The Witch in History: Early Modern and Twentieth-Century Representations* (London: Routledge, 1996), 156–157.

58. Christine Hole, *Witchcraft in England* (New York: Collier Books, 1996), 134.

59. *Wolcott Shorthand Notebook*, 336.

60. *Ibid.*, 348–349.

61. Langdon, 26.

62. *Ibid.*, 348.

63. Perkins, 202.

64. Annie Eliot Trumbull, "One Blank" of Windsor Revelations of a Little Worn Sheepskin Volume," *Hartford Courant*, 3 December 1904, A11–12; "John Youngs' Disease," in *Winthrop Papers*, vol. 6, 160–161.

65. *Winthrop Papers*, vol. 6, 122.

66. *Winthrop Papers*, vol. 4, 77.

67. *Ibid.*, 99.

68. Booth, 142–44

69. *Ibid.*, 148.

70. Lechford, 23.

71. Lechford, 12. In the event a member was admonished they abstained from communion and if they did not "satisfy the Church, else excommunicated. "Excommunication is held a heathen or publican."

72. *Ibid.*

73. *Winthrop Papers*, vol. 2, 16 and 17.

74. Lechford, 25. For example the Boston minister John Cotton, *An Abstract or The Lawes of New England as They Are Now Established*, 10.

75. *Panorama of Life and Literature*, vol. 2 (Boston: Littell and Son, 1866), 148.

76. Lechford, 26.

77. Charles Warren, *History of the Harvard Law School and English Legal Conditions in America* (New York: Lewis, 1908), 19.

78. John Cotton, *Exposition of the Thirteenth Chapter of Revelation by that Reverend and Eminent Servant of the Lord, Mr. John Cotton* (London: Hand and Bible, 1656), 163.

79. *Winthrop Papers*, vol. 2, 36.

80. Warren, 12.

81. Booth, 148.

82. William DeLoss Love, *Colonial History of Hartford* (Hartford: Self Published, 1914), 286; and Booth, 148.

83. Booth, 149.

84. *Ibid.*

85. *Ibid.*, 149–152.

86. *Ibid.*, 152.

87. *Ibid.*, 157.

88. *Ibid.*, 158–160.

89. *Ibid.*, 162–165.

90. Winthrop, vol. 2, 348–349; Harley, 17.

91. *Wolcott Shorthand Notebook*, 345.

92. Perkins, 174–176.

93. Drake, 281.

94. Harley, 6.

95. *Ibid.*, 10.

96. *Ibid.*, 11.

97. *Five Wonders seene in England* (London: Printed by J. C., 1646), 2–3.

98. Julia Rudolph, *Common Law and Enlightenment in England, 1689-1750* (Boydell Press: Woodbridge, 2013), 103.

99. Harley, 12.

100. *Ibid.*, 16–18.

101. *Ibid.*, 11.

102. Increase Mather, *An Essay for the Recording of Remarkable Providences … Especially in New England* (Boston: Samuel Green, 1684), 34–37, on Jane Fyler; Matthew Grant, "Old Church Record 1639-1681," in *Some Early Records and Documents…*, 10; Stiles, vol. 1, 186–187; Bissell, 148–149.

103. Harley, 10; Taylor, 42–43.

104. *Collections*, Connecticut Historical Society, vol. 22, 45–47.

105. *Ibid.*, 45–47; *Collections*, vol. 22, 93; on Ludlow, see Taylor, *Roger Ludlow*, 125–127; and for his opinion on the juries, Taylor, *Roger Ludlow*, 38.

106. Roger Ludlow "was a man inferior to none for good sense and skill in the law." See Roger Wolcott, "Roger Wolcott's Memoir Relating to Connecticut," *Connecticut Historical Society* 3 (1895): 327.

107. *Collections*, vol. 22, 93.

108. Love, 283.

109. Walker, *The Witches of Hertfordshire*, 43.

110. Langdon, 26.

111. *Collections*, vol. 22, 56.

112. *Winthrop Papers*, vol. 4, 77–78 and 99.

113. Langdon, 26.

114. Thomas Hooker, "Sermon," June 1647, 2–7, in *Matthew Grant diary* [transcript].

115. Perkins, 178.

116. John Warham, "Sermon," August 1647, 31–34, in *Matthew Grant diary* [transcript].

117. Stiles, vol. 1, 79.

118. Mather, *Magnalia Christi*, 100.

119. Johnson, *A History of New England*, 76.

120. Langdon, 26; Bernard, 127–137.

121. "Windsor Church Covenant," October 23, 1647, 141, in *Matthew Grant diary* [transcript].

# Chapter 7

1. Gura, 305.

2. Burt, 15; Gura, 305.

3. Stiles, vol. 1, 736; Stephen Innes, *Labor in a New Land: Economy and Society in Seventeenth-Century Springfield* (Princeton, NJ: Princeton University Press, 1983), 6; see for example Walter Fyler of Windsor versus Daniel Brown of Springfield in the Springfield Court. Brown was indebted to Fyler. Smith, *Colonial Justice*, 222–223.

4. Gura, 307.

5. Burt, 19; Innes, 5–12.

6. Katherine Grandjean, *American Passage: The Communications Frontier in Early New England* (Cambridge, MA: Harvard University Press, 2015), passim.

7. Smith, *Colonial Justice*, 219.

8. *Mercurius Politicus*, 1091; Smith, *Colonial Justice*, 22.

9. "Examination of Hugh Parsons, of Springfield on a Charge of Witchcraft, and the Testimonies, before Mr. William Pynchon, at Springfield, 1651," in Drake, *Annals*, 219–258; on Merrick and Sewall see Drake, 220, 245–246; Hale, 19; Gibson, 80–81.

10. Johnson, *Wonder-working providence*, vol. 2 (London: 1654; reprint Andover, 1867), 199.

11. "Examination of Hugh Parsons," in Drake, *Annals*, 219–258.

12. Smith, *Colonial Justice*, 219–21.

13. On the matter of a socio-economic based approach to the witchcraft controversy contained in the trial transcript with no mention of the religious basis and belief in witches as an underlying reality confronting the residents of Springfield see Innes, 136–140; Langdon, 26–29.

14. Smith, *Colonial Justice*, 157.

15. Winsor, 19; Smith, *Colonial Justice*, 24.

16. John Brinsley, *A Consolation for Our Grammar Schooles* (London: Ricahrd Field, 1622), preface; William Bradshaw, *A plaine and pithy exposition of the second Epistle to the Thessalonians* (London: Edward Griffin, 1620), 123; Langdon, 26.

17. *Winthrop Papers*, vol. 5, 45; Burt, 73: and for the justification of Mary Parson's request see Dalton, 277.

18. Ebenezer Clapp, *History of the Town of Dorchester* (Boston: Dorchester Antiquarian and Historical Society, 1859), 75–77.

19. *Winthrop Papers*, vol. 5, 45–46, and 50.

20. Drake, *Annals*, 67.

21. Burt, 73; and "Examination of Hugh Parsons," in Drake, *Annals*, 217–258, passim.

22. Smith, *Colonial Justice*, 219.

23. Gaule, E3; Hole, 129.

24. Hole, 131.

25. Smith, *Colonial Justice*, 219–220.

26. *Ibid.*, 220; and on witches and envy concerning infants and children, Demos, 170 and 198.

27. *Ibid.*, 220.

28. Green, 102.

29. Drake, *Annals*, 250.

30. *Ibid.*, 251.

31. *Ibid.*

32. *Ibid.*, 244.

33. *Ibid.*, 70–71.

34. Drake, *Annals*, 233–234; Tomlinson, 40.

35. Taylor, *Witchcraft Delusion*, 147.

36. Drake, *Annals*, 73.

37. *Ibid.*, 248–249.

38. "it was a means used in England by honest people to finde out witches…." Hoadley, vol. 2, 224; Hole, 145–147. Finding out witches was a dangerous enterprise and was best left to a "cunning person" as the consequences could be disastrous to an innocent party.

39. Hale, 17.

40. Drake, *Annals*, 245.

41. *Ibid.*, 249.

42. *Ibid*, 221–222.

43. Perkins, 314.

44. Drake, *Annals*, 70–71; Burt 74; Dalton, 277.

45. Dalton, 277.

46. *Ibid.,* 277–278
47. Drake, 244.
48. *Ibid.,* 244–245.
49. Dalton, 278.
50. Drake, *Annals,* 245.
51. "confessing their own witchcrafts, and witnessing against the suspected, that they have spirits or markes; that they have beene at their meetings…." Dalton, 278; Bernard, 222–223.
52. Drake, *Annals,* 245.
53. *Ibid.,* 245–246.
54. *Ibid.,* 234.
55. Dalton, 279. "One sign of a witch "That they have imployed their spirit"; Drake, *Annals,* 239–240.
56. *Ibid.,* 227.
57. *Ibid.,* 225–227; and on threatening speech, Dalton, 276.
58. *Ibid.,* 227–229.
59. *Ibid.,* 253.
60. *Ibid.,* 229–30, 230–232, 243, 246. Concerning the beer barrel, Drake noted that the real witch in this case was Goody Mereck but instead Hugh Parsons was already judged guilty of being a witch by his neighbors.
61. Drake, *Annals,* 250.
62. *Ibid.,* 251–252.
63. *Ibid.,* 252–253.
64. *Ibid.*
65. *Ibid.,* 253.
66. Drake, *Annals,* 222.
67. *Ibid.,* 233.
68. *Ibid.,* 235.
69. *Ibid.*
70. *Ibid.,* 236
71. *Ibid.*
72. *Ibid.,* 237.
73. *Ibid.,* 237–238.
74. *Ibid.,* 239.
75. *Ibid.*
76. Dalton, 278; Drake, *Annals,* 245 and 248.
77. Drake, *Annals,* 244 and 248; Smith, *Colonial Justice,* 21–22.
78. Drake, *Annals,* 253–254.
79. *Ibid.,* 240.
80. *Ibid.,* 245.
81. Smith, *Colonial Justice,* 22.
82. Shurtleff, vol. 4, Pt. 1, 47.
83. Shurtleff, vol. 4, Pt. 1, 49; Hale, 19–20.
84. "Mather Papers," *The Collections of the Massachusetts Historical Society* 8 (1868): 58; Malcom Gaskill, "Witchcraft and Power in Early Modern England: the Case of Margaret Moore," in Darren Oldridge, ed., *The Witchcraft Reader* (New York: Routledge, 2002), 345.
85. Michael McDonald, *Mystical Bedlam Madness Anxiety, and Healing in Seventeenth-Century England* (Cambridge, MA: Cambridge University Press, 1981), 82 and 267.

86. Hutchinson, 6; Drake, *Annals,* 66–67; Burt, 75; Green, 107.
87. "From Natick, in New England, July 4, 1651," *Mercurius Politicus,* 25 September 1651; Winsor, vol. 2, 137.
88. Burt, 46 and 78.
89. Booth, 150.
90. Burt, 77; McManus, 194. The Court of Assistants was held twice a year. It was composed of the Governor, the Deputy Governor and Assistants (Puritan magistrates). It "Heard crimes punishable by banishment, dismemberment, or death."
91. Drake, *Annals,* 244–245.
92. Shurtleff, vol. 4, Pt. 1, 96.
93. Smith, *Colonial Justice,* 22–23.
94. Drake, *Annals,* 254–256.
95. *New England Historical and Genealogical Register* (Boston, MA: The Society, 1881), 152–153.
96. Burt, 77.
97. Drake, *Annals,* 68–69.
98. McManus, 194.
99. Burt, 78; Shurtleff, vol. 4, Pt. 1, 96.
100. Burt, 78.

## Chapter 8

1. Tomlinson, 46.
2. Demos, 348–349; "Records of the Particular Court…," vol. 22, 93.
3. Cedric B. Cowing, *The Saving Remnant Religion and the Settling of New England* (Urbana, IL: University of Illinois Press, 1995), 71, 83–84.
4. "Records of the Particular Court…," vol. 22, 26, 30, 45, and 78; *Code of 1650,* 51–54, on decrees and orders concerning trading weapons with the Indians.
5. On gossip in early colonial society see, Mary Beth Norton, *Founding Mothers & Fathers: Gendered Power and the Forming of American Society* (New York: A.A. Knopf, 1996), 252.
6. *Ibid.,* 92–93.
7. *Matthew Grant's Diary,* 95a.
8. "Records of the Particular Court…," vol. 22, 116.
9. Samuel Orcutt, *A History of the Old Town of Stratford and the City of Bridgeport, Connecticut* (New Haven, CT: Tuttle, Morehouse & Taylor, 1886), 140.
10. Trumbull, vol. 1, 201.
11. Orcutt, 140–142.
12. Trumbull, vol. 1, 213.
13. Orcutt, 142.
14. *Ibid.,* 142–143.
15. Hoadley, vol. 2, 48.
16. Taylor, *Roger Ludlow,* 132.

17. Hoadley, vol. 2, 47.

18. Orcutt, 143.

19. Taylor, *Roger Ludlow*, 143.

20. *Ibid.*, 145.

21. Orcutt, 144–145; *Code of 1650*, 51.

22. Clark, 610–611; Isaac Bargrave, *A Sermon Preached Before King Charles, March 27, 1627* (London: Legatt, 1627), 7; and with the restoration of Charles II see rebellion and witchcraft as political theater in John Ogilby, *The entertainment of His Most Excellent Majestie Charles II, in his passage through the city of London to his coronation ... and royal feast in Westminster-Hall* (London: Thomas Roycroft, 1662), 15.

23. Kittredge, 279; Brian P. Levack, "The Great Scottish Witch Hunt of 1661–1662," *Journal of British Studies*, 20 (1980–81): 107–108; Clark, 611–612.

24. Elizabeth Hubbell Godfrey Schenck, *The History of Fairfield, Fairfield County, Connecticut, from the Settlement*, vol. 1 (New York: Self Published, 1889), 73; Wolfgang Beringer, "Weather, Hunger and Fear: Origins of the European Witch-Hunts in Climate, Society and Mentality," *German History* 13 (1995): 1–27; Thomas L. Purvis, *Colonial America to 1763* (New York: Facts on File, 1999), 3.

25. *Ibid.*

26. Trumbull, *The Public Records*, vol. 1, 220; Hoadley, vol. 2, 81.

27. Drake, *Annals*, 72; Donald L. Jacobus, *History and Genealogy of the Families of Old Fairfield*, vol. 4 (Fairfield, CT: Tuttle, Morehouse & Taylor Company, 1930), 954; Tomlinson, 41; Stiles, 158.

28. Tomlinson, 41.

29. Hoadley, vol. 2, 81.

30. *Ibid.*, 85.

31. Burr, 410; Jacobus, vol. 4, 954.

32. Orcutt, 148; William Howard Wilcoxson, *History of Stratford 1639–1939* (Stratford, CT: Brewer Borg, 1939), 197–199.

33. This was highly unlikely for two reasons, Goody had confessed and as a confessed witch her friend would have been immediately "suspicioned" as a witch herself. As we will see in the Staples trial any doubting of the evidence or the fact witches existed raised the suspicion the person doubting the evidence or reality of witches was also a witch.

34. Wilcoxson, 198–199.

35. Jacobus, vol. 4, 955; Levermore, 640.

36. Taylor, 123.

37. *Public Record of the Courts of Connecticut*, 248.

38. Orcutt, 148.

39. Hoadley, vol. 2, 81.

40. Tomlinson, 43; Hoadley, vol. 2, 77–89.

41. Tomlinson, 42–43.

42. http://www.onagocag.com/knappgen/rogerknapp.htm

43. Hoadley, vol. 2, 59.

44. *Ibid.*, 80 and 87.

45. *Ibid.*, 82; for the midwife role in legal proceedings in England, see Harley, 10–11; the New England colonies, see Booth, 97–98.

46. Orcutt, 149.

47. *Ibid.*

48. Hoadley, vol. 2, 85.

49. *Ibid.*, 83 and 85.

50. *Ibid.*, 85.

51. *Ibid.*, 86.

52. *Ibid.*, 85

53. *Ibid.*, 86.

54. *Ibid.*, 87–88.

55. Hoadley, vol. 2, 83; Schenck, 325.

56. Hoadley, vol. 2, 78.

57. *Ibid.*, 81–82.

58. *Ibid.*, 83.

59. *Ibid.*, 84.

60. *Ibid.*, 78–79.

61. Taylor, witchcraft, 38 and 129.

62. Tomlinson, 23–27.

63. We do not know anything about Roger Knapp's trade so we cannot link him with being a carpenter or mason. Unfortunately, he may have been wrongly connected to Thomas Bassett as being one of the four "poor men" that Dr. Thomas Pell of Fairfield, the husband of Lucy Pell (mentioned above) whose debts he remitted. Pell's will only names "these four poor men, Joseph Patton, James Evens, Thomas Bassett, Roger Percy." He remitted debts due to Thomas Bassett husband of the witch Goody Bassett but there is no mention of Roger Knapp in his will. It is likely Roger Knapp was not poor. See Donald L. Jacobus, 4, 955; Tomlinson, 41. For this correction see the Will of Thomas Pell of Fairfield, 1669, AccessGenealogy.com. 13 May 2015. http://www.accessgenealogy.com/new-york/pell-thomas-1669.htm.

64. Wyllys Papers Supplement, 1–2. It is important to note that a close reading of Perkins full essay on the matter of examining a witch is much more cautionary than the abridged version found in the Connecticut archives. (See my appendix).

65. See Perkins, 200–204 for the examination of a witch and 204–209 for a conviction but his recommendations must be used cautiously; Dalton, 277–279.

66. Dalton, 277.

67. Perkins, 203.

68. Perkins, 203; Hansen, 48.

69. Walker, 56–7.

70. Dalton, 277.

71. Stiles, 448; Tomlinson, 53.

72. "Records of the Particular Court...," 106–107.

73. Tomlinson, 54.
74. Stiles, 449–450.
75. Charles William Manwaring, *A Digest of the Early Connecticut Probate Records*, vol. 1 (Hartford, CT: R.S. Peck & Co., 1904–1906), 152.
76. Stiles, 450.
77. Stiles, 450; Taylor, *Witchcraft Delusion*, 148; John Demos, *The Enemy Within, A Short HIstory of Witch-Hunting* (New York: Penguin Press, 2008), 73–79; Tomlinson, 56.
78. Stiles, 450.
79. "Records of the Particular Court," 19; Tomlinson, 56.
80. "Records of the Particular Court," 29; Tomlinson, 57.
81. Tomlinson, 57; and Stiles, 450.
82. "Records of the Particular Court," 131.
83. Tomlinson, 57; Stiles, 449.
84. Hale, 17.
85. Demos, *Entertaining Satan,* 78.
86. Tomlinson, 57.
87. Demos, *Entertaining Satan,* 5–6.
88. Langdon, 28.
89. Robert Blair St. George, *Conversing by Signs: Poetics of Implication in Colonial New England Culture* (Chapel Hill, NC: University of North Carolina Press, 1998), 183.
90. St. George, 190.
91. George Ewart Evans, *The Pattern Under the Plough: Aspects of the Folk-life of East Anglia* (London: Faber & Faber, 1977), 53 and 55.
92. For a discussion on multiple counter magic objects placed in the houses especially in New England see St. George, 193–195; in England see Ralph Merrifield, *The Archeology of Ritual and Magic* (New York: New Amsterdam Books, 1987) 159–175; on the use of witche's bottles in New England see the deposition of Roger Toothaker in Bernard Rosenthal, *Records of the Salem Witch-Hunt* (Cambridge: Cambridge University Press, 2009), 318; on the witches post attached to the lintel or the chimney in East Anglia see Evans, 65–66; and for the relatively new understanding of apotropaic writing in English houses provisionally identified as "witches' marks" or a counter magic inscription carved into beams and attics in English houses in the fifteenth and sixteenth centuries by carpenters and masons see for New England in Marshfield, Massachusetts, the example of the Winslow House that has "Witches marks … or apotropaic marks, or charms … scratched into the wooden beam over the master fireplace in the winter kitchen. A carpenter's compass could be used to create a perfect circle with six flower-like petals meeting in the center (hence the term daisy wheel!), or cruder designs could be created with a knife or nail. These colonial pieces of graffiti prob-

ably represented the sun, or God, or other positive things…. Their purpose? To protect the home from witches and evil spirits … and … were a form of protective folk magic used by colonists to guard doors, windows, and hearths; all places where evil beings were feared to enter," http://www.winslowhouse.org/guarding-the-lintels/; for further discussion in England see Timothy Easton and Jeremy Hodgkinson, "Apotropaic Symbols on Cast-Iron Firebacks" *Journal of the Antique Metalware Society* 21 (2013), http://www.academia.edu/5832596/Apotropaic_Symbols_on_Cast-Iron_Firebacks; on "witches marks" in Dutch dwellings and afterwards by New England people see Orcutt, 145–146.
93. Keith Thomas, *Religion and the Decline of Witchcraft* (New York: Charles Scribner, 1971), 495.
94. Weisman, 71–73.
95. The lesson here was even the town minister could not help his two bewitched children. This demonstration of clerical weakness in the face of bewitchment was not lost on the townspeople of Springfield.

# Chapter 9

1. Levermore, 638; Hoadley, vol. 2, 31.
2. Norton, 250–252; Karlsen, 297–298; Hoadley, vol. 2, 31.
3. Hoadley, vol. 2, 29.
4. News from England during the 1650's generally arrived "erratically," and was "bewildering and depressing"; Cressy, 255; Hoadley, vol. 2, 37–38.
5. Thomas Birch, *A Collection of the State Papers of John Thurloe Papers from the year 1638-1653*, vol. 1 (London: Thomas Woodard and Charles Davis, 1742), 564–565.
6. *Ibid.*, 565.
7. *Ibid.*
8. *Ibid.*
9. "Records of the First Church in Boston," *Publications of the Colonial Society of Massachusetts* 39 (1961): 9–10 in Godbeer, 122.
10. Godbeer, 122.
11. Hall, 78–80.
12. Baldwin, 82.
13. Ernest Hickok Baldwin, *Stories of Old New Haven* (Taunton, MA: C.A. Hack and Son, 1907), B. Baldwin, 78–79 and 81–82.
14. Baldwin, 81–82.
15. Baldwin, 77; Mather, *Magnalia Christi*, vol. 1, 84.
16. Hoadley, vol. 2, passim; Tomlinson, 60–61; Susan M. Hardman, "Hooke, William," *Oxford Dictionary of National Biography* (Oxford University Press), doi:10.1093/ref:odnb/13688.

17. Tomlinson, 60; Hoadley, vol. 2, 31.

18. On legal procedures concerning the recording of depositions see Rosenthal, 46–49; Hoadley, vol. 2, 29. Whether Mrs. Godman could read there is contradictory evidence. See Franklin B. Dexter, *New Haven Town Records 1649–1662* v.1 (New Haven, CT: New Haven Colony Historical Society, 1917), 462–463 and 478–479.

19. Hoadley, vol. 2, 31; Levermore, 639.

20. *Ibid.*, 30–31.

21. *Ibid.*, 32.

22. Hoadley, vol. 2, 31; Dalton, 277–276.

23. Hoadley, vol. 2, 32–33.

24. *Ibid.*, 33.

25. *Ibid.*

26. *Ibid.*, 33–34.

27. *Ibid.*, 34.

28. *Ibid.*, 35–36.

29. *Ibid.*, 29.

30. Hoadley, vol. 2, 29–30; Winslow, *Good Newes…*, 53.

31. Hoadley, vol. 2, 29–30.

32. *Ibid.*, 29–31.

33. Levermore, 640; Gibson, 47–48.

34. *Winthrop Papers*, vol. 6, 300–302; Woodward, 224.

35. The new Haven Court was given to rehabilitation if at all possible. For example, John Knight was nearly put to death for "loathsome filthyness" with Frances Hall's children in an earlier court proceeding. He was allowed back into the community as long as he accepted his initial punishment and behaved. Then on May 28, 1655, he was in court again. The Court noted that public punishments "nor private warnings" could not prevent him from engaging in incorrigible behavior (sodomy, lying and other filthy defiling ways). He was sentenced to death upon the gallows. For more on the trial and others involved in his crimes see Hoadly, *Records of the Colony*, vol. 2, 137–139. Ironically, Goodwife Thorpe who accused Elizabeth Godman of bewitching her cow, claimed she prayed to God to "resist the evill spirit" that possessed her cow on the day John Knight was hanged. She said the cow became well and continued in good health. Dexter, vol. 1, 250.

36. Hoadley, vol. 2, 306.

37. Dexter, vol. 1, 249–252

38. *Ibid.*, 256–257.

39. Hoadley, vol. 2, 152.

40. Hoadley, vol. 2, 152; Dexter, vol. 1, 264. Stephen Goodyeare provided surety at the General Court on Elizabeth Godman's 50 pounds on January 4, 1655 (1656).

41. Dexter, for November 462–63; for December, 464; for February, 466–67; and for April, 478–79.

42. Dexter, 479.

43. Hoadley, vol. 2, 497–498.

44. Woodward, 225; Davenport, 100–102, 103–105, and 108.

45. Woodward, 224–225.

46. *Ibid.*, 226.

47. "Records of the Particular Court…," vol. 22, 86–87; Tomlinson, 49.

48. *Ibid.*, 127.

49. Hoadley, vol. 2, 77–78.

50. *Ibid.*, 78.

51. *Ibid,* 79.

52. *Ibid.*, 79–80.

53. Karlsen, 147; Chadwick Hansen, *Witchcraft at Salem* (New York: George Braziller, 1969), 35.

54. Hall interview on a "Divided Community," in Robert J Tarutis, *Days of Judgment: the Salem Witch Trials of 1692* (Salem, MA: Osram Sylvania, Inc., 1993), DVD; Hoadley, vol. 2, 80.

55. Karlsen, 147.

56. Hoadley, vol. 2, 80.

57. *Ibid.*, 86.

58. *Ibid.*

59. Evans, 74; St. George, 186; For examples of spirits hovering over the chimneys of a house, see the illustration in Joseph Glanvill, *Saducismus triumphatus: or, full and plain evidence concerning witches and apparitions* (London: 1700), frontispiece, Hoadley, vol. 2, 81.

60. *Ibid.*, 80; Dalton, 277.

61. "The Answer of Some Ministers to the Questions Propounded to them by the Honored Magistrates, October 20, 1669," MS. 354, Box 1, Folder 19, *Samuel Wyllys papers*, Ms. Brown Wyllys, University Library; Hansen, 35; Mather, *Wonders*, 83; Clark, 173.

62. Hoadley, vol. 2, 80, 88–89.

63. *Ibid.*, 122.

64. Taylor, *Witchcraft Delusion*, 163.

65. For Connecticut cases in which magistrates required "legal standards of guilt" for the witches and "local residents convinced of their guilt" led to friction in the community see Godbeer, *Escaping Salem*, 53; for an example of a woman hounded by her "outraged neighbors" as a witch, after the jury convicted her of witchcraft and a higher court dismissed the charges see Carolyn S. Langdon, "A Complaint Against Katherine Harrison, 1669," *Bulletin of the Connecticut Historical Society* 34, no. 1 (January 1969): 18–25; Hall, *Witch-Hunting*, 184.

66. See the Connecticut document *Grounds for Examination of a Witch* in the appendix; Taylor, 40; Perkins, 202.

67. Godbeer, *Escaping*, 48.

68. "Findings of the Grand Jury in the Case of Mary Stapels (Mary Staples), Mary Harvy (Mary Harvey), and Hannah Harvy (Hannah Harvey)," *Samuel Wyllys Papers*, Document No. 42, Connecticut State Library, State

Archives, http://cslib.cdmhost.com/cdm/single item/collection/p15019coll10/id/17/rec/23.

69. Godbeer, *Escaping*, 59–60.

70. Taylor, *Witchcraft Delusion*, 140–41.

71. C"ase of Mercy Disbrough (Mercy Disbrow)," *Samuel Wyllys* papers, Document No. 41, Connecticut State Library, State Archives, http://cslib.cdmhost.com/cdm/compound object/collection/p15019coll10/id/188/rec/2.

72. Godbeer, *Escaping Salem*, 61. On spectral evidence see "The Answer of Some Ministers...."

## Chapter 10

1. Sylvester Judd and Lucius Manlius Boltwood, *History of Hadley: Including the Early History of Hatfield, South Hadley* (Northampton, MA: Metcalf and Co., 1863), 12.

2. Lucas, 35.

3. John Hull, "The Diaries of John Hull, Mint-master and Treasurer of the Colony at Massachusetts Bay," *Archeologia Americana: Transactions & Collections of the American Antiquarian Society* 3 (1857): 169–170.

4. "Controversy in the Church in Hartford 1656–1659," *Collections of the Connecticut Historical Society*, vol. 2 (Hartford: The Society, 1870), 66.

5. *Ibid.*

6. G. L. Walker, *History of the First Church in Hartford, 1633–1833* (Hartford, CT: Brown & Gross, 1833), 162.

7. Carol Seager Fuller, *An Incident in Hartford* (Amherst, MA: Private Printing, 1977), 9.

8. Walker, 151.

9. Hull, 189.

10. Cotton Mather, *Late Memorable Providences* (London: Thomas Parkhurst, 1691), p. viii (see preface by Richard Baxter).

11. Walker, 152. See his discussion on the papers published in the Historical Society Collections, vol. 2, 51–125; Trumbull, *Complete History of Connecticut*, 257. Trumbull did not have access to these papers and takes the view the "qualifications for baptism, church membership, and the rights of the brotherhood were most likely the issues in conflict; Demos, 349–350.

12. Trumbull, *Complete History of Connecticut*, 257.

13. Cotton Mather, *Magnalia Christi*, 119.

14. "Controversy...," vol. 2, 54.

15. *Historical Catalogue of the first Church of Hartford 1633–1685* (Hartford, CT: published by the Church, 1885), 5.

16. Walker, 154–155; "Controversy," vol. 2, 58.

17. "Controversy," vol. 2, 54–59, 72; Samuel

Stone, *Samuel Stone's Catechism: Reissued with an Introductory Sketch* (Boston, MA: John Green, 1684), 16.

18. Tom Webster, *Godly Clergy in Early Stuart England: The Caroline Puritan Movement 1620–1643* (Cambridge, MA: Cambridge University Press, 1997), 53.

19. John Hart, D.D. [Jasper Heartwell], *Trodden down Strength by the God of Strength or Mrs. Drake Revived* (London: R. Bishop, 1646), 5.

20. *Ibid.*, 19, 25, 34–35, 40–41.

21. *Ibid.*, 100.

22. *Ibid.*, 101.

23. *Ibid.*, 19.

24. Webster, 53; Hart, 116–117.

25. *Ibid.*, 120.

26. *Ibid.*, 127.

27. *Ibid.*, 128–129.

28. "Records of the Particular Court," vol. 22, 56.

29. Mather, *Memorable Providences*, 62–63.

30. Hall, 178.

31. Webster, 53.

32. Warren W. Lamson, "Connecticut's First Lady: Susannah Garbrand Hooker," *The Connecticut Antiquarian* 37 (1985): 29.

33. *Ibid.*, 24.

34. Stuart Banner, *The Death Penalty: An American history* (Cambridge, MA: Harvard University Press, 2002), 6; Lawrence B. Goodheart, *The Solemn Sentence of Death: Capital Punishment in Connecticut* (Amherst, MA: University of Massachusetts, 2011), 15.

35. *Winthrop's Journal*, vol. 2, 13–14.

36. "Records of the Particular Court," vol. 22, 33.

37. J. Hammond Trumbull, *The Public Records of the Colony of Connecticut 1636–1776*, vol.1 (Hartford: F. A. Brown, 1850), 256.

38. "Controversy," vol. 2, 71.

39. "Records of the Particular Court," vol. 22, 134.

40. Edwin Pond Parker, *History of the Second Church of Christ in Hartford* (Hartford, CT: Belknap and Warfield, 1892), 17.

41. *Winthrop's Journal*, vol. 1, 134; Parker, 17.

42. "Winthrop Papers," *Massachusetts Historical Society. Collections*, vol. 7 (Boston, MA: Massachusetts Historical Society, 1865), 193–194.

43. *Ibid.*, 193.

44. "Records of the Particular Court," vol. 22, 134.

45. Hull, 169–170.

46. Baird Tipson, *Hartford Puritanism: Thomas Hooker, Samuel Stone and their Terrifying God* (New York: Oxford University Press, 2015), 55, 178–179.

47. Lamson, 24.

48. "Records of the Particular Court," vol. 22, 135.
49. *Ibid.*, 134.
50. *Ibid.*, 136.
51. *Ibid.*, 135.
52. Hall, 173–174; *Winthrop Journal*, vol. 1, 329.
53. Lamson, 24; "Records of the Particular Court," vol. 22, 138.
54. Records of the Particular Court," vol. 22, 270 and 272; Manwaring, 313.
55. Booth, 103 and 105.
56. Norton, 7.
57. Hull, 182.
58. Bishop, 228–229.
59. *Ibid.*, 228.
60. Norton, 52–53.
61. "Controversy," vol. 2, 95.
62. "Controversy," vol. 2, 95; Walker, 156.
63. Walker, 156.
64. "Controversy," vol. 2, 72.
65. Walker, 157.
66. "Controversy," vol. 2, 54–55.
67. Walker, 158.
68. Walker, 158; Trumbull *Complete History*, 317.
69. "Controversy," vol. 2, 59–63.
70. *Ibid.*, 66.
71. Trumbull, *Complete History*, 256.
72. "Controversy," vol. 2, 68–70; Walker, 160–161.
73. Hull, 180; Walker, 161–162.
74. Hull, 180.
75. *Richard Mather, A Disputation Concerning Church Members and their Children ... at Boston in New England June 4 1657* (London: J. Hayes, 1659), 2.
76. John Andrew Doyle, *English Colonies in America ...: The Puritan colonies*, vol. 2 (New York: Henry Holt and Co., 1887), 98.
77. Walker, 164; "Controversy," vol. 2, 75–76.
78. "Controversy," vol. 2, 77; Walker, 165.
79. Hull, 183.
80. "Controversy," vol. 2, 114–115.
81. Walker 165; "Controversy," vol. 2, 77–78.
82. *Ibid.*; "Controversy," vol. 2, 79–80.
83. "Controversy," vol. 2, 81.
84. *Ibid.*, 86, 88–93
85. Trumbull, *The Public Records*, 254.
86. *Ibid.*, 254.
87. Trumbull, *The Public Records*, 255; Walker, 168.
88. Judd, 18–19.
89. Trumbull, *The Public Records*, 256; Walker, 168.
90. Trumbull, The *Public Records*, 256.
91. "Controversy," vol. 2, 109.
92. Walker, 172–173; and for the full sentence see "Controversy," vol. 2, 112–125.

93. Walker 174; "Controversy," vol. 2, 120–121 and 123.
94. Paul R. Lucas, *Valley of Discord: Church and Society along the Connecticut River, 1636–1725* (Hanover, NH: University Press of New England, 1976), 48–49.
95. Walker, 175.
96. Trumbull, *The Public Records*, 311; Parker, 38; Lucas, 49.
97. Hull, 188; Josselyn, 203.
98. Lucas, 53–54.
99. Lucas, 63 and 69.
100. Doyle, 77.

## Chapter 11

1. Davenport, 199.
2. Tomlinson, 81.
3. Richard S. Dunn, "John Winthrop Jr., of Connecticut: The first Governor of the East End," in Tom Twomey, ed., *Awakening the Past: The East Hampton 350th Anniversary Lecture, 1998* (New York: New Market Press, 1999), 95.
4. Trumbull, *Public...*, 580–581.
5. Dunn, 95–96.
6. Dunn, 96–97; Great Britain, *Calendar of State Papers, Colonial Series, America and West Indies, 1661–1668*, W. N. Sainsbury, ed. (London: Longman, 1880), 74, 86–88. The Patent is dated in the State Papers April 23, 1662.
7. Dunn, 97; Ernest H. Baldwin, "Why New Haven is Not a State of the Union," *Papers of the New Haven Colony Historical Society*, vol. 7 (New Haven, CT: New Haven Colony Historical Society, 1908), 178.
8. Hoadley, vol. 2, 429 and 456; Dexter, v. 1, 447.
9. Baldwin, 173.
10. Dunn, 97.
11. Great Britain, *Calendar of State Papers*, 27.
12. Ezra Stiles, *A History of Three of the Judges of King Charles I* (Hartford, CT: Elisha Babcock, 1794), 16, 23–25.
13. "Declaration of the Commissioners of the United Colonies Concerning Whalley and Goffe," September 5, 1661, in Ezra Stiles, 59–60.
14. Hoadley, *Records of the Colony*, 422–23.
15. Stiles, 61; Franklin B. Dexter, "Memoranda Respecting Edward Whalley and William Goffe," *Papers of the New Haven Colony Historical Society*, vol. 2 (New Haven, CT: New Haven Colony Historical Society, 1877), 130–131: Great Britain, *Calendar of State Papers*, 33–34.

16. *Ibid.*, 34.
17. John L. Rockey, ed., *History of New Haven County, Connecticut*, vol. 1 (New York: W.W. Preston and Co., 1892), 24; For documents concerning the search for Goffe and Whalley in New England see Great Britain, *Calendar of State Papers*, 15, 27–28, 30, 33–34, 53–54.
18. Great Britain, *Calendar of State Papers*, 33–34.
19. *Mather Papers*, 183.
20. Thomas Bayly Howell, Thomas Jones Howell, "Relation of the arraignment and Trial of those who made the late Rebellious insurrections in London, 1661" in *A Complete Collection of State Trials and Proceedings for High Treason and other Crimes and Misdemeanors*, vol. 6 (London: T.C. Hansard, 1816), 106–107, and 110.
21. *Ibid.*, 106.
22. Great Britain, *Calendar of State Papers*, 110.
23. Hull, 182.
24. *Ibid.*
25. For example see John Marshall and John Locke, *Toleration and Early Enlightenment Culture* (Cambridge, MA: Cambridge University Press, 2006), 297; and a contemporary example is found in Anon., *Strange and Terrible Newes from Cambridge being a True Relation of Quakers Bewitching of Mary Philips* (London: C. Brooks, 1659), 4.
26. Humphrey Norton, *New-England's Ensigne it being the account of cruelty, the professors pride, and the articles of their faith, signified in characters written in blood, wickedly begun* (London: T.L., 1659), 7.
27. Carla G. Pestana, "The city Upon the Hill under Siege-The Puritan Perception of the Quaker Threat to Massachusetts Bay, 1656–1661," *The New England Quarterly* 56 (1983): 336–341.
28. Pestana, 336; Trumbull, *The Public Records*, 282–284.
29. *Ibid.*, 283–284.
30. *Ibid.*, 308.
31. Norton, passim; George Bishop, *New England Judged by the Spirit of the Lord* (London: T Sowle, 1703), passim.
32. Norton, 50.
33. *Ibid.*, 56.
34. George Edward Ellis, *The Puritan Age and Rule in the Colony of the Massachusetts Bay, 1629–1685* (New York: Houghton, Mifflin and Co., 1888), 446–447
35. Norton, 52–53; Nathaniel Goodwin, *Foote Family or the Descendants of Nathaniel Foote* (Hartford, CT: Case Tiffany and Co., 1899), xvi.
36. Bishop, 228.

37. Ellis, 446–447.
38. Norton, 56; Bishop, 173–174; see Dexter, *New Haven Town Records*, 339–343, for Humphrey Norton's trial in New Haven on March 10, 1657/58; Hoadley, vol. 2, 233–234. Norton was sentenced to be "severely whipped and branded on the hand with the letter H."
39. Norton, 56; Bishop, 173–174.
40. Frank D. Andrews, *A Quaker's Visit to Hartford in the Year 1676* (Vineland, NJ: F.D. Andrews, 1914), 8–12.
41. *Ibid.*, 3.
42. Hull, 187–189.
43. *Ibid.*, 189.
44. *Ibid.*, 191.
45. Davenport, 195–199.
46. Great Britain, *Calendar of State Papers*, 55–56.
47. *Ibid.*, 61–62.
48. Murray N. Rothbard, *Conceived in Liberty*, vol. 1 (Auburn, AL: Ludwig von Mises Institute, 1999), 236.
49. Richard Baxter, *Reliquiæ Baxterianæ: Or, Mr. Richard Baxter's Narrative of the Most Memorable Passages of His Life and Times* (London: Matthew Sylvester, 1696), 385–87.
50. *Mather Papers*, 201–202.
51. Baxter, 385.
52. *Mather Papers*, 202.
53. Great Britain, *Calendar of State Papers, Domestic Series, of the Reign of Charles II 1661–1662*, vol. 2, Public Record Office, (London: Longman, Green, Longman and Roberts, 1861), 155.
54. *Mather Papers*, 203.
55. Davenport, 199.
56. *Ibid.*
57. Thurloe, v. 1, 768.
58. Davenport, 194–195.
59. *Ibid.*, 195–196.
60. *Mather Papers*, 202.
61. His first official opportunity came when he presided over his first witch trial in May 1658. Winthrop previously served on the Margaret Jones trial in Boston in 1648. Besides his interest in alchemy it is also possible the execution of Margaret Jones (who also dispensed healing remedies) engendered some sympathy in him. Winthrop later developed a network of elite women who he sent potions to help heal the sick in their communities. Davenport, 127; *Collections of the Massachusetts Historical Society*, vol. 7, 548; Woodward, 198–199.
62. Demos, 233–234; Noel Gish, "Pirates"; Twomey, *Awakening The Past...*, 250.
63. Dunn, in Twomey, *Awakening The Past...*, 91–93.
64. *Ibid.*, 93–94.
65. *Ibid.*, 94.
66. Tomlinson, 69.

67. Henry Parsons Hedges, *Records of the Town of East Hampton, Long Island, Suffolk Co., N.Y.*, vol. 1 (Sag Harbor, NY: John H. Hunt, 1887), 135.
68. King, 116.
69. *Ibid.*
70. Hedges, 134.
71. *Ibid.*, 57.
72. *Ibid.*, 136.
73. *Ibid.*, 135 and 153.
74. Hedges, 129; King, 114 .
75. "Deposition of Mrs. Gardiner, February 24, 1657/58" in Hedges, 133.
76. King, 116. Simons feared Goody Garlick especially when she tried to send herbs earlier into her house. The attack on a more "prominent woman" in the community was the opening she needed to have those with more influence "confront the witch."
77. "Deposition of Goodwife Simons, February 24, 1657/58," in Hedges, 132; "Deposition of Goody Burdsill, March, 11, 1657/58," in Hedges, 139; Tomlinson, 73.
78. "Deposition of Samuel Parsons, February 19, 1657/8," in Hedges, 130.
79. Demos, 323–324. Chimney's and fireplaces come up in depositions on a regular basis. In 1662 there was an indictment issued in Massachusetts but not acted on until 1672 accusing Eunice Cole of entering into a covenant with the Devil. On entering her house two witnesses saw "the shimmering of a red color in the chimney center" an event that terrified the two men; "Deposition of Abraham Perkins, Sr. April 7, 1673," in Suffolk Court Files XIII, no. 1228. The deposition is dated to 1662.
80. "Deposition of Goody Edwards, March 11, 1657/8," in Hedges, 139–140. On salt, "Aubrey says 'salt is inimique to Evil spirits is agrred upon by writers of magic....'" In John Jackson Manley, *Salt, and Other Condiments* (Charing Cross, SW: William Clowes and Sons, 1884), 94.
81. "Deposition of Goody Brooks, February 27, 1657/8," in Hedges, 134.
82. Demos, 217.
83. Demos, 217; Hedges, 140.
84. "Records of the Particular Court," 56, 92 and 93; Trumbull, *The Public Records*, vol. 1, 220; Woodward, 227–228.
85. Schenk, 71.
86. "Records of the Particular Court," 188–189.
87. Woodward, 227.
88. *Ibid.*, 228.
89. "Lion Gardiner to John Winthrop Jr.," 1651, and "Lion Gardiner to John Winthrop Jr.," 1652, in *Massachusetts Historical Society. Collections*, vol. 7 (Boston, MA: Massachusetts Historical Society, 1865), 62–63.

90. Hedges, 134.
91. "John Winthrop Jr. Letter to East Hampton," in Trumbull, *Public Records...*, vol. 1, Appendix 5, 572–573; Woodward, 228–229.
92. William K. Holdsworth, "Law and Society in Colonial Connecticut, 1636–1672," (Claremont Graduate School, Dissertation, 1974), 403, in Woodward, 228.
93. Woodward, 228.
94. "Records of the Particular Court," 238, 240 and 243; Tomlinson, 76–79; Woodward, 230
95. Karlsen, 132–133.

## Chapter 12

1. Gale Ion Harris, "The Earlier Career of Hannah (Wakeman) Hackleton, Edward Whittaker's Wife in the Esopus," *New York Genealogical and Biographical Record* 127 (1996): 67.
2. *Ibid.*
3. Clarence Almon Torrey, *New England Marriages Prior to 1700* (Baltimore, MD: Genealogical Publishing Co., Inc., 1985), 818; James Hammond Trumbull, *The Memorial History of Hartford County Connecticut 1633–1884*, vol. 1 (Boston, MA: Edward L. Osgood, 1886), 265.
4. Charles William Manwaring, *A Digest of the Early Connecticut Probate Records, Hartford District 1635–1700*, v. 1 (Hartford, CT: R.S. Peck and Co., 1904), 40.
5. "Testimony of the Inquest Committee of Elizabeth Kelly, n.d.," no. 5, *Samuel Wyllys papers*, CSL State Archives, http://cslib.cdm host.com/cdm/ref/collection/p15019coll10/id/162; Harris, "The Earlier Career...," 71
6. Lucius Barnes Barbour, *Families of Early Hartford, Connecticut* (Baltimore, MD: Clearfield Co., 1977), 351; Harris, "The Earlier Career," 69; Gale Ion Harris, "William and Goodwife Ayres of Hartford, Connecticut: Witches who Got Away," *The American Genealogist* 75 (2000):197–205.
7. Charles J. Hoadley, "Some Early Post-Mortem Examinations in New England," *Proceedings of the Connecticut Medical Society* (New Haven, CT: Buckingham & Brewer, 1892), 208.
8. "Records of the Particular Court," vol. 22, 237.
9. Harris, "The Earlier Career," 70; for Hartford see "Records of the Particular Court," vol. 22, 204–206 and 208–209.
10. Trumbull, *Public Records*, vol. 15, 542–543; Harris, "The Earlier Career...," 71–72.
11. Terry D. Prall, *Prall, McHugh, Faucett, Crail and allied families: the story of my ancestral heritage* (Baltimore, MD: Gateway Press, 2009), 191 and 213; Demos, 247.

12. Lawrence B. Goodheart, *Solemn Sentence of Death. Crime and Punishment in Connecticut* (Amherst, MA: University of Massachusetts Press, 2011), 36.
13. Peter R. Christoph, Kenneth Kenneth, and Kenn Stryker-Rodda, eds., *New York Historical Manuscripts: Dutch, Kingston Papers*, vol. 1 (Baltimore, MD: Genealogical Pub. Co., 1976), 445–446; Harris, "The Earlier Career," 67.
14. Harris, "The Earlier Career," 66, 68.
15. Harris, "The Earlier Career," 66; Victor H. Paltsitz, ed., *Minutes of the Executive Council of the Province of New York*, vol. 1 (Albany, NY: R.J. Lyon, 1910), 180–181.
16. Harris "The Earlier Career," 70; Hoadley, "Some Early Post-Mortem," 208.
17. Woodward, 230.
18. Gale Ion Harris, "William and Goodwife Ayres," 198.
19. "Records of the Particular Court," vol. 22, 121–122, 185.
20. *Original Distribution of the Lands in Hartford among the Settlers, 1639*, vol. 14 (Connecticut Historical Society, 1912), 408, in Harris, "William and Goodwife Ayres," 200.
21. "Records of the Particular Court," vol. 22, 145.
22. "Testimony of Goody Burr and her son Samuel," no. 3, *Samuel Wyllys Papers*, CSL State Archives.
23. Medical Records of John Winthrop, MS, Massachusetts Historical Society, Boston, 237–238, cited in Harris, "William and Goodwife Ayres…," 200.
24. "Nathaniel Mather to Increase Mather, December 31, 1684," *Massachusetts Historical Society. Collections*, vol. 8 (Boston, MA: Massachusetts Historical Society, 1868), 58.
25. Tomlinson, *Witchcraft Prosecution*, 84.
26. Rembert Dodoens, John Gerard, and John Norton, *The Herball, or, Generall historie of plantes gathered by John Gerard of London, master in chirurgerie* (London: John Norton, 1597), 848.
27. Dodoens, 847; "Testimony of John Kelly and Bethia Kelly his wife concerning the sickness and death of his daughter Elizabeth Kelly aged 8 yrs. and upwards," Series 1, Court records, 1662–1757, MS342, Box 1, Folder 7, May 13, 1662, *Samuel Wyllys papers*, MS, Brown University Library, http://dl.lib.brown.edu/bamco/index.html.
28. "Testimony of John Kelly and Bethia Kelly … May 13, 1662," MS 342, *Samuel Wyllys papers*.
29. "Testimony of Joseph Marsh, March 31, 1661/62," No. 4, *Samuel Wyllys papers*, CSL State Archives, http://cslib.cdmhost.com/cdm/ref/collection/p15019coll10/id/162.
30. "Testimony of John Kelly and Bethia Kelly … May 13, 1662," MS 342, *Samuel Wyllys Papers*.
31. "Testimony of the Inquest Committee," No. 5, *Samuel Wyllys papers*, CSL State Archives.
32. Tomlinson, 84; Hoadley, "Some Early Post-Mortem," 214.
33. Dalton, 277–278.
34. Henry Charles Lea, *Superstition and Force: Essays on the Wager of Law—the Wager of Battle—the* Ordeal—Torture (Philadelphia, PA: Henry C. Lea, 1878), 315–323 passim.
35. James I, King of England, *Daemonologie, In Forme of a Dialogue* (Edinburgh, Scotland: Walter Wald-graue, 1597), 80.
36. "Testimony of the Inquest Committee," No. 5, *Samuel Wyllys Papers*.
37. David R. Senn and Richard A. Weems, eds., *Manual of Forensic Odontology*, Fifth Edition (Boca Raton, FL: CRC, 2013), 49; http://emedicine.medscape.com/article/1680032-overview#a2.
38. Testimony of the Inquest Committee, No. 5, *Samuel Wyllys Papers*.
39. Walter Charleton, *Physiologia Epicuro-Gassendo-Charltoniana, or, A fabrick of science natural, upon the hypothesis of atoms founded by Epicurus* (London: Tho: Newcomb, 1654), 365; Clark, 266; http://emedicine.medscape.com/article/1680032-overview#a2.
40. *Winthrop Journal* 1 (1908): 319–320; Hoadley, "Some Early Post-Mortem," 216.
41. Thomas Robisheaux, "Witchcraft and Forensic Medicine in Seventeenth Century Germany," in Stuart Clark, *Languages of Witchcraft: Narrative, Ideology and Meaning in Early Modern Culture* (New York: St. Martin's Press, 2001), 212.
42. "Testified upon Oath before the Magistrates by Mr. Rossiter and Mr. Pitkin Attests, Daniel Clark Secretary" [Testimony of Dr. Rossiter on death of Kelly's child], MS 341, Box 1, Folder 6, *Samuel Wyllys papers*, Ms. Brown University Library; Stiles, 453.
43. Tomlinson, 88; Woodward, 232; see Robert St. George, 118–119, for a questionable interpretation.
44. "Some Early Autopsies in the United States," *Lancet* (September 1903): 926; Kenneth Iserson, *Death to Dust: What Happens to Dead Bodies?* (Tucson, AZ: Galen Press, 1994), 116.
45. Mather, *Magnalia Christi*, vol. 2, 64.
46. Hoadley, "Some Early Post-Mortem," 216.
47. Lorraine Daston, "Marvelous Facts and Miraculous Evidence in Early Modern Europe," in Helen Parish, ed., *Superstition and Magic in Early Modern Europe* (London: Bloomsbury Press, 2015), 111.
48. *Ibid.*, 114.
49. Robisheaux, 212–213

50. Robisheaux, 213; For example, the English physician Sir Thomas Browne wrote, "I have ever believed, and I now know, that there are Witches...." This belief certainly would have colored his diagnosis in a suspicious death just as it did in a later case of possession. (See below footnote 62.); Thomas Browne, *Religio Medica* [1642], M. A. Murchison, ed., (Cambridge, MA: Cambridge University Press, 1922), 42.

51. "Records of the Particular Court," vol. 22, 247.

52. Harris, "William and Goodwife Ayres...," 201; "Testimony of Joseph Marsh...," No. 4, *Samuel Wyllys papers,* CSL State Archives.

53. "Respecting Goodwife Seager: January 1662, Report of trial. Signed Walt. Fyler. Acquitted," Series 1, Court records, 1662–1757, MS 338, Box 1, Folder 3, January 16, 1662/3, *Samuel Wyllys papers,* Ms. Brown University Library http://dl.lib.brown.edu/bamco/index. html; "Testimony of Goody Burr and her son Samuel," No. 3, *Samuel Wyllys papers,* CSL State Archives.

54. Increase Mather, *Remarkable providences illustrative of the earlier days of American colonization* (London: John Russell Smith, 1856), 99; From a theological perspective as "insufficient proof of witchcraft" see Perkins, *Damned Art,* 208; for legal issues see Clark, *Thinking With Demons,* 590.

55. Gaskill, 217.

56. "Respecting Goodwife Seager: January 1662...," MS 338, *Samuel Wyllys Papers*; Tomlinson, 90.

57. Tomlinson, 90; "Records of the Particular Court," vol. 22, 258–259.

58. Gale Ion Harris and Robert Charles Anderson, "The Later Career of William and Judith Ayres, Escaped Witches from Hartford, Connecticut: Rhode Island Destination and Descendants," FASG, *The American Genealogist* 75 (2000): 302, in Tomlinson, 93.

59. Harris, "The Earlier Career," 205; "Records of the Particular Court," vol. 22, 250–251; Tomlinson, 93.

60. Tomlinson, 182; Woodward, 234; Fuller, 5.

61. "John Whiting to Increase Mather, October 4, 1682," *Massachusetts Historical Society. Collections,* vol. 8 (Boston, MA: Massachusetts Historical Society, 1868), 466–467.

62. Clark, *Thinking with Demons,* 390–391. The physician Thomas Browne gave testimony in the witch trials at Bury St. Edmunds in 1664/65 concerning some possessed children. He testified the "Devil ... did work upon the bodies of Men and Women ... these swooning fits were natural ... heightened to a great excess by the subtilty of the Devil, cooperating with the Malice of these we term

Witches...." *A Tryal of Witches ... Taken by a Person then Attending the Court* (London: 1682), 41–42.

63. John Darrell, *An Apologie, or defense of the Possession of William Sommer* (n.p., n .d.), 11; Clark, *Thinking with Demons,* 402 and 409.

64. Clark, *Thinking with Demon,* 393.

65. *Ibid.,* 408–409, 413.

66. *Ibid.,* 408–409.

67. On the Elizabeth Knapp possession see Demos, 99–131; Samuel Willard, *Useful Instructions for Professing People in Times of great Security and Degeneracy* (Cambridge, MA: Samuel Green, 1673), A2.

68. Willard, 11, 25, 27, 32.

69. Perkins, 215–216.

70. "Cotton Mather to John Richards, December 31, 1692," *Massachusetts Historical Society. Collections,* vol. 8 (Boston, MA: Massachusetts Historical Society, 1868), 392.

71. The date of Ann Cole's initial possession is unknown as is whether she was involved in the original accusations against the Ayres. See Tomlinson, 94. I suspect she began her fits after the initial accusations because in the testimony of Goodman Garret and his wife a gift of parsnips is refused by a neighbor. Parsnips were harvested in the late fall at about the same time as pumpkins. In the lyrics to the song *New England's Annoyances* (circa 1643) there is the following line: "Our pumpkins and parsnips are common supplies, for we can make liquor to sweeten our lips, of pumpkins and parsnips and walnut tree chips." They were likely harvested about the same time. See E. Lewis Sturtevant, "Kitchen Garden Esculents of American Origin III," *The American Naturalist* XIX (Philadelphia, PA: 1885): 658.

72. Whiting, 468.

73. "Testimony of Goody Watson, June 17, 1665, Box 1 Folder," MS 349, *Samuel Wyllys papers,* Ms. Brown University Library, http://dl.lib.brown.edu/bamco/index.html.

74. "Testimony of Goodwife Garrett and Goodman Garett regarding a mess of parsnips," June 15, 1665, MS 340, Box 1, Folder 5," *Samuel Wyllys papers,* Ms. Brown University Library, http://dl.lib.brown.edu/bamco/index.html.

75. "Case of witchcraft against Goodwife Seager and Goodwife Greensmith of Hartford with testimony by Robert Sterne, Stephen Hart and others," No. 1, *Samuel Wyllys papers,* CSL State Archives; "Testimony of Goodwife Garrett and Goodman Garett...," *Samuel Wyllys papers.*

76. *Geneva Bible* (1599), Acts 19: 13–16; Hall, 163.

77. John Henry Benton Jr., *Samuel Slade Benton his Ancestors and Descendants* (Boston, MA: Merrymount Press, 1901), 13.

78. Lucas, 63.
79. Benton, 13–14.
80. "Mather to ... Richards," 391–397.
81. Hall, 157, 173, 174, and 176–178.
82. Whiting, 466.
83. "Testimony of Eliazer Kimmerly...," No. 16, *Samuel Wyllys papers*, CSL State Archives.
84. Whiting, 466.
85. Benton, 15.
86. Hoadley, vol. 2, 29, 33, 34.
87. Winthrop Papers, VI, 301.
88. Manwaring, 108–109.
89. Manwaring, 49–50.
90. Benton, 13; on the Pitkin dispute see Lucas, 94.
91. There have been questions over whether John Cole was related to William Edwards as his half-brother. In a public meeting on January 30, 1672, concerning land division in Hartford the record states "John Cole, son of James [Cole]" (James Cole was also Williams Edwards' step-father); William Smith Porter, *Historical Notices of Connecticut*, No. 1 (1842): 43; Benton, 13.
92. Davenport, 263.
93. *Ibid.*
94. On Watson and Hosmer see above. On Whaples see, "Case of witchcraft against Goodwife Harrison of Wethersfield, testimony of Thomas Waples," No. 7, *Samuel Wyllys papers*, CSL State Archives; on Edwards see Hall, 161.
95. Benton, 14.
96. Benton, 15.
97. Benton, 16.
98. Porter, 38.
99. Tomlinson, 96.
100. Taylor, *Witchcraft Delusion*, 96.
101. "Records of the Particular Court," vol. 22, 81, 86, 107.
102. "Testimony of Rebecca Greensmith in Court, January 8, 1662/63," MS. 337, Box 1, Folder 2, *Samuel Wyllys papers*, Ms. *Wyllys*, Brown University Library, http://dl.lib.brown.edu/bamco/index.html.
103. "Records of the Particular Court," vol. 22, 73, 118, 119.
104. Taylor, *Witchcraft Delusion*, 96; Tomlinson, 96.
105. Porter, 37.
106. "Records of the Particular Court," vol. 22, 247.
107. Whiting, 468.
108. Whiting, 468.
109. "Records of the Particular Court," vol. 22, 258.
110. Whiting, 468.
111. *Annotations upon all the Books of the Old and New Testament* (1645), *Ex xxii*, 18, in Thomas, 441.
112. Increase Mather, *A testimony against several prophane and superstitious customs now practised by some in New-England* (London: 1687), 36. Christmas was not celebrated in colonial New England. That Rebecca would sign a covenant with the devil on Christmas was deeply insulting to Reverend Stone who like other puritan ministers spoke out against Christmas revelry equating it with deviltry and paganism. In 1659 the Massachusetts General Court declared the celebration of Christmas to be a criminal offense. The law was rescinded in 1685. For more information see Penne L. Restad, *Christmas in America: A History* (New York: Oxford University Press, 1995), 14–15.
113. Whiting, 468.
114. Demos, 174.
115. Gaskill, *Witchfinders...*, 44–45.
116. "Testimony of Rebecca Greensmith...," MS 337, *Samuel Wyllys papers*.
117. *Ibid.*
118. "Grounds for the examination of a witch," MS374, Box 1, Folder 39, *Samuel Wyllys papers*, Ms. Brown University Library, http://dl.lib.brown.edu/bamco/index.html (See Appendix).
119. *Ibid.*
120. "Records of the Particular Court," vol. 22, 258.
121. "Records of the Particular Court," vol. 22, 259–260; "Respecting Goodwife Seager: January 1662...," MS 338, *Samuel Wyllys papers*, http://dl.lib.brown.edu/bamco/index.html.
122. Hutchinson, 8–9.
123. Taylor, *Witchcraft Delusion*, 100.
124. Love, 286.
125. Manwaring, vol. 1, 121–122.
126. "Records of the Particular Court," vol. 22, 265.
127. Whiting, 469.
128. Increase Mather, *Remarkable providences,* 53 and 91.
129. Tomlinson, 108.
130. Burr, 18–19; Tomlinson, 93–94.
131. See for example, Katherine Harrison of Wethersfield who moved to Westchester, New York in 1670 following a guilty verdict of witchcraft in the Connecticut Court, and was acquitted by the bench when she promised to remove herself from Connecticut. Following her move to Westchester her neighbors suspected her of witchcraft. She was brought to court in New York. The New York court finally permitted her to remain but her neighbors made her life difficult. She moved away but the accusations followed her. She was in court again and although the case was dismissed public opinion continued to make her life uncomfortable.
132. Trumbull, *Public Records*, v. 2, Appendix, 531.

## Chapter 13

1. "Particular Court Record," vol. 22, 260.
2. "Testimony of Rebecca Greensmith," MS 337, *Samuel Wyllys papers.*
3. "Case of witchcraft against Goodwife Seager and Goodwife Greensmith...," No. 1, *Samuel Wyllys papers.*
4. "Respecting Goodwife Seager: January 1662...," MS 338, *Samuel Wyllys papers.*
5. "Grounds for the examination of a witch," MS 374, *Samuel Wyllys papers,*
6. Woodward, 236–237.
7. Woodward, 210–252, passim.
8. "Testimony of Mrs. Migat," Box 1, Folder 4, MS. 339, *Samuel Wyllys papers,* Ms. Brown University Library, http://dl.lib.brown.edu/bamco/index.html.
9. "Court of Assistants Records," vol. 56, 5, Connecticut State Library, in Hall, *Witch Hunting,* 159.
10. For example, William Goodrich was a deputy from Wethersfield in the general court held in May 15, 1662, and served in the General Assembly of Hartford May 11, 1663. Lafayette W. Case, *The Goodrich Family in America* (Chicago, IL: Fergus Printing Co., 1889), 34.
11. Peter Elmer, *Witchcraft, Witch-Hunting, and Politics in Early Modern England* (New York: Oxford University Press, 2016), 188.
12. Notestein, 267.
13. *Ibid.,* 268.
14. Mather, *Wonders,* 262.
15. Tomlinson, *Witchcraft Prosecution,* 111.
16. "Testimony of Goodwife Garrett," MS. 340, *Samuel Wyllys Papers.*
17. "Case of Goodwife Seager," No. 1, *Samuel Wyllys Papers.*
18. "Testimony of Goodwife Garrett," MS. 340, *Samuel Wyllys Papers.*
19. Woodward, 236.
20. Hinman, *The Blue Laws,* 297.
21. Woodward, 236–237.

22. Hinman, 297
23. Woodward, 237.
24. Tomlinson, *Witchcraft Prosecution,* 113.
25. Thomas, 453; Davies, *Four Centuries,* 188–190; Judd, 236–239
26. "The Answer of Some Ministers to the Questions Propounded to them by the Honored Magistrates, October 20, 1669," MS. 354, Box 1, Folder 19, *Samuel Wyllys papers,* Ms. Brown University Library.
27. *Ibid.*
28. Tomlinson, 135.
29. Woodward, 251.
30. Gersholm Bulkeley, "Will and Doom, Or the Miseries of Connecticut by and Under an Usurped and Arbitrary Power," vol. 3 (Hartford, CT: Connecticut Historical Society, 1895), 233–235; Woodward, 251; Godbeer, *Escaping Salem,* 110–126.

## Appendix

1. Tomlinson, *Witchcraft Prosecution,* 26; Woodward, 233, n. 43.
2. Torture was not legally permitted in England. However, for a theologian who did not have to adhere to specific English laws because he was writing for a wider audience and knowing full well the secret crimes of witches, Perkins advised his readers torture was permissible but only "upon strong and great presumptions." Apparently whoever copied from Perkins may have decided torture needed to remain in the document as a faithful recording of Perkin's recommendations and believed that someday it might be necessary or possible to invoke this harsh measure.
3. The original document is in the Connecticut State Library, State Archives. I have used the transcription in Taylor, *Witchcraft Delusion in Connecticut* (New York: Grafton Press, 1908), 40–42.

# Bibliography

## Manuscript Sources

*Brown University, John Hay Library, Providence Rhode Island*

MS. 337. "Testimony of Rebecca Greensmith in Court January 8, 1662/63." Box 1, Folder 2. *Samuel Wyllys papers.* Ms. *Wyllys,* Brown University Library.

MS. 338. "Respecting Goodwife Seager: January 16:62, Report of trial. Signed Walt. Fyler. Acquitted." Series 1. Court records, 1662–1757. Box 1, Folder 3. January 16, 1662/3. Ms. *Wyllys,* Brown University Library.

MS 339. "Testimony of Mrs. Migat." May 1662. Box 1, Folder 4. *Samuel Wyllys papers.* Ms. *Wyllys,* Brown University Library.

MS. 340. "Testimony of Goodwife Garrett and Goodman Garett regarding a mess of parsnips...." June 15, 1665. Box 1, Folder 5. *Samuel Wyllys papers.* Ms. *Wyllys,* Brown University Library.

MS. 341. "Testified upon Oath before the Magistrates by Mr. Rossiter and Mr. Pitkin Attests, Daniel Clark Secretary" [Testimony of Dr. Rossiter on death of Kelly's child]. Box 1, Folder 6. *Samuel Wyllys papers.* Ms. *Wyllys,* Brown University Library.

MS. 342. "Testimony of John Kelly and Bethnia Kelly his wife concerning the sickness and death of his daughter Elizabeth Kelly aged 8 yrs. and upwards." May 13, 1662. Series 1. Court records, 1662–1757. Box 1, Folder 7. *Samuel Wyllys papers.* Ms. *Wyllys,* Brown University Library.

MS. 349. "Testimony of Goodwife Watson." June 15, 1665. Box 1, Folder 5. *Samuel Wyllys papers.* Ms. *Wyllys,* Brown University Library.

MS. 350. "Testimony of Elizabeth Smith, Regarding Fortune Telling." October 29, 1668. Box 1, Folder 12. *Samuel Wyllys papers,* Ms. Brown University Library.

MS. 354. "The Answer of Some Ministers to the Questions Propounded to them by the Honored Magistrates" October 20, 1669. Box 1, Folder 19. *Samuel Wyllys papers.* Ms. *Wyllys,* Brown University Library.

MS. 374. "Grounds for Examination of a Witch." Box 1, Folder 39. *Samuel Wyllys papers.* Ms. *Wyllys,* Brown University Library.

These documents may be accessed at http://www.riamco.org/render.php?eadid=US-RPB-mswyllys&view=inventory.

*Connecticut State Library (CSL), State Archives, Hartford, Connecticut*

No. 1. "Case of witchcraft against Goodwife Seager and Goodwife Greensmith of Hartford with testimony of Robert Sterne, Stephen Hart and others." *Samuel Wyllys papers.* CSL, State Archives.

No. 3. "Testimony of Goody Burr and her son Samuel." *Samuel Wyllys Papers.* CSL, State Archives.

No 4. "Testimony of Joseph Marsh." March 31, 1661/62. *Samuel Wyllys papers.* CSL, State Archive.

**313**

No. 5. "Testimony of the Inquest Committee of Elizabeth Kelly." *Samuel Wyllys papers*. CSL, State Archives.
No. 6. "Findings of the Grand Jury in the Case of Mary Stapels Mary Harvy, and Hannah Harvy." September 15, 1692. *Samuel Wyllys papers*. CSL, State Archives.
No. 7. "Case of witchcraft against Goodwife Harrison of Wethersfield, testimony of Thomas Waples...." August 7, 1668. *Samuel Wyllys papers*. CSL, State Archives.
No. 16. "Testimony of Eliazer Kimmerly...." *Samuel Wyllys papers*. CSL, State Archives.
No. 41. "Case of Mercy Disbrough." *Samuel Wyllys papers*. CSL, State Archives.
These documents can be accessed at http://ctstatelibrary.org/RG000_samuel_wyllys_papers.html.

### Saint Margaret's Church, Westminster, London, England

Alice Youngs. "Baptism Record, March 2, 1633/34." Saint Margaret's Church. Westminster, London, England. Dean and Chapter of Westminster, London.

### Town of Windsor, Connecticut

"Resolution Concerning Certain Witchcraft Convictions of Windsor Residents in Colonial Connecticut," February 6, 2017

## Primary Sources

Aubrey, John. *Miscellanies Upon Various Subjects*. 4th ed. London: John Russell Smith, 1857.
Bargrave, Isaac. *A Sermon Preached Before King Charles, March 27, 1627*. London: Legatt, 1627.
Baxter, Richard. *Reliquiæ Baxterianæ: Or, Mr. Richard Baxter's Narrative of the Most Memorable Passages of His Life and Times*. London: Matthew Sylvester, 1696.
Bernard, Richard. *A Guide to the Grand-Jury Men*. London: Felix Kingston, 1627.
Birch, Thomas. *A Collection of the State Papers of John Thurloe Papers from the year 1638–1653*. Vol. 7. London: Thomas Woodard and Charles Davis, 1742.
Birch, Thomas, ed. "Mr. Chamberlain to Rev. Joseph Mead February 18, 1624–25." *The Court and Time of James the First*. Vol. 2. London: Henry Colburn, 1848.
Bishop, George. *New England Judged by the Spirit of the Lord*. London: T. Sowle, 1703.
Hubbard, Benjamin. *Sermo Secularis or A Sermon to Bring to Rememberance the Dealings of Jehovah....* London: R.L., 1648.
Bradford, William. *History of Plymouth Plantation*. Boston, MA: Privately printed, 1856.
Bradshaw, William, and Thomas Gataker. *A plaine and pithy exposition of the second Epistle to the Thessalonians*. London: Edward Griffin, 1620.
"A Brief Apologie in defence of the general proceedings of the Court, holden at Boston the ninth day of the fifth month, 1636 against Mr. Wheelwright, a member there, by occasion of a Sermon delivered there in the Same Congregation." In Winthrop, John. *Antinomians and Familists Condemned by the Synod of Elders in New England*. London: Ralph Smith, 1644.
Brinsley, John. *A Consolation for Our Grammar Schooles*. London: Richard Field, 1622.
Brown, William Hande, ed. *Proceedings of the Council of Maryland 1636–1667*. Baltimore, MD: Maryland Historical Society, 1885.
Browne, Thomas. *Religio Medica* [1642]. Murchison, M.A. ed. Cambridge, MA: Cambridge University Press, 1922.
Bulkeley, Gersholm. "Will and Doom, Or the Miseries of Connecticut by and Under an Usurped and Arbitrary Power." *Connecticut Historical Society Collections* 3. Hartford, CT: Connecticut Historical Society, 1895.
Bulkley, Peter. *The Gospel Covenant, or the Covenant of Grace Opened*. London: M.S., 1646.
"Certificate That Joan Guppy, of South Perrott, in the County of Dorset, Was Not a Witch. 1606." *The Antiquary* 33 (July 1897): 215.
Chauncy, Charles. *God's Mercy Shewed to His People Giving Them Faithful MInistry and Schooles of Learning for the Continual Supply Therof*. Cambridge, MA: Samuel Green, 1655.
Clapp, Ebenezer. *History of the Town of Dorchester*. Boston, MA: Dorchester Antiquarian and Historical Society, 1859.

Clapp, Roger. "Memoirs of Roger Clapp. 1630." *Dorchester Antiquarian and Historical Society.* No. 1. Boston: D. Clapp, Jr., 1844.

Clarke, Samuel. *The Lives of Sundry Eminent Persons in this Later Age.* London: 1683.

*Code of 1650: Being a Compilation of the Earliest Laws and Orders, of the General Court of Connecticut.* Hartford, CT: Andrus and Judd, 1833.

Collinson, John and Edmund Rack. *The History and Antiquities of the County of Somerset: Collected from Authentick Records.* Vol. 2. Bath: R. Cruttwell, 1791.

*Connecticut Historical Society Collections.* Vol. 2 Hartford, CT: Connecticut Historical Society, 1870.

*Connecticut Historical Society Collections.* Vol. 3 Hartford, CT: Connecticut Historical Society, 1895.

*Connecticut Historical Society Collections.* Vol. 22 Hartford, CT: Connecticut Historical Society, 1928.

"Controversy in the Church in Hartford 1656–1659." *Connecticut Historical Society Collections.* Vol. 2 Hartford, CT: Connecticut Historical Society, 1870.

Cooper. *The Mystery of Witch-craft.* London: Nicholas Oakes, 1617.

"Correspondence and Documents Chiefly of the Descendants of Gov. George Wyllys of Connecticut 1590–1796." *Connecticut Historical Society Collections.* Vol. 21. Hartford, CT: Connecticut Historical Society, 1924.

Cosin, John. *The Correspondence of John Cosin.* Surtees Society. Vol. 52. George Ormsby, ed. Durham, NC: Andrews & Co., 1869.

Cotton, John. *An Abstract of the Lawes of New England As they are now established.* London: 1641.

Cotton, John. *Exposition of the Thirteenth Chapter of Revelation by that Reverend and Eminent Servant of the Lord, Mr. John Cotton.* London: Hand and Bible, 1656.

Cotton, John. "A Sermon upon the Day of Publique Thanksgiving, from Rev. 15:13." 10 January 1651. In Bremer, Francis J. *Puritan Crisis New England and the English Civil Wars, 1630–1670.* New York: Garland Press, 1989.

Dalton, Michael. *The Countrey Justice.* London: 1618.

Dalton, Michael. *The Countrey Justice.* 3rd Ed. London: 1635

"Damnable Practices of the Three Lincolnshire Witches...." In Pepys, Samuel. *A Pepysian Garland: Black-letter Broadside Ballads of the Years 1595–1639....* Cambridge, England: Cambridge University Press, 1922.

Danforth, Samuel. *An Almanac for the Year of Our Lord 1647.* Cambridge, MA: 1647.

Danforth, Samuel. *An Almanac for the Year of our Lord 1648.* Cambridge, MA: 1648.

Danforth, Samuel. *An Almanac for the Year of Our Lord 1649.* Cambridge, MA: 1649.

Davies, G.J., ed. *Touchying witchcrafte and sorcerye.* Dorset: Dorset Record Society, 1985.

Davies, S.F., Matthew Hopkins, and John Stearn, eds. *Writings of the Witchfinders.* Brighton: Puckrel Publishing, 2007.

Dexter, Franklin B. "Memoranda Respecting Edward Whalley and William Goffe." *Papers of the New Haven Colony Historical Society.* Vol. 2. New Haven, CT: New Haven Colony Historical Society, 1877.

Dexter, Franklin B. *New Haven Town Records 1649–1662.* New Haven, CT: New Haven Colony Historical Society, 1917.

*Diary or an Exact Journal of the Houses of Parliament.* London: 1644.

*A Dog's Elegry or Ruperts Tears, For the Defeat Given Him at Marston Moor Near York.* London: 1644.

Downame, John. *Annotations upon all the books of the Old and New Testament wherein the text is explained....* London: Legatt, 1651.

Drake, Samuel G. *Annals of Witchcraft in New England, and Elsewhere in the United States from Their First Settlement.* Boston, MA: Woodward, 1869.

"Dunster Papers." *Massachusetts Historical Society Collections.* Vol. 2. Boston, MA: Massachusetts Historical Society, 1854.

Eliot, John. *The Christian Commonwealth.* London: 1659

Eliot, John. "To his Excellency, the Lord General Cromwel, Grace, Mercy and Peace." In Eliot, John, and Thomas Mayhew. *Tears of repentance....* London: Peter Cole, 1653.

Eliot, John, and Thomas Mayhew. *The Glorious Progress of the Gospel Amongst the Indians of New England.* London: Edward Winslow, 1649.

Eliot, John, and Thomas Mayhew. *Tears of repentance: or, A further narrative of the progress of the Gospel amongst the Indians in Nevv-England setting forth, not only their present state and condition, but sundry confessions of sin by diverse of the said Indians, wrought upon by the saving power of the Gospel....* London: Peter Cole, 1653.

Elton, Edward. *Exposition of the Ten Commandments of God.* London: 1623.

"Extracts of Letters to Rev. Thomas Prince." *Five Wonders seene in England.* London: J.C., 1646.

Freiberg, Malcolm, ed. "John Youngs' Disease." *Winthrop Papers.* Vol. 6. Boston, MA: Massachusetts Historical Society, 1992.

Freiberg, Malcolm, ed. "Lion Gardiner to John Winthrop Jr." April 27, 1650. *Winthrop Papers.* Vol. 6. Boston, MA: Massachusetts Historical Society, 1992.

Freiberg, Malcolm, ed., *Winthrop Papers.* Vol. 6. Boston, MA: Massachusetts Historical Society, 1992.

Gaskill, Malcolm, ed. *English Witchcraft 1560–1736.* Vol. 3. London: Pickering & Chatto, 2003.

Gaule, John. *Select Cases of Conscience Touching Witches and Witchcrafts.* London: W. Wilson, 1646.

Gifford, George. *A Dialogue Concerning Witches and Witchcraftes.* London: John Windet, 1593.

Glanvill, Joseph, Henry More, and Anthony Horneck. *Saducismus triumphatus: or, full and plain evidence concerning witches and apparitions.* London: 1700.

Grant, Matthew. "Mathew Grant Record, 1639–1681." *Some Early Records and Documents of and Relating to the Town of Windsor Connecticut 1639–1703.* Hartford, CT: Connecticut Historical Society, 1930.

Grant, Mathew. *Matthew Grant's Diary.* Connecticut State Library. http://www.cslib.org/matthewgrant.htm#Description

Grant, Matthew. "Old Church Record 1639–1681." *Some Early Records and Documents of and Relating to the Town of Windsor Connecticut 1639–1703.* Hartford, CT: Connecticut Historical Society, 1930.

Great Britain. *Calendar of State Papers, Colonial Series, America and the West Indies, 1661–1668.* Sainsbury, W.N., ed. London: Longmans, 1880.

Great Britain. *Calendar of State Papers, Domestic Series, of the Reign of Charles II 1661–1662.* Vol. 2. Public Record Office. London: Longman, Green, Longman and Roberts, 1861.

Hale, John. *A Modest Enquiry into the Nature of Witchcraft.* Boston, MA: B. Green and J. Allen, 1702.

Hale, William. *A Series of Precedents and Proceedings in Criminal Causes, extending from the Year 1475–1640 Extracted from Act-Books of the Ecclesiastical Courts in the Diocese of London.* London: F. & J. Rivington, 1847.

Hall, David D., ed. *The Antinomian controversy, 1636–1638: a documentary history.* Middletown, CT: Wesleyan University Press, 1968.

Hall, David D., ed. *Witch Hunting in Seventeenth Century New England.* Boston, MA: Northeastern University Press, 1991.

Hall, Joseph. *Susurrium cum Deo soliloques, or Holy Self-Conferences of the Devout Soul Upon Sundry Choice Occasions.* London: 1651.

Hart. John D.D. [Heartwell, Jasper]. *Trodden down Strength by the God of Strength or Mrs. Drake Revived....* London: R. Bishop, 1646.

Higginson, Francis. "Higginson's Journal of his Voyage to New England." In Andrews, Charles M. *The Colonial Period in American History.* Vol. 3. New Haven, CT: Yale University Press, 1934–1938.

Hinman, R. R. *The Blue Laws of New Haven Colony Usually Called Blue Laws of Connecticut.* Hartford: Case, Tiffany & Co, 1838.

Hinman, R. R. *A Catalogue of the First Puritan Settlers of the Colony of Connecticut.* Hartford, CT: Gleason, 1846.

*Historical Catalogue of the first Church of Hartford 1633–1685.* Hartford, CT: Published by the Church, 1885

Hoadley, Charles J., ed. *Records of the Colony or Jurisdiction of New Haven,* 2V. Hartford, CT: Case, Lockwood and Co., 1858.

Hooker, Thomas. *The Danger of Desertion,* London, George Edwards, 1641.

Hooker, Thomas. *Sermon.* June 1647. In Grant, Matthew. *Matthew Grant diary* [transcript]. http://cslib.cdmhost.com/cdm/ref/collection/p15019coll14/id/548.

Hopkins, Matthew. *The Discovery of Witches.* London: R. Royston, 1647.

Howell, James. *Epistolæ Ho-Elianæ: the Familiar Letters of James Howell.* Boston, MA: Houghton Mifflin, 1908.

Howell, Thomas Bayly, and Thomas Jones Howell. "Relation of the arraignment and Trial of those who made the late Rebellious insurrections in London, 1661." *A Complete Collection of State Trials and Proceedings for High Treason and other Crimes and Misdemeanors.* Vol. 6. London: T.C. Hansard, 1816.

Huit, Ephraim. *Anatomy of Conscience.* London: I.D., 1626.

Hull, John. "The Diaries of John Hull, Mint-master and Treasurer of the Colony at Massachusetts Bay." *Archeologia Americana: Transactions & Collections of the American Antiquarian Society* 3 (1857): 108–306.

Hutchinson, Thomas. *The Witchcraft Delusion of 1692.* Poole, William Frederick, ed. Boston, MA: Privately Printed, 1870.

Johnson, Edward. *A history of New-England. From the English planting in the yeere 1628 untill the yeere 1652.* London: 1654. [1653].

Johnson, Edward. *Wonder-working providence of Sions Saviour in New England.* London: 1654.

Josselyn, John. *An account of two Voyages to New-England.* London: G. Widdowes, 1674.

*Lambeth and the Vatican: Or, Anecdotes of the Church of Rome, of the Reformed Churches and of the Sects and Sectaries.* London: John Knight & Henry Lacey, 1825.

Lechford, Thomas. *New-Englands advice to Old-England.* London: 1644.

"Letter from Henry Dunster's father in Lancashire, England to Henry Dunster, in Massachusetts, March 20, 1640." *Dunster Papers. Massachusetts Historical Society Collections.* Vol. 2, Boston, MA: Massachusetts Historical Society, 1854.

Levack, Brian, P. "The Great Scottish Witch Hunt of 1661–1662." *Journal of British Studies* 20 (1980): 90–108.

"Massachusetts, Marriages, 1695–1910." *Family Search.org.* Symon Beamon and Alis Young, 15 Dec 1654; FHL microfilm 0185414, 0185415, 185416. Accessed 10 November 2014. https://familysearch.org/pal:/MM9.1.1/FCX4-SV.

*Massachusetts Historical Society Collections.* Vol. 7. Boston, MA: Massachusetts Historical Society, 1865.

*Massachusetts Historical Society Collections.* Vol. 8. Boston, MA: Wiggan and Lunt, 1868.

Mather, Cotton. "A Faithful Account of many Wonderful and Surprising Things which happened in the Town of Gloucester, in the Year, 1692." In Mather, Cotton. *Decennium luctuosum An history of remarkable occurrences, in the long war, which New-England hath had with the Indian salvages, from the year, 1688. To the year 1698.* Boston, MA: B. Green and J. Allen, 1699.

Mather, Cotton. *Late Memorable Providences Relating to Witchcrafts and Possessions,* London, Thomas Parkhurst, 1691.

Mather, Cotton. *Magnalia Christi Americana: or, the ecclesiastical history of New-England: from its first planting in the year 1620. unto the year of our Lord, 1698.* Hartford, CT: Silus Andrus and Son, 1853.

Mather, Cotton. *Memorable Providences Relating to Witchcrafts and Possessions,* London, Richard Pierce, 1689.

Mather, Cotton. *Wonders of the Invisible World.* London: John Dunton, 1693.

Mather, Cotton. *Wonders of the Invisible World.* London: John Russell Smith, 1862.

Mather, Increase. *An Essay for the Recording of Remarkable Providences ... Especially in New England.* Boston, MA: Samuel Green, 1684.

Mather, Richard. *A Disputation Concerning Church Members and their Children in Answers to XXI Questions ... is Discussed by an Assembly at Boston in New England June 4 1657.* London: J. Hayes, 1659.

Mather, Richard, and William Tompson. *A Modest and Brotherly Answer to Mr. Charles Herle his Book, Against the Independency of Churches.* London: 1644.

"Mather Papers." *Massachusetts Historical Society Collections.* Vol. 8. Boston, MA: Wiggen and Lunt, 1868.

Mayhew, Thomas. "To the Much Honored Corporation in London, Chosen to Place of Publick

Trust for the Promoting of the Work of the Lord among the Indians of New England,"
    *Massachusetts Historical Society Collections*. Vol. 3. Boston: 1833.
Melton, John. *Astrologaster or The Figure-Caster.* London: Barnard and Alsop, 1620.
*Mercurius Aulicus.* London.
*Mercurius Britannicus.* London.
*Mercurius Politicus.* London.
*Moderate Intelligencer.* London.
Morton, Thomas. *New English Canaan.* Amsterdam: Jacob Frederick Stam, 1637.
*New Englands First Fruits in Respect, First of the Conversion of Some Indian....* London: R.O.
    and G.D., 1642.
New Haven Colony. *New-Haven's settling in New-England: and some lawes for government....*
    London: Livewell Chapman, 1656.
Norton, Humphrey. *New-England's Ensigne it being the account of cruelty, the professors pride,
    and the articles of their faith, signified in characters written in blood, wickedly begun....*
    London: T.L., 1659.
Ogilby, John. *The entertainment of His Most Excellent Majestie Charles II, in his passage
    through the city of London to his coronation ... and royal feast in Westminster-Hall.* Lon-
    don: Thomas Roycroft, 1662.
Ormsby, G., ed. "Richard Montague to Mr. John Cosin, St. Valentines Day, 1624–5" and
    "Richard Montague to Mr. John Cosin, February 1624–25," *The Correspondence of John
    Cosin*, v. 52, Surtees Society Durham, Andrews and Co., 1869.
*Parliaments Post.* London.
"Particular Court 1639–1663," v. 22, *Connecticut Historical Society Collections*, Hartford: Con-
    necticut Historical Society, 1928.
Peacham, Henry. *The worth of a peny, or, A caution to keep money with the causes of the
    scarcity and misery ....* London: 1641.
Pepys, Samuel. *A Pepysian Garland: Black-letter Broadside Ballads of the Years 1595–1639 ..."*
    Cambridge, England: Cambridge University Press, 1922.
*A Perfect Diurnal* London.
Perkins, William. *Discourse of the Damned Art of Witchcraft.* Cambridge: Cantrell Legge, 1608.
"Quarter Session Records for the County of Somerset, Volume I, 1607–1627," v. 23, *Somerset
    Record Society*, London: Butler & Tanner, 1907.
Shepard, Douglas H. *The Wolcott Shorthand Notebook Transcribed.* Dissertation State Uni-
    versity of Iowa, 1957.
Shepard, Thomas. "Memoirs of My Life" in Alexander Young, ed. *Chronicles of the First
    Planters of the Colony of Massachusetts Bay, 1623–1636.*Boston: Little and J. Brown, 1846.
Shurtleff Nathaniel B., ed. *Records of the Governor and Company of the Massachusetts Bay in
    New England 1642–1649,* 3 vols. Boston: William White, 1853.
*Signs and Wonders from Heaven.* London: 1645.
Stearne, John. *A Confirmation and Discovery of Witches and Witchcraft ...* in Malcolm Gaskill,
    *English Witchcraft 1560–1736.* v.3, London: Pickering & Chatto, 2003.
Stiles, Ezra. *A History of Three of the Judges of King Charles I.* Hartford: Elisha Babcock, 1794.
Stone, Samuel. *Samuel Stone's Catechism: Reissued with an Introductory Sketch....* Boston:
    John Green, 1684.
*Strange and Terrible Newes from Cambridge being a True Relation of Quakers Bewitching of
    Mary Philips....* London, C. Brooks, 1659.
T.B. *Observations Upon Prince Rupert's White Dogge Called Boye.* London: 1642.
Trask, William Blake et al. *Suffolk Deeds,* v. 1, Boston: Rockwell and Churchill Press, 1880–1906.
*A True Relation of the Araignment of Eighteene Witches ... St. Edmunds-bury in Suffolke.* Lon-
    don: 1645.
Trumbull, J. Hammond, ed. *Notebook Kept by Thomas Lechford, Esq. Lawyer: In Boston Mas-
    sachusetts Bay From June 27, 1638 to July 29, 1641.* Cambridge: J. Wilson, 1885.
Trumbull, J. Hammond. *The Public Records of the Colony of Connecticut,* 15v., Hartford, CT.
    Brown and Parsons, 1850.
Warham, John. *Sermon.* August 1647. In Grant, Matthew. *Matthew Grant diary* [transcript].
    http://cslib.cdmhost.com/cdm/ref/collection/p15019coll14/id/548.
Webbe, George. *The Arraignment of an Unruly Tongue.* London: John Budge, 1619.

Weld, Thomas, and John Winthrop. *A short story of the rise, reign, and ruin of the antinomians familists & libertines that infected the churches of New-England ... and the lamentable death of Ms. Hutchison....* London: Ralph Smith, 1644.

White, John. *The Planter's Plea or the Grounds of Plantations Examined and Usual Objections Answered.* London: Iones, 1630.

"William Pynchon to John Haynes, May 2, 1639." *Proceedings of the Massachusetts Historical Society.* Vol. 48. Boston, MA: Massachusetts Historical Society, 1915.

"Windsor Church Covenant October 23, 1647." *Matthew Grant diary* [transcript]. http://cslib.cdmhost.com/cdm/ref/collection/p15019coll14/id/548.

Winthrop, John. *Antinomians and Familists Condemned by the Synod of Elders in New England: with the Proceedings of the Magistrates against....* London: Ralph Smith, 1644.

Winthrop, John. *John Winthrop Journal: History of New England.* Hosmer, J. Kendall, ed. New York: C. Scribner and Sons, 1908.

Winthrop, John. *The History of New England from 1630 to 1649.* Savage, J., ed. Boston, MA: Thomas B. Waite, 1825.

"Winthrop Papers." *Massachusetts Historical Society Collections.* Vol. 1–5. Boston, MA: Massachusetts Historical Society, 1929–.

"Winthrop Papers." *Massachusetts Historical Society Collections.* Vol. 7. Boston, MA: Massachusetts Historical Society, 1865.

Wright, T. *Narratives of Sorcery and Magic from the Most Authentic Sources.* London: Richard Bentley, 1851

Young, Alexander, ed. *Chronicles of the First Planters of the Colony of Massachusetts Bay, 1623–1636.* Boston, MA: Little and J. Brown, 1846.

## Secondary Sources

Algeo, John, ed. *Cambridge History of the English Language: English in North America.* Vol. 6. New York: Cambridge University Press, 2001.

Allaben, Frank. "Ancient Agawam-Modern Springfield," *The National Magazine* 16 (1892): 561–585.

Allen, David Grayson. *In English Ways: The Movement of Societies and their Transferal of English Local Law and Custom to the Massachusetts Bay in the Seventeenth Century.* Chapel Hill, NC: University of North Carolina Press, 1981.

Almond, Phillip. *The Lancashire Witches: A Chronicle of Sorcery and Death on Pendle Hill.* London: I.B. Tauris, 2012.

Andrews, Charles M. *The Colonial Period in American History.* New Haven, CT: Yale University Press, 1934–38.

Andrews, Charles M. *River Towns of Connecticut: A Study of Wethersfield, Hartford, and Windsor.* Baltimore, MD: Johns Hopkins University, 1889.

Andrews, Frank D. *A Quaker's Visit to Hartford in the Year 1676.* New Jersey: Vinland, 1914. *Antiquary* 33 (July 1897).

Ashton, John. *The Devil in Britain and America.* London: Ward and Downey, 1896.

Baker, Emerson, and James Kences. "Maine, Indian Land Speculation, and the Essex County Witchcraft Outbreak of 1692." *Maine History* 40: (2001): 159–89.

Baldwin, Ernest H. *Stories of Old New Haven.* Taunton, MA: C.A. Hack and Son, 1907.

Baldwin, Ernest H. "Why New Haven is Not a State of the Union." *Papers of the New Haven Colony Historical Society.* Vol. 7. New Haven: New Haven Colony Historical Society, 1908.

Baldwin, Simeon E. *The Secession of Springfield from Connecticut.* Cambridge, MA: John Wilson and Son, 1908.

Banner, Stuart. *The Death Penalty: An American history.* Cambridge, MA: Harvard University Press, 2002.

Barry, Jonathan. *Witchcraft and Demonology in South-West England 1640–1670.* London: Palgrave MacMillan, 2012.

Beringer, Wolfgang. "Weather, Hunger and Fear: Origins of the European Witch-Hunts in Climate, Society and Mentality." *German History* 13 (1995): 1–27.

Birch, Thomas. *The Court and Time of James the First.* London: Henry Colburn, 1848.

Bissel, Linda A. *Family, Friends and Neighbors: Social Interaction in Seventeenth-Century Windsor, Connecticut.* Ph.D. dissertation. Waltham, MA: Brandeis University, 1973.

Booth, Sally Smith. *Witches of Early America.* New York: Hastings House, 1975.

Boyer, Paul and Stephen Nissenbaum. *Salem Possessed: The Social Origins of Witchcraft.* Cambridge, MA: Harvard University Press, 1974.

Boynton, Cynthia Wolfe. *Connecticut Witch Trials: The First Panic in the New World.* Charleston, SC: History Press, 2014.

Bremer, Francis J. "In Defense of Regicide." *William and Mary Quarterly* 37, no. 1 (1980): 103–124.

Bremer, Francis J. *Puritan Crisis New England and the English Civil Wars, 1630–1670.* New York: Garland Press, 1989.

Brook Benjamin. *Lives of the Puritans Containing a Biographical Account of Those Divines Who Distinguished Themselves on the Cause of Liberty.* London: James Black, 1813.

Burr, G.L. *Narratives of the Witchcraft Cases 1648–1706.* New York: C. Scribner's Sons, 1914.

Burt, Henry M. *The First Century of the History of Springfield; the Official Records 1636–1736.* Springfield, MA: Henry M. Burt, 1898.

Butler, Jon. *Awash in a Sea of Faith: Christianizing the American People.* Cambridge, MA: Harvard University Press, 1990.

Clark, Stuart. *Thinking With Demons: The Idea of Witchcraft in Early Modern Europe.* Oxford: Oxford University Press, 1997.

Clark, Stuart, ed. *Languages of Witchcraft: Narrative, Ideology, and Meaning in Early Modern Culture.* New York: Palgrave Macmillan, 2001.

Coe, Sophia. *Memoranda Relating to the Ancestry of Sophia Fidelia Hall.* Meriden, CT: The Curtiss–Way Co., 1902.

Como, David R. *Blown by the Spirit: Puritanism and the Emergence of an Antinomian Underground in Pre-Civil War England.* Stanford: Stanford University Press, 2004.

Cook, Sherburne F. "The Significance of Disease in the Extinction of the New England Indians." In Kiple, Kenneth and Stephen Beck, ed. *Biological Consequences of the European Expansion, 1480–1800.* Aldershot: Hampshire, 1997.

Cowing, Cedric D. *The Saving Remnant Religion and the Settling of New England.* Urbana, IL: University of Illinois Press, 1995.

Cressy, David. *Coming Over: Migration and Communication between England and New England in the Seventeenth Century.* New York: Cambridge University Press, 1987.

Davenport, John. *Letters of John Davenport.* Calder, Elizabeth, ed. New Haven: Yale University Press, 1937.

Davies, Owen. *Popular Magic: Cunning-folk in English History.* New York: Hambledon and London, 2003.

Davies, Trevor. *Four Centuries of Witch Beliefs.* London: Methuen, 1947.

Davis, Richard Beale. "The Devil in Virginia in the Seventeenth Century." *Virginia Magazine of History and Biography* 65 (1957): 131–49.

Demos, John. *The Enemy Within, a Short History of Witch-Hunting.* New York: Penguin, 2008.

Demos, John. *Entertaining Satan.* New York: Oxford University Press, 1982.

Doyle, John Andrew. *English Colonies in America ...: The Puritan colonies.* New York: Henry Holt and Co., 1887.

Drake, Frederick C. "Witchcraft in the American Colonies, 1647–62." *American Quarterly* 20 (Winter 1968): 694–725.

Dunn Richard S. "John Winthrop Jr., of Connecticut: The first Governor of the East End." In Twomey, Tom, ed. *Awakening the Past: The East Hampton 350th Anniversary Lecture, 1998.* New York: New Market Press, 1999.

Easton, Timothy, and Jeremy Hodgkinson. "Apotropaic Symbols on Cast-Iron Firebacks." *Journal of the Antique Metalware Society* 21 (2013). http://www.academia.edu/5832596/Apotropaic_Symbols_on_Cast-Iron_Firebacks.

Ellis, George Edward. *The Puritan Age and Rule in the Colony of the Massachusetts Bay, 1629–1685.* New York: Houghton, Mifflin and Co., 1888.

Evans, George Ewart. *The Pattern Under the Plough: Aspects of the Folk-life of East Anglia.* London: Faber & Faber, 1977.

Ewen, C. L'Estrange. *Witchcraft and Demonianism.* London: 1933.

Ewen, C. L'Estrange. *Witch Hunting and Witch Trials*. London: Kegan and Paul, 1929.

Felt, Joseph Barlow. *The Ecclesiastical History of New England: Comprising Not Only Religious but also Moral, and other Relations*. Boston: Congregational Library Association, 1855.

Fiske, John. *The Beginnings of New England: Or, the Puritan Theocracy in Its Relations to Civil and Religious Liberty*. New York: Houghton, Mifflin and Co., 1889.

Fletcher, Anthony. "National and Local Awareness in the County Communities." In Tomlinson, Howard, ed. *Before the English Civil War*. London: MacMillan, 1983.

Fuller, Carol Seager. *An Incident in Hartford*. Amherst, MA: Private Printing, 1977.

Games, Alison. *Migration and the Origins of the English Atlantic World*. Cambridge, MA: Harvard University Press, 1999.

Gaskill, Malcolm. "Witchcraft and Power in Early Modern England: the Case of Margaret Moore." In Oldridge, Darren, ed. *The Witchcraft Reader*. New York: Routledge, 2002.

Gaskill, Malcolm. "Witchcraft, Emotion and Imagination in the English Civil War." In Newton, John and Jo Bath, eds. *Witchcraft and the Act of 1604*. Boston, MA: Brill, 2008.

Gaskill, Malcom. "Witches and Witnesses in Old and New England." *Witchfinders: A Seventeenth-Century English Tragedy*. Cambridge, England: Cambridge University Press, 2005.

Gibson, Marion. *Witchcraft Myths in American Culture*. New York: Routledge, 2007.

Gish, Noel. "Pirates." In Twomey, Tom, ed. *Awakening the Past: The East Hampton 350th Anniversary Lecture, 1998*. New York: New Market Press, 1999.

Godbeer, Richard. *The Devil's Dominion Magic and Religion in Early New England*. New York: Cambridge University Press, 1992.

Goodwin, Nathaniel. *Foote Family or the Descendants of Nathaniel Foote*. Hartford, CT: Case Tiffany and Co., 1899.

Grandjean, Katherine. *American Passage: The Communications Frontier in Early New England*. Cambridge, MA: Harvard University Press, 2015.

Greaves, Richard L. "Richard Bernard." *Oxford Dictionary of National Biography*. Vol. 5. New York: Oxford University Press, 2004.

Green, Mason A. *Springfield, 1636–1886: History of Town and City*. Springfield, MA: C.A. Nichols & Co., 1888.

Gura, Philip F. *A Glimpse of Sion's Glory Puritan Radicalism in New England 1620–1660*. Middletown, CT: Wesleyan University Press, 1984.

Hall, David D. *Worlds of Wonder Days of Judgment*. Cambridge, MA: Harvard University Press, 1989.

Hansen, Chadwick. *Witchcraft at Salem*. New York: George Braziller, 1969.

Hardman, Susan M. "Hooke, William." *Oxford Dictionary of National Biography*. doi:10.1093/ref:odnb/13688

Harley, David. "Historians as Demonologists: The Myth of the Midwife-witch." *Social History of Medicine* 3 (April 1990): 1–26.

*Hartford Courant*. Hartford, CT.

Hedges, Henry Parsons. *Records of the Town of East Hampton, Long Island, Suffolk Co., N.Y.* Sag Harbor, NY: John H. Hunt, 1887.

Hewlett, Barry S. and Bonnie L. Hewlett. *Ebola, Culture, and Politics the Anthropology of an Emerging Disease*. Belmont, CA: Thomson Wadsworth, 2008.

Hoadley, Charles J. "Some Early Post-Mortem Examinations in New England." *Proceedings of The Connecticut Medical Society*. Bridgeport, CT: 1892.

Hoffer, Peter Charles. *Law and People in Colonial America*. Baltimore, MD: Johns Hopkins University Press, 1992.

Hole, Christine. *Witchcraft in England*. New York: Collier Books, 1996,

Holmes, Abiel. *American Annals: Or, A Chronological History of America: From Its Discovery....* London: Sherwood, Neely & Jones, 1813.

Hubbard, William. *A General History of New England: From the Discovery to MDCLXXX*. Boston, MA: Charles C. Little and James Brown, 1897.

Innes, Stephen. *Labor in a New Land: Economy and Society in Seventeenth-Century Springfield*. Princeton: Princeton University Press, 1983.

Jacobus, Donald L. *History and Genealogy of the Families of Old Fairfield*. Fairfield, CT: Tuttle, Morehouse & Taylor Company, 1930.

Jones, David S. *Rationalizing Epidemics: Meanings and Uses of American Indian Mortality since 1600*. Cambridge, MA: Harvard University press, 2004.

Judd Sylvester, and Lucius Manlius Boltwood. *History of Hadley: Including the Early History of Hatfield, South Hadley ....* Northampton: Metcalf and Co., 1863.

Kamensky, Jane. "Female Speech and Other Demons: Witchcraft and Wordcraft in Early New England." In Reis, Elizabeth, ed., *Spellbound Women and Witchcraft in America*. Wilmington, DE: Scholarly Resources, 1998.

Karlsen, Carol F. *The Devil in the Shape of a Woman: Witchcraft in Colonial New England*. New York: Norton, 1987.

King, Hugh and Loretta Orion. "It Were As Well to Please the Devil as Anger Him." In Twomey, Tom, ed. *Awakening the Past: The East Hampton 350th Anniversary Lecture Series 1998*. New York: Newmarket Press, 1999.

Kiple Kenneth, and Stephen Beck, ed. *Biological Consequences of the European Expansion, 1480–1800*. Aldershot: Hampshire, 1997.

Kittredge, George L. *Witchcraft in Old and New England*. Cambridge, MA: Harvard University Press, 1929.

Knott, Olive. *Witches of Dorset*. Dorset: Dorset Pub. Co., 1974.

Lake, Peter. *The Boxmakers Revenge, Orthodoxy, Heterodoxy and the Politics of the Parish in Early Stuart London*. Manchester: Manchester University Press, 2001.

Lamson, Warren W. "Connecticut's First Lady: Susannah Garbrand Hooker." *The Connecticut Antiquarian* 37 (1985): 5–34.

Langdon, Carolyn S. "A Complaint against Katherine Harrison, 1669." *Bulletin of the Connecticut Historical Society* 34, no. 1 (January 1969): 18–25.

Langdon, Carolyn S. "Connecticut Witchcraft-What Was It?" *Connecticut Historical Society Bulletin* 38 (January 1973).

Levack, Brian P., ed. *Articles on Witchcraft, Magic, and Demonology: Witchcraft in colonial America*. New York: Garland, 1992.

Levermore, Charles. "Witchcraft in New England." *New Englander and Yale Review* 44 (1885).

Levermore, Charles, H. "Witchcraft in Connecticut." In Levack, Brian P., ed. *Articles on Witchcraft, Magic, and Demonology: Witchcraft in colonial America*. New York: Garland, 1992.

Levermore, Charles H. "Witchcraft in New England." *New England Magazine* 12 (July 1892): 636–44.

Lockridge, Kenneth A. *Literacy in Colonial New England*. New York: Norton, 1974.

Lockwood, John H. *History of Western Massachusetts 1636–1925*. New York: Lewis Historical Publishing Co., 1926.

Love, William DeLoss. *Colonial History of Hartford*. Hartford: Self Published, 1914.

Lucas, Paul R. *Valley of Discord: Church and Society along the Connecticut River, 1636–1725*. Hanover, NH: University Press of New England, 1976.

Macfarlane, Alan. *Witchcraft in Tudor and Stuart England; a regional and comparative study*. New York: Harper & Row, 1970.

Manley, John Jackson. *Salt, and Other Condiments*. London: William Clowes & Sons, 1884.

Manwaring, Charles W. *A Digest of the Early Connecticut Probate Records*. Hartford: R.S. Peck & Co., 1904–1906.

Marshall, John. *John Locke, Toleration and Early Enlightenment Culture*. Cambridge, UK: Cambridge University Press, 2006.

McDonald, Michael. *Mystical Bedlam Madness Anxiety, and Healing in Seventeenth-Century England*. Cambridge: Cambridge University Press, 1981.

McManus, Edgar J. *Law and Liberty in Early New England*. Amherst, MA: University of Massachusetts Press, 1993.

Merrifield Ralph. *The Archeology of Ritual and Magic*. New York: New Amsterdam Books, 1987.

Miller, Edwin. *The Professional Writer in Elizabethan England*. Cambridge, MA: Harvard University Press, 1959.

Miller, Perry. *Errand into the Wilderness*. Cambridge: Harvard University Press, 1956.

Moore, Susan H. *Pilgrims New World Settlers and the Call of Home*. New Haven: Yale University Press, 2007.

Murdock, Kenneth, ed. *Handkerchiefs from Paul Being Pious and Consolatory verses of Puritan Massachusetts*. Cambridge: Harvard University, 1927.

*New England Historical and Genealogical Register.* Boston, MA.

Nichols, J. G. *Narratives of the Days of the Reformation.* Vol. 77. London: Camden Society, 1859.

Norton, Mary Beth. *Founding Mothers & Fathers: Gendered Power and the Forming of American Society.* New York: Vintage Books, 1996.

Norton, Mary Beth. *In the Devil's Snare: The Salem Witchcraft Crisis of 1692.* New York: Alfred A. Knopf, 2003.

Notestein, Wallace. *A History of Witchcraft in England from 1558-1718.* Washington, DC: 1911.

Oldridge, Darren, ed. *The Witchcraft Reader.* New York: Routledge, 2002.

Orcutt, Samuel. *A History of the Old Town of Stratford and the City of Bridgeport, Connecticut.* New Haven, CT: Tuttle, Morehouse & Taylor, 1886.

*Panorama of Life and Literature.* Boston, MA.

Parker, Edwin P. *History of the Second Church of Christ in Hartford.* Hartford, CT: Belknap and Warfield, 1892.

Pestana, Carla G. "The City upon the Hill under Siege-The Puritan Perception of the Quaker Threat to Massachusetts Bay, 1656-1661." *The New England Quarterly* 56 (1983): 336–341.

Pestana, Carla Gardina. *The English Atlantic in an Age of Revolution 1640-1661.* Cambridge, MA: Harvard University Press, 2004.

Powers, David M. *Damnable Heresy: William Pynchon, the Indians and the First Book Banned (and Burned) in Boston.* Eugene, OR: Wipf and Stock, 2015.

Purkiss, Diane. *The English Civil War.* New York: Basic Books, 2006.

Purkiss Diane. *The Witch in History: Early Modern and Twentieth-Century Representations* London: Routledge, 1996.

Purvis, Thomas, L. *Colonial America to 1763.* New York: Facts on File, 1999.

Reis, Elizabeth, ed. *Spellbound Women and Witchcraft in America.* Wilmington, DE: Scholarly Resources, 1998.

Richardson, Margaret and Arthur T. Hertig. "New England's First Recorded Hydatidiform Mole." *New England Journal of Medicine* 260 (March 1959): 544–545.

Robbins, Russell Hope. *The Encyclopedia of Witchcraft and Demonology.* New York: Crown Publishers, 1959.

Rockey, John L., ed. *History of New Haven County, Connecticut.* New York: W.W. Preston and Co., 1892.

Rosenthal, Bernard. *Records of the Salem Witch-Hunt.* Cambridge: Cambridge University Press, 2009.

Rothbard, Murray N. *Conceived in Liberty.* Auburn, AL: Ludwig von Mises Institute, 1999.

Rudolph, Julia. *Common Law and Enlightenment in England, 1689-1750.* Woodbridge, UK: Boydell & Brewer, 2013.

St. George, Robert Blair. *Conversing by Signs: Poetics of Implication in Colonial New England Culture.* Chapel Hill, NC: University of North Carolina Press, 1998.

Schenck, Elizabeth H. G. *The History of Fairfield, Fairfield County, Connecticut, from the Settlement....* New York: Self Published, 1889.

Sharpe, James. *Instruments of Darkness Witchcraft in Early Modern England.* Philadelphia, PA: University of Pennsylvania, 1996.

Sharpe, James. *Witchcraft in Early Modern England.* London: Routledge, 2001.

Smith, Joseph H. *Colonial Justice in Western Massachusetts 1639-1702.* Cambridge, MA: Harvard University Press, 1961.

Stiles, Henry R. *The History and Genealogies of Ancient Windsor Connecticut.* Hartford, CT: Case, Lockwood and Brainard, 1891.

Takaki, Ronald. "The Tempest in the Wilderness: The Racialization of Savagery." *Journal of American History* 79, no. 3 (December 1992): 892–912.

Tarutis, Robert J. *Days of Judgment: the Salem witch trials of 1692.* Salem, MA: Osram Sylvania, Inc., 1993. DVD.

Taylor, John M. *Roger Ludlow, the Colonial Lawmaker.* New York: G.P. Putnam's Sons, 1900.

Taylor, John M. *The Witchcraft Delusion in Colonial Connecticut.* New York: Grafton, 1908.

Thistlethwaite, Frank. *The Story of West County Pilgrims Who Went to New England in the 17th Century.* London: Barrie & Jenkins, 1989.

Thomas, Keith. *Religion and the Decline of Witchcraft.* New York: Charles Scribner, 1971.

Tipson, Baird. *Hartford Puritanism: Thomas Hooker, Samuel Stone and their Terrifying God.* New York: Oxford University Press, 2015.

Tomlinson, Howard, ed. *Before the English Civil War.* London: MacMillan, 1983.

Tomlinson, Richard G. *Witchcraft Prosecution: Chasing the Devil in Connecticut.* Rockland, ME: Picton Press, 2012.

Tomlinson, Richard G. *Witchcraft Trials of Connecticut.* Hartford, CT: Bond Press, 1978.

Tongue, R. L. *Somerset Folklore.* London: Folk-Lore Society, 1965.

Trumbull, Benjamin. *A Complete History of Connecticut, Civil and Ecclesiastical, from the Emigration of its First Planters from England.* Hartford, CT: Hudson & Goodwin, 1797.

Twomey, Tom, ed. *Awakening the Past: The East Hampton 350th Anniversary Lecture Series 1998.* New York: Newmarket Press, 1999.

Walker, G.L. *History of the First Church in Hartford, 1633–1833.* Hartford, CT: Brown & Gross, 1833.

Walker, Simon. *The Witches of Hertfordshire.* Stroud, Gloucestershire: Tempus, 2004.

Watt, Tessa. *Cheap Print and Popular Piety 1550–1640.* New York: Cambridge University Press, 1991.

Webster, Tom. *Godly Clergy in Early Stuart England: The Caroline Puritan Movement 1620–1643.* Cambridge: Cambridge University Press, 1997.

Weismann, Richard. *Witchcraft, Magic, and Religion in 17th Century Massachusetts.* Amherst, MA: University of Massachusetts Press, 1984.

Wilcoxson, William H. *History of Stratford 1639–1939.* Stratford, CT: Brewer Borg, 1939.

Williams, Herbert U. "The Epidemic of the Indians of New England 1616–1620." *Johns Hopkins Hospital Bulletin* 20 (1909).

Winsor, Justin and Clarence F. Jewett. *The Memorial History of Boston: Including Suffolk County Massachusetts 1630–1880.* Boston: Ticknor and Co., 1880–81.

Wolcott, Roger. "Roger Wolcott's Memoir Relating to Connecticut." *Connecticut Historical Society* 3 (1895): 327.

Woodward, Walter W. *Prospero's America John Winthrop, Jr., Alchemy, and the Creation of New England Culture 1606–1676.* Williamsburg, VA: Omohundro Institute of Early American History and Culture, 2010.

# Index

Numbers in **_bold italics_** indicate pages with photographs.

www.ingramcontent.com/pod-product-compliance
Lightning Source LLC
Chambersburg PA
CBHW021120270326
41929CB00009B/972